The Best
AMERICAN
ESSAYS
1992

GUEST EDITORS OF
The Best American Essays

1986 ELIZABETH HARDWICK

1987 GAY TALESE

1988 ANNIE DILLARD

1989 GEOFFREY WOLFF

1990 JUSTIN KAPLAN

1991 JOYCE CAROL OATES

1992 SUSAN SONTAG

The Best AMERICAN ESSAYS 1992

Edited and with an Introduction
by SUSAN SONTAG

ROBERT ATWAN,
Series Editor

TICKNOR & FIELDS · NEW YORK · 1992

ISSN 0888-3742
ISBN 0-395-59935-0
ISBN 0-395-59936-9 (pbk.)

Printed in the United States of America

AGM 10 9 8 7 6 5 4 3 2 1

Contents

Foreword by Robert Atwan   ix

Introduction by Susan Sontag   xiii

ANNE CARSON. *Short Talks*   1
from The Yale Review

JOAN DIDION. *Sentimental Journeys*   6
from The New York Review of Books

E. L. DOCTOROW. *Standards*   48
from Harper's Magazine

RONALD DWORKIN. *Liberty and Pornography*   59
from The New York Review of Books

STANLEY ELKIN. *Some Overrated Masterpieces*   70
from Art & Antiques

PHILIP FISHER. *Thinking About Killing:* Hamlet *and the Paths
Among the Passions*   86
from Raritan

WILLIAM H. GASS. *Exile*   118
from Salmagundi

ADAM GOPNIK. *Audubon's Passion*   139
from The New Yorker

JOHN GUILLORY. *Canon, Syllabus, List: A Note on the Pedagogic
Imaginary*   158
from Transition

ELIZABETH HARDWICK. *Wind from the Prairie* 181
from *The New York Review of Books*

VICKI HEARNE. *What's Wrong with Animal Rights* 199
from *Harper's Magazine*

JAMAICA KINCAID. *On Seeing England for the First Time* 209
from *Transition*

WAYNE KOESTENBAUM. *Opera and Homosexuality:
Seven Arias* 221
from *The Yale Journal of Criticism*

LEONARD MICHAELS. *The Zipper* 244
from *The Threepenny Review*

DAVID RIEFF. *Victims, All?* 253
from *Harper's Magazine*

PATRICIA STORACE. *Look Away, Dixie Land* 268
from *The New York Review of Books*

GEORGE W. S. TROW. *Needs* 297
from *The New Yorker*

JOHN UPDIKE. *First Things First* 300
from *Art & Antiques*

JOHN UPDIKE. *The Mystery of Mickey Mouse* 306
from *Art & Antiques*

GORE VIDAL. *Lincoln Up Close* 314
from *The New York Review of Books*

Biographical Notes 321

Notable Essays of 1991 325

Foreword

VIRGINIA WOOLF put it well: "The art of writing has for backbone some fierce attachment to an idea." Referring specifically to the essay, she was reacting to the type that tries to get by on style alone. Elegance, ease, urbanity, charm, a congenial touch — for decades these would be cited as defining characteristics of the genre. Complex ideas, urgent issues, serious thoughts about books, authors, and culture, were better left to professional philosophers and critics. One of the few great essayists of our century, Woolf wasn't belittling "style"; she simply thought that the easy-chair essay — arch, comfortable, autocratically engaged with trifles or trivia — had seen its day.

This volume has backbone. Though it features some of the finest prose stylists of our time, it never loses touch with the characteristics of the genre Woolf loved best: its passion for thought, its love of controversy. "There's nothing so convincing as an opinion," maintains Stanley Elkin in "Some Overrated Masterpieces." In his inimitable style, he then proceeds with a barrage of his own opinions, most of them — like his comments on Mona Lisa's "gingivitis smile" — refreshingly irreverent.

Susan Sontag has assembled a collection of essays so astonishingly diverse in their range of styles and subjects that this year's book defies any convenient label. Here is humor and commentary, outrageous opinion and crafted argument, personal observation and social criticism. Listing the topics is like browsing along the aisles of a first-class bookstore: popular songs, opera, literary classics, best-sellers, film, photography, history, cartoons.

And these are essays with something to say, something at issue. In "Sentimental Journeys," Joan Didion, one of the very few essayists writing intelligently today about American cities, alerts us to the rhetoric and narratives that surrounded the controversial rape trial involving the Central Park jogger. In "What's Wrong with Animal Rights," Vicki Hearne takes on one of America's ardent causes: "Animal-rights publications are illustrated largely with photographs of two kinds of animals — 'Helpless Fluff' and 'Agonized Fluff,' the two conditions in which some people seem to prefer their animals, because any other version of an animal is too complicated for propaganda." "Victims, All?" asks David Rieff, as he attacks the cant of another popular cause, the "recovery movement." "Imagine a country," Rieff begins, "in which millions of apparently successful people nonetheless have come to believe fervently that they are really lost souls. . . ." When first published, these essays provoked scores of letters in response.

If anything can be said to link these diverse selections together, it is the passion that informs them. Throughout the collection we find many "fierce attachments," either the writer's or the subject's: Audubon's passions, Hamlet's passions, the passions of and for opera, for books and movies, liberty and justice, fact and social sanity, for animals and for ordinary childhood objects. Intellectual passions, to be sure, but erotic ones, too — when, of course, the distinction applies.

The twentieth-century American essay has pursued two different courses, one oriented to the personal anecdote or memoir, the other to a critical or polemical position. We might call these essays of Identity and essays of Ideas — E. B. White, say, as opposed to H. L. Mencken. So far this annual series has given greater play to the personal essay. This year's collection, however, showcases the essay as a genre of ideas. The first-person singular still figures prominently, but even when it's missing, that needn't signify the impersonal. As Sontag reminds us in her introduction, "All the great essays are in the first person. The writer need not say 'I.' "

Nor need the reader always say it. We are well acquainted with readers who automatically pass every literary work they encounter through the fine-mesh filter of some "identity" or another. If they don't see the personal "relevance" of a work, or can't "identify" with an author's stance, or if they've gotten wind that there is something culturally or politically incorrect about the writer, then the game's over before it's begun. More than anything, great essays demand thought, and thought in turn demands the willing suspension of preconceived ideas and identities. When Montaigne launched the modern essay, he also recommended the kind of mental equipment required to read it: "No propositions astonish me, no belief offends me, whatever contrast it offers with my own."

The Best American Essays features a selection of the year's outstanding essays, essays of literary achievement that show an awareness of craft and a forcefulness of thought. Hundreds of essays are gathered annually from a wide variety of national and regional publications. These essays are then screened and turned over to a distinguished guest editor, who may add a few personal favorites to the list and who makes the final selections.

To qualify for selection, the essays must be works of respectable literary quality, intended as fully developed, independent essays (not excerpts) on subjects of general interest (not specialized scholarship), originally written in English (or translated by the author) for publication in an American periodical during the calendar year. Publications that want to make sure their contributors will be considered each year should include the series on their subscription list (Robert Atwan, *The Best American Essays*, P.O. Box 416, Maplewood, New Jersey 07079).

An annual collection involves the efforts and talents of many people. For this seventh volume of the series, I'd like to thank the editorial director of Ticknor & Fields, John Herman, and associate editor Celina Spiegel for their continued enthusiasm, support, and guidance. And I especially want to thank Susan Sontag, whose passion for the essay as a profoundly intelligent genre has enriched this series and given us an invigorating and distinguished book.

R.A.

Introduction

I SUPPOSE I might begin by declaring an interest.

Essays came into my life as a precocious, passionate reader as naturally as did poems and stories and novels. There was Emerson as well as Poe, Shaw's prefaces as well as Shaw's plays, and a little later Mann's *Essays of Three Decades* as well as *Stories of Three Decades,* and "Tradition and the Individual Talent" as well as "The Waste Land" and "Four Quartets," and Henry James's prefaces as well as Henry James's novels. An essay could be as much an event, a transforming event, as a novel or poem. You finished an essay by Lionel Trilling or Harold Rosenberg or Randall Jarrell or Paul Goodman, to mention only some American names, and you thought and felt forever differently.

Essays of the reach and eloquence I am describing are part of a literary culture. And a literary culture — that is, a community of readers and writers with a curious, passionate relation to the literature of the past — is just what one cannot take for granted now. The essayist is more likely a superior ironist or gadfly than a sage.

An essay is not an article, not a meditation, not a book review, not a memoir, not a disquisition, not a diatribe, not a shaggy dog story, not a monologue, not a travel narrative, not a suite of aphorisms, not an elegy, not a piece of reportage, not a —

No, an essay can be any or several of the above.

*

No poet has a problem saying, I am a poet. No fiction writer hesitates to say, I am writing a story. "Poem" and "story" are still relatively stable, easily identified literary forms or genres. The essay is not, in that sense, a genre. Rather, "essay" is just one name, the most sonorous name, bestowed on a wide range of writings. Writers and editors usually call them "pieces." This is not just modesty or American casualness. A certain defensiveness now surrounds the notion of the essay. And many of the best essayists today are quick to declare that their best work lies elsewhere: in writing that is more "creative" (fiction, poetry) or more exacting (scholarship, theory, philosophy).

Often conceived of as a kind of back-formation from other forms of writing, the essay is best defined by what it also is — or what it is not. The point is illustrated by the existence of this anthology, now in its seventh year. First came *The Best American Short Stories*. Then someone suggested, couldn't we also have *The Best American Short* — what? — nonfiction. The most accurate, as well as least satisfying, definition of the essay is: a short, or shorter, prose text that is *not* a story.

And yet it is a very old literary form — older than the story, arguably older than any long narrative that could be called a novel. Essay writing emerged in the high literary culture of ancient Rome, blending the energies of the oration and the formal letter. Not only did the first great essayists, Seneca and Plutarch, write what came to be known as moral essays, with titles like "On the Love of Wealth," "On Envy and Hate," "On Being a Busybody," "On the Control of Anger," "On Having Many Friends," "On Listening to Lectures," and "The Education of Children" — that is, confidently prescriptive accounts of principle, attitude, and conduct — but there are also essays, such as Plutarch's account of the customs of the Spartans, that are purely descriptive. And his "On the Malice of Herodotus" is one of the earliest examples of an essay devoted to the close reading of a master text: what we call literary criticism.

The essay project exhibits an extraordinary continuity, almost to the present day. Eighteen centuries after Plutarch, Hazlitt wrote essays with titles like "On the Pleasure of Hating," "On Going a Journey," "On the Love of the Country," "On the Fear of Death," "On Depth and Superficiality," "The Prose of

Poets" — the perennial topics — as well as essays on slyly trivial themes and reconsiderations of great authors and historical events. The essay project inaugurated by the Roman writers reached its climax in the course of the nineteenth century. Virtually every important nineteenth-century poet and novelist wrote essays, and several of the best writers (Hazlitt, Emerson) were principally essayists. It is also in the nineteenth century that one of the most familiar contemporary transpositions of essay writing — the essay in the guise of a book review — came to prominence. (Most of George Eliot's important essays were written as book reviews for the *Westminster Review*.) And two of the century's greatest minds, Kierkegaard and Nietzsche, could both be considered as practicing a form of the essay — made more concise and discontinuous by Nietzsche; more repetitive and verbose by Kierkegaard.

Of course, to say that a philosopher is an essayist is, from the traditional point of view of philosophy, a demotion. The culture administered by universities has always regarded the essay with suspicion, as a kind of writing that is too subjective, too accessible, merely belle-lettristic. An interloper in the solemn worlds of philosophy and polemic, the essay introduces digressiveness, exaggeration, mischief.

An essay can have any subject in the same sense that a story or a novel or a poem can have any subject. But the assertiveness of the essay-writing voice, the directness of its concern with opinion and argument, makes the essay a more perishable kind of literary enterprise. With a few glorious exceptions, the essayists from the past who were essayists only have not survived. Most essays of the past still of interest to the educated reader are by writers we already care about. One has a chance to discover that Turgenev wrote an unforgettable witness-essay against capital punishment, anticipating the famous essays on the same theme by Camus and Orwell, only because Turgenev is already present as a novelist. We relish Gertrude Stein's "What Are Masterpieces" and her *Lectures in America* because Stein is Stein is Stein.

It is not only that the essay *could* be about anything. It usually was. The good health of essay writing depends on writers continuing to address eccentric subjects. In contrast to poetry and fiction, the nature of the essay is diversity — diversity of level, subject, tone, diction. Essays on being old and falling in love and the nature of poetry are still being written. And there are also essays on Rita Hayworth's zipper and Mickey Mouse's ears.

Sometimes the essayist is a writer, mostly otherwise occupied (with poetry or fiction), who also writes . . . polemics, accounts of travels, elegies, re-evaluations of predecessors and rivals, self-promoting manifestos. Yes. Essays.

Sometimes "essayist" seems no more or less than a sneaky euphemism for "critic." And, indeed, some of the best essayists of the twentieth century have been critics. Dance, for instance, inspired André Levinson, Edwin Denby, and Arlene Croce. Literary studies has produced a vast constellation of major essayists — and still does, despite the engulfment of literary studies by academia.

Sometimes an essayist is a difficult writer who has, happily, condescended to the essay form. Would that more of the important early twentieth-century European philosophers, social thinkers, and cultural critics had done as did Simmel, Ortega y Gasset, and Adorno — who will probably continue to be read with pleasure only in their essays.

The word essay comes from the French *essai,* attempt — and many essayists, including the greatest of all, Montaigne, have insisted that the distinctive mark of the essay is its tentativeness, its disavowal of closed, systematic ways of thinking. Its most obvious trait, however, is assertiveness of one kind or another.

To read an essay properly, one must understand not only what it is arguing for but what it is arguing against. Reading the essays written by our contemporaries, we easily supply the context, the public argument, the opponent, explicit or implicit. The passage of a few decades can make this almost impossible.

Essays end up in books, but they start their lives in magazines. (It's hard to imagine a book of recent but previously unpublished essays.) The perennial comes now mainly in the guise of the topical and, in the short run, no literary form has as great and immediate an impact on contemporary readers. Many essays are discussed, debated, reacted to in a way that poets and writers of fiction can only envy.

The influential essayist is someone with an acute sense of what has not been (properly) talked about, what should be talked about (but differently). But what makes essays last is less their argument than the display of a complex mind and a distinctive prose voice.

While precision and clarity of argument and transparency of style are usually regarded as norms for essay writing, in the same way that the realistic conventions of narrative are taken as normative (and with as little justification), in fact the most durable and compelling tradition of essay writing is as a form of lyrical discourse.

All the great essays are in the first person. The writer need not say "I." A vivid, flavorful prose style with a high aphoristic content is itself a form of first-person writing: think of the essays of Emerson, Henry James, Gertrude Stein, Elizabeth Hardwick, William Gass. The writers I have mentioned are all Americans, and it would be easy to add others. Essay writing is one of the strong American literary forms. It emerges out of the sermon and its secular transposition, the public lecture. Our first great writer, Emerson, is primarily a writer of essays. And a variety of essay writing flourishes in our contemporary contentious, polyphonic culture: from essays that feature an argument to digressive meditations and evocations.

Instead of thinking of contemporary essays according to their subjects — the travel essay, literary and other kinds of criticism, the political essay, cultural criticism, etc. — one could distinguish them by their kinds of energy and rue. The essay as jeremiad. The essay as exercise in nostalgia. The essay as exhibition of a temperament. Etc.

We get out of essays everything a prancing human voice is capable of. Instruction. The bliss of eloquence deployed for its own sake. Moral correction. Entertainment. Deepening of feeling. Models of intelligence.

Intelligence is a literary virtue, not just an energy or aptitude given literary clothing.

It is hard to imagine an important essay that is not, first of all, a display of intelligence. And sheer intelligence of the highest order can in and of itself make a great essay. (Think of Jacques

Rivière on the novel, the Adorno of *Prisms* and *Minima Moralia,* the major essays of Walter Benjamin and Roland Barthes.) But there are as many varieties of essay writing as there are varieties of intelligence.

Baudelaire wanted to call a collection of his essays on painters *Painters Who Think.*

This is quintessentially the essayist's point of view: to convert the world and everything in it to a species of thinking. To the reflection of an idea, an assumption — which the essayist unfolds, defends, or excoriates.

Ideas about literature — unlike ideas about, say, love — almost never arise except in response to other people's ideas. They are reactive ideas. I say *this* because it's my impression that you — or most people, or many people — are saying *that.* Ideas give permission. And I want to give permission, by what I write, to a different feeling or evaluation or practice.

This is, preeminently, the essayist's stance.

I say *this* when you are saying *that* not just because writers are professional adversaries; not just to redress the inevitable imbalance or one-sidedness of any activity that has the character of an institution (and writing is an institution); but because the practice — I also mean the nature — of literature is rooted in inherently contradictory aspirations. A truth about literature is one whose opposite is also true.

Each poem or story or essay or novel that matters, that deserves the name of literature, incarnates an idea of singularity, of the singular voice. But literature — which is an accumulation — incarnates an idea of plurality, of multiplicity, of promiscuity. Every writer knows that the practice of literature demands a talent for reclusiveness. But literature . . . literature is a party. A wake, much of the time. But a party still. Even as disseminators of indignation, writers are givers of pleasure. And one becomes a writer not so much because one has something to say as because one has experienced ecstasy as a reader.

Here are two quotations I have been gnawing on recently.

The first, by the Spanish writer Camilo José Cela: "Literature is the denunciation of the times in which one lives."

The other is by Manet, who told a visitor to his studio in 1882: "Always move in the direction of concision. And then, cultivate your memories; nature will never give you anything but hints — it's like a railing that keeps you from falling into banality. You must constantly remain the master and do as you please. No tasks! No, no tasks!"

SUSAN SONTAG

ANNE CARSON

Short Talks

FROM THE YALE REVIEW

Early one morning words were missing. Before that, words were not. Facts were, faces were. In a good story, Aristotle tells us, everything that happens is pushed by something else. One day someone noticed there were stars but no words, why? I've asked a lot of people, I think it is a good question. Three old women were bending in the fields. What use is it to question us? they said. Well, it shortly became clear that they knew everything there is to know about the snowy fields and the blue-green shoots and the plant called "audacity" that poets mistake for violets. I began to copy out everything that was said. The marks construct an instant of nature gradually, without the boredom of a story. I emphasize this. I will do anything to avoid boredom. It is the task of a lifetime. You can never know enough, never work enough, never use the infinitives and participles oddly enough, never impede the movement harshly enough, never leave the mind quickly enough.

In fifty-three fascicles I copied out everything that was said, things vast distances apart. I read the fascicles each day at the same time, until yesterday men came and took up the fascicles. Put them in a crate. Locked it. Then together we viewed the landscape. Their instructions were clear, I am to imitate a mirror like that of water (but water is not a mirror and it is dangerous to think so). In fact I was the whole time waiting for them to leave so I could begin filling in the parts I missed. So I am left with three fascicles (which I hid). I have to be careful what I set down. Aristotle talks about probability and necessity, but what good is a marvel, what good is a story that does not contain poison dragons? Well, you can never work enough.

Short Talk on Walking Backwards

My mother forbad us to walk backwards. That is how the dead walk, she would say. Where did she get this idea? Perhaps from a bad translation. The dead, after all, do not walk backwards but they do walk behind us. They have no lungs and cannot call out but would love for us to turn around. They are victims of love, many of them.

Short Talk on Le Bonheur d'être bien aimée

Day after day I think of you as soon as I wake up. Someone has put cries of birds on the air like jewels.

Short Talk on Brigitte Bardot

Brigitte Bardot is on the prowl. What does she want, a slave? to satisfy her hungers and make beautiful photographs. Whose slave is it? She does not care, she never blames herself. Using oil she will make the slave shine. Perfect. *La folie,* she will think to herself.

Short Talk on Rectification

Kafka liked to have his watch an hour and a half fast. Felice kept setting it right. Nonetheless, each of us loves the other as he is, he wrote in his diary along with some remarks about her gold teeth, which had for him a really hellish luster in 1912. And for five years they almost married. He made a list of arguments for and against it, including inability to bear the assault of his own life (for) and the sight of the nightshirts laid out on his parents' beds at 10:30 (against). Hemorrhage saved him. When advised not to speak by doctors in the sanatorium, he left glass sentences all over the floor. Felice, says one of them, had too much naked-ness left in her. Healthy teeth? Also horrible in their way.

Short Talk on van Gogh

The reason I drink is to understand the yellow sky, the great yellow sky, said van Gogh. When he looked at the world he saw the nails that attach colors to things and he saw that the nails were in pain.

Short Talk on Sleep Stones

Camille Claudel lived the last thirty years of her life in an asylum wondering why, writing letters to her brother the poet, who had signed the papers. Come visit me, she says. Remember I am living here with madwomen, days are long. She did not smoke or stroll. She refused to sculpt. Although they gave her sleep stones — marble and granite and porphyry — she broke them, then collected the pieces and buried these outside the walls at night. Night was when her hands grew huger and huger, until in the photograph they are like two parts of someone else loaded onto her knees.

Short Talk on Waterproofing

Franz Kafka was Jewish. He had a sister, Ottla, Jewish. Ottla married a jurist, Josef David, not Jewish. When the Nuremberg Laws were introduced to Bohemia-Moravia in 1942, quiet Ottla suggested to Josef David that they divorce. He at first refused. She spoke about night shapes and property and their two daughters and a rational approach. She did not mention, because she did not yet know the word, Auschwitz, where she would die in October 1943, After putting the apartment in order she packed a rucksack and was given a good shoeshine by Josef David. He applied a coat of grease. Now they are waterproof, he said.

Short Talk on the Mona Lisa

Every day he poured his question into her, as you pour water from one vessel into another, and it poured back. Don't tell me he was painting his mother, lust, etc. There is a moment when the water is not in one vessel or in the other — what a thirst it was, and he supposed that when the canvas became completely empty he would stop. But women are strong. She knew vessels, she knew water, she knew mortal thirst.

Short Talk on Sylvia Plath

Did you see her mother on television? She said plain, burned things. She said I thought it an excellent poem but it hurt me. She did not say jungle fear. She did not say jungle hatred wild jungle weeping chop it back chop it. She said self-government she said end of the road. She did not say humming in the middle of the air what you came for chop.

Short Talk on the Total Collection

From childhood he dreamed of being able to keep with him all the objects in the world lined up on his shelves and bookcases. He denied lack, oblivion, or even the likelihood of a missing piece. Order streamed from Noah in blue triangles and as the pure fury of his classifications rose around him, engulfing his life, they came to be called waves by others, who drowned, a world of them.

Short Talk on Seating

Nowadays he is tied to a chair in a room with three madmen but during the war my father was a navigator and flew low over France to drop parcels for spies — once nylon stockings, hard to explain to the Germans who shot down the plane. *Wo ist sie?* they kept asking but Dad had no German and the other three were dead in their seats.

Short Talk on The Anatomy Lesson of Dr. Deyman

A winter so cold that walking on the Breestraat as you passed from sun to shadow you could feel the difference run down your

skull like water. It was the hunger winter of 1656 when Black Jan
took up with a whore named Elsje Ottje and for a time they prospered. But one icy January day Black Jan was observed robbing
a cloth merchant's house. He ran, fell, knifed a man and was
hanged on the 27th of January. How he fared then is no doubt
known to you: the cold weather permitted Dr. Deyman to turn
the true eye of medicine on Black Jan for three days. One wonders if Elsje ever saw Rembrandt's painting, which shows her
love thief in violent frontal foreshortening, so that his pure soles
seem almost to touch the chopped-open cerebrum. Cut and cut
deep to find the source of the problem, Dr. Deyman is saying, as
he parts the brain to either side like hair. Sadness comes groping
out of it.

Short Talk on the Sensation of Airplane Takeoff

Well you know I wonder, it could be love running toward my life
with its arms up yelling *let's buy it what a bargain!*

Short Talk on Orchids

We live by tunneling for we are people buried alive. To me, the
tunnels you make will seem strangely aimless, uprooted orchids.
But the fragrance is undying. A Little Boy has run away from
Amherst a few Days ago, writes Emily Dickinson in a letter of
1883, and when asked where he was going replied, Vermont or
Asia.

Short Talk on Shelter

You can write on a wall with a fish heart, it's because of the phos-
phorous. They eat it, there are shacks like that down along the
river. I am writing this to be as wrong as possible to you. Replace
the door when you leave, it says, now you tell me how wrong that
is. How long it glows. Tell me.

JOAN DIDION

Sentimental Journeys

FROM THE NEW YORK REVIEW OF BOOKS

1

WE KNOW her story, and some of us, although not all of us, which was to become one of the story's several equivocal aspects, know her name. She was a twenty-nine-year-old unmarried white woman who worked as an investment banker in the corporate finance department at Salomon Brothers in downtown Manhattan, the energy and natural resources group. She was said by one of the principals in a Texas oil stock offering on which she had collaborated as a member of the Salomon team to have done "top-notch" work. She lived alone in an apartment on East 83rd Street, between York and East End, a sublet cooperative she was thinking about buying. She often worked late and when she got home she would change into jogging clothes and at eight-thirty or nine-thirty in the evening would go running, six or seven miles through Central Park, north on the East Drive, west on the less traveled road connecting the East and West Drives at approximately 102nd Street, and south on the West Drive. The wisdom of this was later questioned by some, by those who were accustomed to thinking of the park as a place to avoid after dark, and defended by others, the more adroit of whom spoke of the citizen's absolute right to public access ("That park belongs to us and this time nobody is going to take it from us," Ronnie Eldridge, at the time a Democratic candidate for the City Council of New York, declared on the op-ed page of the *New York Times*), others of whom spoke of "running" as a preemptive right. "Runners have Type A controlled personalities and they don't like their schedules interrupted," one runner, a securities trader, told the *Times* to this point. "When people run is a function of their life-style," another runner said. "I am personally very angry," a third said, "because women should have the right to run any time."

For this woman in this instance these notional rights did not prevail. She was found, with her clothes torn off, not far from the 102nd Street connecting road at one-thirty on the morning of April 20, 1989. She was taken near death to Metropolitan Hospital on East 97th Street. She had lost 75 percent of her blood. Her skull had been crushed, her left eyeball pushed back through its socket, the characteristic surface wrinkles of her brain flattened. Dirt and twigs were found in her vagina, suggesting rape. By May 2, when she first woke from coma, six black and Hispanic teenagers, four of whom had made videotaped statements concerning their roles in the attack and another of whom had described his role in an unsigned verbal statement, had been charged with her assault and rape and she had become, unwilling and unwitting, a sacrificial player in the sentimental narrative that is New York public life.

NIGHTMARE IN CENTRAL PARK, the headlines and display type read. *Teen Wolfpack Beats and Rapes Wall Street Exec on Jogging Path. Central Park Horror. Wolf Pack's Prey. Female Jogger Near Death After Savage Attack by Roving Gang. Rape Rampage. Park Marauders Call It 'Wilding,' Street Slang for Going Berserk. Rape Suspect: 'It Was Fun.' Rape Suspect's Jailhouse Boast: 'She Wasn't Nothing.' The teenagers were back in the holding cell, the confessions gory and complete. One shouted "hit the beat" and they all started rapping to "Wild Thing." The Jogger and the Wolf Pack. An Outrage And A Prayer.* And, on the Monday morning after the attack, on the front page of the *New York Post,* with a photograph of Governor Mario Cuomo and the headline NONE OF US IS SAFE, this italic text: "A visibly shaken Governor Cuomo spoke out yesterday on the vicious Central Park rape: 'The people are angry and frightened — my mother is, my family is. To me, as a person who's lived in this city all of his life, this is the ultimate shriek of alarm.' "

Later it would be recalled that 3,254 other rapes were reported that year, including one the following week involving the

near decapitation of a black woman in Fort Tryon Park and one
two weeks later involving a black woman in Brooklyn who was
robbed, raped, sodomized, and thrown down the air shaft of a
four-story building, but the point was rhetorical, since crimes are
universally understood to be news to the extent that they offer,
however erroneously, a story, a lesson, a high concept. In the
1986 Central Park death of Jennifer Levin, then eighteen, at the
hands of Robert Chambers, then nineteen, the "story," extrapo-
lated more or less from thin air but left largely uncorrected, had
to do not with people living wretchedly and marginally on the
underside of where they wanted to be, not with the Dreiserian
pursuit of "respectability" that marked the revealed details (Robert Chambers's mother was a private-duty nurse who worked
twelve-hour night shifts to enroll her son in private schools and
the Knickerbocker Greys), but with "preppies," and the familiar
"too much too soon."

Susan Brownmiller, during a year spent monitoring newspaper
coverage of rape as part of her research for *Against Our Will:
Men, Women and Rape,* found, not surprisingly, that "although
New York City police statistics showed that black women were
more frequent victims of rape than white women, the favored
victim in the tabloid headline . . . was young, white, middle-class
and 'attractive.' " In its quite extensive coverage of rape-murders
during the year 1971, according to Ms. Brownmiller, the *Daily
News* published in its four-star final edition only two stories in
which the victim was not described in the lead paragraph as "attractive": one of these stories involved an eight-year-old child,
the other was a second-day follow-up on a first-day story which
had in fact described the victim as "attractive." The *Times,* she
found, covered rapes only infrequently that year, but what coverage they did "concerned victims who had some kind of middle-
class status, such as 'nurse,' 'dancer' or 'teacher,' and with a favored setting of Central Park."

As a news story, "Jogger" was understood to turn on the demonstrable "difference" between the victim and her accused assailants, four of whom lived in Schomburg Plaza, a federally
subsidized apartment complex at the northeast corner of Fifth
Avenue and 110th Street in East Harlem, and the rest of whom
lived in the projects and rehabilitated tenements just to the north

and west of Schomburg Plaza. Some twenty-five teenagers were brought in for questioning; eight were held. The six who were finally indicted ranged in age from fourteen to sixteen. That none of the six had a previous police record passed, in this context, for achievement; beyond that, one was recalled by his classmates to have taken pride in his expensive basketball shoes, another to have been "a follower." *I'm a smooth type of fellow, cool, calm, and mellow,* one of the six, Yusef Salaam, would say in the rap he presented as part of his statement before sentencing.

> I'm kind of laid back, but now I'm speaking so that you know
> I got used and abused and even was put on the news. . . .
> I'm not dissing them all, but the some that I called
> They tried to dis me like I was an inch small, like a midget,
> a mouse, something less than a man.

The victim, by contrast, was a leader, part of what the *Times* would describe as "the wave of young professionals who took over New York in the 1980's," one of those who were "handsome and pretty and educated and white," who, according to the *Times,* not only "believed they owned the world" but "had reason to." She was from a Pittsburgh suburb, Upper St. Clair, the daughter of a retired Westinghouse senior manager. She had been Phi Beta Kappa at Wellesley, a graduate of the Yale School of Management, a congressional intern, nominated for a Rhodes scholarship, remembered by the chairman of her department at Wellesley as "probably one of the top four or five students of the decade." She was reported to be a vegetarian, and "fun-loving," although only "when time permitted," and also to have had (these were the *Times*'s details) "concerns about the ethics of the American business world."

In other words she was wrenched, even as she hung between death and life and later between insentience and sentience, into New York's ideal sister, daughter, Bachrach bride: a young woman of conventional middle-class privilege and promise whose situation was such that many people tended to overlook the fact that the state's case against the accused was not invulnerable. The state could implicate most of the defendants in the assault and rape in their own videotaped words, but had none of the incontrovertible forensic evidence — no matching semen, no matching fingernail scrapings, no matching blood — commonly

produced in this kind of case. Despite the fact that jurors in the
second trial would eventually mention physical evidence as having been crucial in their bringing guilty verdicts against one de-
fendant, Kevin Richardson, there was not actually much physical
evidence at hand. Fragments of hair "similar [to] and consistent"
with that of the victim were found on Kevin Richardson's clothing and underwear, but the state's own criminologist had testified that hair samples were necessarily inconclusive since, unlike
fingerprints, they could not be traced to a single person. Dirt
samples found on the defendants' clothing were, again, similar
to dirt found in the part of the park where the attack took place,
but the state's criminologist allowed that the samples were also
similar to dirt found in other uncultivated areas of the park. To
suggest, however, that this minimal physical evidence could open
the case to an aggressive defense — to, say, the kind of defense
that such celebrated New York criminal lawyers as Jack Litman
and Barry Slotnick typically present — would come to be construed, during the weeks and months to come, as a further attack
on the victim.

She would be Lady Courage to the *New York Post,* she would be
A Profile in Courage to the *Daily News* and *New York Newsday.* She
would become for Anna Quindlen in the *New York Times* the figure of "New York rising above the dirt, the New Yorker who has
known the best, and the worst, and has stayed on, living somewhere in the middle." She would become for David Dinkins, the
first black mayor of New York, the emblem of his apparently
fragile hopes for the city itself: "I hope the city will be able to
learn a lesson from this event and be inspired by the young
woman who was assaulted in the case," he said. "Despite tremendous odds, she is rebuilding her life. What a human life can do,
a human society can do as well." She was even then for John Gut-
freund, the chairman and chief executive officer of Salomon
Brothers, the personification of "what makes this city so vibrant
and so great," now "struck down by a side of our city that is as
awful and terrifying as the creative side is wonderful." It was precisely in this conflation of victim and city, this confusion of personal woe with public distress, that the crime's "story" would be
found, its lesson, its encouraging promise of narrative resolution.

*

One reason the victim in this case could be so readily abstracted, and her situation so readily made to stand for that of the city itself, was that she remained, as a victim of rape, unnamed in most press reports. Although the American and English press convention of not naming victims of rape (adult rape victims are named in French papers) derives from the understandable wish to protect the victim, the rationalization of this special protection rests on a number of doubtful, even magical, assumptions. The convention assumes, by providing a protection for victims of rape not afforded victims of other assaults, that rape involves a violation absent from other kinds of assault. The convention assumes that this violation is of a nature best kept secret, that the rape victim feels, and would feel still more strongly were she identified, a shame and self-loathing unique to this form of assault; in other words that she has been in an unspecified way party to her own assault, that a special contract exists between this one kind of victim and her assailant.

The convention assumes, finally, that the victim would be, were this special contract revealed, the natural object of prurient interest; that the act of male penetration involves such potent mysteries that the woman so penetrated (as opposed, say, to having her face crushed with a brick or her brain penetrated with a length of pipe) is permanently marked, "different," even — especially if there is a perceived racial or social "difference" between victim and assailant, as in nineteenth-century stories featuring white women taken by Indians — "ruined."

These quite specifically masculine assumptions (women do not want to be raped, nor do they want to have their brains smashed, but very few mystify the difference between the two) tend in general to be self-fulfilling, guiding the victim to define her assault as her protectors do. "Ultimately we're doing women a disservice by separating rape from other violent crimes," Deni Elliott, the director of Dartmouth's Ethics Institute, suggested in a discussion of this custom in *Time*. "We are participating in the stigma of rape by treating victims of this crime differently," Geneva Overholser, the editor of the Des Moines *Register,* said about her decision to publish in February 1990 a five-part piece about a rape victim who agreed to be named. "When we as a society refuse to talk openly about rape, I think we weaken our ability to deal with it." Susan Estrich, a professor of criminal law at Harvard Law School and the manager of Michael Dukakis's 1988 presidential campaign, discussed, in *Real Rape*, the conflicting emotions that followed her own 1974 rape:

> At first, being raped is something you simply don't talk about. Then it occurs to you that people whose houses are broken into or who are mugged in Central Park talk about it *all* the time. . . . If it isn't my fault, why am I supposed to be ashamed? If I'm not ashamed, if it wasn't "personal," why look askance when I mention it?

There were, in the 1989 Central Park attack, specific circumstances that reinforced the conviction that the victim should not be named. She had clearly been, according to the doctors who examined her at Metropolitan Hospital and to the statements made by the suspects (she herself remembered neither the attack nor anything that happened during the next six weeks), raped by one or more assailants. She had also been beaten so brutally that fifteen months later she could not focus her eyes or walk unaided. She had lost all sense of smell. She could not read without experiencing double vision. She was believed at the time to have permanently lost function in some areas of her brain.

Given these circumstances, the fact that neither the victim's family nor, later, the victim herself wanted her name known struck an immediate chord of sympathy, seemed a belated way to protect her as she had not been protected in Central Park. Yet there was in this case a special emotional undertow that derived in part from the deep and allusive associations and taboos attaching, in American black history, to the idea of the rape of white women. Rape remained, in the collective memory of many blacks, the very core of their victimization. Black men were accused of raping white women, even as black women were, Malcolm X wrote in *The Autobiography of Malcolm X,* "raped by the slavemaster white man until there had begun to emerge a homemade, handmade, brainwashed race that was no longer even of its true color, that no longer even knew its true family names." The very frequency of sexual contact between white men and black women increased the potency of the taboo on any such contact between black men and white women. The abolition of slavery, W. J. Cash wrote in *The Mind of the South,*

> in destroying the rigid fixity of the black at the bottom of the scale, in throwing open to him at least the legal opportunity to advance, had

inevitably opened up to the mind of every Southerner a vista at the end of which stood the overthrow of this taboo. If it was given to the black to advance at all, who could say (once more the logic of the doctrine of his inherent inferiority would not hold) that he would not one day advance the whole way and lay claim to complete equality, including, specifically, the ever crucial right of marriage?

What Southerners felt, therefore, was that any assertion of any kind on the part of the Negro constituted in a perfectly real manner an attack on the Southern woman. What they saw, more or less consciously, in the conditions of Reconstruction was a passage toward a condition for her as degrading, in their view, as rape itself. And a condition, moreover, which, logic or no logic, they infallibly thought of as being as absolutely forced upon her as rape, and hence a condition for which the term "rape" stood as truly as for the *de facto* deed.

Nor was the idea of rape the only potentially treacherous undercurrent in this case. There has historically been, for American blacks, an entire complex of loaded references around the question of "naming": slave names, masters' names, African names, call me by my rightful name, nobody knows my name; stories, in which the specific gravity of naming locked directly into that of rape, of black men whipped for addressing white women by their given names.

That in this case just such an interlocking of references could work to fuel resentments and inchoate hatreds seemed clear, and it seemed equally clear that some of what ultimately occurred — the repeated references to lynchings, the identification of the defendants with the Scottsboro boys, the insistently provocative repetition of the victim's name, the weird and self-defeating insistence that no rape had taken place and little harm been done the victim — derived momentum from this historical freight. "Years ago, if a white woman said a Black man looked at her lustfully, he could be hung higher than a magnolia tree in bloom, while a white mob watched joyfully sipping tea and eating cookies," Yusef Salaam's mother reminded readers of the *Amsterdam News*. "The first thing you do in the United States of America when a white woman is raped is round up a bunch of black youths, and I think that's what happened here," the Reverend Calvin O. Butts III of the Abyssinian Baptist Church in Harlem told the *New York Times*. "You going to arrest me now 'cause I said the jogger's name?" Gary Byrd asked rhetorically on his WLIB show, and was quoted by Edwin Diamond in *New York* magazine:

> I mean, she's obviously a public figure, and a very mysterious one, I might add. Well, it's a funny place we live in called America, and should we be surprised that they're up to their usual tricks? It was a trick that got us here in the first place.

This reflected one of the problems with not naming this victim: she was in fact named all the time. Everyone in the courthouse, everyone who worked for a paper or a television station or who followed the case for whatever professional reason, knew her name. She was referred to by name in all court records and in all court proceedings. She was named, in the days immediately following the attack, on local television stations. She was also routinely named — and this was part of the difficulty, part of what led to a damaging self-righteousness among those who did not name her and to an equally damaging embattlement among those who did — in Manhattan's black-owned newspapers, the *Amsterdam News* and the *City Sun,* and she was named as well on WLIB, the Manhattan radio station owned by a black partnership which included Percy Sutton and, until 1985 when he transferred his stock to his son, Mayor Dinkins.

That the victim in this case was identified on Centre Street and north of 96th Street but not in between made for a certain cognitive dissonance, especially since the names of even the juvenile suspects had been released by the police and the press before any suspect had even been arraigned, let alone indicted. "The police normally withhold the names of minors who are accused of crimes," the *Times* explained (actually, the police normally withhold the names of accused "juveniles," or minors under age sixteen, but not of minors sixteen or seventeen), "but officials said they made public the names of the youths charged in the attack on the woman because of the seriousness of the incident." There seemed a debatable point here, the question of whether "the seriousness of the incident" might not have in fact seemed a compelling reason to avoid any appearance of a rush to judgment by preserving the anonymity of a juvenile suspect; one of the names released by the police and published in the *Times* was of a fourteen-year-old who was ultimately not indicted.

*

There were, early on, certain aspects of this case that seemed not well handled by the police and prosecutors, and others that seemed not well handled by the press. It would seem to have been tactically unwise, since New York state law requires that a parent or guardian be present when children under sixteen are questioned, for police to continue the interrogation of Yusef Salaam, then fifteen, on the grounds that his Transit Authority bus pass said he was sixteen, while his mother was kept waiting outside. It would seem to have been unwise for Linda Fairstein, the assistant district attorney in charge of Manhattan sex crimes, to ignore, at the precinct house, the mother's assertion that the son was fifteen, and later to suggest, in open court, that the boy's age had been unclear to her because the mother had used the word "minor."

It would also seem to have been unwise for Linda Fairstein to tell David Nocenti, the assistant U.S. attorney who was paired with Yusef Salaam in a "Big Brother" program and who had come to the precinct house at the mother's request, that he had "no legal standing" there and that she would file a complaint with his supervisors. It would seem in this volatile a case imprudent of the police to follow their normal procedure by presenting Raymond Santana's initial statement in their own words, cop phrases that would predictably seem to some in the courtroom, as the expression of a fourteen-year-old held overnight and into the next afternoon for interrogation, unconvincing:

> On April 19, 1989, at approximately 20:30 hours, I was at the Taft Projects in the vicinity of 113th St. and Madison Avenue. I was there with numerous friends. . . . At approximately 21:00 hours, we all (myself and approximately 15 others) walked south on Madison Avenue to E. 110th Street, then walked westbound to Fifth Avenue. At Fifth Avenue and 110th Street, we met up with an additional group of approximately 15 other males, who also entered Central Park with us at that location with the intent to rob cyclists and joggers. . . .

In a case in which most of the defendants had made videotaped statements admitting at least some role in the assault and rape, this less than meticulous attitude toward the gathering and dissemination of information seemed peculiar and self-defeating, the kind of pressured or unthinking standard procedure that could not only exacerbate the fears and angers and suspicions of conspiracy shared by many blacks but conceivably open what seemed, on the basis of the confessions, a conclusive case to the kind of doubt that would eventually keep juries out, in the trial of the first three defendants, ten days, and, in the trial of the next two defendants, twelve days. One of the reasons the jury in the first trial could not agree, *Manhattan Lawyer* reported in its October 1990 issue, was that one juror, Ronald Gold, remained "deeply troubled by the discrepancies between the story [Antron] McCray tells on his videotaped statement and the prosecution scenario":

> Why did McCray place the rape at the reservoir, Gold demanded, when all evidence indicated it happened at the 102 Street crossdrive? Why did McCray say the jogger was raped where she fell, when the prosecution said she'd been dragged 300 feet into the woods first? Why did McCray talk about having to hold her arms down, if she was found bound and gagged?
>
> The debate raged for the last two days, with jurors dropping in and out of Gold's acquittal [for McCray] camp. . . .
>
> After the jurors watched McCray's video for the fifth time, Miranda [Rafael Miranda, another juror] knew it well enough to cite the time-code numbers imprinted at the bottom of the videotape as he rebuffed Gold's arguments with specific statements from McCray's own lips. [McCray, on the videotape, after admitting that he had held the victim by her left arm as her clothes were pulled off, volunteered that he had "got on top" of her, and said that he had rubbed against her without an erection "so everybody would . . . just know I did it."] The pressure on Gold was mounting. Three jurors agree that it was evident Gold, worn down perhaps by his own displays of temper as much as anything else, capitulated out of exhaustion. While a bitter Gold told other jurors he felt terrible about ultimately giving in, Brueland [Harold Brueland, another juror who had for a time favored acquittal for McCray] believes it was all part of the process.
>
> "I'd like to tell Ronnie some day that nervous exhaustion is an element built into the court system. They know that," Brueland says of court officials. "They know we're only going to be able to take it for so long. It's just a matter of, you know, who's got the guts to stick with it."

So fixed were the emotions provoked by this case that the idea that there could have been, for even one juror, even a moment's doubt in the state's case, let alone the kind of doubt that could be sustained over ten days or twelve, seemed, to many in the city, bewildering, almost unthinkable: the attack on the jogger had by then passed into narrative, and the narrative was about confrontation, about what Governor Cuomo had called "the ultimate shriek of alarm," about what was wrong with the city and about its solution. What was wrong with the city had been identified, and its names were Raymond Santana, Yusef Salaam, Antron McCray, Kharey Wise, Kevin Richardson, and Steve Lopez. "They never could have thought of it as they raged through Central Park, tormenting and ruining people," Bob Herbert wrote in the *News* after the verdicts came in on the first three defendants.

> There was no way it could have crossed their vicious minds. Running with the pack, they would have scoffed at the very idea. They would have laughed.
>
> And yet it happened. In the end, Yusef Salaam, Antron McCray and Raymond Santana were nailed by a woman.
>
> Elizabeth Lederer stood in the courtroom and watched Saturday night as the three were hauled off to jail. . . . At times during the trial, she looked about half the height of the long and lanky Salaam, who sneered at her from the witness stand.
>
> Salaam was apparently too dumb to realize that Lederer — this petite, soft-spoken, curly-haired prosecutor — was the jogger's avenger. . . .
>
> You could tell that her thoughts were elsewhere, that she was thinking about the jogger.
>
> You could tell that she was thinking: I did it.
>
> I did it for you.

Do this in remembrance of me: the solution, then, or so such pervasive fantasies suggested, was to partake of the symbolic body and blood of The Jogger, whose idealization was by this point complete, and was rendered, significantly, in details stressing her "difference," or superior class. The Jogger was someone who wore, according to *Newsday*, "a light gold chain around her slender neck" as well as, according to the *News*, a "modest" gold ring and "a thin sheen" of lipstick. The Jogger was someone who would not, according to the *Post*, "even dignify her alleged attackers with a glance." The Jogger was someone who spoke, according to the *News*, in accents "suited to boardrooms," accents that might therefore seem "foreign to many native New Yorkers." In her first appearance on the witness stand she had been subjected, the *Times* noted, "to questions that most people do not have to answer publicly during their lifetimes," principally about her use of a diaphragm on the Sunday preceding the attack, and had answered these questions, according to an editorial in the *News,* with an "indomitable dignity" that had taught the city a lesson "about courage and class."

This emphasis on perceived refinements of character and of manner and of taste tended to distort and to flatten, and ultimately to suggest not the actual victim of an actual crime but a fictional character of a slightly earlier period, the well-brought-up maiden who briefly graces the city with her presence and receives in turn a taste of "real life." The defendants, by contrast, were seen as incapable of appreciating these marginal distinctions, ignorant of both the norms and accoutrements of middle-class life. "Did you have jogging clothes on?" Elizabeth Lederer asked Yusef Salaam, by way of trying to discredit his statement that he had gone into the park that night only to "walk around." Did he have "jogging clothes," did he have "sports equipment," did he have "a bicycle." A pernicious nostalgia had come to permeate the case, a longing for the New York that had seemed for a while to be about "sports equipment," about getting and spending rather than about having and not having: the reason that this victim must not be named was so that she could go unrecognized, it was astonishingly said, by Jerry Nachman, the editor of the *New York Post,* and then by others who seemed to find in this a particular resonance, to Bloomingdale's.

Some New York stories involving young middle-class white women do not make it to the editorial pages, or even necessarily to the front pages. In April 1990, a young middle-class white woman named Laurie Sue Rosenthal, raised in an Orthodox Jewish household and at age twenty-nine still living with her parents in Jamaica, Queens, happened to die according to the coroner's report from the accidental toxicity of Darvocet in combination with alcohol, in an apartment at 36 East 68th Street in Manhattan. The apartment belonged to the man she had been, according to her parents, seeing for about a year, a minor assistant city commissioner named Peter Franconeri. Peter Franconeri, who was at the time in charge of elevator and boiler inspec-

tions for the Buildings Department and married to someone
else, wrapped Laurie Sue Rosenthal's body in a blanket; placed
it, along with her handbag and ID, outside the building with the
trash; and went to his office at 60 Hudson Street. At some point
an anonymous call was made to 911. Franconeri was identified
only after her parents gave the police his beeper number, which
they found in her address book. According to *Newsday*, which
covered the story more extensively than the *News*, the *Post*, or the
Times,

> initial police reports indicated that there were no visible wounds on
> Rosenthal's body. But Rosenthal's mother, Ceil, said yesterday that
> the family was told the autopsy revealed two "unexplained bruises"
> on her daughter's body.
>
> Larry and Ceil Rosenthal said those findings seemed to support
> their suspicions that their daughter was upset because they received a
> call from their daughter at 3 A.M. Thursday "saying that he had
> beaten her up." The family reported the conversation to police.
>
> "I told her to get into a cab and get home," Larry Rosenthal said
> yesterday. "The next I heard was two detectives telling me terrible
> things."
>
> "The ME [medical examiner] said the bruises did not constitute a
> beating but they were going to examine them further," Ceil Rosenthal
> said.

"There were some minor bruises," a spokeswoman for the office of the chief medical examiner told *Newsday* a few days later,
but the bruises "did not in any way contribute to her death." This
is worth rerunning: a young woman calls her parents at three in
the morning, "distraught." She says that she has been beaten up.
A few hours later, on East 68th Street between Madison and Park
avenues, a few steps from Porthault and Pratesi and Armani and
Saint Laurent and the Westbury Hotel, at a time of day in this
part of New York 10021 when Jim Buck's dog trainers are assem-
bling their morning packs and Henry Kravis's Bentley is idling
outside his Park Avenue apartment and the construction crews
are clocking in over near the Frick at the multi-million-dollar
houses under reconstruction for Bill Cosby and for the owner of
The Limited, this young middle-class white woman's body, showing bruises, gets put out with the trash.

"Everybody got upside down because of who he was," an un-
identified police officer later told Jim Dwyer of *Newsday*, refer-

ring to the man who put the young woman out with the trash. "If
it had happened to anyone else, nothing would have come of it.
A summons would have been issued and that would have been
the end of it." In fact nothing did come of the death of Laurie
Sue Rosenthal, which might have seemed a natural tabloid story
but failed, on several levels, to catch the local imagination. For
one thing, she could not be trimmed into the role of the preferred tabloid victim, who is conventionally presented as fate's
random choice (Laurie Sue Rosenthal had, for whatever reason,
taken the Darvocet instead of a taxi home, her parents reported
treatment for a previous Valium dependency, she could be presumed to have known over the course of a year that Franconeri
was married and yet continued to see him); for another, she
seemed not to have attended an expensive school or to have been
employed in a glamour industry (no Ivy Grad, no Wall Street
Exec), which made it hard to cast her as part of "what makes this
city so vibrant and so great."

In August 1990, Peter Franconeri pleaded guilty to a misde-
meanor, the unlawful removal of a body, and was sentenced by
Criminal Court Judge Peter Benitez to seventy-five hours of
community service. This was neither surprising nor much of a
story (only twenty-three lines even in *Newsday*, on page twenty-
nine of the city edition), and the case's resolution was for many
people a kind of relief. The district attorney's office had asked
for "some incarceration," the amount usually described as a
touch, but no one wanted, it was said, to crucify the guy: Peter
Franconeri was somebody who knew a lot of people, understood
how to live in the city, who had for example not only the apartment on East 68th Street between Madison and Park but a house
in Southampton and who also understood that putting a body
outside with the trash was nothing to get upside down about, if it
was handled right. Such understandings may in fact have been
the city's true "ultimate shriek of alarm," but it was not a shriek
the city wanted to recognize.

2

Perhaps the most arresting collateral news to surface during the
first few days after the attack on the Central Park jogger was that
a significant number of New Yorkers apparently believed the city

sufficiently well ordered to incorporate Central Park into their evening fitness schedules. "Prudence" was defined, even after the attack, as "staying south of 90th Street," or having "an awareness that you need to think about planning your routes," or, in the case of one woman interviewed by the *Times*, deciding to quit her daytime job (she was a lawyer) because she was "tired of being stuck out there, running later and later at night." "I don't think there's a runner who couldn't describe the silky, gliding feeling you get running at night," an editor of *Runner's World* told the *Times*. "You see less of what's around you and you become centered on your running."

The notion that Central Park at night might be a good place to "see less of what's around you" was recent. There were two reasons why Frederick Law Olmsted and Calvert Vaux, when they devised their winning entry in the 1858 competition for a Central Park design, decided to sink the transverse roads below grade level. One reason, the most often cited, was aesthetic, a recognition on the part of the designers that the four crossings specified by the terms of the competition, at 65th, 79th, 85th, and 97th streets, would intersect the sweep of the landscape, be "at variance with those agreeable sentiments which we should wish the park to inspire." The other reason, which appears to have been equally compelling, had to do with security. The problem with grade-level crossings, Olmsted and Vaux wrote in their "Greensward" plan, would be this:

> The transverse roads will . . . have to be kept open, while the park proper will be useless for any good purpose after dusk; for experience has shown that even in London, with its admirable police arrangements, the public cannot be assured safe transit through large open spaces of ground after nightfall.
>
> These public thoroughfares will then require to be well lighted at the sides, and, to restrain marauders pursued by the police from escaping into the obscurity of the park, strong fences or walls, six or eight feet high, will be necessary.

The park, in other words, was seen from its conception as intrinsically dangerous after dark, a place of "obscurity," "useless for any good purpose," a refuge only for "marauders." The parks of Europe closed at nightfall, Olmsted noted in his 1882 pamphlet *The Spoils of the Park: With a Few Leaves from the Deep-*

laden Note-books of "A Wholly Unpractical Man," "but one surface
road is kept open across Hyde Park, and the superintendent of
the Metropolitan Police told me that a man's chances of being
garrotted or robbed were, because of the facilities for conceal-
ment to be found in the Park, greater in passing at night along
this road than anywhere else in London."

In the high pitch of the initial "jogger" coverage, suggesting as
it did a city overtaken by animals, this pragmatic approach to urban living gave way to a more ideal construct, one in which New
York either had once been or should be "safe," and now, as in
Governor Cuomo's "none of us is safe," was not. It was time, ac-
cordingly, to "take it back," time to "say no"; time, as David Dinkins would put it during his campaign for the mayoralty in the
summer of 1989, to "draw the line." What the line was to be
drawn against was "crime," an abstract, a free-floating specter
that could be dispelled by certain acts of personal affirmation, by
the kind of moral rearmament which later figured in Mayor
Dinkins's plan to revitalize the city by initiating weekly "Tuesday
Night Out Against Crime" rallies.

By going into the park at night, Tom Wicker wrote in the
Times, the victim in this case had "affirmed the primacy of freedom over fear." A week after the assault, Susan Chace suggested
on the op-ed page of the *Times* that readers walk into the park at
night and join hands. "A woman can't run in the park at an off-
beat time," she wrote. "Accept it, you say. I can't. It shouldn't be
like this in New York City, in 1989, in spring." Ronnie Eldridge
also suggested that readers walk into the park at night, but to
light candles. "Who are we that we allow ourselves to be chased
out of the most magnificent part of our city?" she asked, and
also: "If we give up the park, what are we supposed to do: fall
back to Columbus Avenue and plant grass?" This was interesting, suggesting as it did that the city's not inconsiderable problems could be solved by the willingness of its citizens to hold or
draw some line, to "say no"; in other words, that a reliance on
certain magical gestures could affect the city's fate.

The insistent sentimentalization of experience, which is to
say the encouragement of such reliance, is not new in New York.
A preference for broad strokes, for the distortion and flattening
of character, and for the reduction of events to narrative has
been for well over a hundred years the heart of the way the city

presents itself: Lady Liberty, huddled masses, ticker-tape parades, heroes, gutters, bright lights, broken hearts, eight million stories in the naked city; eight million stories and all the same story, each devised to obscure not only the city's actual tensions of race and class but also, more significantly, the civic and commercial arrangements that rendered those tensions irreconcilable.

Central Park itself was such a "story," an artificial pastoral in the nineteenth-century English romantic tradition, conceived, during a decade when the population of Manhattan would increase by 58 percent, as a civic project that would allow the letting of contracts and the employment of voters on a scale rarely before undertaken in New York. Ten million cartloads of dirt would need to be shifted during the twenty years of its construction. Four to five million trees and plants would need to be planted, half a million cubic yards of topsoil imported, 114 miles of ceramic pipe laid.

Nor need the completion of the park mean the end of the possibilities: in 1870, once William Marcy Tweed had revised the city charter and invented his Department of Public Parks, new roads could be built whenever jobs were needed. Trees could be dug up, and replanted. Crews could be set loose to prune, to clear, to hack at will. Frederick Law Olmsted, when he objected, could be overridden, and finally eased out. "A 'delegation' from a great political organization called on me by appointment," Olmsted wrote in *The Spoils of the Park,* recalling the conditions under which he had worked:

After introductions and handshakings, a circle was formed, and a gentleman stepped before me, and said, "We know how much pressed you must be . . . but at your convenience our association would like to have you determine what share of your patronage we can expect, and make suitable arrangements for our using it. We will take the liberty to suggest, sir, that there could be no more convenient way than that you should send us our due quota of tickets, if you please, sir, in this form, *leaving us to fill in the name.*" Here a pack of printed tickets was produced, from which I took one at random. It was a blank appointment and bore the signature of Mr. Tweed. . . .

As superintendent of the Park, I once received in six days more than seven thousand letters of advice as to appointments, nearly all

from men in office. . . . I have heard a candidate for a magisterial office in the city addressing from my doorsteps a crowd of such advice-
bearers, telling them that I was bound to give them employment, and
suggesting plainly, that, if I was slow about it, a rope round my neck
might serve to lessen my reluctance to take good counsel. I have had
a dozen men force their way into my house before I had risen from
bed on a Sunday morning, and some break into my drawing-room in
their eagerness to deliver letters of advice.

Central Park, then, for its underwriters if not for Olmsted,
was about contracts and concrete and kickbacks, about pork,
but the sentimentalization that worked to obscure the pork, the
"story," had to do with certain dramatic contrasts, or extremes,
that were believed to characterize life in this as in no other city.
These "contrasts," which have since become the very spine of
the New York narrative, appeared early on: Philip Hone, the
mayor of New York in 1826 and 1827, spoke in 1843 of a city
"overwhelmed with population, and where the two extremes of
costly luxury in living, expensive establishments and improvi-
dent wastes are presented in daily and hourly contrast with
squalid mixing and hapless destruction." Given this narrative,
Central Park could be and ultimately would be seen the way
Olmsted himself saw it, as an essay in democracy, a social experiment meant to socialize a new immigrant population and to
ameliorate the perilous separation of rich and poor. It was the
duty and the interest of the city's privileged class, Olmsted had
suggested some years before he designed Central Park, to "get
up parks, gardens, music, dancing schools, reunions which will
be so attractive as to force into contact the good and the bad, the
gentleman and the rowdy."

The notion that the interests of the "gentleman" and the
"rowdy" might be at odds did not intrude: then as now, the preferred narrative worked to veil actual conflict, to cloud the extent
to which the condition of being rich was predicated upon the
continued neediness of a working class; to confirm the responsible stewardship of "the gentleman" and to forestall the possibility
of a self-conscious, or politicized, proletariat. Social and economic phenomena, in this narrative, were personalized. Politics
were exclusively electoral. Problems were best addressed by the
emergence and election of "leaders," who could in turn inspire
the individual citizen to "participate," or "make a difference."

"Will you help?" Mayor Dinkins asked New Yorkers, in a September address from St. Patrick's Cathedral intended as a response to the "New York crime wave" stories then leading the news. "Do you care? Are you ready to become part of the solution?"

"Stay," Governor Cuomo urged the same New Yorkers. "Believe. Participate. Don't give up." Manhattan Borough President Ruth Messinger, at the dedication of a school flagpole, mentioned the importance of "getting involved" and "participating," or "pitching in to put the shine back on the Big Apple." In a discussion of the popular "New York" stories written between 1902 and 1910 by William Sidney Porter, or "O. Henry," William R. Taylor of the State University of New York at Stony Brook spoke of the way in which these stories, with their "focus on individuals' plights," their "absence of social or political implications" and "ideological neutrality," provided "a miraculous form of social glue":

> These sentimental accounts of relations between classes in the city have a specific historical meaning: empathy without political compassion. They reduce the scale of human suffering to what atomized individuals endure as their plucky, sad lives were recounted week after week for almost a decade. . . . Their sentimental reading of oppression, class differences, human suffering, and affection helped create a new language for interpreting the city's complex society, a language that began to replace the threadbare moralism that New Yorkers inherited from nineteenth-century readings of the city. This language localized suffering in particular moments and confined it to particular occasions; it smoothed over differences because it could be read almost the same way from either end of the social scale.*

Stories in which terrible crimes are inflicted on innocent victims, offering as they do a similarly sentimental reading of class differences and human suffering, a reading that promises both resolution and retribution, have long performed as the city's endorphins, a built-in source of natural morphine working to blur the edges of real and to a great extent insoluble problems. What is singular about New York, and remains virtually incomprehen-

---

*William R. Taylor, "The Launching of a Commercial Culture: New York City, 1860–1930," in John Hull Mollenkopf's *Power, Culture, and Place: Essays on New York City* (Russell Sage Foundation, 1988), pp. 107–133.

sible to people who live in less rigidly organized parts of the country, is the minimal level of comfort and opportunity its citizens have come to accept. The romantic capitalist pursuit of privacy and security and individual freedom, so taken for granted nationally, plays, locally, not much role. A city where virtually every impulse has been to stifle rather than to encourage normal competition, New York works, when it does work, not on a market economy but on little deals, payoffs, accommodations, baksheesh, arrangements that circumvent the direct exchange of goods and services and prevent what would be, in a competitive economy, the normal ascendance of the superior product.

There were in the five boroughs in 1990 only 581 supermarkets (a supermarket, as defined by the trade magazine *Progressive Grocer,* is a market that does an annual volume of two million dollars), or, assuming a population of eight million, one supermarket for every 13,769 citizens. Groceries, costing more than they should because of this absence of competition and also because of the proliferation of payoffs required to ensure this absence of competition (produce, we have come to understand, belongs to the Gambinos, and fish to the Lucheses and the Genoveses, and a piece of the construction of the market to each of the above, but keeping the door open belongs finally to the inspector here, the inspector there), are carried home or delivered, as if in Jakarta, by pushcart.

It has historically taken, in New York as if in Mexico City, ten years to process and specify and bid and contract and construct a new school; twenty or thirty years to build or, in the cases of Bruckner Boulevard and the West Side Highway, to not quite build a highway. A recent public scandal revealed that a batch of city-ordered Pap smears had gone unread for more than a year (in the developed world the Pap smear, a test for cervical cancer, is commonly read within a few days); what did not become a public scandal, what is still accepted as the way things are, is that even Pap smears ordered by Park Avenue gynecologists can go unread for several weeks.

Such resemblances to cities of the Third World are in no way casual, or based on the "color" of a polyglot population: these are all cities arranged primarily not to improve the lives of their citizens but to be labor-intensive, to accommodate, ideally at the subsistence level, since it is at the subsistence level that the work force is most apt to be captive and loyalty assured, a Third World population. In some ways New York's very attractiveness, its promises of opportunity and improved wages, its commitments as a city in the developed world, were what seemed destined to render it ultimately unworkable. Where the vitality of such cities in the less developed world had depended on their ability to guarantee low-cost labor and an absence of regulation, New York had historically depended instead on the constant welling up of new businesses, of new employers to replace those phased out, like the New York garment manufacturers who found it cheaper to make their clothes in Hong Kong or Kuala Lumpur or Taipei, by rising local costs.

It had been the old pattern of New York, supported by an expanding national economy, to lose one kind of business and gain another. It was the more recent error of New York to misconstrue this history of turnover as an indestructible resource, there to be taxed at will, there to be regulated whenever a dollar could be seen in doing so, there for the taking. By 1977, New York had lost some 600,000 jobs, most of them in manufacturing and in the kinds of small businesses that could no longer maintain their narrow profit margins inside the city. During the "recovery" years, from 1977 until 1988, most of these jobs were indeed replaced, but in a potentially perilous way: of the 500,000 new jobs created, most were in the area most vulnerable to a downturn, that of financial and business services, and many of the rest in an area not only equally vulnerable to bad times but dispiriting to the city even in good, that of tourist and restaurant services.

The demonstration that many kinds of businesses were finding New York expendable had failed to prompt real efforts to make the city more competitive. Taxes grew still more punitive, regulation more byzantine. Forty-nine thousand new jobs were created in New York's city agencies between 1983 and 1990, even as the services provided by those agencies were widely perceived to decline. Attempts at "reform" typically tended to create more jobs: in 1988, in response to the length of time it was taking to build or repair a school, a new agency, the School Construction Authority, was formed. A New York City school, it was said, would now take only five years to build. The head of the School

Construction Authority was to receive $145,000 a year and each
of the three vice-presidents $110,000 a year. An executive gym,
with Nautilus equipment, was contemplated for the top floor of
the agency's new headquarters at the International Design Center in Long Island City. Two years into this reform, the backlog
on repairs to existing schools stood at 33,000 outstanding re-
quests. "To relieve the charity of friends of the support of a half-
blind and half-witted man by employing him at the public expense as an inspector of cement may not be practical with reference to the permanent firmness of a wall," Olmsted noted after
his Central Park experience, "while it is perfectly so with reference to the triumph of sound doctrine at an election."

In fact the highest per capita taxes of any city in the United
States (and, as anyone running a small business knows, the widest variety of taxes) provide, in New York, unless the citizen is
prepared to cut a side deal here and there, only the continuing
multiplication of regulations designed to benefit the contractors
and agencies and unions with whom the regulators have cut their
own deals. A kitchen appliance accepted throughout the rest of
the United States as a basic postwar amenity, the in-sink garbage
disposal unit, is for example illegal in New York. Disposals, a city
employee advised me, not only encourage rats and "bacteria,"
presumably in a way that bags of garbage sitting on the sidewalk
do not ("because it is," I was told when I asked how this could
be), but also encourage people "to put their babies down them."

On the one hand this illustrates how a familiar urban principle, that of patronage (the more garbage there is to be collected,
the more garbage collectors can be employed), can be reduced,
in the bureaucratic wilderness that is any Third World city, to
voodoo; on the other it reflects this particular city's underlying
criminal ethic, its acceptance of graft and grift as the bedrock of
every transaction. "Garbage costs are outrageous," an executive
of Supermarkets General, which owns Pathmark, recently told
City Limits about why the chains preferred to locate in the suburbs. "Every time you need to hire a contractor, it's a problem."
The problem, however, is one from which not only the contractor but everyone with whom the contractor does business — a
chain of direct or indirect patronage extending deep into the
fabric of the city — stands to derive one or another benefit,

which was one reason the death of the young middle-class white woman in the East 68th Street apartment of the assistant commissioner in charge of boiler and elevator inspections flickered so feebly on the local attention span.

It was only within the transforming narrative of "contrasts" that both the essential criminality of the city and its related absence of civility could become points of pride, evidence of "energy": if you could make it here you could make it anywhere, hello sucker, get smart. Those who did not get the deal, who bought retail, who did not know what it took to get their electrical work signed off, were dismissed as provincials, bridge-and-tunnels, out-of-towners who did not have what it took not to get taken. "Every tourist's nightmare became a reality for a Maryland couple over the weekend when the husband was beaten and robbed on Fifth Avenue in front of Trump Tower," began a story in the *New York Post* this summer. "Where do you think we're from, Iowa?" the prosecutor who took Robert Chambers's statement said on videotape by way of indicating that he doubted Chambers's version of Jennifer Levin's death. "They go after poor people like you from out of town, they prey on the tourists," a clerk explained last spring in the West 46th Street computer store where my husband and I had taken refuge to escape three muggers. My husband said that we lived in New York. "That's why they didn't get you," the clerk said, effortlessly incorporating this change in the data. "That's how you could move fast."

The narrative comforts us, in other words, with the assurance that the world is knowable, even flat, and New York its center, its motor, its dangerous but vital "energy." FAMILY IN FATAL MUGGING LOVED NEW YORK was the *Times* headline on a story following the September murder, in the Seventh Avenue IND station, of a twenty-two-year-old tourist from Utah. The young man, his parents, his brother, and his sister-in-law had attended the U.S. Open and were reportedly on their way to dinner at a Moroccan restaurant downtown. "New York, to them, was the greatest place in the world," a family friend from Utah was quoted as having said. Since the narrative requires that the rest of the country provide a dramatic contrast to New York, the family's hometown in Utah was characterized by the *Times* as a place where "life revolves around the orderly rhythms of Brigham Young University" and "there is only about one murder a year." The town was in fact Provo, where Gary Gilmore shot the motel manager, both in life and in *The Executioner's Song*. "She loved New York, she just loved it," a friend of the assaulted jogger told the *Times* after the attack. "I think she liked the fast pace, the competitiveness."

New York, the *Times* concluded, "invigorated" the jogger, "matched her energy level." At a time when the city lay virtually inert, when forty thousand jobs had been wiped out in the financial markets and former traders were selling shirts at Bergdorf Goodman for Men, when the rate of mortgage delinquencies had doubled, when fifty or sixty million square feet of office space remained unrented (sixty million square feet of unrented office space is the equivalent of fifteen darkened World Trade Towers) and even prime commercial blocks on Madison Avenue in the Seventies were boarded up, empty; at a time when the money had dropped out of all the markets and the Europeans who had lent the city their élan and their capital during the eighties had moved on, vanished to more cheerful venues, this notion of the city's "energy" was sedative, as was the commandeering of "crime" as the city's central problem.

3

The extent to which the October 1987 crash of the New York financial markets damaged the illusions of infinite recovery and growth on which the city had operated during the 1980s had been at first hard to apprehend. "Ours is a time of New York ascendant," the New York City Commission on the Year 2000, created during the mayoralty of Ed Koch to reflect the best thinking of the city's various business and institutional establishments, had declared in its 1987 report. "The city's economy is stronger than it has been in decades, and is driven both by its own resilience and by the national economy; New York is more than ever the international capital of finance, and the gateway to the American economy. . . ."

And then, its citizens had come gradually to understand, it was not. This perception that something was "wrong" in New York had been insidious, a slow-onset illness at first noticeable only in periods of temporary remission. Losses that might have seemed someone else's problem (or even comeuppance) as the markets were in their initial 1987 free fall, and that might have seemed more remote still as the markets regained the appearance of strength, had come imperceptibly but inexorably to alter the tone of daily life. By April 1990, people who lived in and around New York were expressing, in interviews with the *Times*, considerable anguish and fear that they did so: "I feel very resentful that I've lost a lot of flexibility in my life," one said. "I often wonder, 'Am I crazy for coming here?'" "People feel a sense of impending doom about what may happen to them," a clinical psychologist said. People were "frustrated," "feeling absolutely desolate," "trapped," "angry," "terrified," and "on the verge of panic."

It was a panic that seemed in many ways specific to New York, and inexplicable outside it. Even now, when the troubles of New York are a common theme, Americans from less depressed venues have difficulty comprehending the nature of those troubles, and tend to attribute them, as New Yorkers themselves have come to do, to "crime." ESCAPE FROM NEW YORK was the headline on the front page of the *New York Post* on September 10, 1990. RAMPAGING CRIME WAVE HAS 59 PERCENT OF RESIDENTS TERRIFIED. MOST WOULD GET OUT OF THE CITY, SAYS TIME/CNN POLL. This poll appeared in the edition of *Time* dated September 17, 1990, which carried the cover legend THE ROTTING OF THE BIG APPLE. "Reason: a surge of drugs and violent crime that government officials seem utterly unable to combat," the story inside explained. Columnists referred, locally, to "this sewer of a city." The *Times* ran a plaintive piece about the snatching of Elizabeth Rohatyn's Hermès handbag outside Arcadia, a restaurant on East 62nd Street that had for a while seemed the very heart of the New York everyone now missed, the New York where getting and spending could take place without undue reference to having and not having, the duty-free New York; that this had occurred to the wife of Felix Rohatyn, who was widely perceived as having saved the city from its fiscal crisis in the mid-seventies, seemed to many a clarion irony.

*

This question of crime was tricky. There were in fact eight American cities with higher homicide rates, and twelve with higher overall crime rates. Crime had long been taken for granted in the less affluent parts of the city, and had become in the mid-seventies, as both unemployment and the costs of maintaining property rose and what had once been functioning neighborhoods were abandoned and burned and left to whoever claimed them, endemic. "In some poor neighborhoods, crime became almost a way of life," Jim Sleeper, an editor at *Newsday* and the author of *The Closest of Strangers: Liberalism and the Politics of Race in New York,* noted in his discussion of the social disintegration that occurred during this period:

> . . . a subculture of violence with complex bonds of utility and af-
> fection within families and the larger, "law-abiding" community.
> Struggling merchants might "fence" stolen goods, for example, thus
> providing quick cover and additional incentive for burglaries and
> robberies; the drug economy became more vigorous, reshaping crim-
> inal life-styles and tormenting the loyalties of families and friends. A
> walk down even a reasonably busy street in a poor, minority neighbor-
> hood at high noon could become an unnerving journey into a land-
> scape eerie and grim.

What seemed markedly different a decade later, what made crime a "story," was that the more privileged, and especially the more privileged white, citizens of New York had begun to feel unnerved at high noon in even their own neighborhoods. Although New York City Police Department statistics suggested that white New Yorkers were not actually in increased mortal danger (the increase in homicides between 1977 and 1989, from 1,557 to 1,903, was entirely in what the NYPD classified as Hispanic, Asian, and black victims; the number of white murder victims had steadily declined, from 361 in 1977 to 227 in 1984 and 190 in 1989), the apprehension of such danger, exacerbated by street snatches and muggings and the quite useful sense that the youth in the hooded sweatshirt with his hands jammed in his pockets might well be a predator, had become general. These more privileged New Yorkers now felt unnerved not only on the street, where the necessity for evasive strategies had become an exhausting constant, but even in the most insulated and protected apartment buildings. As the residents of such buildings, the owners of twelve- and sixteen- and twenty-four-room apartments, watched the potted ficus trees disappear from outside their doors and the graffiti appear on their limestone walls and the smashed safety glass from car windows get swept off their sidewalks, it had become increasingly easy to imagine the outcome of a confrontation between, say, the relief night doorman and six dropouts from Julia Richman High School on East 67th Street.

And yet those New Yorkers who had spoken to the *Times* in April of 1990 about their loss of flexibility, about their panic, their desolation, their anger, and their sense of impending doom, had not been talking about drugs, or crime, or any of the city's more publicized and to some extent inflated ills. These were people who did not for the most part have twelve- and sixteen-room apartments and doormen and the luxury of projected fears. These people were talking instead about an immediate fear, about money, about the vertiginous plunge in the value of their houses and apartments and condominiums, about the possibility or probability of foreclosure and loss; about, implicitly, their fear of being left, like so many they saw every day, below the line, out in the cold, on the street.

This was a climate in which many of the questions that had seized the city's attention in 1987 and 1988, for example that of whether Mortimer Zuckerman should be "allowed" to build two fifty-nine-story office towers on the site of what is now the Coliseum, seemed in retrospect wistful, the baroque concerns of better times. "There's no way anyone would make a sane judgment to go into the ground now," a vice-president at Cushman and Wakefield told the *New York Observer* about the delay in the Coliseum project, which had in fact lost its projected major tenant, Salomon Brothers, shortly after Black Monday, 1987. "It would be suicide. You're better off sitting in a tub of water and opening your wrists." Such fears were, for a number of reasons, less easy to incorporate into the narrative than the fear of crime.

The imposition of a sentimental, or false, narrative on the disparate and often random experience that constitutes the life of a city or a country means, necessarily, that much of what happens in that city or country will be rendered merely illustrative, a series of set pieces, or performance opportunities. Mayor Dinkins could, in such a symbolic substitute for civic life, "break the boycott" (the Flatbush boycott organized to mobilize resentment of Korean merchants in black neighborhoods) by purchasing a few dollars' worth of produce from a Korean grocer on Church Avenue. Governor Cuomo could "declare war on crime" by calling for five thousand additional police; Mayor Dinkins could "up the ante" by calling for sixty-five hundred. "White slut comes into the park looking for the African man," a black woman could say, her voice loud but still conversational, in the corridor outside the courtroom where, during the summer of 1990, the first three defendants in the Central Park attack, Antron McCray, Yusef Salaam, and Raymond Santana, were tried on charges of attempted murder, assault, sodomy, and rape. "Boyfriend beats shit out of her, they blame it on our boys," the woman could continue, and then, referring to a young man with whom the victim had at one time split the cost of an apartment: "How about the roommate, anybody test his semen? No. He's white. They don't do it to each other."

Glances could then flicker among those reporters and producers and courtroom sketch artists and photographers and cameramen and techs and summer interns who assembled daily at 111 Centre Street. Cellular phones could be picked up, a show of indifference. Small talk could be exchanged with the marshals, a show of solidarity. The woman could then raise her voice: "White folk, all of them are devils, even those that haven't been born yet, they are *devils*. Little *demons*. I don't understand these devils, I guess they think this is *their court*." The reporters could gaze beyond her, faces blank, no eye contact, a more correct form of hostility and also more lethal. The woman could hold her ground but avert her eyes, letting her gaze fall on another black, in this instance a black *Daily News* columnist, Bob Herbert. "You," she could say. "You are a *disgrace*. Go ahead. Line up there. Line up with the white folk. Look at them, lining up for their first-class seats while *my* people are downstairs behind *barricades* . . . kept behind barricades like *cattle* . . . not even allowed in the room to see their sons lynched . . . is that an *African* I see in that line? Or is that a *negro*? Oh, oh, sorry, shush, white folk didn't know, he was *passing*. . . ."

In a city in which grave and disrupting problems had become general — problems of not having, problems of not making it, problems that demonstrably existed, among the mad and the ill and the underequipped and the overwhelmed, with decreasing reference to color — the case of the Central Park jogger provided more than just a safe, or structured, setting in which various and sometimes only marginally related rages could be vented. "This trial," the *Daily News* announced on its editorial page one morning in July 1990, midway through the trial of the first three defendants, "is about more than the rape and brutalization of a single woman. It is about the rape and the brutalization of a city. The jogger is a symbol of all that's wrong here. And all that's right, because she is nothing less than an inspiration."

The *News* did not define the ways in which "the rape and brutalization of the city" manifested itself, nor was definition necessary: this was a city in which the threat or the fear of brutalization had become so immediate that citizens were urged to take up their own defense, to form citizen patrols or militia, as in Beirut. This was a city in which between twenty and thirty neighborhoods had already given over their protection, which was to say the right to determine who belonged in the neighborhood and who did not and what should be done about it, to the Guardian Angels. This was a city in which a Brooklyn vigilante group, which called itself "Crack Busters" and was said to be trying to rid its Bedford-Stuyvesant neighborhood of drugs, would before September was out "settle an argument" by dousing with gasoline and setting on fire an abandoned van and the three homeless citizens inside. This was a city in which the *Times* would soon perceive, in the failing economy, "a bright side for the city at large," the bright side being that while there was believed to have been an increase in the number of middle-income and upper-income families who wanted to leave the city, "the slumping market is keeping many of those families in New York."

In this city rapidly vanishing into the chasm between its actual life and its preferred narratives, what people said when they talked about the case of the Central Park jogger came to seem a kind of poetry, a way of expressing, without directly stating, different but equally volatile and similarly occult visions of the same disaster. One vision, shared by those who had seized upon the attack on the jogger as an exact representation of what was wrong with the city, was of a city systematically ruined, violated, raped by its underclass. The opposing vision, shared by those who had seized upon the arrest of the defendants as an exact representation of their own victimization, was of a city in which the powerless had been systematically ruined, violated, raped by the powerful. For so long as this case held the city's febrile attention, then, it offered a narrative for the city's distress, a frame in which the actual social and economic forces wrenching the city could be personalized and ultimately obscured.

Or rather it offered two narratives, mutually exclusive. Among a number of blacks, particularly those whose experience with or distrust of the criminal justice system was such that they tended to discount the fact that five of six defendants had to varying degrees admitted taking part in the attack, and to focus instead on the absence of any supporting forensic evidence incontrovertibly linking this victim to these defendants, the case could be read as a confirmation not only of their victimization but of the white conspiracy they saw at the heart of that victimization. For the *Amsterdam News*, which did not veer automatically to the radical analysis (a typical recent issue lauded the FBI for its minority recruiting and the Harlem National Guard for its high morale and readiness to go to the Gulf), the defendants could in this light be seen as victims of "a political trial," of a "legal lynching," of a case "rigged from the very beginning" by the decision of "the white press" that "whoever was arrested and charged in this case of the attempted murder, rape and sodomy of a well-connected, bright, beautiful and promising white woman was guilty, pure and simple."

For Alton H. Maddox, Jr., the message to be drawn from the case was that the American criminal justice system, which was under any circumstances "inherently and unabashedly racist," failed "to function equitably at any level when a Black male is accused of raping a white female." For others the message was more general, and worked to reinforce the fragile but functional mythology of a heroic black past, the narrative in which European domination could be explained as a direct and vengeful response to African superiority. "Today the white man is faced head on with what is happening on the Black Continent, Africa," Malcolm X wrote.

Look at the artifacts being discovered there, that are proving over and over again, how the black man had great, fine, sensitive civilizations before the white man was out of the caves. Below the Sahara, in the places where most of America's Negroes' foreparents were kidnapped, there is being unearthed some of the finest craftsmanship, sculpture and other objects, that has ever been seen by modern man. Some of these things now are on view in such places as New York City's Museum of Modern Art. Gold work of such fine tolerance and workmanship that it has no rival. Ancient objects produced by black hands . . . refined by those black hands with results that no human hand today can equal.

History has been so "whitened" by the white man that even the black professors have known little more than the most ignorant black man about the talents and rich civilizations and cultures of the black man of millenniums ago. . . .

"Our proud African queen," the Reverend Al Sharpton had said of Tawana Brawley's mother, Glenda Brawley: "She stepped out of anonymity, stepped out of obscurity, and walked into history." It was said in the corridors of the courthouse where Yusef Salaam was tried that he carried himself "like an African king."

"It makes no difference anymore whether the attack on Tawana happened," William Kunstler had told *New York Newsday* when the alleged rape and torture of Tawana Brawley by a varying number of white police officers seemed, as an actual prosecutable crime if not as a window on what people needed to believe, to have dematerialized. "If her story was a concoction to prevent her parents from punishing her for staying out all night, that doesn't disguise the fact that a lot of young black women are treated the way she said she was treated." The importance of whether or not the crime had occurred was, in this view, entirely resident in the crime's "description," which was defined by Stanley Diamond in *The Nation* as "a crime that did not occur" but was "described with skill and controlled hysteria by the black actors as the epitome of degradation, a repellent model of what actually happens to too many black women."

A good deal of what got said around the edges of the jogger case, in the corridors and on the call-in shows, seemed to derive exclusively from the suspicions of conspiracy increasingly entrenched among those who believe themselves powerless. A poll conducted in June 1990 by the *New York Times* and WCBS-TV News

determined that 77 percent of blacks polled believed that it was
either "true" or "might possibly be true" (as opposed to "almost
certainly not true") that the government of the United States
"singles out and investigates black elected officials in order to discredit them in a way it doesn't do with white officials." Sixty percent believed that it was true or might possibly be true that the
government "deliberately makes sure that drugs are easily available in poor black neighborhoods in order to harm black people." Twenty-nine percent believed that it was true or might possibly be true that "the virus which causes AIDS was deliberately
created in a laboratory in order to infect black people." In each
case, the alternative response to "true" or "might possibly be
true" was "almost certainly not true," which might have seemed
in itself to reflect a less than ringing belief in the absence of conspiracy. "The conspiracy to destroy Black boys is very complex
and interwoven," Jawanza Kunjufu, a Chicago educational consultant, wrote in his *Countering the Conspiracy to Destroy Black Boys,*
a 1982 pamphlet which has since been extended to three volumes.

> There are many contributors to the conspiracy, ranging from the very
> visible who are more obvious, to the less visible and silent partners
> who are more difficult to recognize.
> Those people who adhere to the doctrine of white racism, imperi-
> alism, and white male supremacy are easier to recognize. Those peo-
> ple who actively promote drugs and gang violence are active con-
> spirators, and easier to identify. What makes the conspiracy more
> complex are those people who do not plot together to destroy Black
> boys, but, through their indifference, perpetuate it. This passive
> group of conspirators consists of parents, educators, and white liber-
> als who deny being racists, but through their silence allow institutional
> racism to continue.

For those who proceeded from the conviction that there was
under way a conspiracy to destroy blacks, particularly black boys,
a belief in the innocence of these defendants, a conviction that
even their own statements had been rigged against them or
wrenched from them, followed logically. It was in the corridors
and on the call-in shows that the conspiracy got sketched in, in a
series of fantasy details that conflicted not only with known facts
but even with each other. It was said that the prosecution was

withholding evidence that the victim had gone to the park to meet a drug dealer. It was said, alternately or concurrently, that the prosecution was withholding evidence that the victim had gone to the park to take part in a satanic ritual. It was said that the forensic photographs showing her battered body were not "real" photographs, that "they," the prosecution, had "brought in some corpse for the pictures." It was said that the young woman who appeared on the witness stand and identified herself as the victim was not the "real" victim, that "they" had in this case brought in an actress.

What was being expressed in each instance was the sense that secrets must be in play, that "they," the people who had power in the courtroom, were in possession of information systematically withheld — since information itself was power — from those who did not have power. On the day the first three defendants were sentenced, C. Vernon Mason, who had formally entered the case in the penalty phase as Antron McCray's attorney, filed a brief which included the bewildering and untrue assertion that the victim's boyfriend, who had not at that time been called to testify, was black. That some whites jumped to engage this assertion on its own terms (the *Daily News* columnist Gail Collins referred to it as Mason's "slimiest argument of the hour — an announcement that the jogger had a black lover") tended only to reinforce the sense of racial estrangement that was the intended subtext of the assertion, which was without meaning or significance except in that emotional deep where whites are seen as conspiring in secret to sink blacks in misery. "Just answer me, who got addicted?" I recall one black spectator asking another as they left the courtroom. "I'll tell you who got addicted, the inner city got addicted." He had with him a pamphlet that laid out a scenario in which the government had conspired to exterminate blacks by flooding their neighborhoods with drugs, a scenario touching all the familiar points, Laos, Cambodia, the Golden Triangle, the CIA, more secrets, more poetry.

"From the beginning I have insisted that this was not a racial case," Robert Morgenthau, the Manhattan district attorney, said after the verdicts came in on the first jogger trial. He spoke of those who, in his view, wanted "to divide the races and advance their own private agendas," and of how the city was "ill-served" by those who had so "sought to exploit" this case. "We had hoped that the racial tensions surrounding the jogger trial would begin to dissipate soon after the jury arrived at a verdict," a *Post* editorial began a few days later. The editorial spoke of an "ugly claque of 'activists,' " of the "divisive atmosphere" they had created, and of the anticipation with which the city's citizens had waited for "mainstream black leaders" to step forward with praise for the way in which the verdicts had brought New York "back from the brink of criminal chaos":

> Alas, in the jogger case, the wait was in vain. Instead of praise for a verdict which demonstrated that sometimes criminals are caught and punished, New Yorkers heard charlatans like the Rev. Al Sharpton claim the case was fixed. They heard that C. Vernon Mason, one of the engineers of the Tawana Brawley hoax — the attorney who thinks Mayor Dinkins wears "too many yarmulkes" — was planning to appeal the verdicts. . . .

To those whose preferred view of the city was of an inherently dynamic and productive community ordered by the natural play of its conflicting elements, enriched, as in Mayor Dinkins's "gorgeous mosaic," by its very "contrasts," this case offered a number of useful elements. There was the confirmation of "crime" as the canker corroding the life of the city. There was, in the random and feral evening described by the East Harlem attackers and the clear innocence of and damage done to the Upper East Side and Wall Street victim, an eerily exact and conveniently personalized representation of what the *Daily News* had called "the rape and the brutalization of a city." Among the reporters on this case, whose own narrative conventions involved "hero cops" and "brave prosecutors" going hand to hand against "crime" (the SECRET AGONY OF JOGGER D.A., we learned in the *Post* a few days after the verdicts in the first trial, was that "Brave Prosecutor's Marriage Failed as She Put Rapists Away"), there seemed an unflagging enthusiasm for the repetition and reinforcement of these elements, and an equally unflagging resistance, even hostility, to exploring the point of view of the defendants' families and friends and personal or political allies (or, as they were called in news reports, the "supporters") who gathered daily at the other end of the corridor from the courtroom.

This was curious. Criminal cases are widely regarded by American reporters as windows on the city or culture in which they take place, opportunities to enter not only households but parts of the culture normally closed, and yet this was a case in which indifference to the world of the defendants extended even to the reporting of names and occupations. Yusef Salaam's mother, who happened to be young and photogenic and to have European features, was pictured so regularly that she and her son became the instantly recognizable "images" of Jogger One, but even then no one got her name quite right. For a while in the papers she was "Cheroney," or sometimes "Cheronay," McEllhonor; then she became Cheroney McEllhonor Salaam. After she testified the spelling of her first name was corrected to "Sharonne," although, since the byline on a piece she wrote for the *Amsterdam News* spelled it differently, "Sharrone," this may have been another misunderstanding. Her occupation was frequently given as "designer" (later, after her son's conviction, she went to work as a paralegal for William Kunstler), but no one seemed to take this seriously enough to say what she designed or for whom; not until after she testified, when *Newsday* reported her testimony that on the evening of her son's arrest she had arrived at the precinct house late because she was an instructor at the Parsons School of Design, did the notion of "designer" seem sufficiently concrete to suggest an actual occupation.

The Jogger One defendants were referred to repeatedly in the news columns of the *Post* as "thugs." The defendants and their families were often said by reporters to be "sneering." (The reporters, in turn, were said at the other end of the corridor to be "smirking.") "We don't have nearly so strong a question as to the guilt or innocence of the defendants as we did at Bensonhurst," a *Newsday* reporter covering the first jogger trial said to the *New York Observer,* well before the closing arguments, by way of explaining why *Newsday*'s coverage may have seemed less extensive on this trial than on the Bensonhurst trials. "There is not a big question as to what happened in Central Park that night. Some details are missing, but it's fairly clear who did what to whom."

In fact this came close to the heart of it: that it seemed, on the basis of the videotaped statements, fairly clear who had done what to whom was precisely the case's liberating aspect, the circumstance that enabled many of the city's citizens to say and think what they might otherwise have left unexpressed. Unlike other recent high-visibility cases in New York, unlike Bensonhurst and unlike Howard Beach and unlike Bernhard Goetz, here was a case in which the issue not exactly of race but of an increasingly visible underclass could be confronted by the middle class, both white and black, without guilt. Here was a case which gave this middle class a way to transfer and express what had clearly become a growing and previously inadmissible rage with the city's disorder, with the entire range of ills and uneasy guilts that came to mind in a city where entire families slept in the discarded boxes in which new Sub-Zero refrigerators were delivered, at twenty-six hundred per, to more affluent families. Here was also a case, most significantly, in which even that transferred rage could be transferred still further, veiled, personalized: a case in which the city's distress could be seen to derive not precisely from its underclass but instead from certain identifiable individuals who claimed to speak for this underclass, individuals who, in Robert Morgenthau's words, "sought to exploit" this case, to "advance their own private agendas"; individuals who wished even to "divide the races."

If the city's problems could be seen as deliberate disruptions of a naturally cohesive and harmonious community, a community in which, undisrupted, "contrasts" generated a perhaps dangerous but vital "energy," then those problems were tractable, and could be addressed, like "crime," by the call for "better leadership." Considerable comfort could be obtained, given this story line, through the demonization of the Reverend Al Sharpton, whose presence on the edges of certain criminal cases that interested him had a polarizing effect that tended to reinforce the narratives. Jim Sleeper, in *The Closest of Strangers*, described one of the fifteen marches Sharpton led through Bensonhurst after the 1989 killing of an East New York sixteen-year-old, Yusuf Hawkins, who had come into Bensonhurst and been set upon, with baseball bats and ultimately with bullets, by a group of young whites.

An August 27, 1989, *Daily News* photo of the Reverend Al Sharpton and a claque of black teenagers marching in Bensonhurst to protest Hawkins's death shows that they are not really "marching." They are

stumbling along, huddled together, heads bowed under the storm of
hatred breaking over them, eyes wide, hanging on to one another and
to Sharpton, scared out of their wits. They, too, are innocents — or
were until that day, which they will always remember. And because
Sharpton is with them, his head bowed, his face showing that he
knows what they're feeling, he is in the hearts of black people all over
New York.

Yet something is wrong with this picture. Sharpton did not invite
or coordinate with Bensonhurst community leaders who wanted to
join the march. Without the time for organizing which these leaders
should have been given in order to rein in the punks who stood wav-
ing watermelons; without an effort by black leaders more reputable
than Sharpton to recruit whites citywide and swell the march, Sharpton was assured that the punks would carry the day. At several points
he even baited them by blowing kisses. . . .

"I knew that Bensonhurst would clarify whether it had been a
racial incident or not," Sharpton said by way of explaining, on a
recent *Frontline* documentary, his strategy in Bensonhurst. "The
fact that I was so controversial to Bensonhurst helped them forget that the cameras were there," he said. "So I decided to help
them . . . I would throw kisses to them, and they would go nuts."
Question, began a joke often told in the aftermath of the first jogger trial. *You're in a room with Hitler, Saddam Hussein, and Al Sharpton. You have only two bullets. Who do you shoot? Answer: Al Sharpton.
Twice.*

Sharpton did not exactly fit the roles New York traditionally
assigns, for maximum audience comfort, to prominent blacks.
He seemed in many ways a phantasm, someone whose instinct
for the connections between religion and politics and show business was so innate that he had been all his life the vessel for other
people's hopes and fears. He had given his first sermon at age
four. He was touring with Mahalia Jackson at eleven. As a teenager, according to Robert D. McFadden, Ralph Blumenthal,
M. A. Farber, E. R. Shipp, Charles Strum, and Craig Wolff, the
New York Times reporters and editors who collaborated on *Outrage: The Story Behind the Tawana Brawley Hoax,* Sharpton was tu-
tored first by Adam Clayton Powell, Jr. ("You got to know when
to hit it and you got to know when to quit it and when it's quittin'
time, don't push it," Powell told him), then by the Reverend Jesse
Jackson ("Once you turn on the gas, you got to cook or burn 'em

up," Jackson told him), and eventually, after obtaining a grant from Bayard Rustin and campaigning for Shirley Chisholm, by James Brown. "Once, he trailed Brown down a corridor, through a door, and, to his astonishment, onto a stage flooded with spotlights," the authors of *Outrage* reported. "He immediately went into a wiggle and dance."

It was perhaps this talent for seizing the spotlight and the moment, this fatal bent for the wiggle and the dance, that most clearly disqualified Sharpton from casting as the Good Negro, the credit to the race, the exemplary if often imagined figure whose refined manners and good grammar could be stressed and who could be seen to lay, as Jimmy Walker said of Joe Louis, "a rose on the grave of Abraham Lincoln." It was left, then, to cast Sharpton, and for Sharpton to cast himself, as the Outrageous Nigger, the familiar role — assigned sixty years ago to Father Divine and thirty years later to Adam Clayton Powell — of the essentially manageable fraud whose first concern is his own well-being. It was for example repeatedly mentioned, during the ten days the jury was out on the first jogger trial, that Sharpton had chosen to wait out the verdict not at 111 Centre Street but "in the air-conditioned comfort" of C. Vernon Mason's office, from which he could be summoned by beeper.

Sharpton, it was frequently said by whites and also by some blacks, "represented nobody," was "self-appointed" and "self-promoting." He was an "exploiter" of blacks, someone who "did them more harm than good." It was pointed out that he had been indicted by the state of New York in June of 1989 on charges of grand larceny. (He was ultimately acquitted.) It was pointed out that *New York Newsday,* working on information that appeared to have been supplied by federal law enforcement agencies, had in January 1988 named him as a federal informant, and that he himself admitted to having let the government tap his phone in a drug-enforcement effort. It was routinely said, most tellingly of all in a narrative based on the magical ability of "leaders" to improve the common weal, that he was "not the right leader," "not at all the leader the black community needs." His clothes and his demeanor were ridiculed (my husband was asked by *Esquire* to do a piece predicated on interviewing Sharpton while he was having his hair processed), his motives derided, and his tactics, which were those of an extremely sophisticated player who counted being widely despised among his stronger cards, not very well understood.

Whites tended to believe, and to say, that Sharpton was "using" the racial issue — which, in the sense that all political action is based on "using" one issue or another, he clearly was. Whites also tended to see him as destructive and irresponsible, indifferent to the truth or to the sensibilities of whites — which, most notoriously in the nurturing of the Tawana Brawley case, a primal fantasy in which white men were accused of a crime Sharpton may well have known to be a fabrication, he also clearly was. What seemed not at all understood was that for Sharpton, who had no interest in making the problem appear more tractable ("The question is, do you want to 'ease' it or do you want to 'heal' it," he had said when asked if his marches had not worked against "easing tension" in Bensonhurst), the fact that blacks and whites could sometimes be shown to have divergent interests by no means suggested the need for an ameliorative solution. Such divergent interests were instead a lucky break, a ready-made organizing tool, a dramatic illustration of who had the power and who did not, who was making it and who was falling below the line; a metaphor for the sense of victimization felt not only by blacks but by all those Sharpton called "the left-out opposition." *We got the power,* the chants go on "Sharpton and Fulani in Babylon: volume 1 the battle of New York City," a tape of the speeches of Sharpton and of Leonora Fulani, a leader of the New Alliance party. *We are the chosen people. Out of the pain. We that can't even talk together. Have learned to walk together.*

"I'm no longer sure what I thought about Al Sharpton a year or two ago still applies," Jerry Nachman, the editor of the *New York Post,* who had frequently criticized Sharpton, told Howard Kurtz of the *Washington Post* in September 1990. "I spent a lot of time on the street. There's a lot of anger, a lot of frustration. Rightly or wrongly, he may be articulating a great deal more of what typical attitudes are than some of us thought." Wilbert Tatum, the editor and publisher of the *Amsterdam News,* tried to explain to Kurtz how, in his view, Sharpton had been cast as "a caricature of black leadership":

He was fat. He wore jogging suits. He wore a medallion and gold chains. And the unforgivable of unforgivables, he had processed hair. The white media, perhaps not consciously, said, "We're going to promote this guy because we can point up the ridiculousness and paucity of black leadership."

Al understood precisely what they were doing, precisely. Al is probably the most brilliant tactician this country has ever produced. . . .

Whites often mentioned, as a clinching argument, that Sharpton paid his demonstrators to appear; the figure usually mentioned was five dollars, but the figure floated by a prosecutor on the jogger case was four dollars (by November 1990, when Sharpton was fielding demonstrators to protest the killing of a black woman alleged to have grabbed a police nightstick in the aftermath of a domestic dispute, a police source quoted in the *Post* had jumped the payment to twenty dollars). This seemed on many levels a misunderstanding, or an estrangement, or as blacks would say, a disrespect, too deep to address, but on its simplest level it served to suggest what value was placed by whites on what they thought of as black time.

In the fall of 1990, the fourth and fifth of the six defendants in the Central Park attack, Kevin Richardson and Kharey Wise, went on trial. Since this particular narrative had achieved full resolution, or catharsis, with the conviction of the first three defendants, the city's interest in the case had by then largely waned. Those "charlatans" who had sought to "exploit" the case had been whisked, until they could next prove useful, into the wings. Even the verdicts in this second trial, coinciding as they did with the most recent arrest of John (the Dapper Don) Gotti, a reliable favorite on the New York stage, did not lead the local news. It was in fact the economy itself that had come center stage in the city's new, and yet familiar, narrative work: a work in which the vital yet beleaguered city would or would not weather yet another "crisis" (the answer was a resounding yes); a work, or a dreamwork, that emphasized not only the cyclical nature of such "crises" but the regenerative power of the city's "contrasts." "With its migratory population, its diversity of cultures and institutions, and its vast resources of infrastructure, capital, and intellect, New York has been the quintessential modern city for more than a century, constantly reinventing itself," Michael Stone concluded in his *New York* magazine cover story, "Hard Times." "Though the process may be long and painful, there's no reason to believe it won't happen again."

These were points commonly made in support of a narrative that tended, with its dramatic line of "crisis" and resolution, or recovery, only to obscure further the economic and historical groundwork for the situation in which the city found itself: that long unindictable conspiracy of criminal and semi-criminal civic and commercial arrangements, deals, negotiations, gimmes and getmes, graft and grift, pipe, topsoil, concrete, garbage; the conspiracy of those in the know, those with a connection, those with a friend at the Department of Sanitation or the Buildings Department or the School Construction Authority or Foley Square, the conspiracy of those who believed everybody got upside down because of who it was, it happened to anybody else, a summons gets issued, and that's the end of it. On November 12, 1990, in its page-one analysis of the city's troubles, the *New York Times* went so far as to locate, in "public spending," not the drain on the city's vitality and resources it had historically been but "an important positive factor":

> Not in decades has so much money gone for public works in the area — airports, highways, bridges, sewers, subways and other projects. Roughly $12 billion will be spent in the metropolitan region in the current fiscal year. Such government outlays are a healthy counterforce to a 43 percent decline since 1987 in the value of new private construction, a decline related to the sharp drop in real estate prices. . . . While nearly every industry in the private sector has been reducing payrolls since spring, government hiring has risen, maintaining an annual growth rate of 20,000 people since 1987. . . .

That there might well be, in a city in which the proliferation of and increase in taxes were already driving private-sector payrolls out of town, hardly anyone left to tax for such public works and public-sector jobs was a point not too many people wished seriously to address: among the citizens of a New York come to grief on the sentimental stories told in defense of its own lazy criminality, the city's inevitability remained the given, the heart, the first and last word on which all the stories rested. We love New York, the narrative promises, because it matches our energy level.

E. L. DOCTOROW

Standards

FROM HARPER'S MAGAZINE

GREAT SONGS and the Men Who Wrote Them. Invariably from poor families, possibly immigrants, coming to light only in their sixties or seventies (uncovered first by the archivists, interviewers, and professors of popular culture, then presented for evenings of song and reminiscence under the auspices of arts councils, then made the subjects of documentary films) because as composers of classics they were thought to have died long ago. And so they rise like vampires from their coffins, toupees slightly askew. They have blondes on their arms who are taller than they, glittery silk-sheathed women highly made-up, past their prime, not as definitively the composers' juniors as they once were but still solemnly sexual. The first thing you notice about the men who wrote the songs is their rampant self-satisfaction. They talk to you nose to nose, grab your lapels, and inform you of everything you have to know about their greatness. They see no contradiction between their established reputation and the need to advise you of it. They want your obeisance even if they have to teach you what you need to know to supply it. Cigars, this is the culture of cigars, and knowledge comes by anecdote. They light their cigars and tell stories from their lives that prove how all the complexities and ambiguities of existence boil down to a few simple lessons that you can learn too if you apply yourself. They are wealthy, having made something that produces income year after year after year without any further effort on their part. They reside in Palm Springs and go regularly to Las Vegas, and to New York every fall to see the new shows. They like Atlantic

City, and Chicago, and New Orleans, but wherever they are they
go to the clubs, they visit clubs as other people visit cathedrals,
and make a point particularly of going to the small rooms where
the new performers are showcasing. They are uneducated men
who are proud of their reading and knowledge of human nature. They favor factual work, not fiction, certainly not poetry,
but popular military histories and the memoirs of statesmen and
inspirational world leaders. From this thin gruel they make a culture by which their minds apprehend the Mysteries. They have
written usually hundreds of songs, perhaps two or three or five
of which you will recognize as standards, ultimate and lasting artifacts of public consciousness. You will not have to encourage
them to sit down at a piano and deliver one of their standards in
their usually bad, gravelly voices and incredibly old-fashioned
sheet music accompaniment. And they will advise you how many
recordings have been made of this song, and by whom, none of
them as right in the phrasing, in the interpretation, as their own.
They will demonstrate by giving you various readings of croon-
ers and belters and chanteuses, and then showing you how the
original, from their throats, is so much better. Tirelessly, exhaus-
tively, they will go through the song again and again, never finding it anything less than fresh though they have been singing it
for decades; the song is thirty, forty, fifty years old and is two or
three minutes long, and they have been singing it and applaud-
ing themselves for it for years, unsated in their wonder for it, the
genius of it, that it exists as an achievement as surely as the Capi-
tol in Washington or the four heads of Mount Rushmore. And
you wonder, the voice not being there and the music barely,
primitively established on the piano, and the words at a level of
composition that would make a poet wince or shake his head in
pity — how is it the song is so good, so truly fine that recognition
surges in you like a current and you laugh for the pleasure of it?
How is it from the vulgar tongue and squawking throat, from the
dulled and cataracted eye, from the lobeless brain of this irre-
mediable dimwit, something has issued that is actually your own
dear and cherished possession, a memory of yourself, a high moment of your own imagining, some precipitate of your best and
most noble expectation for your life, when you were young and
courageous and held her in knightly idealization, turning, turn-

ing around the room in a shuffling trance, as the sweet band turned its measures on the scratchy record, and all your aching, swollen blue desires were given the name of Romance?

The more I think about songs, the more mysterious they become. They stand in our minds as spiritual histories of certain times; they have the capacity to represent in their lyrics and lines of melody wars and other disasters, moral process, the fruits of experience, and, like prayers, the consolations beyond loss. Peoples are brought into being by them. They are a resource both for the loyalists defending their country and for the revolutionists overthrowing it. Yet they are such short and linear things. Little sale tags on life. Their rhythms alone can establish states of mind that are imperially preemptive and, by implication, condescending of all other states of mind. Yet it is essential for their effect that they not go on and on. Not only their single-mindedness but their brevity makes them universally and instantly accessible as no other form is. To cure up life into a lyricized tune is to do tremendous violence to reality, and this is the source of their powerful magic.

What happens in a song that differentiates it from speech, even poetic speech? What makes the spoken voice the singing voice, when does the pitch of a voice become its note, how does the enumeration of a word become the sung word? I've just listened to a song. Words — the vowels of words — are elongated in songs to such an extent that if you spoke the lines of a lyric, without its music but with the vowels held as they are when they are sung, people would not wait to hear the ends of your sentences. This is most particularly true of ballads and love songs, less so of novelty numbers or humorous songs, or songs that take exception to someone's behavior. But it is possible that the appeal of a song lies partly in its deceleration of thought, a release perhaps from the normal race of the mind through its ideas and impressions. Ritually to retard a thought is to dwell in its meaning, to find the pleasures of posed conflicts and their resolutions as you would not in a mere recitation of lyrics.

But everyone understands the difference between song and speech, even children, suggesting that the grunt and the note are equally inborn. The question then arises, why is song for the occasion and speech for the everyday? Why do we not sing most of the time as they do in operas, and speak when we make the especial effort to compact and elevate our feelings?

Lullabies, school songs, anthems, battle hymns, work songs, chanteys, love songs, bawdy songs, laments, requiems. They're there in every age of life, for every occasion, on the sepulchral voices of the choir, in the stomp and shout of the whorehouse piano player. But all songs are songs of justification.

There are no science songs that I know of. No song that tells you the force of gravity is a product of the masses of two objects divided by the inverse ratio of the distance between them. Science is self-justifying and neither seeks nor offers redress. Yet science teaches us something about song: scientific formulas describe the laws by which the physical universe operates and suggest in equations that a balance is possible even when things are in apparent imbalance. So do songs. Songs are compensatory. When a singer asks, why did you do this to me, why did you break my heart? the inhering formula is that the degree of betrayal is equivalent to the eloquence of the cry of pain. The rage is the square root of love multiplied by a power of the truth of the situation. Feelings transform as quickly and recklessly as subatomic events, and when there is critical mass a song erupts, but the overall amount of pure energy is constant. And when the song is good we recognize it as truth. Like a formula, it applies to everyone, not just the singer.

If we sang most of the time, as they do in operas, our lives would resound, as legends; there would be very little room for new data and few occasions genuinely to advance the race, for each small thought or change of direction, each human ploy or representation of feeling, would be monumental. You will notice in classical operas that time moves more slowly than it does before the curtain goes up or after it comes down. There is an actual time warp in every operatic performance between the opening scene of the first act and the closing scene of the last, and that is because the number of narrative events is actually quite small, whereas the reactions to each of them are quite extended. If we sang most of the time, as people do in operas, we would endlessly stand and arrange and rearrange ourselves to offer our solos and the duets and trios and quartets and quintets and choruses of our relationships, and the volatility of the world would diminish, time itself would have to wait for us to register every change of weather with an aria, and we would all move in stately slow motion and rap our staffs upon the earth to bring up the nether spirits, and they would come, because opera is song that has moved outward in all directions and enveloped the entire world in performance, and all the operas ever written are, conglomerately, one song swollen into cosmos.

There are publicly held songs whose authorship is anonymous and there are privately held songs that are the copyrighted property of the composer. Folk songs coming out of the hills, up from the mines, fading behind the night train like its whistle. Measuring the time of the long swings of the sledgehammer between bursts of stone. On the one hand. And on the other, what is worked out at the piano, his burning cigarette scoring a black groove in the lid of the upright, the chord bursts interrupted by urgently penciled notations on the staff.

We make distinctions between what is anonymous and known, historic and contemporary, amateur and professional. We make distinctions of motive, or felt reality. The voice that finds words for the pain. The voice that chooses words to convey the pain.

Yet the basic and defining distinction is between an oral culture and a written. Enduring folk songs are standards composed orally and given directly into the air, without notation and therefore without regard to property rights. Every song, even a so-called folk song, is composed by one person or perhaps by two. But when the song is not written the creator of the song has neither the means of protecting it nor the opportunity of seeing to it that it is replicated, as it is, by other performers. Perhaps this is not even conceived as desirable, or more likely not even thought of as a possibility.

Oral cultures are proud, creative, participatory; the mind gives as it receives; and it is not always clear where the self ends and the community begins. So that over the years if the composed but unwritten song endures, it suffers changes, amendments, revisions, refinements, bevelings, planings, sandings, polishings, oilings, rubbings, handlings, until it stands, as elegantly simple in its presence, as glowing in its grain, as a beautiful piece of country cabinetry.

"Come all you fair and tender ladies, take warning how you court young men, they're like a star of the summer morning, they first appear and then they're gone." The gender sorrow of centuries is in those lines. The counsel is work-pure. You remember how from the porch of the dark mansard house along the railroad track she watched from the open door day after day, night after night, and saw in its blinding sunlight or deep violet starlight the terrible unbroken view of the wide but cultivated plains? At dawn the men appeared on the low horizon flinging the sheaves of hay on the wagons trailing the mechanical reaper, which she heard from this distance as the perturbation of bedclothes, a rasp of breath, a soft and toneless grunt of discovery. Well, it goes back beyond the reaper to the scythe, and back beyond the five-string banjo to the lute: you see her? It's the same woman standing there. But she's in the muck yard, walled by the small shire houses of sod and thatch, with only God and her tight linen cap to protect her from the defilation of her Lord.

Whereas today songs are written on paper and published and copyrighted. They may be interpreted but not changed. And it is as if the spirit voices in the air have gone silent as God has been silent since we wrote down his words in a book. "Tell me how long the train's been gone," says another old song, and that is what it is talking about.

Perhaps the first songs were lullabies. Perhaps mothers were the first singers. Perhaps they learned to soothe their squirming simian babies by imitating the sounds of moving water — the gurgles, cascades, plashes, puddlings, flows, floods, spurts, spills, gushes, laps, and sucks. Perhaps they knew their babies were born from water. And rhythm was the gentle rock of the water hammock slung between the pelvic trees. And melody was the sound the water made when the baby stirred its limbs.

There is the endless delight we take in new beings, the precious fleshlings of our future, our cuntlets and cocklings, our dolls stamped out by God; and there is the antediluvian rage they evoke by their blind, screaming, shitting, and pissing helplessness. So the songs for them are two-faced, lulling in the gentle maternal voice but viciously surrealistic in the words: "Rock-a-by baby in the treetop, when the wind blows the cradle will rock, when the bough breaks the cradle will fall, down will come baby, cradle and all." Imagine falling through a tree, your legs locked and your arms tightly bound to your sides. Imagine falling down into the world with your little head bongoing against the boughs and the twigs and branches whipping across your ears as if you were a xylophone. Imagine being born. Lullabies urge us to go to sleep at the same time they enact for us the terror of waking. In this way we learn for our own sake the immanence in all feelings of their opposite. The Bible, too, speaks of this as the Fall.

"Goober Peas" was a popular song during the Civil War. Goober peas came in a can. They were a ubiquitous field ration. "Peas! Peas! Peas! Peas! Eating goober peas. Goodness how delicious, eating goober peas." This song represents one of the earliest expressions of the irony of ordinary soldiers given to the glory of war. Historians tell us the Civil War was the first instance of modern warfare, by which they mean the moment when the technology of arms became more important than the courage of men. (Yes, if you watch him beheaded in the charge by a shell fired a mile away. Yes, if you have the eyes to watch his body gridded, scored, perforated, and sectioned, quartered, dismembered, and disemboweled with such mechanical efficiency that he is a putrefying blood blob percolating into the earth even as his anguished "Maaa!" still sings in the air.) In recognition of this truth the irony of ordinary soldiers creeps into the campground. We may imagine them marching there singing "The Battle Hymn of the Republic," but in the evening before their action, in contemplation of their death at dawn, when they will run in their chill across the strangely silent meadow, with the familiar beloved scent of hay in their nostrils, and dew loomed in delicate webs of white on the grass, and the woods ahead of them drawn downward by the sunlight, first the treetops and then the slowly thickening trunks, until they see the lead raking toward them as sizzles of light — in contemplation of this they regard one another around the campfire and laugh and sing as raucously as they can, "Peas! Peas! Peas! Peas! Eating goober peas. Goodness how delicious, eating goober peas."

"(She's Only) A Bird in a Gilded Cage" is a song written at the turn of the century. The tone of this song is moralistic, compassionately reproachful. A young girl marries an old man for his money, and having done so dies of lack of love. But popular culture finds its truest expression in the patently moral and covertly lascivious. Think of her drifting through the oppressive rooms of her husband's home — velour drapes, tapestries of the hunt, plush sofas and throne chairs, the thick Persian rugs, the tasseled bellpulls. She wears obsidian bracelets on her arms. Her fingers are ringed and she removes each ring ceremoniously when she sits down to practice the piano. She married money and money keeps even the windows sealed, the cries of the street muted and fading, like her memory. Once she ran free up and down the dank stairwells of poverty, with her cracked ankle shoes slipping off her heels. There was a smart and angry mother upstairs who trained her away from the artless desires and glittering eyes of adoration of the neighborhood boys. There was a father who knew what he had to sell. And now the bird sits and practices her étude, her most taxing physical task of the day. She will be given tea soon, and settled for her afternoon nap, and helped with her bath, and dressed for dinner, and will present herself to her husband at an alluring distance downtable from him. Lonely, pampered, imprisoned in idleness, she will find the one form of expression left to her when at last, in the dark light of her bedroom, with his assistance, she prepares for bed.

"Her beauty was sold for an old man's gold. She's a bird in a gilded cage." If written today, of course, the young woman would not die. The last verse would have her blotting the dribble of oatmeal from the old man's trembling chin and striding off to her classes in medical school. But as a moralistic (if hypocritical) text from the late nineteenth century, the song portrays a common social disaster.

A song written about the same time is "Come Home, Father." The child stands at the bar, pulling on the sleeve of the drunken father. In a sense this is a companion song, a male version of

"(She's Only) A Bird in a Gilded Cage." Both songs describe characteristic recourses of the American working poor in the second half of the nineteenth century.

With Tin Pan Alley, songs became a widely distributed industrial spiritual product. The standards that emerged from this manufactory release us into a flow of imagery that whirls us through our decades, our eras, our changing landscape. For a long while industrialized America looks back longingly at its rural past: "When You Were Sweet Sixteen," it sighs, "In the Evening by the Moonlight," "On the Banks of the Wabash," "In the Good Old Summertime." Then the spirit changes; defiance, rebelliousness is encoded in the sophistications of the double entendre: "(You Can Go as Far as You Like With Me) In My Merry Oldsmobile," "There'll Be a Hot Time (In the Old Town, Tonight)," "It Don't Mean a Thing If It Ain't Got That Swing."

When a song is a standard it can reproduce itself from one of its constituent parts. If you merely recite the words you will hear the melody. If you hum the melody the words will articulate themselves in your mind. That is an indication of an unusual self-referential power — the physical equivalent would be regeneration of a severed limb, or cloning an entire being from one cell. Standards from every period of our lives remain cross-indexed in our brains to be called up in whole, or in part, or, in fact, to come to mind unbidden. Nothing else can as suddenly and poignantly evoke the look, the feel, the smell of our times past. We use standards in the privacy of our minds as signifiers of our actions and relationships. They can be a cheap means of therapeutic self-discovery. If, for example, you are deeply in love and thinking about her and looking forward to seeing her, pay attention to the tune you're humming. Is it "Just One of Those Things"? You will soon end the affair.

Of Great Songs, the men who wrote them will tell you their basic principle of composition. Keep it simple. The simpler, the better. You want untrained voices to handle it in the shower, in the kitchen. Try to keep the tune in one octave. Stick with the four basic chords and avoid tricky rhythms. They may not know that this is the aesthetic of the church hymn. They may not know that hymns were the first hits. But they know that hymns and their realm of discourse ennoble or idealize life, express its pieties, and are in themselves totally proper and appropriate for all ears. And so most popular ballads are, in their characteristic romanticism, secularized hymns.

The principle of keeping it simple suggests why many standards sound alike. One might even say a song can't become a standard unless it is reminiscent of existing standards. Maybe this is why we feel a new good song has the characteristic of seeming, on first hearing, always to have existed. In a sense it has. Just as we in our own minds seem to have always existed, regardless of the date of our birth. A standard suggests itself as having been around all along, and waiting only for the proper historical moment in which to reveal itself.

When people say "our song" they mean they and the song exist together as some sort of generational truth. They are met to make a common destiny. The song names them, it rescues them from the accident of ahistorical genetic existence. They are located in cultural time. A crucial event, a specific setting, a certain smile, a kind of lingo, a degree of belief or skepticism, a particular humor, or a dance step goes with the song. And from these ephemera we make our place in civilization. For good or bad, we have our timely place.

Today different kinds of songs have different venues. Pop in cafés, show tunes in theaters, rock in stadia, country in roadhouses, bluegrass at outdoor festivals, gospel in churches, evangelical pop on TV networks, blues in clubs. It's a kind of fissioning America we find in our songs. And the music of different singing voices, with different lights in the singers' eyes, ingenious idle musical thoughts, and worked-out ideas of different wisdoms, has all hardened into conventions we call genres. And genres we call markets. Songs come in records, tapes, CDs, videos; come in commercials; come in concerts. Songs on the airwaves pour out one right after another, jammed up, no space between them.

If we allow that culture by its nature imprisons perception, that for a poignant creative moment it may enlighten us but then, perversely, transforms itself into a jailhouse walling out reality, then songs comprise the cells of our imprisonment. Behind them rise the tiers and guard towers and electrified fences — sitcoms, sermons, movies, newspapers, presidential elections, art galleries, museums, therapies, plays, poems, novels, and university curricula.

But the bars we grasp are our songs.

RONALD DWORKIN

Liberty and Pornography

FROM THE NEW YORK REVIEW OF BOOKS

WHEN ISAIAH BERLIN delivered his famous inaugural lecture as
Chichele Professor of Social and Political Theory at Oxford, in
1958, he felt it necessary to acknowledge that politics did not at-
tract the professional attention of most serious philosophers in
Britain and America. They thought philosophy had no place in
politics, and vice versa; that political philosophy could be nothing more than a parade of the theorist's own preferences and
allegiances with no supporting arguments of any rigor or respectability. That gloomy picture is unrecognizable now. Political
philosophy thrives as a mature industry; it dominates many distinguished philosophy departments and attracts a large share of
the best graduate students almost everywhere.

Berlin's lecture, "Two Concepts of Liberty," played an important and distinctive role in this renaissance. It provoked immediate, continuing, heated, and mainly illuminating controversy.
It became, almost at once, a staple of graduate and undergraduate reading lists, as it still is. Its scope and erudition, its historical
sweep and evident contemporary force, its sheer interest, made
political ideas suddenly seem exciting and fun. Its main polemical message — that it is fatally dangerous for philosophers to ignore either the complexity or the power of those ideas — was
both compelling and overdue. But chiefly, or so I think, its importance lay in the force of its central argument. For though
Berlin began by conceding to the disdaining philosophers that
political philosophy could not match logic or the philosophy of
language as a theater for "radical discoveries," in which "talent
for minute analyses is likely to be rewarded," he continued by

analyzing subtle distinctions that, as it happens, are even more important now, in the Western democracies at least, than when he first called our attention to them.

I must try to describe two central features of his argument, though for reasons of space I shall have to leave out much that is important to them. The first is the celebrated distinction described in the lecture's title: between two (closely allied) senses of liberty. Negative liberty (as Berlin came later to restate it) means not being obstructed by others in doing what one might wish to do. We count some negative liberties — like the freedom to speak our minds without censorship — as very important and others — like driving at very fast speeds — as trivial. But they are both instances of negative freedom, and though a state may be justified in imposing speed limits, for example, on grounds of safety and convenience, that is nevertheless an instance of restricting negative liberty.

Positive liberty, on the other hand, is the power to control or participate in public decisions, including the decision how far to curtail negative liberty. In an ideal democracy — whatever that is — the people govern themselves. Each is master to the same degree, and positive liberty is secured for all.

In his inaugural lecture Berlin described the historical corruption of the idea of positive liberty, a corruption that began in the idea that someone's true liberty lies in control by his rational self rather than his empirical self, that is, in control that aims at securing goals other than those the person himself recognizes. Freedom, on that conception, is possible only when people are governed, ruthlessly if necessary, by rulers who know their true, metaphysical will. Only then are people truly free, albeit against their will. That deeply confused and dangerous, but nevertheless potent, chain of argument had in many parts of the world turned positive liberty into the most terrible tyranny. Of course, by calling attention to this corruption of positive liberty, Berlin did not mean that negative liberty was an unalloyed blessing, and should be protected in all its forms in all circumstances at all costs. He said later that on the contrary, the vices of excessive and indiscriminate negative liberty were so evident, particularly in the form of savage economic inequality, that he had not thought it necessary to describe them in much detail.

The second feature of Berlin's argument that I have in mind

is a theme repeated throughout his writing on political topics. He insists on the complexity of political value, and the fallacy of supposing that all the political virtues that are attractive in themselves can be realized in a single political structure. The ancient Platonic ideal of some master accommodation of all attractive virtues and goals, combined in institutions satisfying each in the right proportion and sacrificing none, is in Berlin's view, for all its imaginative power and historical influence, only a seductive myth. He later summed this up:

> One freedom may abort another; one freedom may obstruct or fail to create conditions which make other freedoms, or a larger degree of freedom, or freedom for more persons, possible; positive and negative freedom may collide; the freedom of the individual or the group may not be fully compatible with a full degree of participation in a common life, with its demands for cooperation, solidarity, fraternity. But beyond all these there is an acuter issue: the paramount need to satisfy the claims of other, no less ultimate, values: justice, happiness, love, the realization of capacities to create new things and experiences and ideas, the discovery of the truth. Nothing is gained by identifying freedom proper, in either of its senses, with these values, or with the conditions of freedom, or by confounding types of freedom with one another.[1]

Berlin's warnings about conflating positive and negative liberty, and liberty itself, with other values seemed, to students of political philosophy in the great Western democracies in the 1950s, to provide important lessons about authoritarian regimes in other times and places. Though cherished liberties were very much under attack in both America and Britain in that decade, the attack was not grounded in or defended through either form of confusion. The enemies of negative liberty were powerful, but they were also crude and undisguised. Joseph McCarthy and his allies did not rely on any Kantian or Hegelian or Marxist concept of metaphysical selves to justify censorship or blacklists. They distinguished liberty not from itself, but from security; they claimed that too much free speech made us vulnerable to spies and intellectual saboteurs and ultimately to conquest.

In both Britain and America, in spite of limited reforms, the state still sought to enforce conventional sexual morality about

[1] Isaiah Berlin, *Four Essays on Liberty* (Oxford University Press, 1968), p. lvi.

pornography, contraception, prostitution, and homosexuality. Conservatives who defended these invasions of negative liberty appealed not to some higher or different sense of freedom, however, but to values that were plainly distinct from, and in conflict with, freedom: religion, true morality, and traditional and proper family values. The wars over liberty were fought, or so it seemed, by clearly divided armies. Liberals were for liberty, except, in some circumstances, for the negative liberty of economic entrepreneurs. Conservatives were for that liberty, but against other forms when these collided with security or their view of decency and morality.

But now the political maps have radically changed and some forms of negative liberty have acquired new opponents. Both in America and in Britain, though in different ways, conflicts over race and gender have transformed old alliances and divisions. Speech that expresses racial hatred, or a degrading attitude toward women, has come to seem intolerable to many people whose convictions are otherwise traditionally liberal. It is hardly surprising that they should try to reduce the conflict between their old liberal ideals and their new acceptance of censorship by adopting some new definition of what liberty, properly understood, really is. It is hardly surprising, but the result is dangerous confusion, and Berlin's warnings, framed with different problems in mind, are directly in point.

I shall try to illustrate that point with a single example: a lawsuit arising out of the attempt by certain feminist groups in America to outlaw what they consider a particularly objectionable form of pornography. I select this example not because pornography is more important or dangerous or objectionable than racist invective or other highly distasteful kinds of speech, but because the debate over pornography has been the subject of the fullest and most comprehensive scholarly discussion.

Through the efforts of Catharine MacKinnon, a professor of law at the University of Michigan, and other prominent feminists, Indianapolis, Indiana, enacted an antipornography ordinance. The ordinance defined pornography as "the graphic sexually explicit subordination of women, whether in pictures or words . . ." and it specified, as among pornographic materials falling within that definition, those that present women as enjoying pain or humiliation or rape, or as degraded or tortured or filthy, bruised or bleeding, or in postures of servility or submission or display. It included no exception for literary or artistic value, and opponents claimed that applied literally it would outlaw James Joyce's *Ulysses,* John Cleland's *Memoirs of a Woman of Pleasure,* various works of D. H. Lawrence, and even Yeats's "Leda and the Swan." But the groups who sponsored the ordinance were anxious to establish that their objection was not to obscenity or indecency as such, but to the consequences for women of a particular kind of pornography, and they presumably thought that an exception for artistic value would undermine that claim.[2]

The ordinance did not simply regulate the display of pornography so defined, or restrict its sale or distribution to particular areas, or guard against the exhibition of pornography to children. Regulation for those purposes does restrain negative liberty, but if reasonable it does so in a way compatible with free speech. Zoning and display regulations may make pornography more expensive or inconvenient to obtain, but they do not offend the principle that no one must be prevented from publishing or reading what he or she wishes on the ground that its content is immoral or offensive.[3] The Indianapolis ordinance, on the other hand, prohibited any "production, sale, exhibition, or distribution" whatever of the material it defined as pornographic.

Publishers and members of the public who claimed a desire to read the banned material arranged a prompt constitutional challenge. The federal district court held that the ordinance was unconstitutional because it violated the First Amendment to the United States Constitution, which guarantees the negative liberty of free speech.[4] The Circuit Court for the Seventh Circuit upheld the district court's decision,[5] and the Supreme Court of the United States declined to review that holding. The Circuit

---

[2] MacKinnon explained that "if a woman is subjected, why should it matter that the work has other value?" See her article "Pornography, Civil Rights, and Speech," in *Harvard Civil Rights-Civil Liberties Law Review,* Vol. 28, p. 21.

[3] See my article "Do We Have a Right to Pornography?" reprinted as Chapter 17 in my book *A Matter of Principle* (Harvard University Press, 1985).

[4] *American Booksellers Association, Inc. et al.* v. *William H. Hudnit, III, Mayor, City of Indianapolis, et al.,* 598 F. Supp. 1316 (S.D. Ind. 1984).

[5] 771 F. 2d 323 (US Court of Appeals, Seventh Circuit).

Court's decision, in an opinion by Judge Easterbrook, noticed that the ordinance did not outlaw obscene or indecent material generally but only material reflecting the opinion that women are submissive, or enjoy being dominated, or should be treated as if they did. Easterbrook said that the central point of the First Amendment was exactly to protect speech from content-based regulation of that sort. Censorship may on some occasions be permitted if it aims to prohibit directly dangerous speech — crying fire in a crowded theater or inciting a crowd to violence, for example — or speech particularly and unnecessarily inconvenient — broadcasting from sound trucks patrolling residential streets at night, for instance. But nothing must be censored, Easterbrook wrote, because the message it seeks to deliver is a bad one, or because it expresses ideas that should not be heard at all.

It is by no means universally agreed that censorship should never be based on content. The British Race Relations Act, for example, forbids speech of racial hatred, not only when it is likely to lead to violence, but generally, on the grounds that memers of minority races should be protected from racial inbsults. In America, however, it is a fixed principle of constitutional law that such regulation is unconstitutional unless some compelling necessity, not just official or majority disapproval of the message, requires it. Pornography is often grotesquely offensive; it is insulting, not only to women but to men as well. But we cannot consider that a sufficient reason for banning it without destroying the principle that the speech we hate is as much entitled to protection as any other. The essence of negative liberty is freedom to offend, and that applies to the tawdry as well as the heroic.

Lawyers who defend the Indianapolis ordinance argue that society does have a further justification for outlawing pornography: that it causes great harm as well as offense to women. But their arguments mix together claims about different types or kinds of harm, and it is necessary to distinguish these. They argue, first, that some forms of pornography significantly increase the danger that women will be raped or physically assaulted. If that were true, and the danger were clear and present, then it would indeed justify censorship of those forms, unless less stringent methods of control, such as restricting pornography's audience, would be feasible, appropriate, and effective. In fact, however, though there is some evidence that exposure to pornography weakens people's critical attitudes toward sexual violence, there is no persuasive evidence that it causes more actual incidents of assault. The Seventh Circuit cited a variety of studies (including that of the Williams Commission in Britain in 1979), all of which concluded, the court said, "that it is not possible to demonstrate a direct link between obscenity and rape. . . ."[6] A recent report based on a year's research in Britain said: "The evidence does not point to pornography as a cause of deviant sexual orientation in offenders. Rather, it seems to be used as part of that deviant sexual orientation."[7]

Some feminist groups argue, however, that pornography causes not just physical violence but a more general and endemic subordination of women. In that way, they say, pornography makes for inequality. But even if it could be shown, as a matter of causal connection, that pornography is in part responsible for the economic structure in which few women attain top jobs or equal pay for the same work, that would not justify censorship under the Constitution. It would plainly be unconstitutional to ban speech directly *advocating* that women occupy inferior roles, or none at all, in commerce and the professions, even if that speech fell on willing male ears and achieved its goals. So it cannot be a reason for banning pornography that it contributes to an unequal economic or social structure, even if we think that it does.

But the most imaginative feminist literature for censorship makes a further and different argument: that negative liberty for pornographers conflicts not just with equality but with positive liberty as well, because pornography leads to women's *political* as well as economic or social subordination. Of course por-

---

[6] That court, in a confused passage, said that it nevertheless accepted "the premises of this legislation," which included the claims about a causal connection with sexual violence. But it seemed to mean that it was accepting the rather different causal claim considered in the next paragraph, about subordination. In any case, it said that it accepted those premises only for the sake of argument, since it thought it had no authority to reject decisions of Indianapolis based on its interpretation of empirical evidence.

[7] See the *Daily Telegraph*, December 23, 1990. Of course further studies might contradict this assumption. But it seems very unlikely that pornography will be found to stimulate physical violence to the overall extent that nonpornographic depictions of violence, which are much more pervasive in our media and culture, do.

nography does not take the vote from women, or somehow make
their votes count less. But it produces a climate, according to this
argument, in which women cannot have genuine political power
or authority because they are perceived and understood unauth-
entically — that is, they are made over by male fantasy into people very different from, and of much less consequence than, the
people they really are. Consider, for example, these remarks
from the work of the principal sponsor of the Indianapolis ordinance. "[Pornography] institutionalizes the sexuality of male supremacy, fusing the eroticization of dominance and submission
with the social construction of male and female. . . . Men treat
women as who they see women as being. Pornography constructs
who that is. Men's power over women means that the way men
see women defines who women can be."[8]

Pornography, on this view, denies the positive liberty of
women; it denies them the right to be their own masters by re-
creating them, for politics and society, in the shapes of male fantasy. That is a powerful argument, even in constitutional terms,
because it asserts a conflict not just between liberty and equality
but within liberty itself, that is, a conflict that cannot be resolved
simply on the ground that liberty must be sovereign. What shall
we make of the argument understood that way? We must notice,
first, that it remains a causal argument. It claims not that pornography is a consequence or symptom or symbol of how the identity of women has been reconstructed by men, but an important
cause or vehicle of that reconstruction.

That seems strikingly implausible. Sadistic pornography is re-
volting, but it is not in general circulation, except for its milder,
soft-porn manifestations. It seems unlikely that it has remotely
the influence over how women's sexuality or character or talents
are conceived by men, and indeed by women, that commercial
advertising and soap operas have. Television and other parts of
popular culture use sexual display and sexual innuendo to sell
virtually everything, and they often show women as experts in
domestic detail and unreasoned intuition and nothing else. The
images they create are subtle and ubiquitous, and it would not be
surprising to learn, through whatever research might establish
this, that they indeed do great damage to the way women are

[8] See MacKinnon's article cited in footnote 2.

understood and allowed to be influential in politics. Sadistic pornography, though much more offensive and disturbing, is greatly overshadowed by these dismal cultural influences as a causal force.

Judge Easterbrook's opinion for the Seventh Circuit assumed, for the sake of argument, however, that pornography did have the consequences the defenders of the ordinance claimed. He said that the argument nevertheless failed because the point of free speech is precisely to allow ideas to have whatever consequences follow from their dissemination, including undesirable consequences for positive liberty. "Under the First Amendment," he said, "the government must leave to the people the evaluation of ideas. Bald or subtle, an idea is as powerful as the audience allows it to be. . . . [The assumed result] simply demonstrates the power of pornography as speech. All of these unhappy effects depend on mental intermediation."

That is right as a matter of American constitutional law. The Ku Klux Klan and the American Nazi party are allowed to propagate their ideas in America, and the British Race Relations Act, so far as it forbids abstract speech of racial hatred, would be unconstitutional in the U.S. But does the American attitude represent the kind of Platonic absolutism Berlin warned against? No, because there is an important difference between the idea he thinks absurd, that all ideals attractive in themselves can be perfectly reconciled within a single utopian political order, and the different idea he thought essential, that we must, as individuals and nations, choose, among possible combinations of ideals, a coherent, even though inevitably and regrettably limited, set of these to define our own individual or national way of life. Freedom of speech, conceived and protected as a fundamental negative liberty, is the core of the choice modern democracies have made, a choice we must now honor in finding our own ways to combat the shaming inequalities women still suffer.

This reply depends, however, on seeing the alleged conflict within liberty as a conflict between the negative and positive senses of that virtue. We must consider yet another argument which, if successful, could not be met in the same way, because it claims that pornography presents a conflict within the negative liberty of speech itself. Berlin said that the character, at least, of negative liberty was reasonably clear, that although excessive claims of negative liberty were dangerous, they could at least always be seen for what they were. But the argument I have in mind, which has been offered by, among others, Frank Michelman of the Harvard Law School, expands the idea of negative liberty in an unanticipated way. He argues that some speech, including pornography, may be itself "silencing," so that its effect is to prevent other people from exercising their negative freedom to speak.

Of course it is fully recognized in First Amendment jurisprudence that some speech has the effect of silencing others. Government must indeed balance negative liberties when it prevents heckling or other demonstrative speech designed to stop others from speaking or being heard. But Michelman has something different in mind. He says that a woman's speech may be silenced not just by noise intended to drown her out but also by argument and images that change her audience's perceptions of her character, needs, desires, and standing, and also, perhaps, change her own sense of who she is and what she wants. Speech with that consequence silences her, Michelman supposes, by making it impossible for her effectively to contribute to the process Judge Easterbrook said the First Amendment protected, the process through which ideas battle for the public's favor. "[It] is a highly plausible claim," Michelman writes, "[that] pornography [is] a cause of women's subordination and silencing. . . . It is a fair and obvious question why our society's openness to challenge does not need protection against repressive private as well as public action."[9]

He argues that if our commitment to negative freedom of speech is consequentialist — if we want free speech in order to have a society in which no idea is barred from entry — then we must censor some ideas in order to make entry possible for other ones. He protests that the distinction that American constitutional law makes between the suppression of ideas by the effect of public criminal law and by the consequences of private speech is arbitrary, and that a sound concern for openness would be

[9] Frank Michelman, "Conceptions of Democracy in American Constitutional Argument: The Case of Pornography Regulation," *Tennessee Law Review*, Vol. 56, No. 291 (1989), pp. 303–304.

equally worried about both forms of control. But the distinction the law makes is not between public and private power as such, but between negative liberty and other virtues, including positive liberty. It would indeed be contradictory for a constitution to prohibit official censorship while protecting the right of private citizens physically to prevent other citizens from publishing or broadcasting specified ideas. That would allow private citizens to violate the negative liberty of other citizens by preventing them from saying what they wish.

But there is no contradiction in insisting that every idea must be allowed to be heard, even those whose consequence is that other ideas will be misunderstood, or given little consideration, or even not be spoken at all because those who might speak them are not in control of their own public identities and therefore cannot be understood as they wish to be. These are very bad consequences, and they must be resisted by whatever means our Constitution permits. But acts that have these consequences do not, for that reason, deprive others of their negative liberty to speak, and the distinction, as Berlin insisted, is very far from arbitrary or inconsequential.

It is of course understandable why Michelman and others should want to expand the idea of negative liberty in the way they try to do. Only by characterizing certain ideas as themselves "silencing" ideas — only by supposing that censoring pornography is the same thing as stopping people from drowning out other speakers — can they hope to justify censorship within the constitutional scheme that assigns a preeminent place to free speech. But the assimilation is nevertheless a confusion, exactly the kind of confusion Berlin warned against in his original lecture, because it obscures the true political choice that must be made. I return to Berlin's lecture, which put the point with that striking combination of clarity and sweep I have been celebrating:

> I should be guilt-stricken, and rightly so, if I were not, in some circumstances, ready to make [some] sacrifice [of freedom]. But a sacrifice is not an increase in what is being sacrificed, namely freedom, however great the moral need or the compensation for it. Everything is what it is: liberty is liberty, not equality or fairness or justice or culture, or human happiness or a quiet conscience.

STANLEY ELKIN

Some Overrated Masterpieces

FROM ART & ANTIQUES

THERE'S NOTHING so convincing as an opinion, and an odd thing about words is the cockeyed weight they're permitted to bear, so that if I say something as flagrantly meaningless or flat-out arbitrary as that, oh, "He's the sort of person who parts his hair," I've not only suggested something negative about hair-parting, but have made, too, an aspersion on character. He'll think twice before he parts it next time, I bet. And this goes double for written words. "He uses aftershave," I charge, "and his last three cars have been hardtops." "His wife," I continue mercilessly, "dresses the twins alike and pushes them about the streets in a perambulator like one of those wide-load house trailers!"

This isn't just a haughty aesthetic of the supercilious, it's the astonishing Law of the Unframed Indictment, the critical equivalent of holding political prisoners without bringing charges. We condemn a thing simply by mentioning it.

J. M. W. Turner, I claim, as evenly, uninflectedly as I can, paints elements — water and air — in ratios seldom seen in life and got up in murk and slate fug like a foul mood. What's the difference, then, between a Turner and ordinary mall art? Why, merely the weather, only the sobriety of his colors, as if genius were a question of the intervention of light, like sunblock, say. This time, though, by having introduced a reason, however spurious, I seem to have taken higher ground. But in questions of taste there *is* no higher ground. In matters of art and cuisine, reasons are created equal. It's a perfect *democracy* of reasons and, hey, "I know what I like" isn't only a perfectly respectable argument but an absolutely unanswerable one. There *is* nothing so convincing as an opinion.

Am I philistine? What, with *my* up-front heart? Philistine? *Me?* With my sleeves and my hankies and all the other emotional ready-to-wear in the wardrobe of my attentive sentiments? The sucker *I* am for almost any statuary in the open air, in landscape, or any of the kempt green gardens of the world? *This* push-over for the simple human harmonics of any orchestra at work, *any* orchestra, any symphony or pit band, any string quartet, jazz band, pickup bluegrass rhythm jammers, or even just any saw- or jug- or steel-drum-and-washboard skiffle group! What, *this* soft-souled, *nolo-contendere*, hearts-and-minds pussycat? Anybody's fascist, this nose-led company man, as willing — willing? *anxious* — to be stirred as sugar in tea, this lawn-chair enthusiast for all the brass, fife, and oom-pa-pa of high summer's slam-bang reviewing-stand occasions and gazebo patroticals.

But lesser art forms are all collective, I think. Which pretty much — because I know what I don't like, too — puts opera's hyperbolic charms and vocal circus in their place. Because art ought to be as one-on-one as intimacy, something if not actually shades-drawn and pulled-curtain to it, then at least discreet, and the last thing — saving architecture perhaps, which, like that gazebo from which those marches occur, is public, communal — the last thing art ought to be is stirring. And if van Gogh's painted room in Arles can command my tears, all I can tell you is that those are a different sort of tears, *vintage* tears could be, as unlike my public performances in the sculpture garden as Ripple from champagne. Speaking of which, incidentally, with its taste like a mixture of dishwater and sugar substitute, while not one of the overrated masterpieces I mean to consider here, may not be a bad instance. It comes down to us through the bubbles' reputation. Of course that's how everything comes down to us, history working its gravitational will through word of mouth.

Trust me. What I'm talking about has nothing to do with what's in and what's out, what's up and what's down — prepositional aesthetics. There ain't any old Roman pleasure to it, the thumbs-up, thumbs-down joys. I already said I know what I like. It's strictly personal. Because, for me, there *has* to be something personal or I can't function. And there is. Not envy, I *hope* not envy, or not envy exactly, and not sour grapes, *exactly* not sour grapes, with which I've no patience. Sour grapes are pathetic. Just something inimical in me to the overrated, the next guy's hype, a kind of rage like an allergy. It's a myth you don't feel your blood pressure; I *feel* my blood pressure. And for me, the test of time is simply an adjustment of the systolics and diastolics, a subsidence of the personal. So this shall chiefly take place within the precincts of the safely historical, where bygones are bygones (I mean, how long can I reasonably hold a grudge against *The Bonfire of the Vanities*?) and even subjectivity has cooled to a temperature that can't be felt.

Take Leonardo da Vinci, for example, who, with his polymath imagination and sci-fi instinctuals, seems to have been to art what Jules Verne and H. G. Wells were to fiction. Indeed, though many of his designs and sketches seem plausible even today — his tanks and fortifications, his flying machines, catapults, machine guns, hoists and gears, all the heavy arsenal of his Armageddon heart — there's something comic about Leonardo, some after-the-fact humor laid on by perspective and hindsight, the joke, that is, of the primitive, like Fred Flintstone propelling his car by foot power, some principle of the dated operating here. And if this isn't fair, isn't, in fact, specious at the root, if it suggests that a principle of the dated is *always* operable, chipping away and chipping away like a kind of erosion at what was once thought true and beautiful, the water, wind, and temperature of age, why not accept at the outset that *most* things left out in history like the open air oxidize, tarnish, become, finally, subject to the simple human joke of time? The moving finger writes, paints, makes, and having writ, painted, or made, moves on to the next thing. Because a lot of what we talk about when we talk about art is, well, fashion.

Add to my charge against Leonardo that he was a "visionary," this intellectual rover and time traveler, and it's possible to see an instability in him, a certain failure of *sitzfleisch,* an inability, that is, to sit still in his talent, almost as if he took too seriously the burden of being a Renaissance man, or was the sort of guy who parted his hair.

Now, about this Mona Lisa.

See her there in her cat-who-ate-the-canaries, her smug repose and babushka of hair like a face on a buck. A study in browns, in muds and all the purplish earthens of her jaundiced, low-level, f-stop light. See her, see her there, this, well, girl of a certain age, with a faint streak of bone structure blowing off her skin like a plume of jet trail all she has for brow. See her, see the leftward glancing of her color-coordinated eyes inside the puffy, horizontal parentheses of her lashless lids. See the long, low-slung nose dropped inches below the painterly rules of thumb. Now see her famous statelies, her upright, comfortable aplomb, her left forearm along the arm of a chair, her fat right hand covering it, as clubby and at ease as one foot crossed over another. Look at the background through the open casement, the queer topography like mounds of green volcanic vegetable, the strange striated water and all the wavy switchback of the road like something carved from earth by one of the maestro's anachronistic machines, a backhoe, say, some plow or grader of the yet-to-be.

Focus. *Focus!*

In and closer in to the central occasion of her odd, asexual face, in where the mystery lives, the secret agenda, in toward her giacondas, her giaconundrums, the hidden mystery of her guarded gingivitis smile! Because I'm changing my mind here, a little I am, and thinking maybe it's Nat King Cole's version I'm not that crazy about, his viscous syrups I'm thinking of, confusing the box-step cliché and sentimentals with the fact of her face. Because what levers our attention is that nose and those lips, and a truth about art is the company it keeps with the slightly askew, the fly in that woodpile of symmetry, mere balance in painting, equilibrium, a stunt of the "beautiful." What commissions the eye is face. No likeness hangs on the wall of hair, hands, breasts, behinds, the soles of one's feet. Faces are the most private part. It's the face that draws the eye in the Mona Lisa, but I was only kidding about the mystery of that smile. There *is* no mystery. No one ever had to solve a face, and the notion of *this* face's enigmatics has always been a kind of anthropomorphism, only paint's pathetic fallacy, facial phrenology, a horoscopics by bone structure, an astrology of the eye, the palmistry of character, wrongheaded, literary, the racism of beauty, unreliable finally as any other pseudoscience, as if to say, oh, as if to say, "Read my lips."

Next slide.

Georgia O'Keeffe was a painter who rarely depicted human beings. Her desert subject matter is, in a way, the flip, parched, only apparently sunnier side of Turner's wet coin — blanched, bleached landscapes of polished, picked-clean death. This hermit — in New Mexico she lived at "Ghost Ranch" — this prospector type whose unpopulated, desiccated paintings, save for the fossils that appear in them, seem studies in an almost relished absence. The bones and white skulls in O'Keeffe's work signify not decay so much as the evidence of a fled, efficient hunger — the art of the buzzard, the art of the scavenger hunt. Even her rather wonderful cityscapes *(East River No. 1; Shelton Hotel, New York; New York Night)* are alternative versions of shapes found in the desert paintings — the mesa, canyon, adobe variations — and seem deliberate, even perverse, essays in exclusion, as though both nature and the manmade contain value only to the extent that they not only avoid but actually proscribe the human. (Only in *New York Night,* and only if you look carefully, can you make out, in the lower left-hand corner, any people at all — four stick figures of black paint rather more like exclamation points than human beings.) It's as if O'Keeffe were driven by some wilderness, Sierra Club will, vaguely snobbish, a restrictive, country-club vision. She's Edward Hopper without people, without even the saving grace of their dignified loneliness. She's interested only in shapes (my favorite O'Keeffe paintings, her *Sky Above Clouds* series, have always seemed rather like *New Yorker* covers), but where there is no "face" there can be no interest. Even her suggestive, almost gynecological and phallic flora (which almost never appear in bunches and are rarely "arranged") seem parodic, sterile, lush enough but in their issueless isolation really only a sort of sexual floor plan.

Like other private artists she became her greatest achievement, a beautiful woman whose bone structure was her fate and who posed, in a literal sense, in her black clothes, white scarves, and black hats, paring herself down and paring herself down into a piece of art quite like sculpture, a leathery, unsmiling woman of manipulated style, editing herself and disappearing at last behind the very image of a collective, hermaphroditic animism, some perfected, deliberated simulacrum somewhere between ancient squaw and old manitou, a final, showy mysticism complete and functional as the bony infrastructure of those skulls she preferred to the faces that covered them. I think narcissism infrastructures the infrastructure here, the dangerous virus she contracted by being both a subject — all those portraits she permitted Alfred Stieglitz to make of her — and an arranger of subjects.

But it's hard to talk about art. Maybe there should be a law against it, some First Amendment gag order like crying fire in a crowded theater. Still and all, if one knows what one likes, well, where's the harm, eh? And anyway, as I'm writing now, it's the war, day thirteen or fourteen into the Mother of Battles, though it seems longer of course, deeper into time than anything I can remember — and I'm sixty if I'm a day — and I've seen, well, not a lot, but my share, more than, and what I haven't seen, like everyone else, I fill in the blanks, make an allowance, do the Kentucky windage adjustments, write off if not to experience then to helplessness and despair this, well, looting of end times everywhere, this breaking and entering the other guy's turf, with wiser heads figuring — this is a big benefit of the doubt I'm giving away here — that damn near no one has led the right life. The Gulf's a floating filling station, Marines have died, civilians on all sides in God knows what apocalyptic positions fallen on what rubble and hoisted on what shrapnel, and I see that over on the Home Shopping Club, Operation Desert Storm sweatshirts are going for $19.75, over 400 sold and counting, and, jeez, if the world made it, it would have been the millennium in nine years and, in another one and a half, the semimillennium of the discovery of the New World. Some millennium. Some semimillennium. So it's pretty late in the day to be having any Mother of Battles. Ain't going to *study* no war no more! And I take it back about injunctions on art talk, prior restraint. Because maybe that's the only thing we ought to be allowed to talk about, stuff above our station, playing catch-up with culture, sucking up to civilization. And the point is, well, God bless the artists the point is. Here's to those with the paints whether we know whereof we speak or not. Here's to artisans, folks who make violins, cast bells, throw pots, have perfected their pitch. Here's, I mean, to all those whose attentions are engaged in innocent acts, to everyone everywhere who doesn't know where the time has flown. To minders of their own determined business who wouldn't hurt a fly. Here's to occupational therapy even, to doodle and whittle, to whistle and hum and all the preoccupied instrumentals of the head and heart, the *eye-lu-loo-lus* and sweet-dream lullabies of softest yore. And to all those makers of those less-than-masterpieces who lend point to the sermon, and to dilettantes, oh, especially, Lord, to dilettantes, window-shoppers on the artier avenues, friends of the museum, patrons of the symphony, pals of the zoo, to everyone everywhere who's ever tossed a pledge to PBS, NPR, ladies and gentlemen of good will who keep the Sunday. So, waiting for the worst, hoping for the best, it's back I go to my own harmless knitting, an expert self-proclamated but innocent as any.

Now what *I* don't much care for is all the boring, adulatory religious art of dark old early times, the triptychs in their layered gilded frames like great wooden fanfares, I mean; the altarpieces; the madonnas with their malnourished, wizened bundles of infant Jesus in fishbowl, space-helmet halos or under rakish nimbi of beanies (not like Michelangelo's pink, meaty, muscular biblicals so oddly anticipatory of Picasso's great fleshy giants); all the Annunciations running together in our heads like a Pony Express of the holy; all the lugubrious figures making their *there theres* of comfort over the spilled milk and blood of the major players on all that stained glass and shining wood; all that adoration in kings' caucus in the stable like so much political buzz, their baksheesh of gold, frankincense, and myrrh; angels in improbable, heavier-than-air wings; lashed, trussed, hangdog Jesus, pathetic, almost sheepish, shouldering a cross like a T-square, neither a Son of Man to inspire confidence nor a God to reckon with, looking nothing near what he's cracked up to be, looking confused in fact, lost, as if he'd rather be in Philadelphia — all the stupefying *junk* I mean, in Europe raised to the level of an industry, complete with guides yet, scholars of the local (and here's to guides in billed caps, gray creased suits and stuffed pockets), all those panels of unskilled, uninspired piety cartoons which looked at long enough bring on the headache and fog up the mind, and cause, as stated, to run together in the memory this blur of art, this crisis of criticism, this deferential politeness on all sides — *"Bella, bella,"* I assure the guide, *"molti, molti, molti bella"* — in my broken business-as-usual, not only as if no one had ever been afraid of being caught short in church but as if tourists were as anatomically incorrect as all those God-doll altarpieces.

And, God forgive me, *Hamlet* is an overrated play. Well, it's too long, but that ain't it, and too melodramatic of course, *and* familiar, but that ain't it either. For one thing, the premise has always bothered me, or if not the premise then what triggers the play, bothered me, I mean, even back in those old new-critical days of my undergraduate youth when we fastened on the incest thing, or the question of the prince's madness, ruse or consequence, or just plain dug H's brilliant, witty manic depression. He was, for most of us, our first "psychological" hero, more psychological even than Ivan in *The Brothers Karamazov*, which we hadn't read yet anyway. Absolutely, Hamlet was our first interesting guy, a role model even, with his get-thees-to-a-nunnery and all the tortured Ophelia-bashing and secret titillation of the dirty private jokes, his breezy killer instincts, all the full-throated cynicism of his bullying intellect — role model, male bonder, man's man, prince's prince. What puts me off, what *I* can't get past, though, is, quite simply, Hamlet's father's ghost, to me as silly as that cadre of icons in all those triptychs on all those altarpieces, the angels and allegoricals, themselves a band of ghosts, sentimental and sweet-cheeked as zephyrs on maps. I am what I am and cut no slack for the times, the other fellow's world view. Besides, at its core *Hamlet* is a realistic play and having truck with ghosts goes against its grain, botches the unity of its tone, and anyway the ghost's only a device to put the ball in play in the play. In a drama so dependent upon personality, this ghost is a stick figure. It has no character. Nor will it do to write the ghost off as a psychological projection. It comes with too much information for that. A forensic pathologist of a ghost, it fingers Claudius, fine-tunes the terms of its dispatch during its afternoon nap ("Cut off even in the blossoms of my sin, / Unhousel'd, disappointed, unanel'd, / No reck'ning made, but sent to my account / With all my imperfections on my head"), charges Hamlet to avenge it, and even dictates how Hamlet is to treat his mother.

(And like where do *I* get off?)

Some soliloquies bother me — all its vaunted to-be-or-not-to-bes, a speech I've never heard delivered by any actor, *any* actor, who's not managed to make it sound silly.

But finally, it isn't the ghost and it isn't the overblown language which grates so much as the flip side of this "interesting" man, for Hamlet's procrastinations lie as heavily on the belly as bad food. One has the sense that Shakespeare, not Hamlet, is vamping till ready, that Hamlet's frozen will is finally as much a device to stall the play as the ghost is to get it going, because for all the brilliant facets of Hamlet's reckless character, his too-fastidious duty pulls him down and locks up the play like so much left luggage until, well, until we begin to suspect that will paralysis is itself a device, that Hamlet, for all his thoroughbred, live-wire wit, for all his charm and playfulness, is not so much the Dane as one of those paid professionals at an Irish funeral, a bespoke whiner and keener, the ultimate wailer and scold of fate. Brilliant along the brightest edges of its day, the play naps like the old king during the dead, leaden center of its long, endless afternoon.

And get *these* to a nunnery: *Birth of a Nation, The Cabinet of Dr. Caligari* (well, almost every silent movie ever made, including Buster Keaton's, including Charlie Chaplin's). *Citizen Kane, Gone With the Wind,* that documentary about the '36 Olympics, most "screwball" comedies of the thirties (well, most black-and-white films generally). All the Marx Brothers, all the Ritz Brothers, Judy Garland, Fred Astaire. No more "face" to them than the dry, blanched bones of a Georgia O'Keeffe, mask all they *ever* had for a face, as customized as a clown's patented, painted puss. Garland all pixie/gamine/urchin pout and phony hope, that mask out on a ledge somewhere between outrage and melted love and on a kind of red-alert verge of perpetual tears from the tip of her pigtail in *The Wizard of Oz* to the top of her pompadour in *Meet Me in St. Louis,* a face, like the clown's, made for black velvet, crying out for it like a fix, and not much more face to her voice either if you want to know, decibel for decibel its direct weights-and-measure vocal equivalency, all vibrato and belt but slightly off true, and Fred Astaire's fixed puzzled-bumpkin expression more pleasant, perhaps, but as locked-in as Garland's. (Am I cranky, crotchety, under the weather? Are my shoes too tight, is curmudgeon written all over me? Am I this old fogey, is my bite worse than my bark? Or is this still the war news, something fed-up in my bones with hyperbolicized attachment, the red rant of unearned, misunderstood praise?) So take *that*, Fred Astaire, with your vaunted grace in your top hat your white tie and your tails, in your nightclubs, on your patent-leather, art-deco floors, your decks like the seamless, level tiles of chic beauty parlors, barbershops and men's rooms in the basements of world-class hotels. Take that and *that* on your fey, heel/toe, heel/toe bearings in your smug, *noli-me-tangere* aloofness and look-ma-no-hands gravity denials, your tango indifference and vain, vaguely threatening, predatory swoops and leaned inclinations as if, Ginger Rogers or no Ginger Rogers, elegance were only a narcissistic one-man show, *ur* performance art, removed as the elsewhere-engaged attentions of a juggler. Though maybe all movies, could be, fall short of art with their soft blandishments and easy endowments — sound, closeups, an arch, arranged lushness, perfect and unblemished as a gorgeous bay posed on a postcard. (Are my pants too small, is my hat off plumb? Nah, nah, this from a *lover* of movies, one of their easiest marks, privileged to get out of an evening, watch the coming attractions, the trailers, who, settled in his seat in the auditorium, sighs, remarks to the wife, "What could be better?") Because the truth about art *is* the company it keeps with the slightly askew, and the real stunt of the beautiful is not to be *too* beautiful.

And Jasper Johns's flag series — *White Flag* like a plank floor, *Two Flags* like a wall of carelessly mortared bricks and, for my money, the best of them, *Three Flags*, like a box on a board game. Well, I say "for my money," but who's kidding whom here? All that dough and no Hawaii or Alaska? Jasper Johns in a fallen world an easier target than Astaire or Garland, than *Citizen Kane*, than *Gone With the Wind*, though richer people take him more seriously — a desecration not of the flag but of money.

(And once — this would have been in the middlish sixties, Baby Jane Holtzer was a Presence, People Are Talking About, Buzz Buzz and et cetera — I found myself in Frank Stella's East-something brownstone. Uninvited, unintroduced, it being a whimsy intentionally inflicted or a perverse, acceptable usage among certain groups never to make a devoir, as if one's physical, accompanied presence in a place — He's-With-Me understood — were a sort of moral vouchsafe or silent parole like an obscure but flashy idiom of behavior redounding not so much to the credit of the *schlepped* as the honor of the *schlepper,* but no crasher either, given carte blanche like any real guest, special roaming privileges like a range chicken, to mosey, take it all in. I've never forgotten my first impression. Which was, there, surrounded by the astonishing furniture in the setlike rooms — chrome and leather, glass and steel — and several hundred thousand bucks' worth of Stella's frames and canvases, the paintings like patterns on bolts of fabric, the strangely shaped frames like exercises in bizarre carpentry, a realization that what I saw was visionary, but misunderstanding the vision, not recognizing in what was still only the sixties that what I saw was basically only your expensive *de rigueur* restaurant decor of the seventies, eighties, and nineties, maybe even a first take on the higher mall motifs.

(And another time, years later, in Paris at the Rodin Museum, Stella confounded, inverted, in a different mode, on a different scale, some metrics of the monumental, translated really, their differences all there was to run them together in my mind and, miles from the ornamental now, beyond decor or the Wagnerian either, the Tristanic and Isoldic, heroism's warp speeds, into cruel health like bloody organ meats on the redded-up floors of some human abattoir, those monumental sitters or loungers or drowners in their own stone, Rodin's more-than-solid citizens, who can't keep their hands to themselves, whose every pose — think *The Thinker,* think the vats and bone banks in *The Gates of Hell,* think *Adam,* think *Eve, The Crouching Woman, I Am Beautiful, The Prodigal Son, Nymph Kneeling* — suggests, whatever its title, not bodies so much as their functions. Rodin embarrasses finally. He embarrasses *me.* I get, I swear, the penis envy every time I see one of his improbably hung men, I want to sit in the laps of those ladies. Worse yet, and this *is* the war news, prefiguring, to me prefiguring — think of his statue of Victor Hugo — much of the totalitarian art of the last seventy-five years or so — Hitler's, Stalin's, Mussolini's — the romantic, muscular graffiti of all those death trippers.)

And, because a man's got to do what a man's got to do, the *New York Times Book Review.* It puts itself forward, bidding itself up and bidding itself up as the venue of masterpieces — the bourse of books. (Next slide. *Quickly, quickly,* for God's sake!) Harvard. Grappa. Curries. The Book of the Month, the catch of the day. (Acquired tastes generally.) Rolls-Royce automobiles, Vuitton luggage, airports, the configuration of jet planes, all coach-class seating, and any lavatory on every airplane. Into design now but, like the toilets on those planes or the tourists in those churches, anatomically incorrect. Talkin' the truisms, talkin' areas that ought to be taken for granted by now, basic highway design, say, or form-follows-function footwear — talkin' the abhorrent, cryin'-out-to-be-filled vacuums. Like, why are the backs of TVs lopsided, or VCRs lost in a ganglia of connection? Why are cameras badly designed, unbalanced, weighted with topple and as bristled with inexplicable dials and buttons as a camcorder or a fishing reel? (To my way of thinking, the last beautiful camera was the Speed Graphic.) How do you explain the anomalies? Why is it certain articles of men's clothing (their hats, for example — I'm thinking of the fedora, I'm thinking of the borsalino) make a higher fashion statement than women's? Can anyone here say why cutlery is more handsome than dishes, stamps more agreeable to look at than coins, coins easier on the eye than banknotes? (It's the focus of face, the joy of manageable scale.) Or why almost all jewelry, men's *or* women's, is unattractive? (Because it tries to mimic in metals or gems — in dead organics — natural forms, a vaguely frozen machinery of moving parts — insects', the stars'.) And how, this late into time, this far into history, more than two dozen days now into the Mother of Battles (because I can't concentrate, because I'm too old to be a soldier and too far away to be bombed, and because there are no priorities like the priorities of life and death and I can't keep my mind on my business), does one explain the aesthetic downside of furniture?

Compared to many forms that lend themselves to art or craft — drama, the novel, painting, the composition of music, even the *interpretation* of music, like, oh, say, singing the national anthem before the game, infinite other forms that seem to thrive, almost to wallow, in permutation, assuming new content, a mother lode of fresh ideas and differentiated styles as they're taken up by one artist after another — it's extraordinary how

furniture is like most other furniture, as if furniture, alone
among crafts, not only lived along the perimeters of some Platonic Ideal but had somehow actually managed to colonize it: an
imperialism of the conventional. Except for a detail here, a detail
there, inlay, marquetry, the pile-on of money, of pharaohs' or
aristocracy's royal dispensations, a couch is a couch, an escritoire
an escritoire. Beds resemble beds, tables and chairs are like tables
and chairs. In domestic arrangements, form, bound to the custom cloth of human shape, really *does* follow function. The
height of a table has to do with average lap tolerances. Chairs
and beds are the hard aura of a strictly skeletal repose. Even so,
something's busted, I think, in the imagination of furniture designers — I except the art directors of certain major pictures set
in Manhattan apartments; talkin' environment, the ecology of
"life-style," of plot and character, what the principals look like
against the bookcase, propped among the furnishings; one must
learn the script of one's life and be able to afford it; because only
in movies does furniture play well (all lamps and appointments,
all cunning, edge-of-the-field doodad and inspired house-
dower; one has at least the illusion one could live with this stuff,
that it won't vanish in a season like a Nehru shirt) — something
stuck in the vision, some sorcerer's-apprentice effect, which permits to keep on coming and keep on coming with minimal variation, if any, what has come before. It isn't anything as elegant as
highest math happening here, just lump-sum arrangement, ball-
park figure, bottom line. It's the fallacy of the assembly line, the
notion that only costs get cut in such a wide sweep of swath. No,
but really, *isn't* it astonishing that personality, surely as real as the
width of one's shoulders or the breadth of one's beam, should be
so infinite but attention to body so meager and hand-to-mouth
that — chairs, say chairs, I *know* about chairs — there's been less
progress in the design of chairs than in the design of luggage? (I
speak as a cripple full-fledged, confined to a wheelchair. Chairs
are a hang-up with me, but set that aside.) It's as if clothing came
in a single size, pants like tube socks, every dress like a muumuu.
And a rule of the chair seems to be that if it's beautiful it's rarely
comfortable, if comfortable it rarely makes the cut to beauty.

Indeed, there are so few contemporary "museum-quality"
chairs one can almost list them: Marcel Breuer's side chairs, his

Wassily chair like a leather-and-steel cat's cradle; Jacobsen's Egg
chair; Thonet's bentwood rockers; Mies van der Rohe's Barce-
lona; Saarinen's molded plastic chairs on their round bases and
tapered stems like cross sections of parfaits; all Eames's ubiquitous plastic like stackable poker chips or the pounded, hollowed-
out centers of catcher's mitts, as locked into a vision of the fifties
as pole lamps, his famous lounge chair and ottoman. A spectrum
of vernacular chairs — soda-fountain chairs, directors' chairs,
black canvas camp chairs, those crushed — almost imploded —
white or charcoal leather pillow chairs like soft fortresses or
marshmallow thrones, some of the new ergonomic chairs that sit
on you as much as you ever manage to sit on them.

So I *know* about chairs and still have my eye out, never mind
I'm sixty if I'm a day, for that evasive, lost-chord masterpiece of
the genre, which, like love, I'll recognize when I see like a sort of
fate.

Though maybe not. Not because I haven't the imagination to
cut my losses, or even the courage to finesse my life and choose
to sit out the close of my days in desuetudinous splendor, but
because it may not exist. The chair, my gorgeous prosthetic of
choice, may not have been fashioned yet. Because oddly,
strangely, ultimately, chairs are all attitude, molds of the supine
or up on pointe, aggressive or submissive as sexual position. Occupied or unoccupied, they are shadows, ghosts, signs of the
been-and-gone, some pipe-and-slippers choreography of spiritual disposition, how one chooses to acquit oneself, highly personalized as an arrangement of flowers, and oh, oh, if one but
had the body for it one would live out one's days in van Gogh's
room at Arles, eating up comfort and beauty and having it, too,
there in one last fell binge of boyhood in the cane and wood
along those powder-blue walls of the utile, of basin and pitcher,
of military brush and drinking glass, of apothecary bottles clear
as gin on a crowded corner of the nightstand, to be there on the
featherbed, on the oilcloth-looking floor amid one's things. All,
as I say, you have to know is the script of your life. You wouldn't
even have to worry whether you can afford it. What, this poor
Goodwill stuff, these nitty-rubbed-gritty YMCA effects of the
weathered and flyblown pastoral? I'd pay my life out there
gladly, not so much a hero as a loving dilettante of idyll, using

only the plain equipment of beauty. Substituting the hard work
of freedom with the even harder work of contemplation, giving
way to quietude, calm, doing the doldrums in study's Sargasso
Seas, all the light housekeeping of a stock-still ego laced with awe.
There are worse character flaws than sloth. Nationalism, I think,
patriotism, the too-forgiving love of tribe, maybe even of family
itself. All the flaws of a restrictive loyalty, whatever makes us
want to be part of a small idea, whatever makes us dangerous or
allows us to entertain, even for a moment, the idea of a Mother
of Battles. Much better to wait it out at Arles. Much better never
to have seen the flashy dance steps from which we take our
marching orders.

And it's the day before yesterday now. Joan and I are at the
Shady Oak to see *Mr. and Mrs. Bridge.* And it's five o'clock on
Presidents' Day, but that's only irony. It's the Rush Hour Show.
Which is the one we always try to make. It's half price at Rush
Hour but that's not the reason. We're old, we're old people, we
get senior citizen whatever the hour. In spring and summer and
some of the autumn it's still light when the movie lets out. It's
important, that last bit of light. And anyway, though we know no
one, we recognize everyone. Peers, birds of a feather, comfortable at the core as ourselves. We buy our tickets and go in. The
lights are still up, enough to be able to see what I'm doing when
I make the difficult transfer from my wheelchair to the theater
seat. Joan folds the chair and parks it by the screen. "What could
be better?" I ask automatically, but with absolute sincerity, as she
slips in beside me.

The lights go down and something happens that has never
happened before. They're playing "The Star-Spangled Banner."
It's for the war. An American montage like a little music video.
American kids in American suburbs; transparent, billowy, slo-
mo flag collages; purple mountains' majesty from one shining
sea to the next, fields, fruit — all Ma Nature's starched summer
dress whites. And they're standing, they're standing and singing!
Card-carrying AARPers. It's like, well, it's like *church* is what it's
like. They hold, some of them, their hands over their hearts. I
mean there they *are,* singing, or perhaps just lip-synching in the
dark in some key of the common denominator, negotiating the
difficult leaps and bounds of our national anthem. In the dark,

singing to a screen as if it wasn't *Mr. and Mrs. Bridge* they'd come to see but *The Rocky Horror Picture Show.* And not to any orchestra but to a sound track! And the Shady Oak is automated, so not even to a projectionist but to a machine. Which, by default, makes Joan and me the only audience at this odd performance. We're embarrassed, but what embarrasses us, I think, is to be so far out of the loop. Hey, there's *nothing* so convincing as an opinion.

We can't know this yet but G-Day is penciled in. Sunday, February 24, 3:00 A.M. Gulf time — two hours earlier at Arles — a ground war will begin that will last only 100 hours and make a name for this overrated masterpiece of a war. But still Saturday the 23, 7:00 P.M. Shady Oak time. When Rush Hour is winding down and the bigger spenders are lining up for the full-fare show. Who are on the cusp and, when the time comes, may or may not know just what it is they were standing for.

PHILIP FISHER

Thinking About Killing: Hamlet *and the Paths Among the Passions*

FROM RARITAN

ONE OF THE GREAT mysteries within the passions is how one state of vehemence finds itself linked to another. Fear often leads to an intense feeling of shame once the fear has been dispelled, but rarely does shame lead to fear. Jealousy, reaching a pitch of vehemence, transposes into rage. Ambition, as we see it, for example, in Lady Macbeth, redesigns itself as guilt while retaining the same murderousness she now directs at herself. On the other hand, guilt seldom wakes up to find itself ambition. Of these trajectories among the passions the most essential and also most mysterious is the path that leads from wrath to mourning. Two of the greatest works of our literary tradition, the *Iliad* and *King Lear,* are both constructed around an armature where anger, shattered by the death of Patroclus or Cordelia, is reassembled into grief with all intensity preserved, but sublimated into sorrow. Vengeance and mourning preserve but redeploy a common sum of inner excitation, solitude, and prolonged focus on a single object that thins out or cancels any interest in the rest of the world.

To move from killing to mourning, from rage to grief is, at first glance, an obvious and humane progression. The movement from rage to regret and sorrow; from causing death to comprehending — in mourning — the full reality of death; to pass from the most active and volcanic of states to the immobility of mourning: all have about them, as passages, a seeming naturalness little different from going from exertion to exhaustion. But this humanity or obviousness blocks our access to what might really be at stake in these apparently natural passages.

Within the literature of the passions such passages control the unfolding of the work as a whole. Almost alchemical in suddenness, and motivated from without, the metamorphosis of rage into grief or ambition into guilt lies at the heart of the work, where it operates as plot does in the literature of action or as choice and growth do in the literature of character. In *The Winter's Tale* the vehemence is located in King Leontes and passes from jealousy to rage, from rage to remorse, from remorse to mourning, and finally, from mourning to wonder. The life history of the king is of the custodian of a fixed quantity of vehemence that he invests and reinvests, now in rage, now in guilt, now in wonder, until he reaches a serenity that suggests that life itself is already, for him, a matter of the past.

The literature of the passions tells the life history of a quantity of energy that appears first as one state of vehemence, then is redesigned as another, until a finality is reached that is best summed up by the final line of Milton's *Samson Agonistes*, "Calm of mind, all passion spent." The state of serenity, peaceful even to the point of exhaustion, that ends the *Iliad, Oedipus Rex, King Lear, Moby-Dick,* and *Wuthering Heights* is a sign that the inner logic of the work has observed the excitation, transformation, and final exhaustion of a state of vehemence.

The more abstract path that leads from energy to exhaustion is in its essence not a reversible one. But why do we move only from fear to shame or from anger to mourning and not in the other way? Perhaps there is some one state toward which all others tend. Hume thought he could show that many states tend, because of the uncertainty that sets the mind in motion from state to state and from object to object, to degenerate into an unsettled state of fear. It can equally be argued that the social aftermath of many states of passion is embarrassment or shame, once the social world is again noticed. The decline into fear or into shame would then be intrinsic to the mechanism of the passions themselves. But it is no such universal mechanism that leads jealousy to spill over into rage or ambition into guilt. Nonetheless, certain routes of this kind have an almost mechanical predictability within experience. As La Rochefoucauld wrote, "One passes often from love to ambition, but never the other way, from ambition to love."

To turn these paths back upon themselves has never been a casual experiment within art. It is one of the many remarkable features of *Hamlet* that it tries to do just this. What we could call the classical trajectory from anger to mourning — classical, since it describes the economy of the passions in the *Iliad* and *King Lear* — is in Hamlet forced backward. A son, whose inner loss matches the black mourning suit that he alone goes on wearing, is set the problem of passing from the vehement inactivity and world-emptiness of grief into the anger that will make revenge possible. At one level, the resulting paralysis is the outcome of a paradox within the passions: anger and vengeance can precede settled mourning, but cannot follow it. Mourning is, as I will try to show, a passion that results from what we might call an inner reading of the situation of death. Vengeance implies a quite different reading. The two cannot occupy the same place; that is, the same soul at the same time. Within the literature of the passions Shakespeare has designed *Hamlet* as a work that stalemates and then pushes aside the mechanisms of the passions themselves, forcing them to give way to solutions of a different order.

I will try to show that such a reversal within the current of the passions coincides with the aftermath of the passions themselves, meaning by aftermath the historical situation in which the central description of human nature no longer required the passions as one of its elements. The philosopher A. O. Hirshman has recently described the seventeenth century as a period in which accounts of the self move from a vocabulary of the Passions to a vocabulary of the Interests. He spells out, for the inner life, the social changes and their psychological consequences that Max Weber had described in *The Protestant Ethic and the Spirit of Capitalism.* The aftermath of the passions is simply a shorthand for this redistribution of the energies of the inner life into the new categories that were those of a mercantile and family-oriented civilization. Such a civilization strongly values both predictability — that is, regularity — and a concept of privacy and inner

life that is at odds with the very mechanisms of the passions —
their impetuosity and their indiscriminate self-display.

In *Hamlet* the details of the successor world are not spelled out,
and for my purposes it is not important whether that world is the
European one described by Weber and Hirshman or some other.
What I wish to show is how the vocabulary of the passions could
be rearranged so as to spell out, not some new state within the
passions themselves, but their aftermath. The key lies in taking
the single most important trajectory, that from vengeance-seek-
ing anger to mourning, and constructing circumstances in which
only by our being able to pass in the opposite, impossible direction could the laws of vehemence continue to hold sway.

One way to describe the modernity of Hamlet would be to say
that he is incapable of feeling either vehemence or wonder. That
he cannot kill in a vehement act of revenge to carry out his father's demand is the very core of the plot. What he promises to
do when he learns of his father's murder is the one deed impossible for him: "Haste me to know't, that I, with wings as swift / As
meditation or the thoughts of love / May sweep to my revenge."
The oddly chosen words that he finds to express how quickly he
will act — meditation and thoughts of love — predict the play of
counterforces that will immobilize him. A man who plans to kill
as swiftly as "thoughts of love" has weakened his intention with
his very memory of the opposite of vengeance: love. A man who
promises to act as vigorously as "meditation" has already revealed that only a language of thought and inaction can express
his will.

Thus it cannot surprise us that two acts later, and after his
dramatization of the murder has had exactly its intended result,
when Claudius breaks off the performance and then attempts, in
prayer, to confess his terrible crime, Hamlet stands behind the
guilty king unable to "sweep to his revenge." At the center of the
play stands this moment of a killing forgone in the name of a
better, more refined revenge. Alone and with his back turned,
Claudius, kneeling in prayer and unable to resist, survives the
scene of a perfect vengeance. Hamlet outthinks his one perfect
chance.

Yet he can kill in other ways. Impulsively he kills Polonius, who stirs behind the curtain, stabbing "someone" or "whoever it is" without a moment's hesitation. He also kills by delegation when, in his only royal act ("From the King . . ." he wrote), he replaces Claudius's order that would have caused his own death in England. He changes the letter and reseals it with his father's royal seal, which he happens to have in his purse, and brings about the deaths of Rosencrantz and Guildenstern.

More important, he kills by slow provocation. After Hamlet's taunts and rejections and his killing of her father, Ophelia drowns herself, a victim of Hamlet's tortured state. Ophelia takes over literally the madness that had been for him strategic or feigned. She then carries out the suicide that he had so much pondered but never executed. Ophelia shadows Hamlet: he talks of suicide; she kills herself. He plays out a strategic and discardable madness; she goes insane. In these two ways she extends Hamlet into the actual world, becoming his victim and delegate. Like the deaths of Polonius and Rosencrantz and Guildenstern, Ophelia in her madness and suicide seems to absorb or redirect an energy of death present in or aimed at Hamlet himself. The slippage that brings about some death or other than the one that seemed prepared or intended is a fundamental part of the grammar of action in *Hamlet*. Action undergoes a swerve or a zigzag like a knight moves in chess before it lands at its destination. One fundamental contrast between the heroic world of revenge, passion, and certainty and the new world of which Hamlet is the center lies precisely in this slippage of targets within action, specifically within acts of killing. For every Hamlet preoccupied with suicide, an Ophelia drowns herself.

Finally, Hamlet kills by confusion, in the poisonings and stabbings that take Laertes, Gertrude, himself, and, at last, the true target, Claudius. What Hamlet cannot do is to act with vehemence, with single-minded directness, with courage and openness. He is incapable of rage, and thus of the resoluteness that could execute revenge. He seems able to kill anyone but Claudius. One implication of this long list of direct and indirect killings for which Hamlet is responsible is that the alternative to revenge is not peace but slippage, and, finally, slaughter.

Hamlet exists against the background of a world of spirit and action that now, in him, seems ruined. The tragedy of *Hamlet* is the first of Shakespeare's two great aftermath plays, *The Tempest* being the other. Both plays are sustained resolutions, prolonged fifth acts for which the complications and passions are present only in the memory. Twelve years separate the marriage and the approach to marriage that *The Tempest* stages as the quieting of anger from the ferocity that long ago led the ambitious brother to overthrow and plot the death of Prospero. On Prospero's island a dozen years later, revenge is foresworn, and the aftermath of passion acted out in comedy's alternative to vengeance: sexual passion and the transfer to a second generation of the unresolvable, but now effaced, guilt and retribution of the first. In *Hamlet* the cause is fresher. Only weeks separate the poisoning of the king and the seduction of the queen that must have preceded it from the moment when the play begins, but the story that the entire play seeks to conclude has, in its passionate aspect, already taken place before the curtain rises.

Hamlet's heroic and warlike father is now dead. The ambition and lust that drove Claudius to murder the king, the sexual passion that led Gertrude to the hasty wedding that began Claudius's reign: this world of courage, risk, and appetite, of royal power, crimes of ambition and passion, and the answering demands for revenge, serves to outline the diminished thing that we find in the present. At the center of the present, the new world, stands Hamlet himself. That he shares his father's name makes the contrast between them the more imposing. His is an ethos of debate, doubt, self-contempt, and hesitation. Therefore he can neither love nor hate. His love for Ophelia is as reluctant as his hatred for or revenge against Claudius is hesitant. His is a world of wit and plotting, of plays and pretenses, costumes and madness. Even Claudius's stratagem to have him killed he describes as a "Play" which he does no more than rewrite to execute the harmless courtiers. His mixed feelings, irony, cruel sarcasm, contempt and self-contempt, dueling but no murder, sexual puns but no lust, describe the features of a more than personal situation.

Hamlet's is the outline of a successor world to the world of spirit that moves ghostlike in the recent past of Denmark and of Shakespeare's Europe as a whole. Hamlet's is a world of consciousness. It is a mental, bourgeois world based on family drama rather than royal power. The features of that new bourgeois world include a resentful son; a recently remarried mother; a mixed-up courtship with Ophelia; an interrupted education; the blend of grief, guilt, and anger brought on by the death of a father. Alongside Hamlet's own, once royal but now, in his eyes, merely sensual family stands a sententious and moralizing counterfamily that even more fully displays the career and marriage elements of the new world in the windy moralizing father, Polonius, and his son and daughter. Finally, there is that single feature that more than any other indicates the democratic and domestic world of equality: Hamlet's close friendship with Horatio.

The world of kingship and spirit had been singular: the murdered father leaves behind no friend. These features of domesticity, dissatisfaction, and sexual complication are what remain behind in the shell of the now vanished kingly world of duty, courage, revenge, and action. When the ghost demands that his son avenge his murder, the old world is summoning the new to rise to its now archaic laws — those, for example, of revenge and the primacy of the father-son bond. In making this demand, it accomplishes no more than to multiply that new world's self-denunciations, its sense of worthlessness and decline. The new world blunders its way into satisfying the demands for high action imposed by the father, but it consumes itself in the process. The progressive erasing of Ophelia's family prior to Hamlet's own death underlines this toll. Hamlet is incapable of a clean kill.

Hamlet's one vehement and passionate scene is his interview with his mother in her bedroom. Here the single-minded intensity, the driven energy, and the certainty of his words and purposes find voice to confront the sexual picture of his mother and her new husband, an incandescence of the will that the image of the murder of his father never aroused. Sexual disgust and anger with his mother seem to be the one path by which he can imagine the horror of a set of events that have dynastic, familial, and simply criminal components that leave him self-divided and unable to engage unambiguously the complete event that has taken place.

Once he imagines his mother in the bed of Claudius he is brought to a passionate state that neither his own dynastic displacement nor the murder of his father could arouse. Significantly, the ghost of his father gave two commands: first, to take revenge on Claudius, and second, to leave Gertrude unharmed, no matter how great her guilt. The ghost, in this second command, seemed aware that the one direction in which Hamlet's vehemence would carry him to action might be the sexual anger that he feels toward his mother. There is a close parallel between this bedroom scene in *Hamlet* and the scene in *Othello* in which Desdemona is killed in her bed once Othello has roused her from sleep. Hamlet, lucid in his passion, does not harm his mother, but almost by displacement, it is in this bedroom and at this moment of singular vehemence that the first of Hamlet's killings occurs — the impulsive stabbing of "someone" behind the curtain. It is very important that Hamlet kills without knowing whom he is killing. He kills whoever is in his mother's bedroom. In his imagination, at least after the fact, he hopes that it is Claudius, but had he stood facing Claudius instead of the blank curtain, the outcome would not have been a sudden execution of his mission. He kills here an anonymous man, and it is because it is an anonymous, unseen someone that he is able to kill. Having turned away only a few moments earlier from killing Claudius at prayer, the son now kills anyone at all. One further shadow victim can be seen in this curtain murder. The father's extracted promise that Hamlet leave Gertrude unharmed makes Hamlet in his passion at this moment draw and kill someone else, as though to carry out her murder on a surrogate.

This moment of vehemence (directed at his mother) and murder (redirected laterally toward someone behind the curtain), a murder that will contribute to the madness and eventual suicide of Ophelia, is also the scene in which Hamlet himself describes the decline of this new world, here given as a world in which Gertrude can move from the bed of a great and noble king to the bed of his murderer. "Have you eyes? / Could you on this fair mountain leave to feed / And batten on this moor? Ha! Have you eyes?"

The world behind Hamlet that still calls to him "Do not forget!" as the final words of his father in this scene make explicit, is the world of the passions. The passions have a strong center, throughout their history, in the passion of anger. They have, therefore, a close and natural tie to retaliation and to the revenge

plot in narrative. The *Iliad*, the fundamental cultural text of anger, is, in effect, a tracking of Achilles's revenge, first on Agamemnon and his fellow Greeks, and then, after the death of
Patroclus, on Hector and the Trojans.

Anger and the vehement passions that are its many branchings
are the highest evidence of self-identical, undivided being. Hamlet, however, is the best example in our culture of the modern
inability to be undivided. One meaning of vehemence is the capacity to be thoroughly, completely in a given state, whether it be
fear or grief, anger or love. Hamlet's irony, his layers of feeling,
his self-distance, his afterthoughts and reversals, are all features
of a psychology in which the self is no longer self-identical. It is
no longer thorough. It is angry, but able to see the other side of
the matter; in love, but disgusted with love; committed to vengeance, but unable to believe completely in what it is about to do.
The descriptions of the self that we find in the Stoicism of Epic-
tetus and Marcus Aurelius made certain forms of nonidentity
and inner distance, along with the existence of well-defined inner partitions within the self, not only possible but desirable.
Even within personal grief the task set by Stoicism is to reflect
actively against the grain of one's passion until it is neutralized.
In *Hamlet,* however, this self-neutralization, because it takes
place where the claims of a vehement world are still active, brings
on a series of catastrophes: the madness and suicide of Ophelia;
the deaths of her father and brother; the loss of sovereignty in
Denmark; the bungled family deaths of Gertrude and Claudius;
and the death of Hamlet himself.

As Hamlet lives, and knows that he does, in the shadow of vehemence, so too does he live just outside, but still able to summon
up, the philosophical force of wonder.

> It goes so heavily with my disposition that this goodly frame, the
> earth, seems to me a sterile promontory; this most excellent canopy,
> the air, look you, this brave o'erhanging firmament, this majestical
> roof fretted with golden fire: why it appeareth nothing to me but a
> foul and pestilent congregation of vapors. What a piece of work is
> man, how noble in reason, how infinite in faculties, in form and mov-
> ing how express and admirable, in action how like an angel, in appre-
> hension how like a god: the beauty of the world, the paragon of ani-
> mals; and yet to me, what is this quintessence of dust?

The new consciousness in these lines — "quintessence of dust," "sterile promontory," "foul and pestilent congregation of vapors" — has not banished the memory of the glorious language of wonder that it exists in the shadow of. The construction that begins "What a piece of work is man," if only it did not turn at the words "and yet," would demand an exclamation mark. The words "What a . . ." and the (here missing) sign "!" are the very syntax of a language of wonder. In the words that describe the air, along with the pauses and expansions, the inclusion of the hearers, and the reminder that the air is there, right above the head (in the words "look you"), we have a momentary recovery of the feel of wonder. Hamlet's first words are somewhat cold and formal in their praise: "this most excellent canopy, the air." Then, after noticing it and demanding in "look you," that we look again, he goes beyond praise to glorify the air: "this brave o'erhanging firmament," until the state of impassioned wonder is reached with the words "this majestical roof fretted with golden fire." Here Hamlet, from without, reinstates the very feelings that he assures us he no longer feels. To be in the aftermath of vehemence and wonder, while still responsive to their memory, defines Hamlet's state. As the ghost of his father insists, Hamlet must *remember!*

The final lines of Hamlet's speech are, in effect, a retracted encomium on man. With these words Hamlet locates himself in the specific historical aftermath of the Renaissance, with its collective spirit of wonder for which the fundamental topic had been man himself.

> What a piece of work is a man, how noble in reason, how infinite in faculties, in form and moving how express and admirable, in action how like an angel, in apprehension how like a god: the beauty of the world, the paragon of animals; and yet to me, what is this quintessence of dust?

The words "and yet . . ." are for Hamlet a formula that registers the act of doubling back to revoke the steps already taken. They make up the basic pattern of consciousness itself. Their temporal pattern is that of delay. "And yet . . ." invites a lingering that is in the end a postponement. Where the will has begun to engage, "and yet" stalls the forward thrust of the will, undoing resolve.

What Hamlet's delay permits is reconsideration. In normal life the will is often interrupted, as our will to move forward is interrupted by a door that sticks. Instead of being impeded from without, Hamlet's will is self-interrupting. His phrase "and yet" breaks the forward momentum of thought just short of a conclusion. Here the interruption touches only his thought, but within the play itself the "and yet" of consciousness sterilizes the will, as it does when Hamlet stands armed behind Claudius who kneels in prayer; it makes the progress of the play a refusal to progress. The indecisive will is microscopically present in this tiny verbal gesture of afterthought and cancellation.

In those of Shakespeare's plays designed around the passions it is the very opposite of delay that strikes us. The essential trait of the will of Lear or Macbeth, of Othello or Leontes, is that the will is *rash*. It is Banquo who, in the face of the prophecies of the three witches, says the equivalent of Hamlet's "and yet." In the face of the very predictions that have Macbeth so under their spell that, lost within himself, he can speak only in asides, Banquo hesitates and sees that they may mislead: "But 'tis strange; / And oftentimes, to win us to our harm, / The instruments of Darkness tell us truths; / Win us with honest trifles, to betray's / In deepest consequence." Where Banquo sees the "and yet . . ." or "but," Macbeth speeds on in his mind toward his first murder.

Lear listens for only a moment to Cordelia's stubborn refusal to pledge her love before he passes into rage and disowns her. Cordelia passes in a few moments from being "our joy," as Lear addresses her first, or his "best object, / The argument of [his] praise, balm of [his] age, / The best, the dearest" as France reminds him later, to a discarded daughter who is as disgusting to Lear as a cannibal that feeds on its own offspring. Kent interrupts Lear, asking him to delay, to use "consideration." Kent calls what has just taken place "this hideous rashness."

Lear's rashness is not more precipitous than Leontes' in *The Winter's Tale* when he rages at the perfect wife and ideal friend and seeks their deaths. The resoluteness of Macbeth, who never turns aside from murder even when the killings have become monstrous, is the stubbornness that prolongs through time the rash initial momentum of his will. The mechanism of tragedy is more often the dogged persistence of the will, its world-annihilating lack of compromise, than its vacillation and self-cancellation. Rashness and stubbornness are aspects of the inflamed will. Both reveal, by being opposite to, a norm of the will in caution and deliberation, a deliberation that also allows for reconsideration and later adjustment. These normal features of the reasonable will are precisely spelled out in the rashness and stubbornness of passion.

It is Hamlet's single kingly act, the decree that sentences Rosencrantz and Guildenstern to death, sealed with the royal seal of Denmark (the only appurtenance of majesty that Hamlet seems to have inherited from his father, and which he carries with him everywhere in his pocket), for which Hamlet congratulates himself on acting "rashly."

For Aristotle rashness was one of the extremes that defined the virtue of courage; inaction or cowardice defined the other extreme. The close links between rashness, courage, anger, and the will can best be seen, before Shakespeare, in Sophocles' *Oedipus Rex*. The rage of Oedipus at Tiresias, at Creon, and at the shepherd from whom he forces the final evidence defines him as a rash, headstrong man. The warnings of those, including his queen, Jocasta, who plead with him to delay or call off his search only underline his own angry progress. In the present time of the play his rashness is an aspect which lies in his determination to know the truth, no matter what the cost. But in the past it was his rashness that led him to run away to escape his fate, and then, at the crossroads, to slay his father. The killing had been an angry impulse.

One part of the mystery of knowledge in *Oedipus Rex* lies in the interdependence of, on the one hand, the courage that alone suffices to press on to complete knowledge, the courage that had in the past saved society from the monstrous, in solving the riddle of the sphinx by finding the identity of man in general, and now presses on to the personal solution — Who am I? — and, on the other hand, the rashness that produces the monstrous murder of the father and the incestuous marriage and children that follow. Rashness and courage are interwoven, primary aspects of the vehement self which are, as I will show, the self considered as will.

Leaping into Ophelia's grave to discredit Laertes' bombastic claims, Hamlet warns him, "though I am not splenetic and rash, / Yet I have in me something dangerous, / Which let thy wisdom fear." To say that his self-characterization is neither splenetic — the spleen being the seat of anger — nor rash would be an understatement, considering his hesitation within the highest provocations to both rashness and anger. Earlier he acted rashly, stabbing whatever man was hidden behind his mother's curtain. The very essence of rashness lies in the suddenness that does not wait for knowledge. Hamlet's act in his first killing is, in its rashness, remarkably like Oedipus's at the crossroads when he killed "a man" or "someone" who he will only later learn was both king and father. After Hamlet's sword thrust, his mother cries out, "O, what a rash and bloody deed is this!" But Hamlet, pulling aside the curtain to learn whom he has killed, refuses his mother's word and transfers it in speaking to the corpse of Polonius: "Thou wretched, rash, intruding fool, farewell! I took thee for thy better!" The word slides from him as though he were eager to pass it on and relocate it in another spirit. The act of Polonius that Hamlet calls rash is just the opposite, an act of stealth. Polonius has been reckless, and certainly foolish, but his spying is the very opposite of a rash act. The elision of rash and stealthy acts marks either a confusion or a deep complexity in the play.

It is for one of his own most furtive acts that Hamlet happily describes himself as rash. Less than a minute in acting time after the scene in Ophelia's grave where Hamlet threatens Laertes while dismissing as less "dangerous" the traits "splenetic and rash," Hamlet, back in the castle, savors his clever strategy in telling Horatio how he had on board the ship opened the king's sealed commission after stealing it from the sleeping Rosencrantz and Guildenstern: "Rashly, (and praised be rashness for it) let us know, / Our indiscretions sometimes serve us well / When our deep plots do pall." What Hamlet then goes on to describe is exactly such a "deep plot." He rewrote the order so as to have the recipient execute Rosencrantz and Guildenstern instead of himself. The rash act was only to sneak into their room in the dark and dare to open the king's commission. Rashness, which Hamlet gleefully proposes as the alternative to "deep plots," is in his own case wedded to such plots, for which his earlier act of rewriting the play to trick an involuntary confession from Claudius is only the most obvious example. Twice Hamlet rewrites another's play as prologue to a killing.

That *Hamlet* hinges on a world of plots instead of rashness is clear from the fact that it is a world of poison rather than swords. The ghost makes Hamlet swear upon his sword, and the ghost is himself "arm'd" and martial in his bearing. Yet old Hamlet has been poisoned while asleep, a form of death in which the victim cannot know either who his murderer is or even that he is about to die. By leaving no trace, such a death also leaves all others ignorant that such a deed has taken place. The world of poison operates with secrecy and hypocrisy. Laertes and Claudius must disguise their hatred of Hamlet to lure him into the duel where poison will bring about the apparent accidental death of which all will be innocent, even in the eyes of the queen.

Poison debases a passionate world by satisfying only private feelings and the private knowledge of accomplished revenge. In its wake, poison leaves an ever more mystified world. No one knows who killed old Hamlet, nor even that he has been killed. No one, unless Hamlet chose to tell, would ever know what happened to Rosencrantz and Guildenstern. Poison and stratagem are antithetical to the grand public drama of vengeance. The coming of poison, every bit as much as the coming of the locked diary, is an essential moment in the history of *la vie privée*.

In this world of deep plots Hamlet is a symmetrical and equally skilled opponent to Claudius. If Claudius will kill him by a sealed letter once he reaches England, Hamlet will use the same scheme to rid himself of Rosencrantz and Guildenstern. If Claudius will pour poison in the ear of the sleeping king, Hamlet will, with the words of his play, pour poison in the ear of the new king, Claudius. Earlier he had been tempted to use his sword in revenge, only to hesitate at the ironic possibility that to stab the king at prayer would be to send him straight to heaven: "Up, sword, and know thou a more horrid hent." At this moment he blunders past the ferocity of the revenge demanded by his father and falls into the world of stratagems.

The chaotic, blundering climax fuses the world of swords and the new world of poisons. Ostensibly a test of skill with swords, the hidden drama is the uncontrollable flow of poison once set free. The swords are tipped with poison, and to kill the king Hamlet merely needs to nick him. The poison meant for Hamlet has, in the exchange of swords, spilled its revenge to Laertes as well. The poisoned cup meant for Hamlet is drunk accidentally by the queen, and then the rest forced down the throat of Claudius. Like the written death sentence that the king prepared and sealed for Hamlet, the death stored within a poison as often goes astray and finds another victim. The weak aim of death is one of the striking features of this world beyond the passions. Claudius's commission, aimed at Hamlet, strikes Rosencrantz and Guildenstern instead. Hamlet's lunge at the curtain where he thinks Claudius lurks drops Polonius, and in his wake Ophelia. The poisoned cup intended for Hamlet is drunk instead by Gertrude, whom Claudius would least like to kill, and then by Claudius himself. Laertes' excellent poison, of which he is so proud, takes his own life as well as Hamlet's.

The sword on which the ghost insists all swear would have been the instrument of a rash and economical vengeance had Hamlet killed his uncle at once. The poison that now covers the tip of the sword, as the curtain covered Polonius, is the sign of a new, dispassionate, mystified, but finally even more wasteful economy of death.

In *Hamlet* there is a canny review of the central passions of a world of spirit, but seen from the other side of a veil. Anger, wonder, grief, and love are successively evoked and then eluded, melted down and rebuilt within a new vocabulary of consciousness. That world is best described in Hamlet's phrase for the mind in which the dread of something after death "puzzles the will." The puzzled will within his soliloquy is, at the first level, the suicidal will. After listing the universal argument for suicide, Hamlet reaches the "and yet" that keeps us all alive. But the impediment to this act of killing, although it has a different logic, is no different in effect from what puzzles the will and sterilizes the vengeance that would otherwise kill Claudius. The argument of "To be or not to be" proposes that all life be understood as lived within the shadow of a killing that does not take place: the killing of oneself. This universalizes the more local situation of Hamlet, who exists as he does throughout the play because he cannot kill Claudius. The passions that pass barely out of reach, behind the veil, are meditated on by just such a puzzled will.

The scene of wonder is dispelled by Hamlet's "and yet," a phrase that cuts against the grain to deflate the passion of awe. The phrase has its counterpart in the scene of anger at his father's murder that all his later delay will drain of vehemence. The third and equally important passion, one that throughout the history of the passions can be found linked to anger and wonder, is mourning or grief. Neither passion is elicited from Hamlet by the death of Ophelia, staged for us in its painful beauty, and then staged again at the graveyard where Hamlet first learns of it. No grief of his is occasioned by Ophelia's death, just as his father's murder failed to occasion his rash vengeance.

He gives not the slightest hint of any feeling of responsibility for Ophelia's death. Immediately after the graveyard scene, in which he seems more interested in Laertes' false rhetoric of grief than in mourning for Ophelia, we see him boasting to Horatio of his clever killing of Rosencrantz and Guildenstern. The scene so closely follows Ophelia's funeral that it serves to emphasize the part played by distraction, and rapid change of concentration, in all of Hamlet's acts. Ophelia's death has no aftermath. He never mentions her again, nor anything about her. He takes on the fencing contest with Laertes and passes to the final carnage. It is as though Ophelia had dropped out of his mind entirely, just as earlier, when he realized that he had killed Polonius, he dismissed him as merely a bungling courtier, never noticing that he had killed the father of Ophelia and that he might, for that reason, feel some sorrow at least for the suffering that he will have caused her. He notices his mother wringing her hands and turns his attention back to his vehement denunciation of her marriage to Claudius.

> Leave wringing of your hands. Peace, sit you down
> And let me wring your heart, for so I shall
> If it be made of penetrable stuff,
> If damned custom have not brazed it so
> That it be proof and bulwark against sense.
> *Queen.* What have I done that thou dar'st wag thy tongue
> In noise so rude against me?
> *Hamlet.* Such an act
> That blurs the grace and blush of modesty,
> Calls virtue hypocrite, takes off the rose
> From the fair forehead of an innocent love,

And sets a blister there, makes marriage vows
As false as dicers' oaths. O, such a deed
As from the body of contraction plucks
The very soul, and sweet religion makes
A rhapsody of words! Heaven's face does glow
O'er this solidity and compound mass
With heated visage, as against the doom
Is thoughtsick at the act.

The long postponed specification of just what "such an act" or
"such a deed" could be, that in its horror so quickly distracts both
mother and son from the killing that has just taken place, is given
its importance precisely by its capacity to make the killing for-
gettable. This is the simplest case of the use within the literature
of the passions of killing as a form of punctuation or measure-
ment. When later it is Ophelia's death that, like her father's,
seems unable to compel Hamlet's attention or earn his grief for
even a moment, the identical pattern seems to point to some defect within passion itself and not the mere worthlessness of the
dead man, whose body does not distract the angry son from the
subject of his mother's bed, near or on which they both sit. The
opportunity of mourning no longer compels, any more than the
opportunity of love did earlier. The phrase "and yet," which
Hamlet uses as a hesitation within wonder, functions within each
of the passions seen across a gap of feeling. The "and yet" translates, not complication within passion, but a simpler state of affairs. "And yet" is, simply stated, "no longer." Its opposite is the
ghost's strong word for the thoroughness of the passions: "Remember!"

But here we need our own "and yet." Isn't it in his mourning
that Hamlet is the very incarnation of passion? The play begins
with Claudius's reproach to Hamlet for his too prolonged state
of mourning, in which, as Gertrude says, he seems to "seek for
his father in the dust." Unlike the new king and his new wife,
Hamlet has conspicuously refused to lurch from funeral to wedding, from deathbed to marriage bed, from grief to joy. It is here
that he insisted on delay while others rushed to satisfy their passion. His own love for Ophelia, unlike Gertrude's passion for
Claudius, seems unable to push aside rapidly the fact of the old
king's death. He has refused to "cast [his] nighted color off."

What the new king sees as "mourning duties" should last only a certain time, beyond which grief becomes "obstinate condolence" or "stubbornness." After a time "unprevailing woe" must be "throw[n] to earth," and life resumed with a "new father," just as the state has taken a new king.

The features of stubbornness, invariability, and withdrawal from an ever-changing social life to pursue in solitude the course of his passion make Hamlet in his grief a classic picture of an impassioned man, one whose vehemence manifests itself in mourning. What seemed at first a callous response to the deaths of Ophelia, Rosencrantz, Guildenstern, and Polonius might be described instead as the grip of his deep and primal mourning for his father, whose death makes all else trivial. Just as Achilles slaughters twelve prisoners at the pyre of Patroclus, kills and mutilates the body of Hector, and slaughters his way across the Trojan army, all these killings counting as nothing because of his pervasive grief at his friend's death, so Hamlet's carelessness with death in bringing about these four killings might shrink in the face of a mourning for his father so obsessive that it ends only with his own death. That death, and the death of Claudius, lead to the final "death" or vanishing into the afterworld of the ghostly father. By continuing to cause actions within the world, and continuing to appear there, reporting, even if only by hints, on his condition, he remains, in part at least, alive. The play's de facto end is the completion of the father's prolonged dying. And it is this that might be called the end of all mourning. That Hamlet does not survive his mourning is only a further tribute to its vehemence.

Could we go further and say that not only less important grief — as for Ophelia — but all other passions are frozen out by a stubbornness of mourning that Claudius describes for us in the first portrait that is drawn of Hamlet? The anger and vengeance that his father requires of him might then be seen not as a consequence of a paralysis of thought, or doubt, or self-consciousness, but as the stubbornness of a more authentic passion (grief), which holds its own not only against pleasure and the distractions of social life but against love in the presence of Ophelia and wonder in the presence of the natural world, and even against the anger that the murdered father hopes will activate vengeance. What his father requires is not revenge, but for Hamlet to be able to reconfigure his mourning into vengeance. The trajectory from incandescent anger to mourning must, if Hamlet is to obey his father's command, be reversed so as to supply out of the psychology of grief the materials of anger.

Grief and anger are alternative responses to death, or to any loss. That mourning and anger are like two sides of a scale, where a movement of the one requires a reciprocal movement of the other, can be seen as in some ways the central matter in the *Iliad* and *King Lear*. In anger the fact of death is set aside to focus on the cause of death, almost as though the merely static fact were unendurable. The passive suffering of diminution is thrown aside in the new active phase of revenge. Because revenge can be taken, the suffering does not have to be endured as something that simply happened to one. The revenge ethic is the single most powerful rejection of the most damaging emotional conclusion of mourning, its helpless and inactive waiting. Revenge could be called, to alter Clausewitz's phrase about war, the continuation of mourning by other means. When Achilles rolls in the dust and weeps, he mourns Patroclus, but in setting out to kill Hector he transposes mourning into vengeance. Most of all, he is able to set aside the paralytic passivity of grief that pays honor to death by simulating so many of its effects within the life of the mourner — not eating, for example, or refusing to continue with one's concerns, or being unable to feel strongly for others. In Hamlet's words, "How weary, stale, flat, and unprofitable / Seem to me all the uses of this world!"

The most important split between the strategy of anger and that of grief occurs around the component of guilt and self-reproach within all mourning. A feeling of responsibility for the death, or at least a guilt at not having prevented it, hovers over every loss almost as a misunderstanding of death itself, or a refusal of the passivity built into losses that happen to us, a refusal so urgent that it would prefer to imagine the self responsible, if that would make it seem less passive. With anger and revenge the guilt is discovered to lie not in the self, but concretely in the outer world, where it can be attacked and punished.

Revenge and anger work out a simplification of grief in which the self, instead of accepting responsibility, presents itself as the defender of the dead, representing him in acts that if alive he certainly would do for himself. Had he been only wounded by his murderer, his first act would have been to retaliate. In revenge we execute for the victim the acts that the extremity of his suffering has made him unable to do for himself, like a victim who has subsequently been blinded by an attacker so that he cannot later identify him in court. In revenge, the death is taken as just such a preemption of retaliation, since the one thing that pushing aggression to the final point of homicide seems certain to prevent is any later settling of accounts. Thus the killing of old Hamlet by Claudius is, from the point of view of revenge, not the central crime, but rather the secondary act that seemed to ensure that the real crime (whether that be the seduction of Gertrude or the usurpation of the throne) could never be avenged. The mythological story of the rape of Philomel, in which Tereus cuts out the tongue of his victim so that she can never say what has happened to her, is the model for this act. This is the structure that guarantees the innocence of revenge. The revenge asked of Hamlet by his father is no more than the simple deed that if he still lived he would do for himself.

It is this that the end of the play makes clear. The plot to poison Hamlet with the drink or to kill him with the poisoned sword is interrupted and revealed before its completion. Claudius's final plot restages the poisoning of the first Hamlet, but with the difference that this time there exists a pause before death. In that brief pause the facts are all made clear to the victim (Hamlet) just before his death. Hamlet thus becomes his own avenger in killing Claudius and Laertes, an act that he, unlike his father, can execute this side of the curtain of death. Hamlet therefore requires no delegate, and the acts of killing hover between prevention and vengeance. They cannot be seen as prevention, since he has already been touched by the poison and will soon die. Yet because he is still within a zone of ambiguity between life and death, about to die but still able to strike, he can act. This zone in which he is already doomed but not yet dead creates a mirror image, on this side of death, for the similar zone of ambiguity on the other side, within which his dead father is still partially active. It is within these two zones that all acts of revenge within the play occur.

Legally, we draw an absolute distinction between acts of violence to prevent our own death and acts done by others after that death to avenge it. But in experience the finality of the moment of death that converts innocent prevention into culpable revenge is not clear. A man who comes upon a murderer just finishing the grisly slaughter of the man's child appears justified in our eyes if then and there, in his rage, he strikes the murderer dead. Lear kills Cordelia's murderer on the spot. But if he were to have done so just one day later, our doubts about vengeance and revenge would begin to come into play. If he takes revenge a month later, we feel that he is at fault, because now the matter should be in the hands of the state — transferred to the hands of objective justice. Should the father take his revenge twenty years later, we would pity him but think him mad.

When he acts on the spot, having discovered the killer just finished with his work, the immediacy of grief and rage gives a rightness to the revenge, as if it were little more than the *defensive* blows he would have struck had he in fact arrived in time to defend his child. Ten minutes earlier, even the death of the assailant would have seemed nothing could the blow have saved the child. Arriving a few moments too late, his murderous stroke has the effect of being "as if" in defense, "as if" to prevent, although slightly too late.

Here vengeance and prevention, revenge and defense seem so near as to be inextricable. So Lear says, "I might have saved her; now she's gone for ever! / Cordelia! Cordelia! stay a little. Ha!? What is't thou say'st? Her voice was ever soft, / Gentle and low, an excellent thing in a woman. / I killed the slave that was a-hanging thee." This is the purest case of vengeance, of mourning and grief threaded together. Cordelia seems still alive, and the moment Lear imagines that she is still speaking, but in her customary soft voice, disguises the line between life and death. This in turn erases the line between prevention and revenge, between Lear's act of killing the one who was *about to hang her but had not yet completely done so,* an act designed to prevent a death that, once complete, makes his killing into vengeance.

Vengeance always has this aspect of prolonged, as-if-but-too-late prevention. That is the innocence at the heart of revenge. It is to show just what would have been done to prevent the act and defend the victim if these acts had been, as they were not, *in time*. This is a second aspect of the innocence of vengeance; the first is the identification or delegation so intimate that the acts of vengeance are no more than those very acts that the victim himself would have done had the plot been interrupted short of success.

Both features are conspicuous in the revenge required of Hamlet. First of all, in *Hamlet* it is the "as-if-alive" presence of the old king's ghost that blurs this line between prevention and vengeance. The king, although already murdered, is incompletely dead. He has not ceased to be an active presence in the world. The curtain within time that divides before death from after death is incompletely closed, permitting an ambiguous zone. The entire play takes place within this zone, since it begins by noticing the presence of the ghost and ends with the death of Claudius, which will permit the old king to be completely dead; that is, no longer active on earth. Second, *Hamlet* takes up the most familiar form of revenge, where the delegation takes place within a family. In fact, the identification of victim and revenger is made complete by giving victim and avenger the same name.

In the drama of vengeance, which has always had an almost operatic public character, one thing displayed for all to see is the militant alliance between the avenger and the victim for whose sake vengeance is now being taken. This solidarity is made so prominent that it pushes aside any suspicion that just this angry avenger, so eager that the guilty one be punished, is himself responsible or partly guilty. It is this relation between guilt and the eagerness for justice that Sophocles so brilliantly knots together in *Oedipus Rex*. The hunger for justice functions as a distraction that moves the questions about the guilt of everyone or the specific guilt of this avenger out of sight so as to concentrate on a single outer target. The part played by the uniqueness of the target in revenge is fundamental. If we call that target "the one who must be killed" (Claudius in *Hamlet*, Hector in the *Iliad*, the white whale in *Moby-Dick*), then one convenience of the revenge narrative is to concentrate guilt in a single outer figure and demonstrate the innocence of all others in their pursuit of that figure. By pursuing Hector, Achilles blanks out the prior question of his own part in the death of Patroclus, who had been sent into battle dressed in Achilles' armor. Anger and mourning supply alternative solutions to both passivity and responsibility in the face of death. Hamlet's inability to carry out revenge is in part a sign of his rejection of the simplification offered by anger to the deepest internal problem of grief, the inescapable feeling of responsibility and even the sense of having done nothing to prevent death.

The psychological questions of innocence within revenge or of the alternatives of anger and mourning within grief make up only one part of the carefully designed zone of ambiguity around the acts of killing within *Hamlet*. I have already mentioned the first of Hamlet's own killings, where he kills "whoever" stands behind a curtain. This curtain filters out the identity of his victim at the moment of attack. The curtain makes the identity of the victim into "someone hiding in my mother's bedroom." It is not that Hamlet has killed the wrong person, but only that the generic murder happens to cover a wider field than he, in advance, could picture. Similarly, a letter that when opened orders the receiver to execute whoever has just handed the letter to him functions as a similar curtain to prepare a generic murder. It is behind this curtain that Rosencrantz and Guildenstern are killed instead of Hamlet.

We might think of sleep as a third form of curtain separating the killer and his victim. The old king's afternoon nap hides the identity of the killer from his victim, reversing the function of the curtain that hid the identity of his victim from Hamlet. Finally, it is poison, as we see in the final scene, that erects this curtain in an unusually casual way. Gertrude drinks from the poisoned cup intended for Hamlet. In his turn, Hamlet then forces the rest of the poison, deliberately, down the throat of the poisoner. And in the exchange of swords, Laertes is nicked by the sword that, unknown to Hamlet, was intended to kill him. The curtain in Gertrude's bedroom through which Hamlet strikes provides the play's master image for the stealth and redirection of death in a no longer face-to-face social realm. Poison on the tip of a sword is a curtain over that sword, as is the envelope that conceals the contents of the letter from the one who carries it to the recipient. Sleep is the envelope or curtain within which each of us, like the king, spends a third of life. Each of these curtained experiences filters out or makes impossible aspects of the total situation of deliberately inflicted death. The play as a whole rotates the aspects of death so as to bring now one and now another to the front. At the same time, the filter removes and calls attention to its act of removal, one after another, of the appurtenances within consciousness, of the act of killing. That Shakespeare works out so many variations, subtracting now this, now that aspect of knowledge and feeling from the moment of killing, shows that the staging of this act in its totality is one of his goals in the play.

These many killings and variations on the puzzle of knowledge at the moment of death entail the mystification of the slayer and the slain, each hidden from the other's sight. Polonius cannot know that he is about to die, since he cannot see that on the other side of the curtain, Hamlet has drawn and is about to strike. On his side of the curtain, Hamlet cannot know whom he is about to slay. The same mystifications occur for each of the secondary killings. But it is in the design and reiteration of the original act of murder upon which all these later acts depend — Claudius's killing of the sleeping king in his garden by pouring poison in his ear — that the most remarkable version of this paradox takes place.

The ghost describes his murder with these words:

> Sleeping within my orchard,
> My custom always of the afternoon,
> Upon the secure hour thy uncle stole
> With juice of cursed hebona in a vial,
> And in the porches of my ear did pour
> The leperous distillment, whose effect
> Holds such an enmity with blood of man
> That swift as quicksilver it courses through
> The natural gates and alleys of the body,
> And with a sudden vigor it doth posset
> And curd, like eager droppings into milk,
> The thin and wholesome blood. So did it mine,
> And a most instant tetter barked about
> Most lazarlike with vile and loathsome crust
> All my smooth body.
> Thus was I, sleeping, by a brother's hand,
> Of life, of crown, of queen at once dispatched.

Before describing in detail this extraordinary scene of a killing of a sleeping king, I want to notice its reiteration in Shakespeare. Like *Hamlet*, *Macbeth* concerns the chain of killings that follows from a similar murder of a sleeping king. In *Macbeth* the act itself is staged in the tension of present time even though the actual killing occurs offstage. Every moment of preparation and aftermath is represented with an almost hallucinatory intensity. The murder of the sleeping king in *Hamlet* has, like most of the passionate acts of the play, taken place before the play itself begins. But the care with which it is visualized in the king's own narrative and then pantomimed in the play within the play that Hamlet presents to the court two acts later keeps it active as a scene within the time of the play, even though it has occurred earlier. The killing occurs three times: once in fact, once in the king's narration to his son, and finally in the play performed for the court. Within *The Tempest* the murder of two different sleeping rulers is plotted by entirely different bands of would-be murderers, and once the king himself awakes to find the drawn swords pointed at his heart.

In *Othello* a scene with significant differences occurs. Desdemona wakes up just as she is about to be killed, but her death is set in relation to a moment between sleep and waking that calls attention to awareness of impending death in a careful way. The difference that Desdemona is not a royal figure makes conspicuous the first of the layers built into the killings or would-be killings within *Hamlet, The Tempest,* and *Macbeth:* a sleeping king is simultaneously the most powerful of men and a man utterly without power. He is all-powerful, but in his sleep as helpless as an infant.

In his analysis of the passions in *A Treatise of Human Nature,* Hume has a remarkable comment on such killings.

> 'Tis an aggravation of a murder, that it was committed upon persons asleep and in perfect security; as historians readily observe of any infant prince who is captive in the hands of his enemies, that he is the more worthy of compassion the less sensible he is of his condition. As we ourselves are here acquainted with the wretched situation of the person, it gives us a lively idea of a sensation of sorrow, which is the passion that *generally* attends it; and this idea becomes still more lively, and the sensation more violent by a contrast with that security and indifference which we observe in the person himself.

These points are made as a final turn to Hume's important account of sympathy, the power to feel passions in relation to the experience of others. We are able to suffer when another suffers, or to feel elation when another triumphs. We even feel shame or embarrassment for someone else who has done something that they themselves seem unashamed or unembarrassed by. What interests Hume, however, is the paradox that very often we feel even more strongly those passions that the other does not or cannot feel. If someone reacts modestly to a great honor, we feel, in our sympathy, greater and not less pride for him. A man in extreme suffering often elicits our sympathy even more if outwardly he minimizes his expressions of distress and bears his sufferings patiently. What we might have expected in cases of sympathy — that we feel in proportion to what we see another feel — is challenged by these cases. We seem to operate, Hume suggests, with an idea of what is commonly felt, of what seems generally appropriate to the occasion, and we apply that measure to our own response.

Hume's extreme example is a man murdered while sleeping. To be able to fall asleep is the very proof of security and ease. A young prince who cannot even understand that he has fallen into the hands of his enemies is a similar case. What Hume is proposing is that in these cases we can see clearly that our sympathy does not simply replicate whatever the other is feeling; asleep, he is feeling comfortable and secure. Instead, in the act of sympathy we step in and replace him. We appoint ourselves his representative and feel what *generally* would be felt. We do it for him because he cannot do it for himself. For the sleeping king, we take over the passions of fear or horror that the sleeping man, about to die, cannot feel because of the curtain of sleep. We reinsert a full degree of humanity into the situation. The young prince who has fallen into the hands of his enemies cannot know that he is about to die, nor can he comprehend the many more than personal consequences of that death for his country, which will have lost its future king. We supply for him the missing passions in the face of the dreadful act.

In doing this we perform an act of delegation similar to the act of revenge. In carrying out revenge, we perform only those acts that the victim would have done had he been able to do them to save himself. If he had only been wounded by the first stroke, he would have tried to kill his attacker to prevent any second, fatal one. As revenger Hamlet is only asked to replace his father in those very acts that, had he not died, he would have found it natural to do. Hume's examples point out that the case of a murdered sleeper represents a general relation of delegation for which revenge is only a special instance. In Hamlet's case, his father remains enough alive to tell him exactly what he would do, and to whom, were he able. His being alive (although as a ghost) after his murder, so as to sponsor revenge, is fundamentally linked to his being asleep just before that murder, so as to sponsor the more general delegation of passion.

In *Hamlet* the extraordinary conditions that surround the killing of the king, Hamlet's father, refine out with an ingenious precision the connections between consciousness and murder. As a result they expose a normally hidden or confused relation of the passions to that ultimate violation of the will: one's own murder. If all passions occur as part of the technology of the will, and most often as consequences of an insult to the will or an impairment of it — as anger and grief make clear — then there can be no greater paradox within the passions than the fact that although they are able to respond to the smallest nuances of impairment of the will, as when we kick angrily at a door that we had expected to open easily, they are unable to respond to the final and total destruction of the will in murder.

King Hamlet's death inverts the ordinary conditions for one's own killing. A murdered man usually is conscious of what is about to happen in the moments just before his death. This is what it means to face death, and it is precisely this that Hector does when he stops running and turns to face Achilles. Were he overtaken while still running, he would be killed from behind and never know the moment of oncoming death. He does know already just who it is that is chasing him and that if he cannot outrun him he is about to die. Since it is by a blow of a sword that he will die, he also knows the means, whether he chooses to stop, turn, and face death or not.

On the other side of death, the opposite is true. It is the one event about which no later reflections are possible. Death deprives the victim of the power to react to the event. Therefore, the many passions that are passions only in relation to the past — such as anger, guilt, regret, grief, which only begin once the event has taken place — are impossible for that very event for which, proportionally, they would be most important. Only those passions directed toward a future event, such as fear, hope, anxiety, and courage, are possible in relation to an event that will have no aftermath within which the victim can look back at it and respond. Sleep blocks the passions of anticipation as well. To be murdered while sleeping thus cancels both the passions directed toward the future and those directed at the past. Sleep erases the will, and the passions that are the very texture of the will, in the one event for which they would be ultimately legitimate. The moment of being murdered is the ultimate case in which the very fear that hovers over the many everyday threats or possibilities of destruction — most of which evaporate or have only a possible threat within them — at last must be fully present if fear itself is to be grounded.

Killing plays the role that it does in the literature of the passions in part because it breaks off the response and counter-response of action by means of the one act that removes the possibility of any further personal response. It becomes the final act of a will that can be certain that it is not to be limited by the answering act of the other. It becomes for that reason the direct translation in the field of action for the unilateral assertion of the self that the passions imply in general in the realm of inner life.

These ordinary conditions of death or murder provide an intense moment prior to death, a moment in which, along with the awareness that death is about to occur, there is the passion of hope somehow to avoid it, or the passions of fear or serenity, of courage or resignation. But after the event has occurred, no consciousness or passion is possible. In King Hamlet's death these conditions are reversed. Asleep at the moment of his murder, he has no consciousness that he is about to die. But present after his own death as a ghost, he can experience and express that ordinarily unlighted side of the moon of awareness that the finality of death keeps hidden. To be asleep at the moment of being murdered and to be awake afterward and able to describe it exactly as though one had been present during the event but separate from oneself and at a distance from the scene — these are symmetrical reversals of ordinary experience. To be a ghost in this sense, armed with a complete eyewitness account of one's own murder, is almost a compensation for the lack of consciousness during the moment just before death, which in a killing is probably a more charged moment of awareness than any that proceeded it in life. To be asleep at just the crucial passage of life is thus illuminated from the other side, where the ghost is awake and aware within the normally darkened sphere of death.

To put the problem only in terms of consciousness is to make it seem that knowledge is the subject that Shakespeare has in mind by playing with the conditions of death. This is to some extent the case. The essence of poison, especially poison poured into the ear of a sleeper, is that it makes it possible for the murder to go unknown. A realm of secrecy and privacy is opened up. The victim often does not know who has killed him, and, in most poisonings, does not know that he is actually being killed. To know one's killer and to know that one is being murdered at all (as opposed to falling asleep or feeling sick) are both already mystified awarenesses within a world of poisons, unlike a world of swords. Being asleep only represents more clearly what is the basic barrier to knowledge already located in poison itself, the means of death. But it transfers that barrier to the victim from the external means. Asleep, he did not know he was about to die. Nor did he know at whose hand. These epistemological facts of sleep were, however, already facts of poison itself.

Just as the murder is unknown to the victim, it mystifies the society of survivors, who in King Hamlet's case think that he died of a snakebite. That the old king remains as a ghost who does know the exact details of his death draws a line between knowledge shared by the victim and his killer — both of whom now know every detail of the act — and the false account believed by all others. When young Hamlet is informed by his father, he enters the secret society of the murderer and the victim. In a society of mystified knowledge made possible by poison, only those three share a full understanding of what took place.

Shakespeare times the opening of the play no less significantly than he does the end, which I have described as the moment when at last the murdered king will be completely dead. The play begins two months after the death of Hamlet's father, but at the moment when, in effect, his father dies for him again in the scene of murder described by the ghost. Of the murder Hamlet had suspected nothing. This second version of his father's death factors out the two possible responses: on the one side, and for the first two months, mourning for the father lost by accident; on the other side, vengeance for the father murdered. What appear as alternative stories (accidental death while sleeping due to a snakebite or murder at his brother's hand by a poison poured into his ear) manifest opposed internal passions open to Hamlet as the bereaved son. Here we do not have two different stories but two successive stories, each of which lasts long enough to call forth the passionate response that is its due.

The story of murder, coming late in the process of grief — two months after the death — invites Hamlet to cast off any guilt and convert the paralysis of mourning into the activity of vengeance. It is crucial that Shakespeare shows us Hamlet in the second scene of the play, before he has spoken to his father but after we, though not Hamlet, know that the father's ghost has begun to walk at night. The Hamlet of act 1, scene 2 — whom we first observe acting socially, then hear described in the portraits drawn by his mother and stepfather, and finally witness describing himself in his soliloquy — is a Hamlet with only the fact of grief and without the possibility of vengeance.

The first words of his soliloquy reveal within his grief a core of suicidal thought. The father's death has stimulated a will to action, but against himself. Death is sensuously imagined, but first as a melting that might come of itself, supplying the advantage of suicide without the need to kill. "Oh that this too, too solid flesh would melt, / Thaw, and resolve itself into a dew." If this melting or dispersal were to happen of itself, suicide would not even be necessary, and it is interesting that even here, in contemplating aggression against himself, Hamlet begins by imagining and preferring an alternative to suicide that just happens by itself, without the necessity of agency. But he does go on to a second possibility: "Or that the Everlasting had not fixed / His canon 'gainst self-slaughter." Here, too, where the act is proposed it is also barred, figuring as a wish that can be entertained because it has been crippled in advance.

There rests within his protraction of mourning this merely wished aggression against his own life. The disgust with his mother upon which the rest of the soliloquy will turn adds a second aggressive element to his grief. Blamed not for his father's death, but for her sexual haste in marrying a lesser man too soon, she is nonetheless the target, as Hamlet himself is, of a stewing anger. His anger has the impotence of grief, which can never change the fact that caused the grief, but it is now transferred to sexuality and self-disgust. Just as the Everlasting has fixed a ban on self-slaughter, the ghostly father will erect an equal ban on any vengeance on the mother. So, while redirected in his anger to a new target by the ghost, who informs him that Claudius was his killer, Hamlet is simultaneously encouraged to revenge and blocked explicitly from taking any vengeance on what had until then appeared to be his true targets, his mother and himself.

In wishing that his flesh would melt or dissolve, Hamlet proposes a third alternative to the passivity of grief and the active anger of revenge. He dreams that what is hated will simply go away by itself. The two stories of the father's death translate, or seem motivated by, the two alternative passions within Hamlet. All things known to only one person, whether hallucinatory or not, have no public substance that makes it important to distinguish between inner and outer world. Because these two stories are known only to Hamlet, they are, in effect, not facts at all but details of his inner life made concrete in this narrative form. The words "melt" and "dissolve" invert this conversion, since what they describe is not the outer world of flesh but the ordinary actions of the passions within the mind. It is the passion that over time will melt or fade away, while flesh continues to require both slaughter and self-slaughter.

A ghost is the temporary aftermath of a life, as smoke is of an extinguished fire. Shakespeare's play, as the prolonged and subdivided fifth act to a series of events that are over before the curtain rises, draws a line between a world of passions prior to the time of the play and a new world made up of the aftermath of passion. The ambition and lust of Claudius; the desire that provoked Gertrude's infidelity to the king; the military valor and power of the king himself, who years before had fought with Fortinbras and slain him, thus extending Denmark's borders; even the love of which we hear only later, and from Ophelia, that led Hamlet before the time of the play to utter "almost all the holy vows of Heaven" in making tenders of his love to Ophelia: each of these states of passion is regarded from the other side of a gulf.

Since of all the passions mourning is the one that regards all experience across a similar tear within time, it is mourning that personalizes the wider meanings of an aftermath into an individual case. It seems the one passion that stands in the aftermath of the passions themselves, imitating in a passionate state the very world-weariness and indifference of such dispassionate states as boredom, fatigue, or indifference. When Freud sets mourning within the wider state of melancholy, or as we would call it, depression, he looks at a pathological loss of interest in the world that seems at first to have no center in a loss. "In grief the world becomes poor and empty, in melancholy it is the ego itself."

The German word for tragedy, *Trauerspiel*, places mourning *(Trauen)* at the heart of what our word *tragedy* only notices as an incident of a certain kind. If *Hamlet* is a *Trauerspiel* but disguised within the shell of a revenge tragedy, then the atmosphere of prolonged mourning and the settlement with mourning that the play enacts point toward the kind of world lost in the death of the former king. The unsuccessful heir of the same name will never live to embody his virtues in the new world that follows. The world in which young Hamlet might have been or ought to have been king passes over to the "rights of memory" that young Fortinbras invokes, in living on to avenge at last the political losses of his own father's death.

Denmark itself passes away as a distinct kingdom, along with the fading ghost and the son who dies, as his father did, by poison. Around these occur all the accessory deaths, the most important of which wipe out the entire family of Polonius, in which the new values of calculation, love, and family occur on a scale that is domestic and not royal. The liquidation of the world which the fading ghost takes with him translates Freud's phrase, "the world becomes poor and empty." But in the other half of his formula, the inner loss of territory — "in melancholy it is the ego itself" — welds the political fact to a psychological blank spot on the map: a mourning for the passions themselves. Emptied out from among the categories of action, the passions are noticed where they once occurred, but now only in their absence.

WILLIAM H. GASS

Exile

FROM SALMAGUNDI

for Heide Ziegler

LET US BEGIN where we began — in darkness: a darkness in which there was yet no color to the skin, no distinction between thine and mine, no tangle of tongues, no falsely alluring ideas, no worries which might spread like an oil slick over our amniotic ocean; hence no hither-and-thithering either, no mean emotions, treacheries, promises, prohibitions, no lifelong let-downs. We began in a place where darkness really did cover the face of things, and not because the shades were drawn and the lights were out, but because darkness was our ether, and let us sleep. It was a world where *qué pasa?* could be honestly answered, *nada*.

What colored this darkness with calamity? We soon grew too big for our boots, our britches, and our own good. So the walls of our world moved against us like a wrestler's hold, squeezing us out as though we were a stool: what a relief for the old walls, loose at last, lax as a popped balloon; but what confusion for us, now overcome by sensation, seared by the light. Some still call it a trauma — birth — and the earliest Greek poets bewailed the day just as the babies themselves bewailed it, explaining that we cried out at the cruelty of being cast into the harsh bright air where perceptions and pain were one, where screaming was breathing.

Before, we had been in nurture and in nature's care, and although poisons may have seeped into us, or our genetic codes been badly garbled, all our exchanges had been innocent and au-

tomatic and regular, as was our pulse. Now, suddenly, we were
in the hands of Man; that is, in the hands of Mom and Dad,
proud in their new possession, proud because they have fulfilled
their function, happy because they are supposed to be happy,
cooing their first coos, which will be our first words — *coup de
coude, coup de bec, coup de tête, coup de main, coup d'état, coup de
grâce* — while we wonder why we are wet and where the next
suck is coming from, or why there is so much noise when we
bawl, why we are slapped and shaken, why we are expected to
run on empty and not scream when stuck or cry when chafed,
not shit so much, and not want what we want when we want it.

Life is itself exile, and its inevitability does not lessen our grief
or alter the fact. It is a blow from which only death will recover
us, and when we are told, as we lie dying, that we are going
home, we may even be ready to welcome the familiar darkness,
the comforting *nada* of the grand old days when days were nothing but nights. Perhaps that is the last lie we shall be told, however, for the advancing darkness is a darkness we shall never
even dream in. It will not be the sincere zero of a release after
long suffering — a quilt-covered quiet, the past recaptured, a
womb reoccupied — but the zero with the zero in it. It will not be
the Nothing from which nothing comes, but the Nothing that is
nothing but its no — and a no, in addition, that is nothing but
the pure brief round of its "o."

When Adam and Eve were expelled from Paradise, according
to the Christian story, death, pain, and labor followed them to
serve as punishments for their transgressions — for falling for
the first apple that fell in their lap. With an orchard of pears,
plums, and cherries to choose from — the Tree of High Times,
the Vine of Accomplishment, the Hedge of Military Hardware,
and the dense Bush of Indecision — what must they do but pick
a piece of fruit a worm has recommended. For the Greeks, far
wiser in my opinion, life was a sentence, the Denmark that made
our world a prison, and the body was the coffin of the soul. That
attitude became a poetic tradition, so that centuries after the
Greek poets had grumbled that the worst thing that could happen to a man was to be born, while the best was to get to the end
as quickly and painlessly as possible, Guillaume, Seigneur du
Bartas was writing:

> You little think that all our life and Age
> Is but an *Exile* and a Pilgrimage.

That things were better for us once upon a time — before the revolt of the angels (all those puissant legions, Milton wrote, whose exile hath emptied heaven), before the Fall, back in the Golden Age, prior to the Flood, the destruction of the Tower of Babel, when giants walked the earth, when there were real heroes, honest kings, and actual dragons, in any case before we were brought, through birth, into this brutality — is a belief which constantly accompanies us and somehow gives us comfort. The comfort, of course, is in the note of grace it lets us sound: that wretched things will one day be put right, and the wrongs of our distant forefathers finally paid for in full, and death will release us from present pain, and we can go home again to paradise.

We continue to mimic these mythological banishments with ones of our own. The Greeks punished people by driving them out of their cities, by sending them into exile the way unwed former maidens were sent away from the door of their family home — with babe and blanket and much weeping — into the cold and falling snow. Even Hades was considered just another foreign country, a lot like Persia, where the barbarians bowed down to their superiors, sniffing the dust of their lordling's feet.

As we invariably exclaim, how things have changed! A vast reversal of value has taken place. Children wish to leave home and home town, the sooner the better. Down-on-the-farm has been replaced by up-on-the-town. High on the hog is not where we choose to feed but on the shrimp and the sole and the slaw, in our low-cal life, a life through which — in lieu of jig — we jog. Money is our country now. We go where it goes — we followers of the cash flow. There is nothing more seductive than the bottom line. Money makes the world go round, the song says, but the word keeps the wheel of fortune spinning, and that's as warming as the Gulf Stream to us all.

Money. The Japanese make it, Hong Kong smuggles it, Singapore launders it, the Swiss horde it for everybody, the Italians style it, the French flavor it, the Germans mark it, Americans lose it, the English pout, the Russians long, the Chinese make change.

Increasingly, to be exiled means to be sent to a place where you can't conduct any business.

In our brave new world, there isn't a single exciting word that won't fit upon a billboard. Pictures contain our immediate information. We go blank when the screen does. Our previous definition of the human — that we reason; that we reflect upon ourselves; that we make tools; we speak — is in the shop for microchip repairs. We are really, when you count performance and tabulate behavior, not supercomputers, but a lot like locusts, little chafing dishes maybe, small woks, modest ovens, simple furnaces, barbecue pits and picnic grills: we consume. A universe is burning — a forest for our flame.

We number ourselves now in billions, a profusion so dangerous that were we, all told, to fart in unison, we would windsweep and poison the world; and were one to strike a match to such a methane-colored cloud . . . boom would not be the half of it.

We also live in an age of migration and displacement. Driven by war, disease, or famine, out of fear of genocide or starvation, millions are on the move, by boat, mostly, as it has always been. Not every foot of ocean is under someone's boot. But boot people don't let boat people land. And, as if to balance those who have been thrust out of their country like a dog to do its business, there are an equal number who have been shut up inside it; who would leave, if they could, in search of freedom, a better living, compatible ideals.

So we have learned to punish people by keeping them home as well as by kicking them out. Yes. Stay home at the range, with Mom and Dad and their ideas, stay home by the monitored telephone, out of the shops and markets, behind the bamboo, lace, or iron curtain, stay home where home rules rule, and the roost has already got its rooster. Then, when the walls come tumbling down (as, eventually, they always do), the confined will run away in search of freedom, unaware that they have been sent into exile by circumstances.

We should always allow the Greeks to instruct us. You may remember how the soothsayers came with their worry to the king when Oedipus was barely born and scarcely asleep in his cradle. They foretold what every father fears: your son will succeed you, and enjoy all you now enjoy, and possess the love of your wife in her role as a mother; her breasts will be no longer yours, nor her caresses, nor her looks of love; your son's youthful vigor shall shade you and stunt your growth; and he shall slowly edge you into your grave with the negligent side of his shoe. In heed of these warnings, the babe was taken to the mountains during the night, his ankles pinned the way a skinned kid is trussed for the spit, and there he was abandoned in the belief that the cold wind would freeze his heart, and his lungs would expel his soul with their last outcry of breath; hence no human hand could be blamed by the gods for the child's demise.

Of course the infant is rescued and raised by a shepherd who finds him in among the rocks or under a bush, or by an animal who takes him to her den (the stories vary), and he grows up in increasing puzzlement about his nature, because he doesn't resemble a wolf or a bear, or the parents who adopted him. Twice an exile, first into life, as we all are exiled, then into another country, and now an alien among his so-called kin. Why wasn't he drowned in a butt of malsy, a method favored by the English kings? Or simply swallowed as Saturn swallowed his children, or the whale did Jonah, or Mount Etna vain Empedocles?

This becomes an important theme. The dead have relatives, sons have mothers, few expungements are really complete. Six million erasures were realized, yet there remained still more Jewish names. The mother arms the swallowed son with a dagger, and there in the darkness of his father's belly, center of his father's powers, he slits his way out while the Titan is asleep, or (the stories vary) the Titan is given an emetic and vomits the gastrically scalded boy, or a stone is substituted for the baby's body (stories vary), and a gluttonous Saturn swallows that. In any case, the saved child seizes a sickle and cuts his father's cock, his father's balls off, and heaves them out an embrasure, over a parapet, across a cliff edge, into the sea. It is an instructive story. More morals than an evangelist's sermon. The Greeks were great educators. Aphrodite, the goddess of love, rose from the ocean in the splash, and, blood borne, rode to shore on a shell formed from the foam of what had fallen. We could go on — it is tempting — but the tale would take us toward another lesson, rather than the one we are intent on now.

Let us move, for a moment, from myth to history. You recall how the friends of Socrates had arranged his escape. Athens had no desire to make a martyr of a man who had practically pushed them into voting his execution. His enemies would be well satisfied if the troublesome sage would go into exile like his protégé, Alcibiades, and encourage the decay of some other city. Let the gadfly bite another rump. Here was one horse, at least, who was weary of being kept awake. But Socrates declined, nettlesome to the last, claiming, among other things, to be a son of the State, and unable to renounce his parentage. His arguments are interesting, although their reasons are hidden, and one of them can tell us something of what exile is. He claims, of course, to have gotten fair treatment at his trial. All he, or you or I, can correctly ask of the judicial system is that it give us our due, and Socrates felt that he had received it. If the umpire's call goes against him, he can't then take himself out of the game in a snit, a game whose rules he has accepted and whose advantages he has enjoyed. Above all, exile is amputation, a mutilation of the self, because the society Socrates lives in is an essential part of his nature, a nature he cannot now divide.

In short, Socrates invokes three principles, none precisely put, but each profound: he affirms the importance of due process (which means he places a sound method above any result, however right it might chance to be, if it remains unsubstantiated); he believes in the correlativity of rights and duties (which means that none is inalienable, but that each right is earned through the discharge of a corresponding and defining obligation); he takes for granted a kind of anatomical connection between individuals and their society (which means that our community is to each of us like a shared arm, and is thus a vital increase of the local self).

We are generally related to other things and persons in one of three ways: instrumentally, as Locke saw us connected, in terms of our interests, so that the State, for example, is seen as a means to the individual happiness of each of its citizens; collectively, as Hegel saw us constituted, in which we are all functional elements contributing to the health of the whole; and, as I shall call it, Socratically, where the community is an essential organ of the self, but not the sum of that self.

Families, societies, governments, are properly dissolved, on the instrumental view, when they fail to serve the interests of their members, just as we would replace a broken drill bit with another, or an incompetent business associate with a go-getter, or a losing football coach with one who will win. Let us suppose I am a bachelor troubled by nerves, acne, and anorexia. Life seems pointless, i.e., without sexual direction. My doctor advises me to marry. "Marriage will clear your complexion, calm your nerves, fatten you up." So I decide to say, "I do," and wait the benevolent consequences. After several years, however, my zits return, my nerves refrazz, once again I can't keep my pasta down. Clearly, divorce is indicated.

Under the concept of the collective, on the other hand, individuals can be substituted for others when they fail to perform their function, the way a pitcher is replaced on the mound, because it is the team which will continue (doesn't our alma mater?), even though the coach and those who played for him have passed into history. The bachelor who happened to have bad skin was admitted to the family in order to perform his function there, as husband and father, even grandfather eventually. If, however, his performance is poor, then he may be removed for a better breadwinner, or for one whose social standing is on steadier stilts. Families, in this ruthless fashion, sometimes survive centuries of misfortune and calamity. We have seen teams limp through losing season after losing season, with coaching staffs dismissed and players continually shuffled.

This example allows us to observe that although the team itself may be collectively constituted, the owner's relation to it may be completely instrumental. If the club not only loses games but also loses money, he may sell it and establish instead a line of ladies' hosiery. Money, of course, is the pure and perfect emblem of instrumentality, and that is why, though so universally desired, it has always been, by the better sort, despised. The true fan, of course, thinks of the team as a mutuality, and through it the community participates in its varied fortunes, and maintains a common temperature, as if its members shared the same heart.

A common blood is the common bond in the case where the community is defined as the shared self, like a public park or a library, belonging to all but owned by none. If my arm is injured, I feel sorry for it; I worry for it; I tend it, heal it; and even if it has offended me, I do not cut it off. Only when the whole self is threatened would that remedy be recommended. The loss would be mourned, and considered irrevocable. So if the bachelor's skin breaks out again, or if the family's fortunes decline because of him, he is not to be turned out of doors. Rather, the reasons for his earlier happiness must be discovered, the healthy state of affairs restored, and the family's welfare in that way sustained.

Exile, as I am trying to define it, is not a condition which can arise for the instrumentalist. I can, of course, be separated from my rod and reel, my hamburger franchise, my seventh wife, and that separation might be costly, especially if the fish are biting, or my wife is wealthy or especially litigious; but exile would always be far too strong a word for what really would be an inconvenience and a disappointment, even if these were severe.

Under the collective conception, exile is an unmitigated catastrophe for the person expelled, since the entire self would depend upon the definition given to it by the State. On the other hand, the State which has cast that person out need suffer nothing, nor the other citizens sense a loss, so long as the job which was once done continues to be done obediently and well.

Athens may wish him out of the way, but Socrates will be missed, because his contribution, and the contribution of every citizen to the State, has to be regarded as unique, so long as we are speaking of society as a shared self. Only here does each man's death truly diminish me, in Donne's famous phrase, because only here is each individual, without any sacrifice of self or its sovereignty, a part of the whole.

City-states were small, both in population and in territory, so that when the city felt it had a dangerous element in its midst — a cell which was becoming cancerous — expulsion was the reasonable recourse. But a body beset by enemies may not only attack and kill them, or send them away with a violent sneeze, it may seal them off inside itself, forming a sort of Siberian cyst. Countries with colonies can penalize one of them by shipping it idealists, convicts, and religious zealots. Individual malcontents, if simple disappearance isn't feasible, can be tossed overboard, marooned, or left to the mercies of the wilderness, as Oedipus was. For its victim, exile has two halves like a loaf cut by a knife. Heart, home, and hearth fill one side — the land the exile loses; while foreignness, strangeness, the condition of the alien, occupy the other — the strand on which the castaway is washed.

Despite the grim character which the Greeks gave it, the term nowadays has many honorific, romantic, even poetical applications. Paris is clearly the most favored modern island of exile, but it is difficult to take seriously the punishment which sends you there. American writers who took extended vacations along Saint Germain because Paris was Paris, and because of the favorable rate of exchange, liked to think of themselves as exiles, although they readily went home when their money gave out, or to further their careers.

Henry James and T. S. Eliot became expatriates out of sympathy and convenience, and from a vague distaste for their place of birth. In a way, they had been English all along, and the move merely confirmed their identity. Only Ezra Pound was ever a real exile, and that didn't occur until his incarceration in St. Elizabeths. Shut away in an asylum for the insane (a common resort), he achieved, after those many years in Europe, exile's dubious status among the discomforts of home. These days there are a lot of things you can become besides an exile: you can be an immigrant, an undesirable alien, a displaced or stateless person, a dissident, an expatriate, a deportee, a wetback, a criminal, a colonist, a tourist, a Flying Dutchman, a Robinson Crusoe, a Wandering Jew.

To be exiled is not to be flung out of any door, but out of your own door; it is to lose your home, where home suggests close emotional belonging and the gnarled roots of one's identity. I cannot be exiled from café society because I never had a home there. I can be blackballed from my club or cashiered from the army, expelled from school or ejected from the game, but I cannot be exiled from any of them. However, those black people who were enslaved and carried out of Africa — they were being exiled from the human race and reduced to instrumentalities, to machines, to money. Black people have not yet been let into America. They are the dark artery that is denied.

I can be forced from my homeland by a usurper, or by a conquering army, but so long as I cannot feel I have been excluded by the country itself, I am not really an exile. Exile involves rejection by a loved one, as if the face in your mirror grimaced when it looked out and saw you looking in. It is a narcissistic wound.

Our species cannot regenerate a limb. Only in rare cases, and immediately, can any severed member be reattached, sewn back like the finger of a glove. Perhaps one can pretend to be a tourist for thirty years as Gertrude Stein did, and never be an exile, just a Yank on an extended trip abroad. Perhaps one can write in Trieste, Zurich, and Paris while becoming more Irish than ever, a Dubliner of dreams. Perhaps.

A friend has told me how it felt to leave East Germany as a child of ten, and to leave behind the real companions of her heart. She had a number of dolls which she cared for in a most motherly way, and she told them everything that happened to her, and shared with them what she read, and explained to them how she felt and what she thought. Above all, she invented stories for each one, since each was an individual and had personal preferences. It was natural that the stories would begin to intertwine, creating a single enriched narrative, one part of which she would then relate to the doll most deserving of it, while another part she would tell to the doll desiring that. So she had a special listener for each part of her life, a listener who listened as she listened, and sympathized, and supported, and forgave perhaps more perfectly than she could. She was told that when she left she could take only one doll. The family's exit would be illegal, and they would travel light. But to choose? And to leave the others to take their chances, to be neglected, to be abused? To leave one thread intact and snap the others as if you were your own malignant fate? She never played with dolls again, and never invented another story. She says that for a time she closed down her soul like a shop.

She could return now to "her native haunts," of course. But her doll days are over. When you are exiled from a space, you are also exiled from a time — in my friend's case, a childhood. The hurt heart heals, but the healed heart still hurts.

What exactly is the crime for which exile seems such an appropriate punishment? There are scoundrels aplenty in our midst: murderers, muggers, robbers, rapists, vandals, addicts, extortionists, kidnappers, car thieves, safe crackers, embezzlers, arsonists, pickpockets, purse snatchers, drug dealers, skimmers, usurers (so many scoundrels we may be in their midst); those who make obscene phone calls, beat babies, steal from the poor box, drink or gamble away somebody else's savings, adulterate and poison, forge and deceive, or are guilty of cheating at Parcheesi, counterfeiting, bribery, kickbacks, pollution, jury rigging, tax evasion, libel, misrepresentation, plagiarism, peeping, high crimes and misdemeanors, including terrorism and treason; and all of these, and all those I haven't listed who nevertheless belong there, like those whose dogs foul the walkways and who litter our alleys and deface our walls, who chop down old trees and old buildings, who poison the air and offend the eye and din their dins in our ears, they are simply put in the pokey, and kept securely penned for varying periods of unpleasant time; but none of them, including those who threaten the welfare of the State by running from the enemy, selling secrets, disobeying their superiors, or abusing their high office, are sent into exile.

Rulers frequently suffer this demeaning fate, often as a simple consequence of usurpation; but we must remember that in any game of king-of-the-hill, it is the hill which must send you spinning if you are to taste true exile, not a knock on the head by some kid who wants your job. And if a kid anyway, then only by your son (the classic configuration, although nowadays a daughter will also do), who has to have the people behind him, as well as an army and a couple of international cartels. Then it will be the hill, indeed, that gives you the heave and the humiliation. At other times, the rulers we lose are simply scoundrels who would have a place or two reserved for them on my list if they didn't happen to be playing Big Daddy behind some polished desk, and, like Ferdinand Marcos, probably ought to be jailed for bad taste, murder, and theft, but for many reasons, most of them morally obnoxious, escape this result through exile.

Who else? People of the wrong race sometimes. Yes. However, the ghetto is not a place of exile, or even a sealed-off area of infection. It is a convenient circle of moral and religious confinement which has the further advantage for the State of being economically useful. Like the slums in which black people are put, the occupants are encouraged to go out to do the Turk's work, the Mexican's, the Yugoslav's labor, to dig holes and touch caps, to fare forth upon a bus to ma'am the ma'ams and wipe cracks.

Who else? Artists. And among artists, it is only occasionally painters, sculptors, architects, who may have their shows closed, their buildings reviled, their casts smashed, but who are rarely banished for the reason of their work. Nor are musicians — who may have performances disrupted, who may find that the concert halls are closed to them, who will receive excoriating reviews and then an ornately orchestrated silence — ordinarily ushered out of the country on account of a run of seditious notes.

The case of Socrates continues to be instructive. It was Socrates who felt, and taught, that the soul was the only true mover of the body, and that therefore it behooved us to learn its makeup, and something of the way it went about its business. Like plants, we had appetites, and these impelled us; in league with the animals, we had feelings and perceptions as well, and these sent us in search of satisfactions; but in addition, and unlike any other creature, we could direct ourselves by means of reason to responsible ends. Speech was the principal organ of influence. Through speech we made our thoughts known to others, and through speech each aspect of ourselves endeavored to persuade our differing desires, by reasoning, flattery, or shouts, to fall silent. More often than not, the exiled are novelists and poets, journalists and playwrights, or any others, whatever their occupation, who speak out or up. Put generally, though I think centrally, what is exiled is nearly always someone's word.

And when a musician is sent away in disgrace, it is what his music is said to say that is the cause; and when the painter is put out like a wildfire, it is because of what his paintings are supposed to mean; it is the words which can be pulled from them, the ideas they then can be alleged to support, for which they are excluded. Socrates did not corrupt the youth by laying his lustful hands on them; he did not corrupt them by omitting to pay ritual homage to the gods; he corrupted them by teaching them intelligent talk; he taught them to quiz the wizards of the marketplace and the heavies of the politburo and the swifties of the courts, and to confront them in their places of power where their walk would be most swaggery and their talk most confident, and there, in that advantageous atmosphere, were there words to be examined, weighed in a just debate with other words.

The pimps and prostitutes, cardsharps, bid riggers, and legal liars on my list: why should we suffer the expense of their long stays in our iron-bar hotels, and the pay of the guards who must guard them, and the cost of the high walls which hedge them in? why should death row be crowded with criminals who have grown old on appeals and three square meals a day? why not wrap up our undesirables and ship them to Cuba? goons and contract killers and burglars by the boatload.

Couldn't we pay some country to be our penal colony? Like radioactive waste, nobody wants wife beaters, bad-check artists, and confidence men. And so I wonder: why are writers always able to find a welcome in some country, when other kinds of bad guys are turned away at the border? Well, why are miserable and misunderstood wives so valued by the husbands of their neighbors? Over and over again, one nation's persecuted artists have become another's national treasure. The word which sounded foul in one ear may ring sweetly in someone else's. It was brave of Solzhenitsyn to tell the truth we wanted to hear about the USSR, and we were glad to give him a mountaintop from which to broadcast, so long as he set off his charges in the right direction.

Rarely is an exile lucky enough to be kicked out of New Jersey only to fall on his feet in Devon. Normally he is taken from his family and friends, deprived of his livelihood, his habits, his haunts; his ordinary avenues of expression are closed, his countryside is altered utterly, snow begins to fall in a world which had heretofore held a Hawaiian heart, the birds no longer sing the right songs, the flowers wear the wrong colors, nor are the car horns happy; the winds blow in different directions, the cities smell of fish or beer or paper, clothing is uncomfortably odd, and the words which once came to your tongue like your own soul freely, unashamed, naked to a wife or husband, now have to hide in your head, for there is no one to speak to, no one to read what you've written, no one to know about and protest your case, or understand the conditions of virtue which were called your crime.

You are no longer you when even your present daily life is as remote as a memory. You are no longer you, if — especially — you were defined by your way of life, the things you loved, the ideals you esteemed, your language.

Against this, celebrity exiles have often reported improved conditions: they got better jobs, were lionized, given opportunities to express themselves — in dance, in painting, in design — in directions they could scarcely have foreseen. They were put on TV, asked their opinion, smiled at by strangers in the street, by the CIA debriefed. And there was tea on the terrace following the replay of their defection. Universities paid them to speak, and offered them even more to teach. They had assumed, in effect, the mantle of a new profession: Herr Doktor Dissident, Professor of Exilese. And ease it is for some, and easy for some to shift tongues, to pick up this word and that and grammarize themselves, to adapt to a new, far richer life than they earlier could have dreamed.

They might remarry, adopt a team (the Washington Redskins, most likely), disco around a lot, acquire a taste for scotch, begin to forget the wretched whom they once resembled and who lay in prison still or slid still in fear down gray streets or slept lightly as the cat sleeps when in the pound. It became equally easy to discount or forget their fellow exiles who hadn't landed in swimming pools with surrounding lawns, but who found themselves taken down every peg possible, driving a taxi through streets they couldn't recognize or pronounce, selling bruised fruit, cleaning house when before they had owned one, patronized or ignored, handed a visored cap or a broom, and cast adrift where there was neither water nor a boat.

To enjoy such success, cold wars need to be kept hot. To enjoy such success, other exiles are unwanted competition: for limelight, available sympathies, restricted access to the goodies of the new life. Back in the old country, they had often cultivated a fine hatred for one another, so why should they change this comforting relation just because both were in a new place? Besides, only they, of this country or that, region or that, race or that, language or that, this or that kind of cruel repression, grim persecution, special pain and particular rage, only they, that is, were exiles really, exiles in extremis, with an island in their name, exiles in essence. Others were carbons, copies, no-accounts, unable to muster up the misery, the enmity, the enemies who might give them an honest exile's status and an entry into the aristocracy of the properly deposed.

Who are those who make this transition most easily? those for whom exile almost turns out not to be? The lucky ones scarcely cared about their native soil, were into making it one way or in one place or other, were cosmopolitan in their dress and tones and taste and bones, and had early on freed themselves from clan and family, from countryside and climate — perhaps they lived in an apartment complex on a city block amidst a lot of similarly anonymous buildings, and saw only the sky through a sooty window, and wrote on mimeograph paper. Coca-Cola and corn dogs comfort them now; their microwave knows how much better off they are — with clean sheets and a car, some good dope and their own towel. The region they had always cared about remained a region of the mind, and the mind was mainly a midden made of texts, of pages of reportage and consignment, and drama, of course, sentiment, sob-stuff, high-minded alignments of rhymes recited in a Racinean hurry before being shot or having a head cut off; and they understood geography as a text, history as a text, texts as texts, and were able then to transfer themselves as on library loan from one book depository to another, suffering only the ordinary wear and tear of careless usage.

In particular, those who did well in their adoptive country were those who learned the new language quickly, and who stepped smartly into the idioms and lingo of the times, who wrote in their new home as they had written when in the old one: rapidly, breezily, glibly, satirically. For them, the forced switch from one language to another put both the new one and the old one in a revelatory light. They saw their mother tongue no longer as a daughter might see her mother, but as Mother's seducer might, or the baker whom she owed for last week's rolls. And they saw their adopted tongue as an entirely new, wholly free, wonderfully energized way of thinking, because nothing of their rejected history clung to it, the lint of a past life didn't remain; it was as clean of guilt and memory and old emotion as algebra is (one reason why algebra has always been a haven for the haunted).

There was guilt enough. The old days had gathered it like cloud. That was one more factor in favor of another language, another country; because every difference was desirable, and every distance; because no matter what wrong your motherland had done you, or how clearly mistaken in you it had been, or how unjustly you had been treated, how severely you had suffered, how bitterly you had been made to play Job, you were nevertheless still haunted by your father figures, your idols of the family; you were bitten by your conscience regardless; you called your- self an ungrateful whelp, disgraceful offspring, rotten kid — all the regular stuff — while knowing that your voice, at such times, was only the flavored echo of your enemies, that it was your own arm they were using to bring the gavel down, and *your* mouth which dolefully pronounced *their* sentence. That was another un- fairness. Perhaps the final one.

Well, it is certainly sensible, under such circumstances, to make yourself over in the image of another culture, if you can, because you are going to want to call cabs and order croissants, and you may want to blow the whistle on the bastards who drove you from your homeland — a vigorous article in the local language might do that — or cash in on your new celebrity. It may be, however, as I've already suggested, that you used your first lan- guage as superficially as you will use every other, just to request cold toast and tea, or to kiss off an unwanted lover, get a good lie going; and it may also be that you know no other way to use it but badly, as if it were a laundry basket or a paper cup you could crush and throw away after use.

The scientist, for example, is presumed to be working at a level of concept which escapes the parochial, so that although the summaries of his experiments are in German or French, they are not in French and German but in perception records and loga- rithms. Suppose our words spilled from our mouths as palpably as spit; suppose some were encased in soft pink clouds like cotton candy or encircled like comic strip balloons, or came out in Gothic; suppose they filled up small rooms, and we waded through them to reach the phone or the door, and little language ladies spent the night collecting them in nets, hosing them into vats, and at earliest dawn trucks laden with the *logos* slunk through the streets to great dictionary-shaped dumps. I suppose it only to indicate how well rid of our words we are. No sooner spoken than absorbed by the wide, though increasingly worried, sea of air around us. As for the similarly useless written word . . . well, we may die of our records; bad writing is more contagious than a cold; and if it isn't pieces of plastic and those wormy twist- ties that get us, it will be vast memo slides, best-seller blowups or stock certificate subsidence.

But if your language is supposed to be the medium of an art;

if you, its user, are an artist and not a reporter, a persuader, a raconteur; if you aren't writing principally to get praise or pay, but wish to avoid the busy avenues of entertainment, to traffic in the tragic maybe, dig down to the deeply serious; then (although there are a few exceptional and contrary cases) you will understand right away how blessed you are by the language you were born with, the language you began to master in the moment you also started to learn about life, to read the lines on faces, the light in the window which meant milk, the door which deprived you of Mother, the half-songs sung by that someone who loaned you the breast you suckled — the breast you claimed as more than kin.

Only if you spring fully grown from the brow of Zeus can you escape being born, and learning a language before you get big, and losing that language along with growing old. It is like living under a certain sort of sun, except that the word begins as merely the wind and weather of the spirit, because what occurs in the outside world initially as a kind of din is slowly made sense of and assimilated. Gradually, too, is a style formed, like the hardening of your bones and physiognomy, by degrees, the way your character comes into being — assertive and tough, mild and weak. That you will learn a language, then, is likely; that you will learn it well is unlikely; that you will live well is unlikely; that you will have a shape is certain; that your soul — that old ghost — will be the source of your speech and the words you write is a Socratic conjecture I support; the word is all the soul is.

So what is sent away when we are forced out of our homeland? Words. It is to get rid of our words that we are gotten rid of, since speech is not a piece of property which can be confiscated, bought or sold, and therefore left behind on the lot like a car you have traded, but is the center of the self itself. The excruciation of exile lies in this: that although the body is being sent into the world as Adam and Eve were sent by the angel, the soul is being cast into a cell of the self where it may mark the days with scratches on the wall called writing, but where it will lose all companions and survive alone.

This claim of mine concerning the centrality of the spoken word is, of course, not believed. In our picture-perfect time, who should believe it? So on your next date, draw a picture of your

passion. Thus explain your needs. How far into real feeling will
it take you? Will it not inadvertently possess a certain lavatory
style? When next you are alone and pondering some problem
(should you call him? will she or won't she? does he like the am-
plified guitar better than the cradled bass? in what will she prefer
that I express myself, chalk or crayon?), try posing your questions in terms of the flickering image so many say they love and
is the future's salutatory wave. Think through anything. Start
small. Continue simple. But doodle the solution into being.

If we can read, it is expected that we also ought to be able to
write, or, anyway, type. How many of us, in our camera-crafted
age, can take a really good photograph, or copy a pictured face,
or form an interesting image in any medium, or read a blueprint,
understand a map or set of architectural plans, or even follow
the right arrows when trying to catch a suburban train? If this is
a visual age, why is our visual literacy next to nil? We can't even
doodle with any skill.

We could say, of Saturn swallowing his children, that he had
sent them to hell inside himself. For quite a few of its sufferers,
exile is a spiritual condition, not merely a geographical one. This
is what many of our American writers of the teens and twenties meant when they described themselves as exiles, and when
they weren't just putting on airs. Gertrude Stein said that when
American expansion had reached the Pacific, there was nowhere
else to go but "west in the head." And into the head we went.
Then sent our luggage east of us to Paris. Where we spent our
exile wasn't the real issue. James Baldwin wasn't sent into exile in
France. His exile began before he was born, when the darkness
of all our beginnings darkened his skin.

The expression "spiritual exile" is a metaphor, of course, but a
significant one, since there is a large number for whom exile is
only a *pro forma* punishment: they are doing well and have found
a happy home in their adoptive country. "Alienation" pretty well
describes the condition of heart and mind which constitutes the
inner content of actual, of effective, exile. While alienation can
be mutual, as it often is with married pairs, it is often as solitary
as masturbation. Citizens can become alienated from their government without the nation noticing. That failure to notice is
often part of it. Still, being indifferent to someone or something

does not imply that you once upon a time felt otherwise, or that you must continue to mourn your separation.

"Alienation," as a philosophical term, is no longer in vogue, so perhaps it is safe to pick it up again, if only for a moment. What is more familiar than your own face — the one there in the mirror, the face you are shaving? But what is that behind the head? It is a wall you've never seen, a wall the mirror has invented, and the head, too, wobbles on its neck now, as if it were under water. Remember how it felt to return after many years to the high school of your youth: how small the halls were; how tattered the blinds; how grim the lockers — a greasy green, and dented without design. Reality and memory were out of tune then, and now they are again.

The movement of the razor over the face, the scrape of the blade, the cream being pushed here and there like suds across a floor, have all leaped over oddity and reached the surreal. The operation of doorknobs is inexplicable. Doorknobs ought to be easy. We only expect bidets to be mysterious. But as alienation settles over our souls like a fog, features, operations, relations, without actually altering, offer us different points of reference, their aims shift, their essences dissolve. An inner weariness wells up, everything is an obstacle, asking us questions we do not understand. We issue the same old orders to our will, but after that our limbs flair awkwardly; walking cautiously straight ahead, we still back into things as though blind; we forget how to sneeze.

At the same time, of course, how vividly, how accurately, how freshly we see; for everything we had known well, we had long since ceased to know: the flag was noble, the flag always waved, priests, presidents, and poets were worthy of respect. And now the bathroom wall surprises us; so does the tone in our wife's voice when she says "no" once again — a sound which suddenly seems the same as the scrape of our razor. We really hear, perhaps for the first time, the guggle of water down the drain — down the drain like the departure of all hope. In the blink of an eye, we've placed a Duchamps here, another there, until we have a world full of the familiar made strange.

We have spent a lifetime making things a part of ourselves, constructing, as they say, a second nature: learning to walk, to speak, to ride a bike, pick a lock, spoil a party, dance the fandango, wash dishes, shovel snow, swim, do our job, turn on, turn off, go to the bathroom, stoop to conquer. We had felt at home in our neighborhood, safe and sound, until houses were looted, purses snatched, and Pakistanis moved in. So now we walk a fierce dog. We had felt at home in our yard with its swimming pool until someone threw an open can of paint in it, until adolescents made a habit of swimming nude there in the middle of the night, until a squirrel drowned. We had felt at home in our home, freshly done in chintz and lacquer, until the kids brought their noisy punk friends in the den, the dog began pooping in a corner, robbers ripped us off, and the wife stopped making the bed. We had felt at home in our flesh until our flesh grew old, grew flabby, went fat, and then there was that stranger in the mirror with his red-rimmed eyes, and the stubble every morning like an early field gray with frost.

Then strangers invaded our private hunk of public space with their hands out and their staring eyes. Then strangers came too close to us in the subway, and sat down beside us with empty seats on every side. So now we come warily up to the ports of our eyes, and go about, even when alone, hidden deep within like a pip in a pumpkin, and protected from the actuality of everything, especially every touch, as we always did at rush hour, so as not to feel felt when packed in the train like a tin.

Alienation is the exile of the emotions — of hope, of trust — sent away somewhere so they won't betray us.

The exile that I personally know about is an exile far less gruesome than the fate which befell Saturn's children; it is not at all dramatic like the epic of Oedipus, not a bit lyric, either, like a ballad bemoaning the old days from the lute of a Slavic poet. It does not even concern the exile of a person whose speech was found to be offensive, and who was sent away where his message could be heard no more. I am talking about the loss of a use of language, in my opinion its fundamental employment — the poetic in the broadest sense — and how that limb of our language has been cut off and callously discarded.

This has been, of course, my subject all along. And someone may ask, so complete has been its disappearance, what is this special use of language, and what makes it so special? Alas, to answer would require another essay and an honesty absent from most hearts. It is, first of all, a use of language which refuses to be a use. Use is abuse. That should be the motto of every decent life. So it treats every word as a wonder, and a world in itself. And it walks between them, even over dizzy heights, as confidently as a worker on beams of steel. And it does not care to get on, but it dwells; it makes itself, as Rilke wrote, into a thing, mute as the statue of an orator. It reaches back into the general darkness we — crying — came from, retouches the terrors and comforts of childhood, but returns with a magician's skills to make the walls of the world dance.

Paul Valéry divided buildings thus: into those that were dumb, and therefore would be, on my account, soulless, dead; those that spoke, and would be, on my account, solid citizens and a worthy norm, provided their speech was clear and honest and unaffected; and those that sang, for these found in themselves their own true end, and rose like Shelley's lark through the heaviest atmosphere.

We have grown accustomed to silence from this sort of singing. We make other noises. Yet it is an old rule of history that exiles return, that they return wrathfully, whether a banished people, a forbidden idea, or a barricaded way, to reclaim what should have been their heritage. They return wrathfully, not only because they remember and mourn the life they were taken from, but because the past can never be recovered, not even by a Proust, not if you wish to take up residence in it again. To listen to our stories other selves have been invented to replace the dolls, who, if any remain, are alive somewhere in other arms. But of course poetry, if it returns, will never make us pay. No. It will not put us to death or in prison or send us, as it was sent, so sadly away. It will simply put us to shame.

ADAM GOPNIK

Audubon's Passion

FROM THE NEW YORKER

IN 1803, an eighteen-year-old Frenchman who had been born in Haiti, as Jean Rabin, and who had lived in Paris just long enough to take a few drawing lessons and learn how to ice-skate, arrived in New York. For the next seventeen years, he wandered through Pennsylvania and Kentucky and Ohio and Louisiana, pursuing one quixotic money-making scheme after another. Then, in 1820, he was seized by what he afterward called his "Great Idea," and for the next thirty years — until his death, in 1851 — he raced from Florida to Labrador, drawing a picture of every American bird and every American beast, beginning with the wild turkey, and including even such minor Americans as the knobbed-billed phaleris, the annulated marmot squirrel, and Richardson's meadow mouse, and ending, five hundred and eighty-four paintings later, with the silvery shrew mole. He signed his work John James Audubon, and became the nearest thing American art has had to a founding father.

Lewis Mumford once described him as an "exuberant French coxcomb" who "changed his silks for leather hunting clothes and let his hair grow down to his shoulders; and . . . gradually turned into an archetypal American, who astonishingly combined in equal measure the virtues of George Washington, Daniel Boone, and Benjamin Franklin." Already in Audubon's lifetime, his person and his legend had begun to blend backward into the first generations of American patriots. The Vanderlyn portrait of Andrew Jackson that hangs in New York's City Hall, for instance, is a composite — Jackson's head mounted on a drawing of Audubon's body. In the last portraits of Audubon, painted by his son John Woodhouse Audubon, Audubon's light, fencing master's features have even begun to fuse indistinguishably with those of General Washington.

Yet Audubon's strange origins, his slow start, and the long period of shady struggle in his middle years add to the clear, eighteenth-century glow of his legend a more peculiarly nineteenth-century American touch — of frontier purification and renewal and reform. Audubon's self-transformation from the dilettante in a ruffled shirt arriving in America into the American woodsman eventually returning in triumph to France is one of the great awakenings in American biography. In his poem "Audubon: A Vision and a Question for You," Robert Penn Warren called this transformation a "passion," lending a Christian overtone to the story of Audubon's rebirth in the wilderness.

In the popular imagination, Audubon remains an archetypal American, though perhaps he now stands on the second shelf of American curios — somewhere between Betsy Ross and Johnny Appleseed. Although the last couple of years have marked no particular Audubon occasion and seen no Audubon exhibitions, he has still been the most visible of all American artists. Last year, Wellfleet Press reprinted the octavo edition of *Birds of America,* to complete a republication program that began in 1989 with the reproduction of Audubon's *Quadrupeds,* so that now, for the first time, both of Audubon's masterpieces are available in cheap editions in something like their original form. Then, later last year, the Audubon Society arranged for the republication of Roger Tory Peterson's "Baby Elephant" folio of *Birds of America,* in which the birds have been reorganized along modern ornithological lines. Also, Dover Books has republished Audubon's accounts of his trips to Europe, the Missouri Valley, and Labrador, and Alice Ford's exhaustive biography, out of print for more than two decades, was republished in 1988 by Abbeville.

With his reputation as the father of bird sanctuaries and the begetter of the duck postage stamp, however, Audubon the artist has become more familiar than really known. We come to him sideways, repeating by rote a set of pious attitudes that his successors have intoned (nature true, nature wild, nature as it really is) and then catching out of the corner of our eye the uncanny intensity of his art — its haute-couture theatricality and ecstatic

animation, its pure-white backgrounds and shadowless, cartoon-
ish clarity — which still proves so unexpected that we are inclined either to explain it away as technique or write it off as naiveté. Yet to turn the pages of even the inadequately printed
Wellfleet volumes is to recognize that Audubon remains the supreme stylist of American art, and that his formal daring enabled him to achieve a new kind of emotional concentration,
which invested each of his birds and beasts with some heightened
facet of his own complicated character.

Audubon was not an abstract artist, and he wasn't a mere pat-
ternmaker, but he recognized that his greatest achievement was
the invention of what he referred to, modestly but pointedly, as
"my style" — an American idiom as pared-down, sturdy, and
adaptable as a Shaker box. (It was a style so knowingly wrought
that he could teach it to John Woodhouse and trust him to execute and complete many of the last plates in *Quadrupeds* in a manner almost, though not quite, indistinguishable from his own.)
The current flood of Auduboniana reaches us today in a time
when an uncertainty about the future of the American wilderness, which Audubon made his subject, reinforces a larger uncertainty about American manners and American appetites —
about the origins of our picture of ourselves. So the questions
that we put to Audubon, perhaps like those we put to any founding father, both increase in urgency and simplify in form, and
have now become one indivisible question, half biographical and
half formal: what was it in the man that produced the passion,
and what was it in the passion that produced the style?

Everyone agrees that Audubon was French and was a nearly
compulsive liar; everyone also agrees that he was an archetypal
American and was obsessed with scientific truth. The conventional, idealizing accounts make those Audubons successive ones,
but the truth seems to be that Audubon was all these things at
once. The two roles he liked best to play were the aristocratic
Frenchman with a mysterious past and the simple American man
of the woods. What is amazing is how gracefully he managed to
inhabit both inventions, and how quickly he could exchange one
for the other.

Audubon was not a small or a mean liar — he is extremely reliable on the details concerning his animals — but he had a vivid

imagination, and when he was depressed he liked to entertain or console himself by making up stories about his origins, his history, and his adventures. He lived with these stories, and eventually they began to slip out in public. He suffered from *folie circulaire:* one day he would sign a letter to his wife "The Great, the Wonderful Audubon"; the next he would sink into despair.

The most ambitious lie Audubon seems to have told was about his own birth: that he was the lost Dauphin of France, whisked out of prison during the Revolution and entrusted to the care of a loyal seaman. The development of this story is typical of the process of Audubon's self-inventions. It turns up in his surviving journals for the first time when he is in France in 1828, trying to find subscribers for the first edition of *Birds*. After a particularly discouraging day, he writes, "I walk the streets. I bow! I ask permission to do this or that! . . . I, who should command all." (Alice Ford thinks that his journals were bowdlerized by his granddaughters, in order to emphasize the Dauphin legend. But the fantasy is entirely in Audubon's style; only twenty-five years ago someone as hard-nosed as Mumford thought there might be something to it.) The legend is interesting not so much for its absurdity as for the way it combines his two national modes: the story may use French stock properties, but it is an *American* story, a tall tale. It places Audubon, properly, in both his worlds — halfway between Marie Antoinette and Mark Twain.

The truth about Audubon's origins may reveal why he found the Dauphin story so seductive. His father, Jean Audubon, was a sea captain. (Audubon made him an admiral; eventually, he would have him fighting with General Washington at Valley Forge, although — as Audubon perhaps knew, perhaps did not — no battle took place there.) Captain Audubon became a slave trader in Haiti. He left behind a wife in France, and took a series of mistresses. One of them, a Jeanne Rabin, gave birth to a boy in 1785. Audubon's father accepted the boy fully, though in the father's papers the son is referred to, flatly, as "Jean Rabin, Créole of Saint-Domingue." Haiti (Saint-Domingue then) was a violent place, and Audubon's father had intimations of the revolt that would erupt there in 1790. Just before it began, he took two of his illegitimate Saint-Domingue children (there was at least one other) back to France, where they were embraced by Mme. Audubon. So the Dauphin story is a truth told slant: Audubon's birth *was*, in a sense, mysterious, and the lie allowed him to make the story of his illegitimacy glorious rather than shaming.

The Audubons arrived home, in Nantes, in the middle of the Revolution. Audubon's father, slave dealer and plantation owner, made an about-face and became a fanatical Republican. He turned into a kind of Jacobin commissar in the area, responsible for writing up reports on the loyalty of the region's towns and villages. Though Audubon lived in Nantes in some luxury — for the rest of his life he loved fancy clothes, parties, skating, dancing, violin playing — he was always aware of the violence around him. Another of his repeated stories was that he had seen one of his aunts dragged through the streets during the Revolution and murdered; the truth is that none of his aunts were murdered, and in any case, his father was more likely to have been the one doing the dragging.

In 1789, Audubon's father, on a trading expedition, had stopped in Pennsylvania and — partly because he thought there was a promising vein of lead on the property — bought a farm, outside Philadelphia, called Mill Grove. In 1803, Audubon *père* shipped Jean to America to save him from being conscripted into the Napoleonic armies (the senior Audubon had by now become a fanatical Bonapartist, though not one inclined to have his son fight). By then, Pennsylvania seemed to occupy a special place in the lore of the Audubon family. In Haiti and in France, the Audubons had been surrounded every day by cruelty — the horrors of the slave system, and then the excesses of the Revolution. Pennsylvania, by contrast, was a safe place, a treasure house, a big back yard. For Audubon, the opposition between the Old and the New World was not one that balanced elegant European artificiality against the honest and limitless wilderness. Instead, it set the violence and danger of the Old World against the promise of safe bourgeois comforts and pleasures in America.

Audubon remained all his life unmistakably French. He spoke with an impenetrable Inspector Clouseau accent. (Someone who ran into Audubon long before he was famous transcribed his speech just because it sounded so funny: "Hi emm en Heenglishmen," he has Audubon saying, "becas hi got a Heenglish wife.") The grammar of all his writings, though cleaned up by various editors, was always that of his first language. His vision remained French, too. All his life, he claimed that before he left for Amer-

ica he had studied drawing in the atelier of Jacques-Louis David.
While older biographies accepted this as gospel, Ford finds it improbable. If it was a lie, though, it must have concealed another
kind of truth. Audubon told the story to people who could easily
have checked up on him, and he repeated it in the private journals that were intended only for his beloved wife, Lucy: "I had
studied under the instruction of the celebrated David," "the
pupil of my old master, David," "the lessons which I had received
from the great David." Perhaps Audubon had told Lucy that
story while he was courting her ("We are what we make ourselves," Audubon wrote once; it could have been the family
motto) and was stuck with it.

Still, if he wasn't trained by David, he was certainly schooled
in his style. At a low moment in his life, he made a living by drawing charcoal portraits entirely in the linear, neoclassical manner
that David had perfected. That manner couldn't have been a
stranger springboard for someone who wanted to draw birds
and mammals in their natural habitats. John Constable, nearly
an exact contemporary of Audubon, said once that if David's
shallow, artificial, theatrical style ever became widely accepted, it
would mark the end of nature painting in England. But for Audubon the vague intimations of the sublime were indistinguishable from the blurry generalizations of ignorance; he called the
early Romantic landscapes and bird pictures he saw in England
"washy, slack, imperfect messes." He took it for granted that the
hard-edged draftsmanship of French neoclassicism was the one
good grammar of art, and he remained faithful to it all his life.
(He had the advantage, too, of a parallel tradition, exemplified
by the flower painter Redouté, that married the precision of neoclassicism to scientific illustration. Redouté was almost the first
painter in Paris to whom Audubon showed the early drawings of
Birds of America.) Audubon's animals are, in a way, distant offspring of the profile figures in the *Death of Socrates,* and the di-
orama-like boxes in which so many of his birds are suspended
are a miniaturization of David's sober stage spaces. Audubon's
paintings, like L'Enfant's designs for Washington, D.C., were
one of those early American achievements that developed an overblown Romantic eccentricity from a strict French neoclassical
model.

Audubon also inherited the French mania for the systematic. He couldn't paint one shrike without thinking about the next one, around the corner. He was a catalogue waiting to happen; he said that as a teenager he had tried his hand at a *Birds of France*. Though the idealized account has him throwing off his "coxcomb" sophistication in America to become a birdman and an artist, submitting himself humbly to the discipline of science and nature, the truth seems to be almost the reverse. Drawing birds, making art, inventing catalogues, producing beautiful books — all these things he thought of as French, and part of his "aristocratic" past. (An early attempt at an American bird catalogue, which Audubon might have known, had been made by another émigré Frenchman.) For Audubon, a real American was someone who went out into the woods and came back with a fortune. He wasted the first sixteen years of his life in the United States trying to become such an American, and it was only when every circumstance conspired against him, and drove him back to the French manner he had intended to abandon, that he at last found his way.

Audubon's enduring strength and weakness was his grandiosity. Immediately after his arrival in Pennsylvania, he fell in love with a beautiful local girl named Lucy Bakewell. His love for her remained the single ennobling passion of his life. (He courted Lucy in a cave, and took her to watch pewees, wearing fancy shirts that he had had made at the best haberdashery in Philadelphia — a typically Audubonian combination of Eagle Scout and Beau Brummel.) When the lead mine at Mill Grove had to be sold (Audubon claimed that he was swindled out of it), he found another large ambition — to become a retail tycoon. In 1808, he and Lucy were married, and they set out for Louisville, Kentucky, where he and a partner had gone into business as dry-goods merchants.

When Audubon arrived in Louisville, it was already a stable, mercantile, provincial city. He had to make regular trips back East on business, and it was during these trips — not trailblazing journeys away from the city and into the wilderness but trips from one town to another through well-charted country — that he drew many of his first American birds. His ecstatic sense of

American nature had from the beginning a touch of the outing and the expedition — a sense of the wilderness as a park between two houses.

Audubon loved to watch birds. But his was not the spirit of so many present-day birders, for whom the birds might just as well be stamps or baseball cards. He was drawn to them as familiars, and he was interested in them as social animals. (Lucy Audubon once said, "I have a rival in every bird.") In his journals (and in his collections of bird biographies as well), what he chooses to describe is almost never the markings or the profiles — the appearance — of birds. What interests him is their behavior, their habits, their movements — the "manners" of birds, as he called them. Here he is on a trip to Labrador, describing the varied reactions of birds to a rainstorm: "The Great Black-backed Gull alone is seen floating through the storm, screaming loudly and mournfully as it seeks its prey; not another bird is to be seen abroad; the Cormorants are all settled in the rocks close to us, the Guillemots are deep in the fissures, every Eider Duck lays under the lee of some point, her brood snugly beneath her opened wings, the Loon and the Diver have crawled among the rankest weeds, and are patiently waiting for a return of fair weather, the Grouse is quite hid under the creeping willow, the Great Gray Owl is perched on the southern declivity of some stupendous rock." It is like the opening of *Bleak House* — a portrait of the weather in a world, and of the characters within it.

The dry-goods store soon failed, and for sixteen years Audubon moved around Kentucky and Ohio and Louisiana. The Audubons had four children, two girls and two boys, and Audubon cheerfully set himself up in one unrealistic project after another. They all ended in debts and recriminations, with the again unsuccessful capitalist wandering off to watch swallows.

In 1810, Audubon had been introduced to a Philadelphia ornithologist named Alexander Wilson, who was planning a complete catalogue of American birds. Audubon recognized that Wilson's drawings were niggling and undramatic compared even with his own roughest sketches, but he would probably never have made bird painting his occupation if he had not gone finally and irredeemably bankrupt in 1819. This last bankruptcy was the consequence of a crazy scheme of his to build a mill and run a steamboat in a little Kentucky town called Henderson. It went so badly that Audubon ended up in a local jail for a few nights. He had persuaded a recent English émigré named George Keats to invest money in the plan. Some of the money belonged to George's brother, John, who was back in England, writing poems. The venture helped ruin Keats, and the name Audubon tolls in his letters like a funeral bell: "I cannot help thinking Mr Audubon a dishonest man" and "Mr Audubon has deceived you."

Bankrupt, Audubon began to make a living by drawing charcoal portraits of local merchants, at five dollars a profile. Many of the profile portraits that he was asked to draw were made on the sitter's deathbed. He was once even asked to draw the portrait of a child exhumed from the grave, and make her look beautiful and alive. He was thirty-five years old, and he had failed at everything else. It must have been heartbreaking to know the Audubons at that moment. They were a subject for a Tennessee Williams play: the overworked and beautiful and distressed mother (both of her daughters had died, one just around the time of the bankruptcy), and the young man with the accent and the frayed lace cuffs, still talking compulsively about his studies with David, about his admiral father, about his mysterious birth.

He was thrown back on his birds. They were all he had left, and Lucy thought there might be a little money in them. "It seems my Genius (if I have any) was intended that way," he wrote to her sadly. Then, cheering up, as he always did, he added that he would present the drawings to "the High Judges of Europe." In the 1820s, he perfected the new way of drawing birds that he called his style. He eventually placed on his drawings and watercolors the notation "Drawn from nature," but that was shorthand for a long and contrived process. Audubon would shoot his birds — sometimes hundreds at a time — and then skin them and take them home to stuff and paint. That was what every bird painter did. But Audubon hated the unvarying shapes and Roman-coin profiles that traditional taxidermy produced, so he began to make flexible armatures of bent wire and wood, and he arranged bird skins and feathers — sometimes even whole, uneviscerated birds — on them in animated poses. That is why his birds look, in every sense, so *wired*. He would paint a bird in a single session, recording the outline of the invented pose in firm brushstrokes and then filling in between, like a child with a coloring book, in bright, generalizing watercolor. "My plan," he wrote, "was to form sketches in my mind's eye, each representing each family in their most constant and natural associations, and to complete those family pictures as chance might bring perfect specimens." Over the years, he accumulated not so much a jumble of nature notes and sketches as a vocabulary of firmly delineated, stylized, and even artificial shapes.

In time, Audubon began to refine these "family pictures" into a few simple formats. He invented organizing stories on which he could pin little feathery truths: petrels and terns seen from overhead, as chevrons; upright water birds, their long throats always curving close to their bodies in compressed arabesques; songbirds spread out flat, like bats. For these shapes to be articulate, they had to be seen whole and clear and close up, and so, for all their vivacity, they also began to take on an obviously "studio" quality. (Around 1824, Audubon decided that they would have to be printed life-size — an almost unprecedented conception.) It is impossible to imagine any rational point of view from which the birds might have been seen in nature; his flamingos and herons and swans fill the frame of the picture from top to bottom, as if they had come indoors to sit for the artist. Pure, isolated shapes set against a white background, they become symbols of themselves.

When Audubon had to include more than one bird (a mate or a variant) in a single drawing, he often rejected the conventional compositional system of elegantly varying the poses and places of his subjects. Instead, he repeated a single shape, varying only its size, or "pinning" it down on the background in a new way, as Matisse later did with his fixed shorthand of cutouts. Sometimes this exact repetition of forms can create an odd mixture of geometric abstraction and backwoods lyricism: in the drawing of two violet-green swallows, the same chevron is almost mechanically replicated, so that the echoing shapes, placed beside each other with a chevron of white in between, form an implied fan shape of happy green union. And sometimes the repetition can be comic, as when the little female snakebird thrusts her long throat out in exact imitation of her open-beaked mate, all the while curled safely just beneath him. At other moments — for ex-

ample, in his drawing of two petrels — Audubon will spin or
rotate a fixed schematic shape to show its back or its underside,
so that the picture, with a single form rotating across it, is like
a stop-action photograph. Yet Audubon's birds always reveal
themselves (the undersides of his ducks, the splayed-out bodies
of his cocks) without being reduced to specimens.

Audubon's birds were more high-keyed in color than almost
any other American art would be until the next century. They
were flatter, too, since modeling depends on the kind of slow
graying-out of tone that Audubon thought would distract from
his precise notation of the birds' true colors. (This flatness was
noticed and attacked in his lifetime.) Flatness is in bad odor right
now, and it is hard to recall that there was a time when it was an
empirical, rather than a metaphysical, issue in American art — a
problem of light instead of virtue. In most American abstract
painting, flatness produces brightness; in Audubon's art, brightness produced flatness. Audubon had invented an imaginary,
unnaturally radiant light of a kind that was not seen again in descriptive art until the photographs of Avedon and Penn in the
fifties: the searching, even illumination that fills in detail and
casts a staring, blank white light along smooth surfaces — a light
at once blinding and particularizing. Sometimes, as with the flamingos and herons, Audubon's light is like light at noon on a
white sand beach, picking out each grain of sand, yet still unify-
ing the scene in an all-over, shadowless brightness. Audubon
made American light tropical.

Earlier European bird books had been hierarchical, with the
birds lined up by status. Audubon's birds come at us, for the most
part, in democratic disorder, and so can be taken only as individuals. We judge them, as Americans are supposed to judge other
Americans, by their character. (A Martian coming upon Audubon's birds would have absolutely no notion that birds use feathers for camouflage.) Audubon saw that the behavior of birds,
their instinctual code of greetings and seductions, could be recorded as affectations: the heron's dainty, bent-wristed greeting
to its fellows; the red-necked grebe sapiently lecturing its child;
the great horned owls staring down their accusers. Mated birds
in Audubon are not slaves of instinct but married couples; they
are always in cahoots. Or else his birds stand alone in fancy dress

and become worldly types: the senatorial pelican, the demagogic shrike, the seigneurial blue heron, the outlaw vulture. Even in his lesser paintings, the birds can be struck off in characterizations of the kind that filled his notebooks as humors: the peevish scaup duck, the proud egret, the suspicious snowy owls, the wise-guy cormorant, the hysterical whooping crane, the serene violet-green swallows. Although Audubon is famous as the first bird painter to show birds in their environments, and eventually began to have various landscape painters — among them Joseph Mason and, later, George Lehman — assist him by painting backgrounds, in his greatest bird pictures his subjects completely dominate the environments. They don't fill a natural niche; they oversee an estate, assuming poses that in European art had been allowed only to the landed gentry standing in their parks, their stately homes off in the distance. It may be that in a democratic culture only things that come by their beauty naturally — birds or models or movie stars — are permitted to be shown with such aristocratic self-importance. Audubon's snowy heron, with its bald head and noble posture, is so large and commanding that it can only be taken as the owner of the Colonial estate in the background.

If Audubon's birds are subjects rather than specimens, they are never merely allegorical or archetypal; their very birdness forbids that. They are, above all, *alive,* and their wildness seems to exist — and to be recorded by him — for its own sake. It burns through in their beady, wide-open, wondering eyes, their thrusting serpentine necks, their chattering mouths — a whole new language of recorded ardor. Audubon's birds are always glamorous and always greedy. His swan is unlike any earlier swan in art — not "graceful" or raising its wings, like the swans he described in the parks in France, but sharp-eyed, grasping, its ugly black-webbed foot propelling its beautiful ivory body forward, its eye on the main chance.

"Does there not exist a high ridge where the mountainside of 'scientific' knowledge joins the opposite slope of 'artistic' imagination?" Vladimir Nabokov, another émigré with a love of American wildlife, asked once about Audubon. (Nabokov didn't think that Audubon's occasional drawings of butterflies walked along that ridge.) But at least in his birds Audubon walked along it more bracingly and with a finer equilibrium than any artist be-

fore or since. He sought facts — the exact things, peculiarities —
and found them by inventing a style. In Audubon, the pattern-
ing impulse and the explanatory impulse were always the same.
"What is love?" Robert Penn Warren wrote in his poem about
Audubon. "One name for it is knowledge."

In 1826, Audubon traveled to Europe, carrying the first set of
watercolors for *Birds of America*. (He thought that there were not
enough potential subscribers in America to pay for the book, and
also that there was no one here who could engrave it properly.)
Armed only with a few standard letters of introduction, he went
first to Liverpool. The bird paintings were an enormous success
there, and he went on to Edinburgh, where he found the first of
his engravers, W. H. Lizars. Lizars began to produce sample
plates using the aquatint process — a tonal printing technique
that translated Audubon's drawings into big compositional areas
and increased their blocky, Japanese-woodcut quality. Later, Audubon rather callously traded in Lizars for a still better engraver,
a Londoner named Robert Havell, who further sharpened the
clarity of the watercolors. Looking for an ornithologist who
could supply the necessary scientific expertise for the text, Audubon went back to Scotland and eventually found a tough-
minded young naturalist named MacGillivray, who wound up
editing most of Audubon's writings on birds. Then he went to
Paris, and managed to get King Charles X and much of his court
to subscribe to *Birds*. Audubon understood that while in America
it paid him to be very French, in France it paid him to be very
American — the noble rustic rather than the rusticated noble.
He claimed that when the painter Gérard (an authentic student
of David's) saw some of his *Birds*, he cried, "Who would have expected such things from the woods of America?" In the salons of
Paris, Audubon at last became an American.

Birds of America was a multinational effort, and in the end
was more European than American — French style and English
technique and Scottish realism presiding over the creation of a
picture of the New World. For the next decade, while *Birds* was
being produced, Audubon spent about as much time in Europe
as he did in America. (The last two years of the project, from
1837 to 1839, he spent almost entirely in England, supervising
Havell's engravings and writing the last of a series of accompany-

ing essays.) *Birds* appeared between 1827 and 1838, in irregular installments of five plates, along with a series of complementary volumes, the *Ornithological Biography*, which was issued between 1831 and 1839. By 1835, Audubon was an international celebrity. He lunched with presidents, met famous authors, and wrote, "I have laboured like a cart Horse for the last thirty years on a Single Work, have been successful almost to a miracle in its publication so far, and am now thought a-a-a- (I dislike to write it, but no matter, here goes) a Great Naturalist!!!"

He had enemies. Philadelphia, where he had started his American life, was filled with other, more skeptical naturalists, who had an intellectual investment in the Scottish precision and plainness of Alexander Wilson's more drily "scientific" catalogue of birds. They recognized, perceptively, that beneath the illusion of empirical truth in Audubon's work, increasingly surrounded, as it was, by a pious P.R. atmosphere of expedition-making and sample-gathering (at one point Audubon even had a navy man-of-war take him on a drawing expedition), there lay a not very well concealed element of melodramatic fantasy. One Philadelphian, the naturalist George Ord, mounted a vicious campaign against Audubon, which continued relentlessly for the rest of Ord's life. Audubon's critics attacked the "frenzy and ecstasy" that he showed for his subjects. Fortunately for him, the cases that his critics chose to make an issue of — for instance, whether the nest of the mockingbird could ever actually be invaded by a rattlesnake, as Audubon had shown it to be — were ones on which Audubon happened to have the goods. (It could have turned out differently.)

Audubon shrewdly recognized that the way to cash in on his fame was to release a second, affordable edition of *Birds*, and between 1840 and 1844 he published an octavo edition, several times smaller. It sold extremely well; its seven volumes sat on American shelves as a reassuring presence — a kind of museum of a wilderness that was already becoming remote. The octavo edition of *Birds* was one of the books that helped invent America. It is hard to recall how regional all America's ideas of place were until after the Civil War — how rooted in the love of a state, a provincial locality. Although Audubon's birds, of course, belong to particular places, and although the landscape artists he employed tried to show particular locations, Audubon saw America as an idealized whole. The Audubon family had reached across America, traveling from north to south, from New York to Boston to Florida to Ohio, and Audubon's compositions — the unchanging light, and blank, cloudless skies, and long, uninterrupted horizons — are recognizably American without ever being quite situated. This almost mystical idea of Americanness, expressed as a spare, underpopulated thinness, an endless backdrop, begins in Audubon and continues right through to John Ford Westerns and to Georgia O'Keeffe.

Every bird or animal picture book before had tried to make a point beyond the blind, flat empirical record; for Audubon, the enrichment of the empirical record was all the point there was. The French naturalist Buffon's ornithology was structured to mimic the surrounding social order — the noble birds first and the lesser ones behind. Audubon's book begins *in medias res*, with the wild turkey, proceeds to the songbirds, and then abruptly turns to the lyrical swallows, the arctic terns, the water birds. The sequence loosely follows Audubon's own voyages and discoveries as much as any biological program — a kind of autobiography written in birds. He took the French mania for systematization and made it into a recognizably American love of facts for their own sake — single observations connected by "ands."

Pictures of birds are, like pictures of babies, easy to love. Audubon's beasts — or *Viviparous Quadrupeds of North America,* to give them their proper name — have never been as popular as his birds. The only critic to recognize their power and what is in some ways their superiority was Edmund Wilson, who devoted one and a half uncharacteristically rapturous pages to them in *Patriotic Gore,* under the chapter heading "Poetry of the War." Perhaps what drew him to Audubon's beasts was their unsentimental realism and their violence. The first bird to appear in *Quadrupeds* is dead — a partridge being mouthed by a fox, which, torn between fear and greed, is staring back at an unseen hunter. The accompanying text that Audubon wrote, in collaboration with the naturalist John Bachman, tells what happens to the fox when the hunter releases his dog:

> The Fox has no time to double and shuffle, the dog is at his heels almost, and speed, speed, is his only hope for life. Now the shrill baying of the hound becomes irregular; we may fancy he is at the throat

of his victim . . . every bound and plunge into the snow, diminishes
the distance between the fox and his relentless foe. . . . One more desperate leap, and with a sudden snappish growl he turns upon his pur-
suer. . . . For a moment he resists the dog, but is almost instantly overcome. He is not killed, however, in the first onset; both dog and fox,
are so fatigued that they now sit on their haunches facing each other,
resting, panting, their tongues hanging out, and the foam from their
lips dropping on the snow. After fiercely eyeing each other for a
while, both become impatient — the former to seize his prey, and the
latter to escape. At the first leap of the fox, the dog is upon him; with
renewed vigour he seizes him by the throat, and does not loose his
hold until the snow is stained with his blood, and he lies rumpled,
draggled, with blood-shot eye, and frothy open mouth, a mangled
carcass on the ground.

Desperate leaps, panicky darting and plunging, hanging
tongues and foaming lips, fierce eyes — these are constants of
Quadrupeds. Violence, seen with a curious equanimity, almost a
kind of relish, is the leitmotiv. There are many trapped animals:
the red fox with his hind leg caught in a steel jaw, his body
turned in an oddly composed and graceful twist of pain; the
Canada otter betrayed by his own greed, his small, delicate paw
still reaching for the fish after the trap has snapped shut, his
mouth turned toward us, screaming in disbelief. (The trapped
otter was an obsessive image for Audubon. He first imagined it
in the early 1820s, and drew and painted it many times after.)
Other animals scream to create fear: the wolverine, with his
wrinkled nose, who stretches open his fanged mouth to intimi-
date some unseen predator (the prints are filled with unseen
predators: noises off); the mink, with its beautiful sleek body
and ugly webbed feet, who turns away from his arching mate to
howl; the plumed-tail skunk snarling to defend her young hidden in a tree hollow. Instead of using aquatint, Audubon had the
beasts printed as lithographs, so that in place of the animated
contours of the birds there are soft, blurred edges of fur and
microscopically particularized curling hairs. The light in *Quadrupeds* is less intense and even than in *Birds;* it is soft but shadowless, sculpting out breasts and muscular bodies.

In the endless plates of small rodents and moles and shrews,
which fill the book, the violence is less explicit, but they have

a lurid, horror-movie quality anyway. The common American shrew moles, for example, with their weird, flapping paws and obscene blind faces, seem to be casing the little American farmhouse in the background like extraterrestrials stalking a schoolyard. Sometimes this same note of panic becomes vaguely comic: Wilson's meadow mice, delicately and improbably separating the high grass on their little hill to peer out for enemies; the marsh hare and his mate looking dolefully away from each other, like an old Beckett couple; the Canada pouched rats, meeting and exchanging battle stories like a team of exhausted football players. Tree animals are allowed almost the only moments of calm: the orange-bellied squirrels meet in the notch of a tree and stare at each other; the wise and fat raccoon looks down from a tree and scratches his head. The movement of the birds is upward: limbs lift, heads turn, beaks point. The mammals move down, in little, burrowing worm shapes.

The violence that marks *Quadrupeds* is also the dominant note of Audubon's wilderness journals, but the slaughter of birds and animals, which is the theme of the journals, has, in retrospect, a justification in Audubon's work: the birds and beasts bought with their deaths immortality for their kind. "On leaving the wood we shot a Spruce Partridge leading her young," he writes. "On seeing us she ruffled her feathers like a barnyard hen, and rounded within a few feet of us to defend her brood; her very looks claimed our forbearance and clemency, but the enthusiastic desire to study nature prompted me to destroy her, and she was shot, and her brood secured." The relentlessness of Audubon's descriptions of his slaughters and the almost giddy excitement that the killing inspires in him lend an underside to his accounts which is genuinely alien to modern sensibilities; sometimes the journals have an almost drunken violence, and read like an ad for the National Rifle Association: "Next, Sprague shot an adult yellow-winged male, with the markings principally such as are found in the Eastern States. Harris then shot a young Redshafted, just fledged, with a black stripe on the cheek. His next shot was a light-colored Red-shafted male, with black cheeks, and another still, a yellow Red-shafted with a red cheek. After all this Mr. Culbertson proposed to run a sham Buffalo hunt again. He, Harris, and Squires started on good horses, went about a mile, and returned full tilt, firing and cracking. Squires fired four times and missed once. Harris did not shoot at all; but Mr. Culbertson fired eleven times, starting at the onset with an empty gun, snapped three times, and reached the fort with his gun loaded."

Audubon threw himself into *Quadrupeds* with a passion that surprised even his family. But he fell ill when the book was about half completed; contemporary accounts of the illness sound like a clinical description of the progression of Alzheimer's disease. He became "crabbed, uncontrollable," demanded kisses, and called for old French songs. At the end of his life, he fell into a silent reverie, and was roused only once, when an old friend came to visit, and Audubon suddenly called out, "Yes, yes, Billy! You go down that side of Long Pond, and I'll go this side, and we'll get the ducks."

Audubon was buried in Manhattan; there is a monument to him in Trinity Church Cemetery, on 155th Street. In the hundred and forty years since his death, many of his admirers have tried to translate his example into a conservation program. (The details of this translation, and all its accomplishments, are related in Frank Graham, Jr.'s new book about the National Audubon Society, *The Audubon Ark*, published by Knopf.) Yet the more time one spends in Audubon's company, the more certain it seems that the mission of the society that bears his name — to protect birds and other wildlife — would not have stirred him much. Today, it seems, we can see wild creatures only as waifs or wards; Audubon's wild creatures are always sure of themselves — are never appealing to or looking for a protector. He loved them because they were not needy. It's hard to imagine Audubon within the Audubon Society: once his subjects had to be protected, the splendor that drew him to them in the first place would be gone.

But if Audubon is a relic as a "scientific" naturalist, as a naturalist in the other, literary sense he is still alive. He was the first American artist to look at abundance and see isolation. His animals do not belong to a large "ecology" or have a rank within a secure hierarchy. Instead, their life is lived in a constant present, in which they are always watchful. The only respite comes when an animal is with its mate. Audubon is a poet of married life, who pictures twoness as mutual protection, a midpoint around which a hostile world revolves. His pictures of mated animals can have a horrible delicacy, as in the wonderful plate of two black vultures cuddled within each other's wings and about to peck out and share the eye of a dead deer, or in the plate of a barn owl coming home on a starry winter night, climbing up a branch and opening his beak with delight as his mate turns her head coquettishly, and lifts her snowy-white wing to reveal the hanging squirrel they will share for dinner.

Audubon's passion produced a style by transforming his extravagances into a chastened, dispassionate-seeming language of hard facts, through which the original ardor still shines. The outward sign that his ardor settled on was simply stylized movement; it seems right that George Balanchine thought that Audubon's art could be the subject of a ballet — for forty years, he and Lincoln Kirstein planned to collaborate on a *Birds of America* ballet. (A score exists, by Morton Gould, and bits and pieces of the plan can be reconstructed from accounts by Balanchine's biographer.) The ballet would have turned on the Dauphin legend: the rightful king wandering in America and creating a court of birds. In the third act, apparently, the scene would have leaped ahead to Hollywood in the thirties, with an eternal Audubon transferring his attentions from the white egret to the platinum blonde. Balanchine's Audubon might have fixed forever one image of Audubon, that of the émigré classicist, lost in America.

It also makes sense, though, that in the end Balanchine decided to leave the Audubon ballet alone. Perhaps he recognized that there was nothing much to reinterpret. The constant animation that Audubon imposed on his creations, and that to his contemporaries could look so unnatural, has come to seem at the end of his two volumes as beautifully contrived as ballet, and has the same equanimity. In Audubon's world, as in classical dancing, heightened action of any kind — struggle, escape, seduction, threat, violent death — becomes an opportunity for grace: "And speed, speed, is his only hope for life." Attempting to fix each animal as his imagination grasped it, Audubon ended up painting a catalogue of five hundred and eighty-five aspects of what is still an American theme: that natural life is lived in fear, ruled by habit, and relieved by flight.

JOHN GUILLORY

Canon, Syllabus, List: A Note on the Pedagogic Imaginary

FROM TRANSITION

RECENT CRITICAL DEBATES have tended to generate their own controversial vocabularies, by means of which the milieu of an entire debate can be evoked with great economy, in a word or two. Such a word is "canon" — the name of a debate. I would like to begin by observing the tacit historical displacement that permits the currency of this word: the displacement of the word "classic" by the word "canon." The latter term does not now signify the same relatively uncritical regard for the great works of Western literature as its predecessor, but rather a critique of that very regard, a critique that has all but retired the word "classic" as the signifier of a precritical era of criticism itself. I foreground this simple historical observation by way of emphasizing the more important point that the word "canon" is not so much the name for a historically stable collection of texts as it is the sign of a particular crisis in the history of literary criticism within the university. For it is only within the university that the critique of the canon has currency, in the form of an ongoing debate about the syllabus, the curriculum. The critique of the canon has eventuated in many new curricular programs, from which I do not intend to dissent here. On the contrary, I would like to provide such programs with a different and better defense of their necessity. The business of this argument is not to question the neces-

as genius did, why the texts the author produces are, or are not, canonical.

The institutional context for the return of the author as a "social identity" is now familiar to everyone: the entrance of various socially defined minorities in larger numbers into the university system. The movement to open the canon to noncanonical authors submits the syllabus to a demographic demand, the demand of representation: authors *stand for* social groups. This demand follows upon a transformation of the educational system, a "democratization" of that system, or more accurately, a redistribution of cultural or educational capital.[1] With this political agenda, I am wholeheartedly in agreement; in fact, I shall argue that the democratization of the educational system is scarcely begun, much less accomplished. There is indeed a relation between the representation of minorities in the university and the representation of minorities in the canon, but as soon as one examines this relation closely, the difference between "representation" in the one context and "representation" in the other is immediately apparent. It may very well be easier to make the canon representative than the university itself, and the discrepancy here raises the question of the political efficacy of "representation" in what I shall call the "imaginary" field. The sense in which a noncanonical author "represents" a socially defined minority is continuous with the sense in which the noncanonical work is believed to be immediately expressive of the author's *experience* as a representative member of a social group. The subordination of the text to the author in the current critique of the canon determines that a pedagogy of interpretation will move inevitably in the direction of valorizing the author's experience, the latter usually conceived under the univocal categories of race, class, or gender. Much contemporary theory calls the valorization of experience itself into question, in my view for good political reasons. The reduction of the text to the "voice" of an author has been without question politically strategic in the short term, but at a certain long-term cost. Sooner or later the reduction will be paid for in the failure to *relate* race, class, and gender to one another in a systemic analysis of the modes of domination. It is evident now that while new "voices" are heard expressing themselves, the multivocity of the social system, in which none of us speaks with *one*

voice, has retreated beyond the horizon of analysis. The tele-
graphic invocation of race/class/gender punctuating current critical discourse is the unmistakable symptom of a failure to produce a systemic analysis.

Let me clarify the politics of this position: I am offering a critique from the Left of a liberal consensus whose name is "plural-
ism" and whose pedagogic agenda has been exhausted in the
gesture of "opening the canon." We can indicate briefly what is
at stake in the difference between a Left critique and a liberal
critique by insisting upon the *incommensurability* of the terms race,
class, and gender: the modes of domination and exploitation
specific to each of these socially defined minorities cannot be re-
dressed by the *same* strategy of representation. It is by no means
apparent that the representation of blacks in the literary canon
has quite the same social effects as the representation of women,
precisely because the representation of blacks *in the university* is
not commensurable with the representation of women. What
does it mean that the study of literature by African-American authors has been modeled on the paradigm of "women's studies"?
One consequence of that paradigm is the theoretical and practical indifference of race and gender as *social identities,* as identities
defined primarily by the experience of marginalization. A politics presuming the ontological indifference of all minority social
identities (the "identity politics" which is increasingly being questioned within feminism itself) can only recover the differences
between social identities at the level of individual "experience,"
which in turn yields no other politics within the university than
the politics of self-affirmation. It is scarcely surprising that differences between, for example, black men and black women are
now so readily acknowledged, since it is just such differences
which were effaced in the first place by the politics of self-affirmation, itself the consequence of reducing the categories of race
and gender to univocal social identities. Even more obvious and
troubling is the entire inadequacy of the politics of self-affirmation to address the category of *class*; for while it is easy enough to
conceive of an affirmative racial or sexual identity, it makes very
little sense to posit an affirmative (lower-) class identity, as such
an identity would have to be grounded in the experience of de-
privation *tout court.* The existence of an elitist *Proletkult* notwith-

standing, and granting also the presence of certain admirable elements of resistance in working-class culture, the *affirmation* of a lower-class identity is hardly compatible with a program for the abolition of want. The incommensurability of the category of class with that of race or gender — class cannot be constructed as a social identity in the *same way* as race or gender — does not, on the other hand, disenable a description of the relation between these social modalities. Incommensurability is the condition for an accurate description of the systemic relations between race, class, and gender, relations which are obviously multiply overlapping and mutually determining. The fact of incommensurability also explains why the revisionist critique of the canon has in practice been incapable of identifying or "canonizing" any texts by lower-class writers who are not also identifiable according to race or gender terms. Within the liberal critique, with its identity politics of self-affirmation, the category of class is likely to remain an empty invocation.

On these grounds one may also question the easy elision by which adding "a *text* by a woman" to the syllabus becomes "adding a *woman*." The difference between the two phrases points to the presence of an *imaginary representation,* and thus to the difference between the syllabus and the canon. A certain social problem — the lack of representation — has been addressed by changing the syllabus. But the social problem itself would never have been conceived as accessible to redress by altering the syllabus if the syllabus had not been taken to represent in a fairly straightforward way a selection from the canon itself. I would on the contrary argue that no syllabus really performs such a representative function, and thus that we have entertained certain unrealistic assumptions about the effects of simply changing the syllabus. It is perhaps time to reflect now upon the consequences of an overinvestment in the syllabus, as that pedagogic instrument is supposed to embody of itself a critique of the canon and a critique of all those exclusionary social forces apparently represented by the canon. Nowhere is this overinvestment more apparent than in the distortion which transforms a list of texts into a list of representative authors or social identities.

Let us consider next a more pragmatic question: what does it mean in the classroom, with its physical and institutional con-

straints, to open the syllabus of canonical works to works regarded in this context as noncanonical; that is, works by authors
belonging to socially defined minorities? I want to suggest that
the objective of canonical revision entails in practice shifting the
weight of the syllabus from older works to *modern* works. In fact,
the history of canon formation, if it is at base the history of curricular revision, has always displayed just this drive to modernize
the syllabus at the expense of older works. The opening of the
classical curriculum to vernacular writing in the eighteenth-century school system is one rather momentous example, perhaps
more socially consequential than the current opening of the
canon, since it was responsible for the creation and dissemination of "standard English" as the cultural and administrative
language of the bourgeoisie.[2] Closer at hand, and slightly less
momentous, are the generic modernizations of the canon, the inclusion of the novel in syllabi of the later nineteenth century, or
film since the 1960s. By constructing the canonical text as determined by the social identity of the author, the current critique of
the canon both discovers and also mystifies the obvious fact that
the older the literature, the less likely it will be that texts by socially defined minorities exist in sufficient numbers to answer the
demand of representational diversity. Yet critics of the canon
have not assimilated the simple determinism of this fact. The
reason more women authors, for example, are not represented
in older literatures is hardly that their works were routinely excluded by invidious or prejudicial standards of evaluation. The
historical reason is that with few exceptions before the eighteenth century, women were routinely excluded from access to
literacy or were proscribed from composition or publication in
the genres considered to be serious rather than ephemeral. If
current research has recovered a number of otherwise forgotten
women writers, even before the eighteenth century, this fact
does not relate directly to canon formation as a process of evaluation or selection, but to the present institutional context of a
valid and interesting *research program* whose subject is the history
of women writers and writing. No other defense is required than
the requisites of the research program in order to justify an in-
quiry into unpublished literary productions such as letters or di-
aries, as well as published works that are now obscure or "non-

canonical"; certainly it is not necessary to claim canonical status for these works, as the archive has always been the legitimate resource of historical scholarship.[3] If the feminist research program has recovered from the archives the works of a number of published women writers now relatively forgotten, such as Elizabeth Cary or Katherine Phillips, it must also be borne in mind that while the archives preserve (and bury) hundreds and thousands of writers of various social origins and identities, the social conditions governing access to literacy determined that before the emergence of the middle-class educational system, the greater number of *writers,* canonical or noncanonical, were men. The number of "canonical" texts represents in turn only the minutest percentage of these works, and canonical authors could never in that case have reflected the actual social diversity of their periods (not even, it might be added, women authors of the early modern period, who were literate by and large as a consequence of being aristocratic).[4] The retro-construction of these writers as expressing the experience of the social identity of the woman in general is only the obverse of the error of regarding their writings as excluded from the canon merely as a consequence of the fact that they were written by women. Once the fact of exclusion is located primarily and most effectively at the level of access to *literacy,* it should no longer be possible to speak of the canon as either succeeding or failing to represent a demographically accurate picture of the social world by virtue of prejudicial principles of evaluation. A distinction must be made between the conditions of a text's *production* and the conditions of its *reception* in order to see the real historical relation between these conditions and the process of canon formation.

One might nevertheless want to object here that even if the process of exclusion is primarily located at the level of access to literacy, it might still be the case that canon formation functions to exclude works by minority writers who do manage to acquire the means to literary production. For reasons I will now indicate, I believe even this qualified formulation is inaccurate. It may well be the case that some writers have been unjustly neglected; indeed, the history of canon formation offers many examples of writers rediscovered after periods of obscurity. What seems historically dubious is that such cases can be *generally* explained by invoking the categories of race, class, or gender as the immediate criteria of evaluation. These categories might well explain at the present time why some writers have been recovered from the archive, but not necessarily why they ceased to be read in the first place. Nor does the circumstance of their being read now mean that they have become canonical — only that they are read now. To conclude otherwise is to mistake the current research program (the necessity and interest of which is not at issue here) for an irrevocable act of canonization, as though the effect of the historical process on canon formation could be overturned by a single referendum. Consider once again the category of gender as a hypothetical criterion for exclusion from the canon: the existence of *some* canonical women authors, even before the revisionary movement of the last two decades, vitiates in a strictly logical sense the category of gender as a *universal* criterion of exclusion; which is to say that in any case of an excluded woman author, it will not be sufficient merely to invoke the category of gender in order to explain the lack of canonical status. The principle that explains the exclusion of Harriet Beecher Stowe from the canon on the basis of gender is inadequate to account for the reception of Stowe's work, if only because this principle cannot also account for the counterexample of Jane Austen's canonical status. Nor does the argument being made here necessarily discard the category of gender as a *factor* in the reputation of a given author; we can expect that many factors will enter into the situation of the reception of a given author's work, and that these factors will advance and recede at different moments in the history of the work's reception. The point is rather that the historical process of canon formation is too complex to be reduced to determination by the *single* factor of the social identity of the author. Furthermore, these identities are themselves historically constructed; they mean different things at different historical moments, and thus their relation to the entitlements of cultural capital will be differently construed at different times. The categories of race, class, and gender are in this sense *our* categories of canon formation, and they can only operate as such in a cultural environment in which, first, these groups are discursively constituted as *minorities* (objects of repression and subjects of resistance), and second, no social group has an actual monopoly on the means of literary production. The latter circumstance is, to say the least, mere social justice, but it means that curricular revision to include the works of minority writers is contingent upon all the other conditions of production which permit socially defined minorities access to cultural capital, in the forms of literacy and access to publication. The identity of groups which have in some historical conditions been denied access to the particular form of cultural capital in question has not always been defined by race, class, or gender in the modern sense of those categories as constitutive of minorities. The eighteenth-century bourgeoisie, for example, was by no means a materially disadvantaged class, but it did conceive of itself as *culturally* disadvantaged, and its campaign to raise the status of vernacular, as opposed to classical, education (institutionalizing thereby a vernacular canon of English literature) eventually permitted it to narrow the gap between its material and its cultural capital. The caste against which it struggled, the aristocracy, was itself culturally disadvantaged with respect to the clergy during the feudal era, and it too campaigned at a certain moment in its history to acquire a literacy it had up to then considered unnecessary to its rule, but without ever constituting itself as a "minority." The historical record suggests that the history of canon formation will scarcely be intelligible at all unless it is seen in relation to the history of literacy; and in that context, the process of canonization cannot be reduced to determination by categories specific to the present social formation.

At this point I would like to advance a series of polemical hypotheses. I would argue, first, that the process of canon formation (as opposed to the condition of basic literacy) has never really been a process of *exclusion*. There is no historical, social act which corresponds to the notion of exclusion from the canon. Historical instances of canonical evaluation, in the institutional context in which they are performed (ordinarily, the school), are always instances of inclusion. If every act of inclusion is also, logically speaking, an act of exclusion, the difference between an *intention* to include and an *intention* to exclude is just what is historically significant. If the latter motive were indeed the more urgent in the institutional context of literary canon formation (as it is, perhaps, in the institutional context of the church, where scripture must be dogmatically consistent), the literary canon would in fact be far more ideologically homogeneous than it is; for what force would prevent the "canonizers" from excluding *any* work of a heterodox nature, regardless of the social identity of its author?

Second, the historical pressures governing this process have always been biased toward the widest possible strategies of inclusion, and the literary canon has never been in any real sense like scripture, closed to particular works for any transhistorical ideological reason. It has always been relatively open, a continuously expanding aggregate of texts, continuously subject to the pressures of *modernization*. Once the various historical reformations of the canon are recognized as examples of its modernization, the rhetoric of the "anticanonical," of overthrowing the principle of canonicity itself, can be discarded as unhistorical.

Third, works which have become canonical have by and large been those which their readers have found most interesting, beautiful, or good; that is, the selection of texts for reproduction, dissemination, or for study in the classroom occurs for *positive* reasons. This hypothesis, so far from flaunting an unforgivable political naiveté, is intended to acknowledge the fact that the act of evaluation has as its immediate object a text, not an author. The social identities of author and reader, on the other hand, are *preconditions* of evaluative acts, but they are not expressed immediately as principles of evaluation, except possibly as *analogies* for the positive qualities valued in a text. We know, for example, that the caste traits of the aristocracy could double during the classical period for positive aesthetic criteria (the *classici* were the highest stratum in the Roman caste system); nevertheless, the difficulty of generalizing even class as a criterion of evaluation is evident in the adjacent field of visual art, of which a good deal was produced by slaves, whose social identities have rendered them anonymous but whose works have survived. We may use the classical period to raise an analogous question about whether aesthetic criteria can be generalized from *racial* categories, as these categories are quite modern. There is no sense in which Sophocles or Virgil could be judged in their own time on the basis of such a racial identity as "white," and hence any explanation of their canonicity by reference to these terms would be fun-

damentally anachronistic. Evaluation itself is historically much
more complex than the simple act of accepting or rejecting the
social credentials of the *author*. This thesis does not deny, then,
that criteria of evaluation are historically determined and certainly also compromised by the social conditions of their formulation and use. A history of evaluative criteria would have to
address, however, the *ex post facto* status of these criteria, in themselves insufficient to account for the canonicity of specific works,
since quite different and even incompatible criteria of positive
value are advanced at different times to account for the canonicity of the *same* works.

Lest one conclude from this argument that the process of
canon formation is exempt from any complicity in the systematic
repressions which characterize human societies, let me under-
score what I have argued elsewhere more fully, that the process
of canon formation has an institutional context, the school, and
it is this institution which is responsible for the systematic regulation of reading and writing as social practices.[5] The school con-
trols access to literacy, and the dissemination of its cultural capital to *some* of the population is better served by selections of texts
on principles of evaluation not directly based upon the social
identity of the author. With regard to the social function of the
educational system, the identity of the author matters less than
the capacity of the text to interest students sufficiently to acquire
the knowledge the school has the function of disseminating.
(This point is true by default where certain writers are concerned about whose identity very little is known; but it is also
valid in the exceptional, and laudable, case in which minority
writers are used to teach minority students how to read — that
is, when the social identity of the author is a relevant *pedagogic*
fact. The immediate object of such a syllabus is still the dissemination of literacy.) It is the function of dissemination, not the
judgment of works for eternal canonization, for which the syllabus exists, and it is a mistake therefore to believe that individual
judgments about which works to include on a given syllabus are
in any sense except *cumulatively*, over periods of time, judgments
about canonicity.

In retrospect it appears to me that the critique of the canon has
all along simply assimilated the syllabus, a list of works one might

read in a particular *class,* to the canon — the supposed sum total of works considered in a serious institutional context to be worth reading or studying. Any syllabus will necessarily be limited by the constraints of the particular class and its rubric, even by the irreducibly material constraint that only so much can be read or studied in a given class. In no classroom is the canon itself the object of study. Where does it appear, then? It would be better to say that the canon is an *imaginary* totality of works. No one has access to the canon. This fact is true in the trivial sense that no one ever reads every canonical work; no one can, because the works invoked as canonical change continually according to many different occasions of conflict or contestation. But this point is not as trivial as it may sound. What it means is that the canon is never other than an imaginary list; it never appears as a complete and uncontested list in any particular time and place, not even in the form of the omnibus anthology, which remains a selection from a larger list which does not itself appear anywhere in its table of contents. In this context, the distinction between the canonical and the noncanonical can be seen not as the form in which judgments are actually made about individual works but as an effect of the form of the syllabus, the fact that works not included on a given syllabus appear to have no status at all. The historical condition of literature is a rather more complex continuum of major works, minor works, interesting works, works read primarily in research contexts, works as yet simply shelved in the archive. But even these distinctions are insufficiently nuanced to represent the continuum of preserved writing; what should be clear is that the category of the "noncanonical" is entirely inadequate to represent the status of works which do not appear on a given syllabus.

What does have a concrete location as a list, then, is not the canon but the syllabus, the list of works one reads in a given class, or the curriculum, the list of works one reads in a program of classes. When teachers believe they have in some way challenged or overthrown the canon and its principles, what they have always really done is devise or revise a particular syllabus, as it is only through the syllabus that they have any access to the imaginary list which is the canon. While this point is in some respects quite obvious, it nevertheless usefully exposes the fallacy of using a revision of the syllabus against the *principle* of the canon. So far from being the case that the canon determines the syllabus in the simple sense that the syllabus is constrained to select only from canonical works, it is much more historically accurate to argue that the syllabus projects the canon as its imaginary totality. The imaginary list is projected out of the multiple individual syllabi functioning within individual pedagogic institutions over a relatively extended period of time. Changing the syllabus cannot mean in any historical context overthrowing the canon because every construction of a syllabus *institutes* once again the process of canon formation.

To illustrate the latter point we might consider briefly one exemplary syllabus, which has been taken to embody the canon of Western classics, the recently controversial "Western culture" course offered at Stanford University, now considerably revised so as to include works by various minorities as well as works by non-Western writers. If one glances over the list of works on this syllabus, one sees that there are no women (unless the nineteenth-century novel category makes a slot for a woman available). There are, of course, no nonwhite authors (depending upon how one defines the race of St. Augustine — and the difficulty of this determination is not an uninteresting complication); and the farther back one goes in the list, the more likely that the author comes from a privileged class, priestly or noble. Obviously, in order to "open" this canon, one would have to *modernize* it, to displace the preponderance of works from earlier to later. And there are of course many good reasons to do so. The pressure to modernize the curriculum has succeeded again and again despite the inertial conservatism of the educational institution, and it is this pressure which is largely responsible for many historically significant *exclusions:* the fact that we read Plato but not Xenophon, Virgil but not Statius, has nothing to do with the social identities of Xenophon or Statius, something more to do with later evaluations of their relative interest; but the necessity of choosing between them has everything to do with the modernization of the curriculum, with the imperative of *making room* for such later writers as Locke and Rousseau. The totality of the canon as an imaginary list is always in conflict with the finite materiality of the syllabus, the fact that it is constrained by the limits imposed by its institutional time and space (and it is also the case with this, as with any other list, that it is subject to "sampling error," to representational inaccuracy, as a consequence of the small number of works capable of being included on a given syllabus). Nevertheless, this fact has been hard to acknowledge, perhaps because none of us will ever be familiar with more than a fraction of what has been written that might be considered to be worth reading or studying. Everything that counts as "knowledge" is a selection from a continually expanding aggregate. What sense would it make, then, to argue that the Stanford curriculum "excludes" Herodotus, Ovid, two of the three major Greek tragedians, medieval romances, Rabelais, Calvin, Montaigne, Bacon, Kant, Hegel, the Romantic poets, Proust, Joyce, Mann, not to mention Virginia Woolf, Simone Weil, Richard Wright, or Zora Neale Hurston? If one replaced some of the entries on the Stanford syllabus with names just cited, would the course have been more (or less) representative of something called "Western culture"? I would suggest that it would be better to begin a critique of this course with the notion of Western culture, the umbrella term under which all these different texts take shelter from the labor of critique, the labor of reading. (It is perhaps worth emphasizing that the concept of "Western culture" is itself of relatively recent origin — perhaps no earlier than the eighteenth century — and that it is constructed by suppressing the elements of African and Asian culture it has assimilated, as well as the difficult suturing of the Judaic and the Hellenic.) The homogenizing concept of "Western culture" hints that all these texts are in accord about certain fundamental issues, or that they all share something that might go by the same name. I do not believe that they necessarily share anything, and I say this at the same time that I would also happily acknowledge that they are all worth reading. It would be absurd to conclude from a critique of the canon that one should not read any particular work; one should of course read as much as one can. But the construction of a syllabus begins with selection; it does not begin with a "process of elimination." What is excluded from the syllabus is not excluded in the *same way* that an individual is excluded as the member of a social minority, socially disenfranchised. What is wrong with the Stanford curriculum has less to do with its inclusions or exclusions than with the fact that it is not and *cannot* be a course on Western culture. As soon as any of the works on the syllabus begin to be taught as expressive of a homogeneous and overarching culture extending absurdly from the fifth century B.C. to the present, these works begin to be *misread*.

What one would like to comprehend with a finer set of terms is the relation between the material constraints of the syllabus as an instrument of pedagogy and the various imaginary totalities projected out of historical curricula. The syllabus has the form of a list, but the items on the list are given a specious unity by reference to a whole of which they are supposed to be a part, a synecdoche. This specious unity indeed characterizes not only the canon but the syllabi we call English literature, Romantic literature, women's literature, Afro-American literature. The canon achieves its imaginary totality, then, not by embodying itself in a really existing list but by retroactively constructing its individual texts as a *tradition*, to which works may be added or subtracted without altering the impression of totality or cultural homogeneity. A tradition is "real," of course, but only in the sense in which the imaginary is real. A tradition always retroactively unifies disparate cultural productions (and this is no less true for the tradition of women writers or the tradition of Afro-American writers), and while such historical fictions are perhaps impossible to dispense with, one should always bear in mind that the concept of a given tradition is much more revealing about the immediate context in which the concept of the tradition is formulated than it is about the works retroactively so organized. Also, and perhaps more interestingly, the larger and more disparate the body of works to be retroactively unified, the more urgent and totalizing the concept of tradition will be. Hence it is that the monumental fiction of the Western tradition comes into *political* conflict with the alternative (if only slightly less fictional) traditions of writing by women, African-Americans, etc. If the principle of specious unity is implicit in the construction of any syllabus, this means that the form of the syllabus sets up the conditions within which it is possible to forget that the syllabus is just a list, that there is no concrete cultural totality of which it is a part. The confusion of the syllabus with the canon thus inaugurates a pedagogy of misreading, the obliteration of the text's specificity as it is absorbed into the unity of the syllabus/canon. Here it will be possible to raise a question about the historical context of the present canonical reformation, since the construction of alternative canons (that is, alternative syllabi) is very much concerned to reassert the *unity* of certain subcultural or countercultural formations, women's culture or African-American culture. The syllabus functions in a pedagogical context to embody that unity by immediately projecting an alternative or oppositional canon out of the synecdochic list which is the syllabus. I would suggest that the present very anxious fixation on the canon (and on the syllabus as its avatar) by both its defenders and its critics can be read as symptomatic of a certain anxiety associated with the perceived unity or disunity of contemporary culture. Provisionally we may say that the perceived disunity of the culture as a whole, as a *fragmented* whole, is recuperated by reconstituting cultural unities at the level of gender, race, or, more recently, ethnic subcultures, or gay and lesbian subcultures (excepting always, of course, lower-class culture, which cannot be assimilated to the identity politics of self-affirmation). The social pressure reconstituting such unities is expressed in the present debate about the canon as the characteristic insistence upon the social identity of the author (a *unitary* identity) as the only relevant consideration in the context of canon formation.

The discursive form which mediates between the pedagogic scene of debate about the canon and the social scene of perceived cultural fragmentation is the *list itself*. I would like to suggest that an obsession with the form of the list characterizes what Cornelius Castoriadis calls the "social imaginary," the entire realm of imaginary significations organizing social life as something in excess of the satisfaction of material needs or functions. What I will call the "pedagogic imaginary" is a subset of that social imaginary, and it organizes the discursive and institutional life of teachers in excess of the simple function of disseminating knowledge. In *The Imaginary Institution of Society*, Castoriadis elaborates the concept of the social imaginary in the following terms:

> Beyond the conscious activity of institutionalization, institutions have drawn their source from the *social imaginary*. This imaginary must be interwoven with the symbolic, otherwise society could not have "come together," and have linked up with the economic-functional compo-

nent, otherwise it could not have survived. It can be placed, and it must be placed, in their service as well; there is, of course, a *function* of the institutional imaginary, although here too, we observe that the effect of the imaginary *outstrips* its function.[6]

The example I would like to address briefly, the list which is appended to E. D. Hirsch's *Cultural Literacy,* has the simple function of communicating what Hirsch believes to be a quantity of knowledge prerequisite to functional literacy. For the purposes of the example I am less interested in disputing Hirsch's argument (it has been well and thoroughly contested by others)[7] than in explaining why this knowledge must take the form of a *list*; and in fact I would argue that it is really the form of the list which has allowed Hirsch's book to produce effects of fascination in both the social and the pedagogic imaginary. The list which defines a common culture of the "culturally literate" (that is, the culturally advantaged) is itself an exemplary artifact of *mass culture,* with its lists of ten best everything. As such, the form of the list is a significant instance of the social imaginary; but within that imaginary, what does it signify? One would have to invoke Lukács or Adorno to convey the context of the nostalgia for totality that pervades this aspect of mass culture, in the midst of its carnival of cultural diversity, its infinite dispersal and fragmentation of knowledge. The fetishized list is one symptom of what Lyotard has described as the "postmodern condition of knowledge." Indeed, nothing can be more alienating (in the full range of Marxian senses) than to read through Hirsch's list, from which I excerpt (almost arbitrarily) the following sequence: Agamemnon, aggression, Agnew (Spiro), agnosticism, agreement (grammar), agribusiness, air pollution, air quality index, Akron, Ohio.[8] From Agamemnon to Akron, Ohio, is, to be sure, quite a stretch; it is Western culture on the rack. Nothing *makes sense* of the sequence, least of all its origin in the house of Atreus. Nevertheless, the relations among these terms are not so difficult to recover at another level of analysis, at the level of a critique which is explicitly proscribed by the form of the list, the form which unifies these terms as constitutive of that cultural capital called "cultural literacy." The latter form of capital has everything to do with a knowledge of *grammar,* the kind of knowledge conveyed by a literary education, but it does not of itself reveal the relation between agribusiness and air pollution, or between Spiro Agnew and aggression. Its specious unity is a repression of the *systemic* relations between the very terms which might signify (with surprising accuracy) the world of late capitalism, where the detritus of "Western" culture is merely juxtaposed to the name of Akron, Ohio, the center, as *The Dictionary of Cultural Literacy* tells us, of rubber production in the United States. The form of the list forecloses any systemic analysis between its own terms on behalf of a nostalgia in which Agamemnon and Akron, Ohio, might truly belong to a "common culture." The nonexistence of this culture, or its actual existence as *mass* culture, is just the fact which Hirsch's list both denies and manifests.

I would suggest further that the fetishized mass cultural form of the list, as an instance of the social imaginary, determines within the university the form of the critique of the canon, its fixation on the syllabus as an *exclusive* list. A nostalgia for totality pervades the debate about the canon on *both sides* of the debate — on the one side as the unity of Western culture, and on the other as the unity of its countercultures, each represented by its canon of "noncanonical" works. Both unities contend with the actual dominance of mass culture by projecting an imaginary totality out of mass culture's image of cultural diversity — the form of the list. There is no question that such unities, especially unities in *opposition*, are politically strategic, that the concept and experience of "solidarity" is essential to any struggle. But the pedagogic imaginary within which the critique of the canon has been advanced is at once in excess of that solidarity, because it constructs out of its alternative canon/syllabus/list a homogeneous culture (of women writers, of African-American writers, etc.), and in defect of that solidarity, because the image of cultural homogeneity it disseminates is only an image *for* those who consume it in the university, where it is consumed *as* an image. The "open" canon can lay claim to representational validity in the experience not of "women" or "blacks" but of women or blacks in the university — which is not itself a *representative* place. The university is nevertheless a locus of real power (the distribution of cultural capital) and therefore a good place for a political praxis to define its object. Such an object should not be the imaginary alone, the image which is the "canon," even if such a praxis must include the image or mobilize the potent force of the imaginary. The imaginary has real and sometimes beneficial social effects, but these effects are always mediated by the institutional form within which they are expressed. We might now begin to defetishize the imaginary list, the canon, by recognizing that while canonical texts are indeed a form of cultural capital, they are not the only form of capital disseminated in the school, and perhaps not even the most important form. It would entail a major reconsideration of the politics of pedagogy if the cultural capital we disseminated were to be called *reading* rather than the "canon." Different forms of this capital (from basic literacy to the sophisticated critical hermeneutics of the graduate schools) are disseminated (or fail to be disseminated) across the vertical and horizontal scope of the educational system.

The difference between the canon and the syllabus, then, is the difference between the pedagogic imaginary, with its images of cultural or countercultural totality, and the form of the list as the instance of mass culture's social imaginary, with its simultaneous denial and manifestation of cultural heterogeneity. As teachers we should of course never let the syllabus *determine* pedagogy, even or especially when we "change the syllabus." The fact that we have conceived of the latter project as changing or even overthrowing the canon itself means that the form of the *syllabus* fails to be recognized as a mediating structure in its institutional place. To decline the theoretical and practical labor of analyzing pedagogic structures in their mediating institutional sites is to cede everything to the imaginary totality, to play the game of culture without understanding it. It is only in the pedagogic imaginary that changing the syllabus means in any *immediate* sense changing the world; what is required now is an analysis of the institutional location and mediation of such imaginary structures as the canon in order first to assess the real effects of the imaginary and then to bring the imaginary itself under more strategic political control. It is a fact, to be sure, that many more women authors are taught in literature classes than used to be, just as it is a fact that there are now many more women authors, and just as it is a fact that there are now many more women in professional and managerial fields. It is also a fact that the burden of poverty in the last decade has been shifted more and more onto the shoulders of women. What is the relation between these facts? The critique of the canon can at present offer no analysis of the relation between the forms of cultural and material capital, and it never will if it settles for the goal of projecting the imaginary ego ideal of a newly constituted professional-managerial class, no longer exclusively white or male. Those who have never been taught, or have been very inadequately taught, the *practice* of reading have little occasion to rejoice at being "represented" in the canon. Such representation does not address or compensate for their situation so long as the school continues to distribute cultural capital unequally. Let us recognize, then, that the university belongs to an educational *system*, inclusive of every level and every kind of school, however apparently autonomous. If we have accomplished a necessary curricular revision in the last decade, a modernization of the curriculum, we should reflect upon the fact that what has been revised is the *university* curriculum, in response to social pressures registered much more ambiguously at the lower levels of the system, where the democratization of the school has been simultaneously subverted by the withdrawal of public funding, the "de-skilling" of teachers, and the virtual removal of texts, literary or otherwise, from the classroom.[9] What would it mean to redefine the object of our critique as the institution of the school, of which the syllabus is only an instrumentality? It would mean acknowledging that the canonical reformation has somewhat less social effect as an agency of change than it claims, by which I mean, precisely, "less." To have drawn up a new syllabus is not yet to have begun teaching, nor is it yet to have begun reflection upon the institutional form of the school.

N O T E S

1. The term "cultural capital" throughout invokes the work of Pierre Bourdieu and Jean-Claude Passeron, *Reproduction in Education, Society, and Culture*, translated from the French by Richard Nice, with a foreword by Tom Bottomore (London, Beverly Hills: Sage, 1977). The knowledge the school provides is *capital* because, like capital, it can be used to make more of itself; it can also be translated into the forms of material capital, such as money. (The belief in education for upward mobility expresses this truth in the language of ideology.) Bourdieu's "transformation problem," the mutual convertibility of

cultural and material capital, is at once the greatest theoretical difficulty in his work and its most important theoretical advance.

2. On the introduction of vernacular works into the schools of the eighteenth century, see Richard Altick's invaluable *The English Common Reader: A Social History of the Mass Reading Public 1800–1900* (Chicago: University of Chicago Press, 1957), pp. 47ff.

3. The difference between a research program and canonical revaluation is symptomatically confused in such statements as that by Marilyn L. Williamson, *Raising Their Voices: British Women Writers, 1650–1750* (Detroit: Wayne State University Press, 1990), p. 9, which I quote for its representative language:

> I do not therefore make aesthetic judgments the goal of my reading, and some readers will doubtless find much of the writing covered in this study deficient in quality and therefore not worth much attention. My work and that of other feminist critics offers the possibility of breaking out of the cycle of assuming that what is unknown or obscure deserves to be so. I do not claim to have discovered inglorious Miltons among the score of writers in this study, but I believe their work deserves attention nonetheless. The neglect is historical: most were well-known, some quite famous, in their own time. Just as historians are beginning to read popular pamphlets along with Hobbes and Locke, so literary historians are reading far beyond the canon and the taste and values it informs.

Historians will be surprised to learn that they are just beginning to read archival material in connection with works by major authors. But historical scholarship has been practiced by literary critics too. The dovetailing of new forms of historical scholarship with a critique of the canon has produced the quite interesting misapprehension that writing *about* a given author is equivalent to canonization. It seems doubtful that permanent revisions to the canon can be undertaken without recourse to strong arguments for the revaluation of specific works or authors, but this condition has always obtained in the circumstance of canonical revision.

4. On this question I am relying on the work in progress by Margaret W. Ferguson, *Limited Access: Studies in Female Literacy and Literary Production in the Renaissance,* forthcoming from Routledge Press.

5. I have developed this argument at greater length in "Canonical and Non-Canonical: A Critique of the Current Debate," *ELH* 54 (1987), 483–527. I would add parenthetically here that while the school is not exclusively the agent of canon formation — obviously publishing houses, commercial anthologies, and the mass market enter into the process of establishing the contemporary reputation of a given author — even the most successful contemporary reputation is insufficient to ensure the canonicity of an author. Canonicity is a function of the reproduction of a work over time, and the market for such reproduction is the school. This point is particularly clear in the apparently anomalous case of an author such as Harriet Beecher Stowe, who has remained popular without, until recently, entering the canon. The fact that feminist critics can now argue for the canonicity of Stowe confirms that can-

onical status is meaningless outside the context of the school syllabus, and hence that reputation and canonicity are quite different phenomena. With regard to anthologies, my own research into eighteenth-century vernacular anthologies suggests that such anthologies only have canonical force (that is, have a social function above and beyond that of entertaining the reading public) when these anthologies are employed in the school system.

6. Cornelius Castoriadis, *The Imaginary Institution of Society*, translated by Kathleen Blamey (Cambridge, England: Polity, 1987), p. 131. Castoriadis's critique of pure functionalism might explain the innate conservatism of institutions as well as the fact that all institutions are unstable and subject to radical change, to being reimagined. Throughout this argument I have attempted to credit the social *force* of the imaginary, irreducible to mere social function, but also the political ambiguity of imaginary constructions, like the canon, which are not recognized as such.

7. See, for example, the recent Modern Language Association publication *Profession 88* (New York, 1988), with articles by Andrew Sledd and James Sledd, Helene Moglen, Robert Scholes, and Paul B. Armstrong.

8. E. D. Hirsch, Jr., *Cultural Literacy: What Every American Needs to Know* (Boston: Houghton Mifflin, 1987). Hirsch comments on the form of the list in the following remarks:

> Not least among the virtues of a list of cultural literacy is the fact of its finiteness. As soon as one thinks about it, it is obvious that shared information in a large nation like ours must be limited. . . . Just to illustrate the finiteness of literate culture is useful. It should energize people to learn that only a few hundred pages of information stand between the literate and the illiterate, between dependence and autonomy. (143)

Hirsch does not go on to draw the appropriate conclusion, which is that the infinitude of information in our culture corresponds to, is the "postmodern condition" of, the irreducible heterogeneity of the culture. The handy "finiteness" of the list is the ideological denial of that heterogeneity.

9. It has been both instructive and alarming in this context to read the work of Michael W. Apple, *Teachers and Texts: A Political Economy of Class and Gender Relations in Education* (New York: Routledge, 1988), or Stanley Aronowitz and Henry Giroux, *Education Under Siege: The Conservative and Radical Debate over Schooling* (South Hadley, Mass.: Bergin & Garvey, 1985), on the problem of curriculum at the primary and secondary levels of the American educational system. The absence of these names from the debate about the canon, and indeed the absence of comment about the relation between the university curriculum and the curriculum at lower levels of the system, testifies to how entirely the debate about the canon has been conducted in the realm of the pedagogic imaginary of university teachers.

ELIZABETH HARDWICK

Wind from the Prairie

FROM THE NEW YORK REVIEW OF BOOKS

Roll along, Prairie Moon,
Roll along, while I croon.

AROUND World War I, writers from the American middle western states began to appear on the literary scene. In fiction, there were Dreiser, Sinclair Lewis, and Sherwood Anderson, and also the three known as the "prairie poets," Carl Sandburg, Vachel Lindsay, and Edgar Lee Masters.

Looking into the new biography of Carl Sandburg, a work of exhaustive, definitive coziness in the current American mode of entranced biographical research, I was reminded of having some years ago taken from the library stacks a curiosity, a biography of Lindsay written by Edgar Lee Masters. If Carl Sandburg may be said to have managed shrewdly the transactions of his declamatory, bardic career as a national treasure born in Illinois on a corn-husk mattress, the other two rose and fell disastrously, and literally. Vachel Lindsay committed suicide and Masters died in want, having been found broke and sick in the Chelsea Hotel in New York and rescued to die in a nursing home.

The two men, Lindsay and Masters, are not quite soulmates. Their union is geographical, a territorial circumstantial linkage to a mythographic Middle West, the putative spiritual grasslands of the vast native country. Lindsay was a naive, manic evangelist, preaching the Gospel of Beauty and carrying with him on his incredible cross-country hikes the Christian fundamentalism and

Anti-Saloon teachings of his youth. Along with, of course, Illinois, the prairie, the conviction of being the voice of some real America, *in situ,* that must be honored, as if under threat of extinction by a flood. As a versifier, he had no more caution than a hobo hitching a ride, but somehow his voice prevailed for a time, even with some of the respected critics of the day. He appeared and appeared, willing to recite at a high school reunion as well as in London, where, according to a later biographer, Eleanor Ruggles, "he and his mother met Robert Bridges, venerable laureate and defender of the tongue [sic], and John Masefield, always Vachel's admirer, came in from Boars Hill to pay his respects." Feverish days, but toward the end in Washington, D.C., an audience of two hundred walked out, puzzling the performer and Edgar Lee Masters, but attributed in the Ruggles biography to a microphone failure of which the poet was unaware. A miserable moment, for as Robert Frost, a rival from the Northeast, observed, "Hell is a half-filled auditorium."

Edgar Lee Masters, for a good part of his life a successful lawyer in Chicago, was, one would need to say, a lot smarter than Vachel Lindsay and certainly more worldly — but then everyone was more worldly than Lindsay. Masters was in religion a freethinker, set against the "hypocrisy" of the preachers, even more exasperated by the Temperance Movement, and along the way set against puritanical sexual inhibitions. He was a handsome man who, step by hesitating step, nevertheless made a rashly uncomfortable marriage to a fundamentalist, teetotaler young woman. He had children, stayed on, was unfaithful, listing in his autobiography nearly as many female loves as Goethe; finally divorced, and remarried a young woman, indeed thirty years younger than he. Lindsay was one of those too-friendly boosters with their often strange imperviousness and faltering sense of the appropriate. Masters was splenetic, the cemetery headstone his natural memorial, cranky in opinion, and although he was very productive and for a time immensely successful, there was in his life a feeling of being undervalued, and even of seeing the whole country in an enormous displacement from virtue, pioneer and otherwise.

Of Lindsay, Masters said he was "impelled to write something about the poet who was native to Illinois, as I am in reality, and who knew the same people and the same culture that I do, and who practiced the art of poetry, as I have, in the same part of America, and under the same social and political conditions." In the end, as he reaches Lindsay's declining audience and death, he begins to see the life as a social rather than a personal tragedy, to view the native "singer" as a victim of the East, the money-grubbing, alienated world that preferred the poems of Robert Frost and E. A. Robinson, poets Masters finds essentially "English" in tone and landscape rather than American.

There's more to it than that from this strange man about his stranger fellow bard:

> The motley stocks and alien breeds which have taken America cannot be American until there is an America to mold them into Americans. . . .
>
> Lindsay might sing himself hoarse of the old courthouse America, the old horse and buggy America, the America of the Sante Fé Trail, of Johnny Appleseed. . . . Did the East, did these alien stocks want to be American? This is what Lindsay was up against. In this connection mention must be made of the Jews who are enormously numerous, powerful and influential. Jews are not Americans in the sense that the Jews are English or French, according to habitat. . . .

Ezra Pound described Vachel Lindsay as a "plain man in gum overshoes with a touching belief in W. J. Bryan." Yes, there was "Bryan, Bryan, Bryan, Bryan," the poem celebrating the Free Silver populist, fundamentalist, and prohibitionist in his losing campaign against McKinley. Almost three hundred lines in which Bryan is seen as "the prairie avenger . . . smashing Plymouth Rock with his boulders from the West." His defeat was the "victory of Plymouth Rock and all those inbred landlord stocks" (perhaps it was) and also, in a wild extension, somehow the defeat of the "blue bells of the Rockies and the blue bonnets of old Texas."

Lindsay's life was one of intense, sentimental aggressiveness: and yet there is something unprotected about him. His unanchored enthusiasm has the dismaying aspect of being genuine and unforced, a sort of hysterical innocence, or so it seems. The cheerful, round-faced, fair-haired country boy was in fact town bred, born in Springfield, Illinois. Fate put his birthplace next to the house in which Lincoln had lived and this had the effect of igniting the boy like a firecracker — the nearness to the great, solemn son of the prairie, like himself, the hallowed walker of the streets of Springfield. Lincoln in Illinois had quite a contrary effect on Edgar Lee Masters, who wrote a long, scathing biography of the fallen president, composed with the racing eloquence of contempt for the man and for the "tyrannous plutocracy" that followed the Civil War.

Both Lindsay and Masters came from professional families. Masters's father was a self-made lawyer, a conscientious man of some influence in Illinois and given, at least in part, to liberal causes and worthy cases. The Lindsay family was an odder combination of beliefs and habits. The father, as a young man in impecunious circumstances, worked his way through an Ohio medical school, set up practice in Illinois, and, after the death of his first wife, somehow saved enough for further study in Vienna. On the boat going to Europe, he met his future wife, a teacher of art and other subjects in Kentucky. Throughout their lives, with or without their children, the couple traveled quite a lot, going several times to Europe and even as far as Japan and China, but there were less cosmopolitan strains in the mother. She passed on to her son the ornamental, provincial "art-loving" claim of certain small-town American wives, and also a good measure of the missionary qualities he displayed. Mrs. Lindsay was the organizer of church spectacles, liked to officiate in group meetings, attend conferences, and so on.

Her family was attached to the Campbellite Church, also known as the Disciples of Christ, or just as the Christian Church. The church had been founded by Alexander Campbell and his son Thomas, originally Presbyterians and then, coming to believe in baptism by immersion, uniting their flock with the Baptists, before finally breaking away — in one of those organizational disputes so peculiar to the Protestant denominations — to found their own Campbellite sect. From these roots Vachel Lindsay got his fundamentalism and prohibitionism, the Gospel of Beauty, and a flair for expounding preacher-style. He was sent to the Art Institute in Chicago and later, in New York in 1905, studied with William Merrett Chase and Robert Henri, but did not make notable progress as a painter or as a cartoonist.

All the time Lindsay had been writing verses in his hymn-tune rhythms, reciting at the YMCA, and turning himself into a peddler. With his verses and drawings, the plain, open-faced, clean young man wandered the streets of New York, knocking on the doors of fish markets, Chinese laundries, bakeries, stopping people to listen to his wares, canvassing, as it were, Hell's Kitchen. A curious, impervious nuisance, bringing to mind the intrepid appeals of the Jehovah's Witness bell-ringers. And then he began his years of quite literally tramping across the country, pamphlets and verses for sale, doing missionary work for the Gospel of Beauty. He carried with him a character reference from the YMCA.

It was in California that Lindsay learned of the death of General William Booth, founder of the Salvation Army. And thus he came to write one of his first bizarre incantations, an unaccountable success for which the mind glancing back on our literary history is, well, *dumbstruck.*

GENERAL WILLIAM BOOTH ENTERS INTO HEAVEN.

> (To be sung to the tune of "The Blood of the Lamb"
> with indicated instrument)

The work opens with bass drumbeats and:

> Booth led boldly with his big bass drum —
> (Are you washed in the blood of the Lamb?)
> The Saints smiled bravely and they said: "He's come."
> (Are you washed in the blood of the Lamb?)

The thing flows on apace and concludes:

> He saw King Jesus. They were face to face,
> And he knelt a-weeping in that holy place.
> Are you washed in the blood of the Lamb?

This submission appeared in an early issue of *Poetry,* and Harriet Monroe in the annual prize-giving of 1913 awarded it $100. A prize for $250 went to William Butler Yeats, the latter having been pushed for by Ezra Pound. Sometime later, when Yeats was in Chicago, Miss Monroe invited Lindsay to a dinner at which the various important writers on hand were invited. That evening Vachel Lindsay recited the whole of "The Congo," and was ap-

parently "well-received" in spite of its being over two hundred
fiercely resounding lines. This most extraordinary embarrassment in our cultural history achieved a personally orated dissemination scarcely to be credited. Anywhere and everywhere he
went with it — the Chamber of Commerce, high schools, ladies'
clubs, the Lincoln Day Banquet in Springfield, the Players Club
in New York, where Masters tells that its noise greatly irritated
certain members.

"The Congo" is the supreme folly of Lindsay's foolhardy career. There is a sad, no doubt unconscious complacency in its
concussive hilarity, the compositional shove coming from

> an allusion in a sermon by my pastor, F. W. Burnham, to the heroic
> life and death of Ray Eldred. Eldred was a missionary of the Disciples
> of Christ who perished while swimming a treacherous branch of the
> Congo.

The work is subtitled "A Study of the Negro Race," and part one
lies under the heading "Their Basic Savagery." The imagery, if
such it can be called, is black-face American minstrel, except for
a strophe about Leopold of Belgium in hell with his hands cut
off.

With a "deep rolling bass," the prairie evangelist sets out on his
crusade:

> Fat black bucks in a wine-barrel room,
> Barrel-house kings, with feet unstable . . .
> Beat an empty barrel with the handle of a broom . . .
> Boomlay, boomlay, boomlay, Boom. . . .
>
> Then I saw the Congo, creeping through the black,
> cutting through the jungle with a golden track. . . .
>
> Tattooed cannibals danced in files;
> Then I heard the boom of the blood-lust song. . . .
> Boom, kill the Arabs,
> Boom, kill the white men,
> Hoo, Hoo, Hoo. . . .
> Mumbo-Jumbo will hoo-doo you.

The second section has the title "Their Irrepressible High
Spirits." Here, on the Congo River, we run into a round of crap-
shooting, whoops and yells, witch-men dressed to kill, "cakewalk

princes" in tall silk hats, coal-black maidens with pearls in their hair, and more Boom, Boom, Boom. In the third section, "The Hope of Their Religion," the Apostles appear in coats of mail and, to the tune of "Hark, ten thousand harps and voices," ordain that "Mumbo-Jumbo will die in the jungle." The forests, the beasts, and the "savages" fade away, whispering, in a pianissimo, the dying strains of "Mumbo-Jumbo will hoo-doo you." The "bucks" are thus converted, all now down-home Campbellites.

What the far-flung audiences made of this infernal indiscretion is hard to imagine. There is always a market for "carrying on" in public, as we can confirm today. No doubt there was more condescension in the air than the reports would suggest. A performance was organized in 1920 at Oxford University by Robert Graves and can be read as an elaborate prank on the pretensions of the dons rather than as a tribute to the prairie poet — indeed, the sweating reiterations of the amateur elocutionist might recall Tom Thumb at Queen Victoria's court.

In any case, scholars can excavate in the old magazines many alarming commendations of this native genius, fresh voice, America's Homer, and so on. Harriet Monroe, a promoter of poetry and of the Middle West in tandem, wrote the introduction to the book publication of *The Congo and Other Poems*. The praise is short but unfortunately ranging in reference like a kangaroo leaping over rich and spacious plains. Whistler and Whitman are called forth before a landing by Miss Monroe on the "old Greek precedent of the half-chanted lyric." The "Greek precedent" is one of those critical jokes like "the Jane Austen of the Upper West Side," but the claim of the prairie poets, and subsequent idolators, to the example of Whitman is an unending irritation.

"The Santa-Fé Trail" is another noisy work, the theme seeming to be that the sound of the automobile, Crack, Crack, Crack, is trying without success to overwhelm the song "sweet, sweet, sweet" of a local Southwest bird known as Rachel-Jane. Then there is a salute to the firemen, "Clang, Clang, Clang," and an evocation of Jesus in "I Heard Immanuel Singing."

> He was ruddy like a shepherd.
> His bold young face how fair.
> Apollo of the silver bow
> Had not such flowing hair.

Tramping and reciting, forever in manic locomotion with note-book in hand to scribble whatever came into his head, head to be laid down at night on a YMCA pillow, Lindsay had little time left for romantic life. Actually Lindsay comes across as more than a little girl-shy in spite of crushes here and there, one falling on the poet Sara Teasdale. But she married a rich shoe manufac-turer and for a time was set up grandly in New York, until she too was mowed down by the drastic scythe of taste and died di-vorced, no longer rich, reclusive and embittered. At last Lindsay married a young woman from Spokane, a high-school teacher of English and Latin. She was twenty-three and he was forty-six. They had two daughters and were always in financial distress, since his income came largely from recitations and a good por-tion went to agents and expenses. On the road, the listeners for-ever calling for "Congo" and "General Booth," Lindsay was to experience the pathos of repetition: exhaustion and insolvency.

Along the way, uphill and downhill, Lindsay wrote a most in-teresting book, fortunately in prose: *The Art of the Moving Picture,* first issued in 1915, revised in 1922, and later reprinted with an excellent appreciation of its worth in the introduction by Stanley Kauffmann. After the rant and carelessness of the verses, Lind-say concentrated his mind on the movies. Here it is, he must have decided as he rested his vocal cords in the darkness of the old cinemas — American, popular, infinite in variety, flung out to the folk with a prodigality very similar to his own production methods. He tries to organize what the films can do, sort out the types, explain the power of directors like D. W. Griffith.

For instance, "The Action Picture":

> In the action picture there is no adequate means for the development of full-grown personal passion. The Action Pictures are falsely adver-tised as having heart-interest, or abounding in tragedy, but though the actors glower and wrestle and even if they are the most skillful lambasters in the profession, the audience gossips and chews gum.

There are the Intimate Photoplay, the Splendor Pictures, which divide into Crowd Splendor, Patriotic Splendor, Religious Splendor, and so on. Concerning the intimate photoplay, he writes:

> Though the intimate and friendly photoplay may be carried out of doors to a row of loafers in front of the country store, or the gossiping

streets of the village, it takes its origin and theory from the snugness of the interior. The restless reader replies that he has seen photoplays that showed ballrooms that were grandiose, not the least cozy. These are to be classed as out-of-door scenery so far as theory goes, and are discussed under the head of Splendor Pictures. The intimate Motion Picture . . . is gossip *in extremis*.

The movies and their vagrant images for him, the lonely traveling man, had the seductive power of the saloon for others of his kind. He was seduced into a contemplation and wish for coherence absent from his verse-making. Thus he finds "noble views of the sea," common to early camera effects, allied to "the sea of humanity spectacles":

> the whirling of dancers in ballrooms, handkerchief-waving masses of people on balconies, the hat-waving political ratification meetings, ragged, glowering strikers, and gossiping, dickering people in the market-place. Only Griffith and his disciples can do these as well as almost any manager can reproduce the ocean. Yet the sea of humanity is dramatically blood-brother to the Pacific, the Atlantic, or Mediterranean. . . . So, in *The Birth of the Nation*, the Ku Klux Klan dashes down the road as powerfully as Niagara pours over the cliff.

A film version of Ibsen's *Ghosts* came to town, and Lindsay reports that it was not Ibsen and should have been advertised under the title "The Iniquities of the Fathers. An American Drama of Eugenics, in a Palatial Setting." The style of these reflections, offhand and colloquial, is usefully attuned to the subject and to his casual, but transfixed, attentions. Returning from a showing of Larry Trimble's *The Battle Hymn of the Republic*, he will record that the girl at the piano played "Under the Shade of the Old Apple Tree" throughout. Among the virtues of the films will be their usefulness, nonalcoholic, to the working classes, who in the heat of summer, "under the wind of an electric fan, can witness everything from a burial at Westminster to the birthday parade of the ruler of the land of Swat."

Los Angeles is the Boston, the Florence of this great flowering, and the stars are national monuments. He pens a tribute to Mary Pickford, "doll divine," which will proceed to rhyme with "valentine." And Blanche Sweet: "Stately are her wiles / filling oafs with wisdom, / Saving souls with smiles." *The Art of the Moving Picture* is the prairie singer's finest, most lasting tribute to the American West, to Hollywood.

He was fifty-two years old when he committed suicide. It is not easy to be certain what was going on in his mind, but there seem to have been frightening mood swings, ups and downs, suspicions followed by remorse, in every way a sad collapse. Doctors were called in, but before a decision could be made for treatment, Lindsay drank Lysol, saying, "I got them before they got me — they can just try to explain this if they can."

Edgar Lee Masters was asked by Lindsay's wife to write a biography and given access to the papers — a very large fund of jottings, since Vachel Lindsay showed a self-preoccupation quite precocious, if that is the way to look at his keeping a daily diary almost from the time he first learned to write. Masters's work is rich in thorny attitudes, and that gives it a certain cross-grained interest, especially when compared to the ruthless coverage of the pertinent and impertinent, the sense of being on a long trip with the subject in the family car, that defines the research of Lindsay's other biographer, Eleanor Ruggles, as it does so many other conventional and academic biographies.

Lindsay's limitations are, if not stressed, at least acknowledged, when Masters writes:

> Lindsay dwelt forever in cuckoo cloudland. . . . He never grew up. The curled darling became a man of great emotional strength; but the memory of himself as the apple of his mother's eye, as the child wonder of grammar school. . . . Jesus, with him, after all, was a sort of Santa Claus grown up and made suitable for adult wonder and devotion.

On the other hand we are asked to view the fantastical footnote, Lindsay, in conspiratorial terms:

> Not being Eastern American he made only a slight impact upon it; and after the first excitement about his poetry subsided he was treated with supercilious indifference, and the field he had broken and harrowed and sowed was taken and reaped by pro-English artists. . . . They preferred the Arthurian legends to Johnny Appleseed and Andrew Jackson.

The accent of grievance, neatly correspondent to Masters's cast of mind, is not to the point in the matter of Vachel Lindsay, and in any case the shape of an individual career is mixed with so many contingencies it cannot easily support a translation to the general. But all that is nothing beside the fact that if poor Lindsay had some sort of talents, they were not for poetry. He did not write poetry, he wrote jingles and hymns and scenarios for his public appearances. The true melancholy of the life lies in the broad encouragement of his naiveté, the span of his performances which would inevitably weary. His books were published, he was "famous," and yet somehow he remained a door-to-door peddler.

An academic study of Edgar Lee Masters* has chapter titles that run "Masters, Goethe, and the Greeks"; "The Natural Child of Walt Whitman"; "Shelley and Masters." That's the way things go, these wondrous, inflationary assignations coming about from the list of Masters's readings. The peculiar deformities of the scholars' trade, at least of those with a provincial aspect to their orderings, are indeed the disabilities of the lover, freshly enthralled. And as the multiculturalists assume their posts in the academy, we may see more loving resurrections from the dust, rising to drape their togas in the Pantheon. Masters himself can speak, as a throwaway, of Vachel Lindsay's "very Platonic sense of shadows" and find him "more Greek than German."

Edgar Lee Masters was born in 1869, and his major work, *Spoon River Anthology*, did not appear until 1915, although a few of the portraits had been published earlier under a pseudonym. He entered his father's profession of law and practiced in Chicago for almost thirty years. He was unhappily married and wrote in his autobiography: "Somehow little by little I got the feeling that my wife in spite of her almost meek compliance was enervating me and cutting off my hair and putting out my eyes." A bitter divorce quite naturally finally came about, and Masters moved to New York with his very young bride and settled into the Chelsea Hotel, his wife going back and forth to teach in Pennsylvania.

In many ways a companionable man, friend of Mencken, Dreiser, and others who liked their cigars and schnapps, member of the Players Club, somehow Masters seemed to drift into

*Ronald Primeau, *Beyond "Spoon River": The Legacy of Edgar Lee Masters* (University of Texas Press, 1981).

reclusion. We may notice that although he was in partnership for almost eight years with Clarence Darrow in Chicago, the well-known lawyer does not appear in the autobiography. Masters's son, by the first wife, in a memoir attributes this gap to the scandal of the divorce and the appearance on the scene of her replacement, some thirty years younger. Perhaps, he suggests, Darrow took at best a neutral attitude and the estrangement followed. Also the son tells of his difficulties in getting through to his father at the Chelsea, and when they did meet, Ellen Masters, now his stepmother, did not seem to be on hand. On hand, however, was another young woman, Alice Davis, who lived in the hotel and helped with manuscripts and whatever else she helped with.

In 1944 the *New York Times* printed a story telling that Masters had been taken to Bellevue Hospital suffering from pneumonia and malnutrition. The Authors League and the American Academy came to his rescue, the wife packed him off to a Pennsylvania nursing home near where she was teaching, and there he died at the age of eighty-one. Not a happy roundup, even if there is a hint of self-willed recoil and collapse when one remembers the great industry Masters showed throughout his life in the production of works in many forms: verse, plays, novels, biography, and autobiography.

Spoon River Anthology (1915) — a book could scarcely be more of a success. Said to have sold more copies than any previous work of American poetry, it was translated into all the European languages as well as into Arabic, Korean, and Chinese; also transformed for the stage and used as the libretto for an opera, performed at La Scala. The book is an "anthology" of the gravestones around Spoon River, an area near Lewistown, Illinois, where Masters grew up. The dead come forth to speak the epitaphs of their lives, each one a short free-verse recollection, a sort of *conte*, very often remembering injuries or spoken with a surly ruefulness. The unquiet graves, some 214 of them, "all, all, are sleeping on the hill," were thought to be somewhat cynical and degrading to the quality of life lived in the Illinois villages of Masters's youth and from which he drew his ruminating characters.

The first one is "Hod Putt," who died by hanging for a robbery in his days of poverty after a life of toil. Seeing an opportunity for the last word, he notes with satisfaction that he lies next to a crook who prospered from clever uses of the possibilities of bankruptcy. "Now we who took the bankrupt law in our respective ways, / Sleep peacefully side by side." The verses today strike one not as acerb so much as generally soulful, "filled with longing" poems; good, simple people seeking transcendence. "Of what use is it / To rid one's self of the world, / When no soul may ever escape the eternal destiny of life?"

The public appeal of the work must have been in the framing: first the lachrymal country churchyard with the darkening granite of the tombstones lying in random placement as in village life; then the brief, anecdotal summations, many of them reading like those civil court cases that scrape the skins of the litigants into eternity. To this must be added the candid moral framing of the little stories, the accent on the scorned, the unlucky, the eccentric from whom the smothering "hypocrisy" of the village would exact its punishments.

The "valiant" departed one, "Jefferson Howard," is "Foe of the church with its charnel darkness, / Friend of the human touch of the tavern" and hounded by the "dominating forces" — Republicans, Calvinists, merchants, bankers. In Spoon River fate deals out repetitive cards, like the equalizing aspect of death itself. The aesthetic default of the work, pressing upon the mind as one name after another approaches its declaration, is that it could go on forever, the flat proseness of the language contributing, as the rocks in the sod are turned over again and again. There was indeed a second collection of Spoon River tales, a replication and consequent deflation of the original invention. (Another monologue-portrait was published during these years, "The Love Song of J. Alfred Prufrock.")

A biography, *Lincoln: The Man*, appeared in 1931. Hara-kiri, blood on the floor, Masters's as well as Lincoln's, an insult to the prairie, to Illinois, and perhaps to Carl Sandburg, or so Vachel Lindsay thought. Sandburg's Lincoln book, Volume I, *The Prairie Years*, had been out for six years, and if its success embittered Masters, the emotion had its source in the picture of Lincoln rather than in the author's success in the market.

Masters's character is a puzzle, and it is hard to understand why this attractive and intelligent man, successful as a lawyer and a writer, should be such a sorehead. He is the village iconoclast, atheist, free-lover, and more than a bit paranoid in the matter of local and national forces. He has *ideas* as some have freckles, and the book on Lincoln puts many of them on display with a good deal of eloquence, however alienating. The notion of the book is that the Civil War should not have been fought and that the aftermath, the domination of plutocrats, merchants, bankers, and the later imperial adventurism, was a disastrous drift. "Hebraic-Puritanism" is Masters's phrase for the moral insufficiency of the country. By this he does not appear to indicate anti-Semitism; instead he felt a corrosive resentment of the Bible, Old Testament and New, and its power to shape the ethical climate of the nation. After the Civil War,

> as if in sublime malice, the choking weeds of Hebraic-Puritanism were sown; and thus the evils of empire and ancient privileges began to thrive, scarcely before the new wheat was started. Ages may be required for creative vision to stand externally in this field and its epos. . . .

The overwhelming offense of the biography was its picture of the character of Lincoln, who is seen as a creature of swamp-bred shrewdness, a sort of wary, calculating Snopes, retaining in the midst of certain superficial refinements the qualities of his father, Thomas Lincoln, who out of shiftlessness had sunk into the fetid habits of the "poor white" class. Masters stresses the fact that Nancy Hanks, Lincoln's mother, was illegitimate, and in the enveloping mist of parental uncertainty had discovered or imagined her supposed father to be a well-bred Virginia planter. Lincoln claimed the presence of his more promising qualities to have come from the absent grandfather. "Lincoln was profoundly ashamed of the poverty of his youth, and of the sordid surroundings in which he grew up." Thus his life was ruled by the determination to rise above his beginnings, "unlike the more honest Andrew Jackson and Walt Whitman."

The distinction and beauty of Lincoln's prose and of his platform style must be conceded — and also reduced. For Masters this accomplishment and talent are suffused and diseased with the poison of the Bible: "Lincoln, whose only literacy was out of the Bible, and who developed an oratory from it, inspired by its artifice of emotional reiteration, and equipped with its sacred curses and its dreadful prophecies, its appeal to moralities where there was no thought, no real integrity . . ." The Gettysburg Address is unfavorably compared to Pericles' funeral oration and subjected to a textual analysis on the matter of truth: "It was not true that our fathers in 1776 had brought forth a new nation; for in that year our fathers brought forth thirteen new nations, each of which was a sovereign state." Lincoln as a statesman and a thinker is accused of the "Hebraic-Puritan principle of assuming to act as one's brother's keeper, when the real motive was to become one's brother's jailer."

Out of indignation and obsession, Masters dug his own grave and sadly inscribed his own tombstone with the acid of the Spoon River meters. The resentment of the Civil War soldier "Knowlt Hoheimer," killed in battle and lying up on the hill, might be his epitaph:

> Rather a thousand times the county jail
> Than to lie under this marble figure with wings,
> And this granite pedestal
> Bearing the words, "Pro Patria."
> What do they mean, anyway?

Carl Sandburg lived to be eighty-nine years old, and he spent those years going here and yon, a hardy tumbleweed of a populist, blown by the wind across the plains. More than forty books to his credit and what for some would have been a burdensome accretion of honors, each one to be accepted and attended like the duties on the court calendar. Of course he was sustained by the old pioneer energy, and his act as an early pop-art king, writing free-verse poems, collecting and performing *The American Songbag*, was inexhaustible. The seven volumes on the life of Lincoln — "a folk biography," some critic was happy to describe it — spread over more than ten years, but of course he was on the hoof a good deal of that time.

These reflections come about from the strenuous busyness of Penelope Niven's new biography of Sandburg: over seven hundred pages, followed by another hundred of notes. The effort is a sort of rival to Sandburg's *Lincoln: Prairie Years, Chicago Years, National Hero Years.* Professor Niven says in her preface that her previous scholarship was of the sort to exclude the claims of this bygone figure, fallen from eminence, but "a decade after his death, I went to his Carolina mountain home," and then it appears that she fell into the corncrib, so to speak; that is, the vast Sandburg papers in libraries, in possession of the family, lying about in cartons. After this great haystack, the fodder of the book, was pulled apart, she began the Carl Sandburg Oral History Project of more than 150 interviews.

Having gone through the heap, settled into the poet and each member of the family, reliving their nights and days with an intrusive intimacy, the biographer will want to put each scrap down. The index cards or data sheets come to have a claim of their own, and the affirmation, the yes, yes, of Sandburg's scurry through life is her own affirming journey. The book is tedious and sentimental and long, long, four score and ten years long. She likes descriptions such as "hearty and vigorous," or "erect and vigorous" — and who can doubt that's exactly what the wily old campaigner was, even though the biographer had never encountered him in life. The scholar of the papers, of *the life of,* knows, like some celestial Xerox machine, details that consciousness erases overnight.

One of the amusements of this biography is that it is a kind of informal history of the radio and television shows of the period, not unlike listening to the "golden oldies." Sandburg hit them all: the *George Jessel Show,* the *Milton Berle Show,* the *Dave Garroway Show,* the *Ed Sullivan Show,* the *Bell Telephone Hour.* Ed Murrow comes in more than once, and with Norman Corwin, the prince of radio Americana, Sandburg had a "fruitful" relationship. At the Philharmonic Auditorium in Los Angeles he was introduced by Edgar Bergen (sold out, standing ovation); the publication of the *Second American Songbag* had an introduction by Bing Crosby. Penelope Niven again and again calls Sandburg the "eternal hobo," but as his fame grows he is usually on his way to the studio or to the auditorium.

For a number of years, or for a good part of them, the prairie poet was in Hollywood under contract. Two producers from MGM sought his services for an "epic film about the USA," an undertaking not designed to be a mere motion picture, but a "great, ringing message to the people." Sandburg was to write a novel, following in shape a scenario written by Sidney Franklin. The novel would be published and then made into a film. For this he was given $100,000, and the project was a "challenge Sandburg could not resist." The end of it all, after story conferences, residence in the film colony, after years and years, was that the novel appeared under the name of *Remembrance Rock*, 1,067 pages of the American Dream, never made into a film, a critical failure, but in no way a money loss for the author. The second Hollywood adventure was a year and a half of work with George Stevens on *The Greatest Story Ever Told*. "HE was not only a pioneer, but an adventurer and an explorer, in his own words a Seeker," the biographer writes, her words ever echoing those of her subject.

Sandburg made a bold identification between his own career and the history of the great country itself. Roosevelt wanted him to run for Congress, we are told. He collected Harvard and Yale honorary degrees, among many others, Pulitzer Prizes for history and poetry, invitations to address a session of Congress — a lot of this adulation arising from his assuming the mantle of Lincoln as a friend of the Family of Man, and so on. He missed out on a few things such as the Nobel Prize and felt a certain annoyance when President Kennedy, whom he had supported, invited Robert Frost to read a poem at the Inaugural rather than himself.

Oscar Wilde called the prairies "blotting paper" and if they are so looked at, Carl Sandburg can be said to have sucked up all the nutrients in the soil. His beginning voice in *Chicago Poems* (1916), celebrating the "City of the Big Shoulders" and lamenting the lot of the dispossessed, would sustain him, it seems, into the Depression period, and the years of the New Deal. As a child of Swedish immigrants, Sandburg was part of the Social-Democratic movement in the middle western states, and that marked the rhythm of his life: the little man, the striker, the dreamer, the immigrant toiler, friend of all mankind. His particular politics were New Deal and the Democratic party. On and on he goes, each of his affirmations self-affirming.

The People, Yes is 179 pages long, with 107 sections — a statistical plenitude as typical of the prairie poets as of the wheat acreage of the region. In his notes, Sandburg writes of the work as coming out of "Piers Plowman, seven hundred years ago, a far better handbook and manual of democracy than either Dante or Donne" — a statement of such historical incongruity that it raises questions of familiarity with the last two and maybe also the first of the antecedents named. No matter, the sprawl of the work is a "modern epic" and an "odyssey deep into the American Experience," in the reading by the biographer. In some ways her spacious accommodations arouse sympathy, since an attempt to analyze Sandburg's lines flowing down the pages would be profitless. His people, yes or no, are actually just indentured servants, and they did his work, sunup to sundown. The poet's acres and the house in the Carolinas are "open to the public as a National Park and National Historic Site." And that's it.

To spend time with the metered, or unmetered, minstrels of the Middle West is to invite a special melancholy, one not only aesthetic, although that defect predominates, since they come into history as poets, not as preachers, philosophers, politicians, or entertainers. Birth or youth in Illinois marked them, a tattoo appropriate enough as experience, the turf of the imagination. Still, they were not ordinary citizens, state proud, but ones making a claim for what were, for the most part, hasty, repetitive, and formless verses, unlike, for instance, the inspirations of Hart Crane of Ohio.

Elitism, which is merely the existence of exceptional talents, will here be scorned as a threat to the demotic voices of the prairie. Of course they too, by publication, must make their entrance into the long tradition, an inescapable transition in the arts, like the onset of puberty. As outlandishly successful as these poets were, this happy circumstance was, as usual, not sufficient, because of the wish for a higher validation that haunts the dreams of the popular in the manner of a concealed felony.

We note that the three have a proprietary feeling about the country, a longing to transform its restless genetic material into a *folk*, to fashion the inchoate strains into a hardy stock with the name "American" on it, like a packet of sunflower seeds. A futile parochialism for a nation that has ever been, to expropriate a phrase from Kafka, "a cage seeking a bird."

VICKI HEARNE

What's Wrong with Animal Rights

FROM HARPER'S MAGAZINE

NOT ALL happy animals are alike. A Doberman going over a hurdle after a small wooden dumbbell is sleek, all arcs of harmonious power. A basset hound cheerfully performing the same exercise exhibits harmonies of a more lugubrious nature. There are chimpanzees who love precision the way musicians or fanatical housekeepers or accomplished hypochondriacs do; others for whom happiness is a matter of invention and variation — chimp vaudevillians. There is a rhinoceros whose happiness, as near as I can make out, is in needing to be trained every morning, all over again, or else he "forgets" his circus routine, and in this you find a clue to the slow, deep, quiet chuckle of his happiness and to the glory of the beast. Happiness for Secretariat is in his ebullient bound, that joyful length of stride. For the draft horse or the weight-pull dog, happiness is of a different shape, more awesome and less obviously intelligent. When the pulling horse is at its most intense, the animal goes into himself, allocating all of the educated power that organizes his desire to dwell in fierce and delicate intimacy with that power, leans into the harness, and MAKES THAT SUCKER MOVE.

If we are speaking of human beings and use the phrase "animal happiness," we tend to mean something like "creature comforts." The emblems of this are the golden retriever rolling in the grass, the horse with his nose deep in the oats, the kitty by the fire. Creature comforts are important to animals — "Grub first, then ethics" is a motto that would describe many a wise Labrador retriever, and I have a pit bull named Annie whose continual quest for the perfect pillow inspires her to awesome feats. But there is something more to animals, a capacity for satisfactions that come from work in the fullest sense — what is known in philosophy and in this country's Declaration of Independence as "happiness." This is a sense of personal achievement, like the satisfaction felt by a good wood-carver or a dancer or a poet or an accomplished dressage horse. It is a happiness that, like the artist's, must come from something within the animal, something trainers call "talent." Hence, it cannot be imposed on the animal. But it is also something that does not come *ex nihilo*. If it had not been a fairly ordinary thing, in one part of the world, to teach young children to play the pianoforte, it is doubtful that Mozart's music would exist.

Happiness is often misunderstood as a synonym for pleasure or as an antonym for suffering. But Aristotle associated happiness with ethics — codes of behavior that urge us toward the sensation of getting it right, a kind of work that yields the "click" of satisfaction upon solving a problem or surmounting an obstacle. In his *Ethics,* Aristotle wrote, "If happiness is activity in accordance with excellence, it is reasonable that it should be in accordance with the highest excellence." Thomas Jefferson identified the capacity for happiness as one of the three fundamental rights on which all others are based: "life, liberty, and the pursuit of happiness."

I bring up this idea of happiness as a form of work because I am an animal trainer, and work is the foundation of the happiness a trainer and an animal discover together. I bring up these words also because they cannot be found in the lexicon of the animal-rights movement. This absence accounts for the uneasiness toward the movement of most people, who sense that rights advocates have a point but take it too far when they liberate snails or charge that goldfish at the county fair are suffering. But the problem with the animal-rights advocates is not that they take it too far; it's that they've got it all wrong.

Animal rights are built upon a misconceived premise that rights were created to prevent us from unnecessary suffering. You can't find an animal-rights book, video, pamphlet, or rock concert in which someone doesn't mention the Great Sentence, written by Jeremy Bentham in 1789. Arguing in favor of such rights, Bentham wrote: "The question is not, Can they *reason?* nor, can they *talk?* but, can they suffer?"

The logic of the animal-rights movement places suffering at the iconographic center of a skewed value system. The thinking of its proponents — given eerie expression in a virtually sado-pornographic sculpture of a tortured monkey that won a prize for its compassionate vision — has collapsed into a perverse conundrum. Today the loudest voices calling for — demanding — the destruction of animals are the humane organizations. This is an inevitable consequence of the apotheosis of the drive to relieve suffering: death is the ultimate release. To compensate for their contradictions, the humane movement has demonized, in this century and the last, those who made animal happiness their business: veterinarians, trainers, and the like. We think of Louis Pasteur as the man whose work saved you and me and your dog and cat from rabies, but antivivisectionists of the time claimed that rabies increased in areas where there were Pasteur Institutes.

An anti-rabies public relations campaign mounted in England in the 1880s by the Royal Society for the Prevention of Cruelty to Animals and other organizations led to orders being issued to club any dog found not wearing a muzzle. England still has her cruel and unnecessary law that requires an animal to spend six months in quarantine before being allowed loose in the country. Most of the recent propaganda about pit bulls — the crazy claim that they "take hold with their front teeth while they chew away with their rear teeth" (which would imply, incorrectly, that they have double jaws) — can be traced to literature published by the Humane Society of the United States during the fall of 1987 and earlier. If your neighbors want your dog or horse impounded and destroyed because he is a nuisance — say the dog barks, or the horse attracts flies — it will be the local Humane Society to whom your neighbors turn for action.

In a way, everyone has the opportunity to know that the history of the humane movement is largely a history of miseries, arrests, prosecutions, and death. The Humane Society is the pound, the place with the decompression chamber or the lethal injections. You occasionally find worried letters about this in Ann Landers's column.

Animal-rights publications are illustrated largely with photographs of two kinds of animals — "Helpless Fluff" and "Agonized Fluff," the two conditions in which some people seem to prefer their animals, because any other version of an animal is too complicated for propaganda. In the introduction to his book *Animal Liberation,* Peter Singer says somewhat smugly that he and his wife have no animals and, in fact, don't much care for them. This is offered as evidence of his objectivity and ethical probity. But it strikes me as an odd, perhaps obscene underpinning for an ethical project that encourages university and high school students to cherish their ignorance of, say, great bird dogs as proof of their devotion to animals.

I would like to leave these philosophers behind, for they are inept connoisseurs of suffering who might revere my Airedale for his capacity to scream when subjected to a blowtorch but not for his wit and courage, not for his natural good manners that are a gentle rebuke to ours. I want to celebrate the moment not long ago when, at his first dog show, my Airedale, Drummer, learned that there can be a public place where his work is respected. I want to celebrate his meticulousness, his happiness upon realizing at the dog show that no one would swoop down upon him and swamp him with the goo-goo excesses known as the "teddy-bear complex" but that people actually got out of his way, gave him room to work. I want to say, "There can be a six-and-a-half-month-old puppy who can care about accuracy, who can be fastidious, and whose fastidiousness will be a foundation for courage later." I want to say, "Leave my puppy alone!"

I want to leave the philosophers behind, but I cannot, in part because the philosophical problems that plague academicians of the animal-rights movement are illuminating. They wonder, do animals have rights or do they have interests? Or, if these rightists lead particularly unexamined lives, they dismiss that question as obvious (yes, of course animals have rights, prima facie) and proceed to enumerate them, James Madison style. This leads to the issuance of bills of rights — the right to an environment, the right not to be used in medical experiments — and other forms of trivialization.

The calculus of suffering can be turned against the philosophers of festering flesh, even in the case of food animals, or exotic animals who perform in movies and circuses. It is true that it hurts to be slaughtered by man, but it doesn't hurt nearly as much as some of the cunningly cruel arrangements meted out by "Mother Nature." In Africa, 75 percent of the lions cubbed do not survive to the age of two. For those who make it to two, the average age at death is ten years. Asali, the movie and TV lioness, was still working at age twenty-one. There are fates worse than death, but twenty-one years of a close working relationship with Hubert Wells, Asali's trainer, is not one of them. Dorset sheep and polled Herefords would not exist at all were they not in a symbiotic relationship with human beings.

A human being living in the "wild" — somewhere, say, without the benefits of medicine and advanced social organization — would probably have a life expectancy of from thirty to thirty-five years. A human being living in "captivity" — in, say, a middle-class neighborhood of what the Centers for Disease Control call a Metropolitan Statistical Area — has a life expectancy of seventy or more years. For orangutans in the wild in Borneo and Malaysia, the life expectancy is thirty-five years; in captivity, fifty years. The wild is not a suffering-free zone or all that frolicsome a location.

The questions asked by animal-rights activists are flawed, because they are built on the concept that the origin of rights is in the avoidance of suffering rather than in the pursuit of happiness. The question that needs to be asked — and that will put us in closer proximity to the truth — is not, do they have rights? or, what are those rights? but rather, what is a right?

Rights originate in committed relationships and can be found, both intact and violated, wherever one finds such relationships — in social compacts, within families, between animals, and between people and nonhuman animals. This is as true when the nonhuman animals in question are lions or parakeets as when they are dogs. It is my Airedale whose excellencies have my attention at the moment, so it is with reference to him that I will consider the question, what is a right?

When I imagine situations in which it naturally arises that A defends or honors or respects B's rights, I imagine situations in which the relationship between A and B can be indicated with a possessive pronoun. I might say, "Leave her alone, she's my daughter" or "That's what she wants, and she is my daughter. I think I am bound to honor her wants." Similarly, "Leave her alone, she's my mother." I am more tender of the happiness of my mother, my father, my child, than I am of other people's family members; more tender of my friends' happinesses than your friends' happinesses, unless you and I have a mutual friend.

Possession of a being by another has come into more and more disrepute, so that the common understanding of one person possessing another is slavery. But the important detail about the kind of possessive pronoun that I have in mind is reciprocity: if I have a friend, she has a friend. If I have a daughter, she has a mother. The possessive does not bind one of us while freeing the other; it cannot do that. Moreover, should the mother reject the daughter, the word that applies is "disown." The form of disowning that most often appears in the news is domestic violence. Parents abuse children; husbands batter wives.

Some cases of reciprocal possessives have built-in limitations, such as "my patient / my doctor" or "my student / my teacher" or "my agent / my client." Other possessive relations are extremely limited but still remarkably binding: "my neighbor" and "my country" and "my president."

The responsibilities and the ties signaled by reciprocal possession typically are hard to dissolve. It can be as difficult to give up an enemy as to give up a friend, and often the one becomes the other, as though the logic of the possessive pronoun outlasts the forms it chanced to take at a given moment, as though we were stuck with one another. In these bindings, nearly inextricable, are found the origin of our rights. They imply a possessiveness but also recognize an acknowledgment by each side of the other's existence.

The idea of democracy is dependent on the citizens' having knowledge of the government; that is, realizing that the government exists and knowing how to claim rights against it. I know this much because I get mail from the government and see its "representatives" running about in uniforms. Whether I actually have any rights in relationship to the government is less clear, but the idea that I do is symbolized by the right to vote. I obey the government, and, in theory, it obeys me, by counting my ballot, reading the *Miranda* warning to me, agreeing to be bound by the Constitution. My friend obeys me as I obey her; the government "obeys" me to some extent, and, to a different extent, I obey it.

What kind of thing can my Airedale, Drummer, have knowledge of? He can know that I exist and through that knowledge can claim his happinesses, with varying degrees of success, both with me and against me. Drummer can also know about larger human or dog communities than the one that consists only of him and me. There is my household — the other dogs, the cats, my husband. I have had enough dogs on campuses to know that he can learn that Yale exists as a neighborhood or village. My older dog, Annie, not only knows that Yale exists but can tell Yalies from townies, as I learned while teaching there during labor troubles.

Dogs can have elaborate conceptions of human social structures, and even of something like their rights and responsibilities within them, but these conceptions are never elaborate enough to construct a rights relationship between a dog and the state, or a dog and the Humane Society. Both of these are concepts that depend on writing and memoranda, officers in uniform, plaques and seals of authority. All of these are literary constructs, and all of them are beyond a dog's ken, which is why the mail carrier who doesn't also happen to be a dog's friend is forever an intruder — this is why dogs bark at mailmen.

It is clear enough that natural rights relations can arise between people and animals. Drummer, for example, can insist, "Hey, let's go outside and do something!" if I have been at my computer several days on end. He can both refuse to accept various of my suggestions and tell me when he fears for his life — such as the time when the huge, white flapping flag appeared out of nowhere, as it seemed to him, on the town green one evening when we were working. I can (and do) say to him either, "Oh, you don't have to worry about that" or, "Uh oh, you're right, Drum, that guy looks dangerous." Just as the government and I — two different species of organism — have developed improvised ways of communicating, such as the vote, so Drummer and I have worked out a number of ways to make our expressions known. Largely through obedience, I have taught him a fair

amount about how to get responses from me. Obedience is reciprocal; you cannot get responses from a dog to whom you do not
respond accurately. I have enfranchised him in a relationship to
me by educating him, creating the conditions by which he can
achieve a certain happiness specific to a dog, maybe even specific
to an Airedale, inasmuch as this same relationship has allowed
me to plumb the happiness of being a trainer and writing this
article.

Instructions in this happiness are given terms that are alien
to a culture in which liver treats, fluffy windup toys, and miniature sweaters are confused with respect and work. Jack Knox, a
sheepdog trainer originally from Scotland, will shake his crook
at a novice handler who makes a promiscuous move to praise a
dog, and will call out in his Scottish accent, "Eh! Eh! Get back, get
BACK! Ye'll no be abusin' the dogs like that in my clinic." America is a nation of abused animals, Knox says, because we are always swooping at them with praise, "no gi'ing them their freedom." I am reminded of Rainer Maria Rilke's account in which
the Prodigal Son leaves — has to leave — because everyone loves
him, even the dogs love him, and he has no path to the delicate
and fierce truth of himself. Unconditional praise and love, in
Rilke's story, disenfranchise us, distract us from what truly ex-
cites our interest.

In the minds of some trainers and handlers, praise is dishon-
esty. Paradoxically, it is a kind of contempt for animals that mas-
querades as a reverence for helplessness and suffering. The idea
of freedom means that you do not, at least not while Jack Knox
is nearby, helpfully guide your dog through the motions of,
say, herding over and over — what one trainer calls "explainy-
wainy." This is rote learning. It works tolerably well on some
handlers, because people have vast unconscious minds and can
store complex preprogrammed behaviors. Dogs, on the other
hand, have almost no unconscious minds, so they can learn only
by thinking. Many children are like this until educated out of it.

If I tell my Airedale to sit and stay on the town green, and
someone comes up and burbles, "What a pretty thing you are,"
he may break his stay to go for a caress. I pull him back and correct him for breaking. Now he holds his stay because I have
blocked his way to movement but not because I have punished

him. (A correction blocks one path as it opens another for desire to work; punishment blocks desire and opens nothing.) He holds his stay now, and — because the stay opens this possibility of work, new to a heedless young dog — he watches. If the person goes on talking, and isn't going to gush with praise, I may heel Drummer out of his stay and give him an "Okay" to make friends. Sometimes something about the person makes Drummer feel that reserve is in order. He responds to an insincere approach by sitting still, going down into himself , and thinking, "This person has no business pawing me. I'll sit very still, and he will go away." If the person doesn't take the hint from Drummer, I'll give the pup a little backup by saying, "Please don't pet him, he's working," even though he was not under any command.

The pup reads this, and there is a flicker of a working trust now stirring in the dog. Is the pup grateful? When the stranger leaves, does he lick my hand, full of submissive blandishments? This one doesn't. This one says nothing at all, and I say nothing much to him. This is a working trust we are developing, not a mutual congratulation society. My backup is praise enough for him; the use he makes of my support is praise enough for me.

Listening to a dog is often praise enough. Suppose it is just after dark and we are outside. Suddenly there is a shout from the house. The pup and I both look toward the shout and then toward each other: "What do you think?" I don't so much as cock my head, because Drummer is growing up, and I want to know what he thinks. He takes a few steps toward the house, and I follow. He listens again and comprehends that it's just Holly, who at fourteen is much given to alarming cries and shouts. He shrugs at me and goes about his business. I say nothing. To praise him for this performance would make about as much sense as praising a human being for the same thing. Thus:

A. What's that?
B. I don't know. [Listens] Oh, it's just Holly.
A. What a goooooood human being!
B. Huh?

This is one small moment in a series of like moments that will culminate in an Airedale who on a Friday will have the discrimination and confidence required to take down a man who is at-

tacking me with a knife and on Saturday clown and play with the
children at the annual Orange Empire Dog Club Christmas
party.

People who claim to speak for animal rights are increasingly devoted to the idea that the very keeping of a dog or a horse or a
gerbil or a lion is in and of itself an offense. The more loudly
they speak, the less likely they are to be in a rights relation to any
given animal, because they are spending so much time in air-
planes or transmitting fax announcements of the latest Sylvester
Stallone anti-fur rally. In a 1988 *Harper's* forum, for example,
Ingrid Newkirk, the national director of People for the Ethical
Treatment of Animals, urged that domestic pets be spayed and
neutered and ultimately phased out. She prefers, it appears,
wolves — and wolves someplace else — to Airedales and, by a
logic whose interior structure is both emotionally and intellec-
tually forever closed to Drummer, claims thereby to be speaking
for "animal rights."

She is wrong. I am the only one who can own up to my Airedale's inalienable rights. Whether or not I do it perfectly at any
given moment is no more refutation of this point than whether I
am perfectly my husband's mate at any given moment refutes
the fact of marriage. Only people who know Drummer, and
whom he can know, are capable of this relationship. PETA and
the Humane Society and the ASPCA and the Congress and
NOW — as institutions — do have the power to affect my ability
to grant rights to Drummer but are otherwise incapable of creating conditions or laws or rights that would increase his happiness. Only Drummer's owner has the power to obey him — to
obey who he is and what he is capable of — deeply enough to
grant him his rights and open up the possibility of happiness.

JAMAICA KINCAID

On Seeing England for the First Time

FROM TRANSITION

WHEN I SAW England for the first time, I was a child in school sitting at a desk. The England I was looking at was laid out on a map gently, beautifully, delicately, a very special jewel; it lay on a bed of sky blue — the background of the map — its yellow form mysterious, because though it looked like a leg of mutton, it could not really look like anything so familiar as a leg of mutton because it was England — with shadings of pink and green, unlike any shadings of pink and green I had seen before, squiggly veins of red running in every direction. England was a special jewel all right, and only special people got to wear it. The people who got to wear England were English people. They wore it well and they wore it everywhere: in jungles, in deserts, on plains, on top of the highest mountains, on all the oceans, on all the seas, in places where they were not welcome, in places they should not have been. When my teacher had pinned this map up on the blackboard, she said, "This is England" — and she said it with authority, seriousness, and adoration, and we all sat up. It was as if she had said, "This is Jerusalem, the place you will go to when you die but only if you have been good." We understood then — we were meant to understand then — that England was to be our source of myth and the source from which we got our sense of reality, our sense of what was meaningful, our sense of what was meaningless — and much about our own lives and much about the very idea of us headed that last list.

At the time I was a child sitting at my desk seeing England for the first time, I was already very familiar with the greatness of it. Each morning before I left for school, I ate a breakfast of half a grapefruit, an egg, bread and butter and a slice of cheese, and a cup of cocoa; or half a grapefruit, a bowl of oat porridge, bread and butter and a slice of cheese, and a cup of cocoa. The can of cocoa was often left on the table in front of me. It had written on it the name of the company, the year the company was established, and the words "Made in England." Those words, "Made in England," were written on the box the oats came in too. They would also have been written on the box the shoes I was wearing came in; a bolt of gray linen cloth lying on the shelf of a store from which my mother had bought three yards to make the uniform that I was wearing had written along its edge those three words. The shoes I wore were made in England; so were my socks and cotton undergarments and the satin ribbons I wore tied at the end of two plaits of my hair. My father, who might have sat next to me at breakfast, was a carpenter and cabinet maker. The shoes he wore to work would have been made in England, as were his khaki shirt and trousers, his underpants and undershirt, his socks and brown felt hat. Felt was not the proper material from which a hat that was expected to provide shade from the hot sun should be made, but my father must have seen and admired a picture of an Englishman wearing such a hat in England, and this picture that he saw must have been so compelling that it caused him to wear the wrong hat for a hot climate most of his long life. And this hat — a brown felt hat — became so central to his character that it was the first thing he put on in the morning as he stepped out of bed and the last thing he took off before he stepped back into bed at night. As we sat at breakfast a car might go by. The car, a Hillman or a Zephyr, was made in England. The very idea of the meal itself, breakfast, and its substantial quality and quantity was an idea from England; we somehow knew that in England they began the day with this meal called breakfast and a proper breakfast was a big breakfast. No one I knew liked eating so much food so early in the day; it made us feel sleepy, tired. But this breakfast business was Made in England like almost everything else that surrounded us, the exceptions being the sea, the sky, and the air we breathed.

At the time I saw this map — seeing England for the first time — I did not say to myself, "Ah, so that's what it looks like," because there was no longing in me to put a shape to those three words that ran through every part of my life, no matter how small; for me to have had such a longing would have meant that I lived in a certain atmosphere, an atmosphere in which those three words were felt as a burden. But I did not live in such an atmosphere. My father's brown felt hat would develop a hole in its crown, the lining would separate from the hat itself, and six weeks before he thought that he could not be seen wearing it — he was a very vain man — he would order another hat from England. And my mother taught me to eat my food in the English way: the knife in the right hand, the fork in the left, my elbows held still close to my side, the food carefully balanced on my fork and then brought up to my mouth. When I had finally mastered it, I overheard her saying to a friend, "Did you see how nicely she can eat?" But I knew then that I enjoyed my food more when I ate it with my bare hands, and I continued to do so when she wasn't looking. And when my teacher showed us the map, she asked us to study it carefully, because no test we would ever take would be complete without this statement: "Draw a map of England."

I did not know then that the statement "Draw a map of England" was something far worse than a declaration of war, for in fact a flat-out declaration of war would have put me on alert, and again in fact, there was no need for war — I had long ago been conquered. I did not know then that this statement was part of a process that would result in my erasure, not my physical erasure, but my erasure all the same. I did not know then that this statement was meant to make me feel in awe and small whenever I heard the word "England": awe at its existence, small because I was not from it. I did not know very much of anything then — certainly not what a blessing it was that I was unable to draw a map of England correctly.

After that there were many times of seeing England for the first time. I saw England in history. I knew the names of all the kings of England. I knew the names of their children, their wives, their disappointments, their triumphs, the names of people who betrayed them, I knew the dates on which they were born and the dates they died. I knew their conquests and was made to feel glad if I figured in them; I knew their defeats. I knew the details of the year 1066 (the Battle of Hastings, the end of the reign of the Anglo-Saxon kings) before I knew the details of the year 1832 (the year slavery was abolished). It wasn't as bad as I make it sound now; it was worse. I did like so much hearing again and again how Alfred the Great, traveling in disguise, had been left to watch cakes, and because he wasn't used to this the cakes got burned, and Alfred burned his hands pulling them out of the fire, and the woman who had left him to watch the cakes screamed at him. I loved King Alfred. My grandfather was named after him; his son, my uncle, was named after King Alfred; my brother is named after King Alfred. And so there are three people in my family named after a man they have never met, a man who died over ten centuries ago. The first view I got of England then was not unlike the first view received by the person who named my grandfather.

This view, though — the naming of the kings, their deeds, their disappointments — was the vivid view, the forceful view. There were other views, subtler ones, softer, almost not there — but these were the ones that made the most lasting impression on me, these were the ones that made me really feel like nothing. "When morning touched the sky" was one phrase, for no morning touched the sky where I lived. The mornings where I lived came on abruptly, with a shock of heat and loud noises. "Evening approaches" was another, but the evenings where I lived did not approach; in fact, I had no evening — I had night and I had day and they came and went in a mechanical way: on, off; on, off. And then there were gentle mountains and low blue skies and moors over which people took walks for nothing but pleasure, when where I lived a walk was an act of labor, a burden, something only death or the automobile could relieve. And there were things that a small turn of a head could convey — entire worlds, whole lives would depend on this thing, a certain turn of a head. Everyday life could be quite tiring, more tiring than anything I was told not to do. I was told not to gossip, but they did that all the time. And they ate so much food, violating another of those rules they taught me: do not indulge in gluttony. And the foods they ate actually: if only sometime I could eat cold cuts after the-

ater, cold cuts of lamb and mint sauce, and Yorkshire pudding
and scones, and clotted cream, and sausages that came from up-
country (imagine, "up-country"). And having troubling thoughts
at twilight, a good time to have troubling thoughts, apparently;
and servants who stole and left in the middle of a crisis, who were
born with a limp or some other kind of deformity, not nourished
properly in their mother's womb (that last part I figured out for
myself; the point was, oh to have an untrustworthy servant); and
wonderful cobbled streets onto which solid front doors opened;
and people whose eyes were blue and who had fair skins and who
smelled only of lavender, or sometimes sweet pea or primrose.
And those flowers with those names: delphiniums, foxgloves, tu-
lips, daffodils, floribunda, peonies; in bloom, a striking display,
being cut and placed in large glass bowls, crystal, decorating
rooms so large twenty families the size of mine could fit in com-
fortably but used only for passing through. And the weather was
so remarkable because the rain fell gently always, only occasionally in deep gusts, and it colored the air various shades of gray,
each an appealing shade for a dress to be worn when a portrait
was being painted; and when it rained at twilight, wonderful
things happened: people bumped into each other unexpectedly
and that would lead to all sorts of turns of events — a plot,
the mere weather caused plots. I saw that people rushed: they
rushed to catch trains, they rushed toward each other and away
from each other; they rushed and rushed and rushed. That
word: rushed! I did not know what it was to do that. It was too
hot to do that, and so I came to envy people who would rush,
even though it had no meaning to me to do such a thing. But
there they are again. They loved their children; their children
were sent to their own rooms as a punishment, rooms larger than
my entire house. They were special, everything about them said
so, even their clothes; their clothes rustled, swished, soothed.
The world was theirs, not mine; everything told me so.

If now as I speak of all this I give the impression of someone
on the outside looking in, nose pressed up against a glass window, that is wrong. My nose was pressed up against a glass
window all right, but there was an iron vise at the back of my
neck forcing my head to stay in place. To avert my gaze was to
fall back into something from which I had been rescued, a hole

filled with nothing, and that was the word for everything about
me, nothing. The reality of my life was conquests, subjugation,
humiliation, enforced amnesia. I was forced to forget. Just for
instance, this: I lived in a part of St. John's, Antigua, called Ovals.
Ovals was made up of five streets, each of them named after a
famous English seaman — to be quite frank, an officially sanctioned criminal: Rodney Street (after George Rodney), Nelson
Street (after Horatio Nelson), Drake Street (after Francis Drake),
Hood Street, and Hawkins Street (after John Hawkins). But
John Hawkins was knighted after a trip he made to Africa, opening up a new trade, the slave trade. He was then entitled to wear
as his crest a Negro bound with a cord. Every single person living
on Hawkins Street was descended from a slave. John Hawkins's
ship, the one in which he transported the people he had bought
and kidnapped, was called *The Jesus*. He later became the trea-
surer of the Royal Navy and rear admiral.

Again, the reality of my life, the life I led at the time I was
being shown these views of England for the first time, for the
second time, for the one-hundred-millionth time, was this: the
sun shone with what sometimes seemed to be a deliberate cruelty; we must have done something to deserve that. My dresses
did not rustle in the evening air as I strolled to the theater (I had
no evening, I had no theater; my dresses were made of a cheap
cotton, the weave of which would give way after not too many
washings). I got up in the morning, I did my chores (fetched
water from the public pipe for my mother, swept the yard), I
washed myself, I went to a woman to have my hair combed
freshly every day (because before we were allowed into our classroom our teachers would inspect us, and children who had not
bathed that day, or had dirt under their fingernails, or whose
hair had not been combed anew that day, might not be allowed
to attend class). I ate that breakfast. I walked to school. At school
we gathered in an auditorium and sang a hymn, "All Things
Bright and Beautiful," and looking down on us as we sang were
portraits of the Queen of England and her husband; they wore
jewels and medals and they smiled. I was a Brownie. At each
meeting we would form a little group around a flagpole, and
after raising the Union Jack, we would say, "I promise to do my
best, to do my duty to God and the Queen, to help other people
every day and obey the scouts' law."

Who were these people and why had I never seen them, I mean really seen them, in the place where they lived? I had never been to England. No one I knew had ever been to England, or I should say, no one I knew had ever been and returned to tell me about it. All the people I knew who had gone to England had stayed there. Sometimes they left behind them their small children, never to see them again. England! I had seen England's representatives. I had seen the governor general at the public grounds at a ceremony celebrating the Queen's birthday. I had seen an old princess and I had seen a young princess. They had both been extremely not beautiful, but who of us would have told them that? I had never seen England, really seen it, I had only met a representative, seen a picture, read books, memorized its history. I had never set foot, my own foot, in it.

The space between the idea of something and its reality is always wide and deep and dark. The longer they are kept apart — idea of thing, reality of thing — the wider the width, the deeper the depth, the thicker and darker the darkness. This space starts out empty, there is nothing in it, but it rapidly becomes filled up with obsession or desire or hatred or love — sometimes all of these things, sometimes some of these things, sometimes only one of these things. The existence of the world as I came to know it was a result of this: idea of thing over here, reality of thing way, way over there. There was Christopher Columbus, an unlikable man, an unpleasant man, a liar (and so, of course, a thief) surrounded by maps and schemes and plans, and there was the reality on the other side of that width, that depth, that darkness. He became obsessed, he became filled with desire, the hatred came later, love was never a part of it. Eventually, his idea met the longed-for reality. That the idea of something and its reality are often two completely different things is something no one ever remembers; and so when they meet and find that they are not compatible, the weaker of the two, idea or reality, dies. That idea Christopher Columbus had was more powerful than the reality he met, and so the reality he met died.

And so finally, when I was a grown-up woman, the mother of two children, the wife of someone, a person who resides in a powerful country that takes up more than its fair share of a continent, the owner of a house with many rooms in it and of two automobiles, with the desire and will (which I very much act upon) to take from the world more than I give back to it, more than I deserve, more than I need, finally then, I saw England, the real England, not a picture, not a painting, not through a story in a book, but England, for the first time. In me, the space between the idea of it and its reality had become filled with hatred, and so when at last I saw it I wanted to take it into my hands and tear it into little pieces and then crumble it up as if it were clay, child's clay. That was impossible, and so I could only indulge in not-favorable opinions.

There were monuments everywhere; they commemorated victories, battles fought between them and the people who lived across the sea from them, all vile people, fought over which of them would have dominion over the people who looked like me. The monuments were useless to them now, people sat on them and ate their lunch. They were like markers on an old useless trail, like a piece of old string tied to a finger to jog the memory, like old decoration in an old house, dirty, useless, in the way. Their skins were so pale, it made them look so fragile, so weak, so ugly. What if I had the power to simply banish them from their land, send boat after boatload of them on a voyage that in fact had no destination, force them to live in a place where the sun's presence was a constant? This would rid them of their pale complexion and make them look more like me, make them look more like the people I love and treasure and hold dear, and more like the people who occupy the near and far reaches of my imagination, my history, my geography, and reduce them and everything they have ever known to figurines as evidence that I was in divine favor, what if all this was in my power? Could I resist it? No one ever has.

And they were rude, they were rude to each other. They didn't like each other very much. They didn't like each other in the way they didn't like me, and it occurred to me that their dislike for me was one of the few things they agreed on.

I was on a train in England with a friend, an English woman. Before we were in England she liked me very much. In England she didn't like me at all. She didn't like the claim I said I had on England, she didn't like the views I had of England. I didn't like England, she didn't like England, but she didn't like me not liking it too. She said, "I want to show you my England, I want to show you the England that I know and love." I had told her many times before that I knew England and I didn't want to love it anyway. She no longer lived in England; it was her own country, but it had not been kind to her, so she left. On the train, the conductor was rude to her; she asked something, and he responded in a rude way. She became ashamed. She was ashamed at the way he treated her; she was ashamed at the way he behaved. "This is the new England," she said. But I liked the conductor being rude; his behavior seemed quite appropriate. Earlier this had happened: we had gone to a store to buy a shirt for my husband; it was meant to be a special present, a special shirt to wear on special occasions. This was a store where the Prince of Wales has his shirts made, but the shirts sold in this store are beautiful all the same. I found a shirt I thought my husband would like and I wanted to buy him a tie to go with it. When I couldn't decide which one to choose, the salesman showed me a new set. He was very pleased with these, he said, because they bore the crest of the Prince of Wales, and the Prince of Wales had never allowed his crest to decorate an article of clothing before. There was something in the way he said it; his tone was slavish, reverential, awed. It made me feel angry; I wanted to hit him. I didn't do that. I said, my husband and I hate princes, my husband would never wear anything that had a prince's anything on it. My friend stiffened. The salesman stiffened. They both drew themselves in, away from me. My friend told me that the prince was a symbol of her Englishness, and I could see that I had caused offense. I looked at her. She was an English person, the sort of English person I used to know at home, the sort who was nobody in England but somebody when they came to live among the people like me. There were many people I could have seen England with; that I was seeing it with this particular person, a person who reminded me of the people who showed me England long ago as I sat in church or at my desk, made me feel silent and afraid, for I wondered if, all these years of our friendship, I had had a friend or had been in the thrall of a racial memory.

I went to Bath — we, my friend and I, did this, but though we were together, I was no longer with her. The landscape was al-

most as familiar as my own hand, but I had never been in this
place before, so how could that be again? And the streets of Bath
were familiar, too, but I had never walked on them before. It was
all those years of reading, starting with Roman Britain. Why did
I have to know about Roman Britain? It was of no real use to me,
a person living on a hot, drought-ridden island, and it is of no
use to me now, and yet my head is filled with this nonsense, Roman Britain. In Bath, I drank tea in a room I had read about
in a novel written in the eighteenth century. In this very same
room, young women wearing those dresses that rustled and so
on danced and flirted and sometimes disgraced themselves with
young men, soldiers, sailors, who were on their way to Bristol or
someplace like that, so many places like that where so many adventures, the outcome of which was not good for me, began.
Bristol, England. A sentence that began "That night the ship
sailed from Bristol, England" would end not so good for me.
And then I was driving through the countryside in an English
motorcar, on narrow winding roads, and they were so familiar,
though I had never been on them before; and through little villages the names of which I somehow knew so well though I had
never been there before. And the countryside did have all those
hedges and hedges, fields hedged in. I was marveling at all the
toil of it, the planting of the hedges to begin with and then the
care of it, all that clipping, year after year of clipping, and I wondered at the lives of the people who would have to do this, because wherever I see and feel the hands that hold up the world,
I see and feel myself and all the people who look like me. And I
said, "Those hedges" and my friend said that someone, a woman
named Mrs. Rothchild, worried that the hedges weren't being
taken care of properly; the farmers couldn't afford or find the
help to keep up the hedges, and often they replaced them with
wire fencing. I might have said to that, well if Mrs. Rothchild
doesn't like the wire fencing, why doesn't she take care of the
hedges herself, but I didn't. And then in those fields that were
now hemmed in by wire fencing that a privileged woman didn't
like was planted a vile yellow flowering bush that produced an
oil, and my friend said that Mrs. Rothchild didn't like this either;
it ruined the English countryside, it ruined the traditional look
of the English countryside.

It was not at that moment that I wished every sentence, every-thing I knew, that began with England would end with "and then it all died; we don't know how, it just all died." At that moment, I was thinking, who are these people who forced me to think of them all the time, who forced me to think that the world I knew was incomplete, or without substance, or did not measure up be-cause it was not England; that I was incomplete, or without sub-stance, and did not measure up because I was not English. Who were these people? The person sitting next to me couldn't give me a clue; no one person could. In any case, if I had said to her, I find England ugly, I hate England; the weather is like a jail sen-tence, the English are a very ugly people, the food in England is like a jail sentence, the hair of English people is so straight, so dead looking, the English have an unbearable smell so different from the smell of people I know, real people of course, she would have said that I was a person full of prejudice. Apart from the fact that it is I — that is, the people who look like me — who made her aware of the unpleasantness of such a thing, the idea of such a thing, prejudice, she would have been only partly right, sort of right: I may be capable of prejudice, but my prejudices have no weight to them, my prejudices have no force behind them, my prejudices remain opinions, my prejudices remain my personal opinion. And a great feeling of rage and disappoint-ment came over me as I looked at England, my head full of per-sonal opinions that could not have public, my public, approval. The people I come from are powerless to do evil on grand scale.

The moment I wished every sentence, everything I knew, that began with England would end with "and then it all died, we don't know how, it just all died" was when I saw the white cliffs of Dover. I had sung hymns and recited poems that were about a longing to see the white cliffs of Dover again. At the time I sang the hymns and recited the poems, I could really long to see them again because I had never seen them at all, nor had anyone around me at the time. But there we were, groups of people longing for something we had never seen. And so there they were, the white cliffs, but they were not that pearly majestic thing I used to sing about, that thing that created such a feeling in these people that when they died in the place where I lived they had themselves buried facing a direction that would allow them to see the white cliffs of Dover when they were resurrected, as surely they would be. The white cliffs of Dover, when finally I saw them, were cliffs, but they were not white; you would only call them that if the word "white" meant something special to you; they were dirty and they were steep; they were so steep, the correct height from which all my views of England, starting with the map before me in my classroom and ending with the trip I had just taken, should jump and die and disappear forever.

WAYNE KOESTENBAUM

Opera and Homosexuality: Seven Arias

FROM THE YALE JOURNAL OF CRITICISM

Listening speaks.
— ROLAND BARTHES

Donna Elvira's "Ah! chi mi dice mai" (Vengeance)

I devoted my twenty-first winter to Mozart's *Don Giovanni* (1787) and to the search for a boyfriend. In my dorm room, I listened to Donna Elvira's "Ah! chi mi dice mai" again and again; I wanted the boy next door to hear it while he studied and slept. *Give me back the rapture that the gods and the male powers have taken away! Hear me regain, in thrillingly angry vocal vibrations, the bliss I thought was lost!*

Don Giovanni seduced Donna Elvira and then abandoned her. She enters proclaiming her wish to claw his heart out. If you listen only to the music, she sounds simply angry. If you follow the words, she desires reclamation more than retribution: she wants Don Giovanni back.

Donna Elvira's anger simplifies her. The key is firmly E-flat major. Her first phrase, and all its recurrences, begin on the downbeat; decisive, she's partial to dotted rhythms. She never doubts herself, never vacillates. She only retraverses the harmonic structure already displayed, a coat of arms, before she entered.

Even the rests — the silences — convey her confidence. Her repeated phrase ("gli vo' cavare il cor": "I'll tear out his heart") comes in forte after three beats' rest; her steady quarter notes have the orchestra's full support, a regatta; her strong "Sì!" is almost a caricature of wronged womanhood.

She sings to the audience, unaware that Don Giovanni and his companion Leporello are listening. (They don't yet recognize her.) She sings to male duos: Don Giovanni and Leporello, Mozart and Da Ponte. Brief, haunting, ambiguous excursions into the minor key occur in Don Giovanni's mocking asides. Does he sing "Poverina! Poverina!" ("Poor darling! Poor darling!") in and out of G minor with lilting lullaby motion because he really wants to rescue her, because he truly sympathizes?

Elvira extracts most gold from the word "cavare": to dig out. She performs arpeggiated E-flat major vocalism on the word's second syllable, "va." How delighted she is to go nowhere with her vengeful impulses, to dig out the heart of her own voice by lingering on that word! She is her own enemy: vengeful desires harm the throat before they reach their intended object (the rake). Sing "vengeance" and you will be doomed to find it in your own larynx. Kiri Te Kanawa is most idiosyncratic on the syllable "tor" in the phrase "Ah! se ritrovo l'empio, e a me non *tor*na ancor": "Ah! if I find the traitor and he will not *return* to me. . . ." She rolls the "r" and finds a veiled, covered sound for the three-beat-long B-flat: the rolled "r" of the celibate, the rolled "r" of the woman whose passions are never reciprocated, the rolled "r" of the woman who wants to occupy the center of a "vengeance" opera but finds herself to be, instead, comic, imitable, only one of Don Giovanni's many sexual conquests. And her vengeance aria seems quaint, borrowed from another genre — opera seria.

Donna Elvira has the gall and righteousness — churchgoer! — to fall straight down the B-flat major chord when she sings "Ah! se ritrovo l'empio" ("Ah! if I find the traitor . . ."). She must be confident if she can descend that unambiguously, if she can say, "I'll give you the chord you want, I'll bravely plumb the depths of my degradation. I love Donna Elvira for her complacency, upright uptight woman expressing a botched and irregular love affair in a countenanced, forgiven key. And then in the next phrase she shows her Jack-the-Giant-Killer ability to leap whole octaves: "vo' farne orrendo scempio!" ("I'll kill him most horribly"). In the background, the pulse-setting orchestra gives us the tonality by seeming to disturb it.

Queer vengeance: identifying with wronged women; desiring erotic impossibilities. Donna Elvira expresses eroticism not as pining lyricism but as juridical confidence: I sit at the center of a sexual discourse because a rake abandoned me.

During my days of "Ah! chi mi dice mai" I was certain that my love affair with the boy next door would end any moment. I placed my erotic eccentricity within the fantasy-discourse of *the woman about to be jilted:* I counted the days of my romance because I was convinced I would soon become Donna Elvira, crying on the streets. Only the abandoned are entitled to speak of their reprobate loves. And so I hid the discourse I wanted to occupy, *boy meets boy,* like a nested box inside a larger, more authoritative discourse: *the wronged woman.* In order to speak to myself about *boy meets boy,* I entered the vocal consciousness of a woman who can sing boldly about her erotic life only because she's been deserted.

The Countess's "Dove sono" (Serenity)

In Mozart's *Le Nozze di Figaro* (1786), the Countess, alone on stage, sings "Dove sono," a melody so delicately accompanied by woodwinds and strings, so content to dwell within C, E, and G — pitches which remind our bodies of what C major holds out as promise and bier — that I am driven to ask why operatic female serenity appeals to a body (mine) culturally marked as queer.

From the opera's comic intrigue and identity-confusion the Countess stands remote, though she is morally central. She is arbiter, sufferer. She is the preeminent "soul" in the opera: her two arias, "Porgi amor" and "Dove sono," which render *female interiority* more richly than others in the opera, define introspection as a trait of women and encourage listeners to recognize that "feminine" state in themselves.

When the second act opens with the Countess musing mournfully in "Porgi amor," we are chastened out of our former carefree investment in comic situations. I thought this opera was a divine joke, and now, suddenly, I have found my point of tragic identification: the oversensitive woman, on whom no slight is lost, and who has the cathedral-capaciousness of soul to contemplate her condition while she endures it.

The Countess is not the victimized, sad object of our listening. Listening involves more than brutish audition. We take the Countess into our body as she sings — or, when she sings, she peers into our interior; she exposes us. And so we associate our inward-looking moments with the sound of a woman thinking aloud.

In the recitative, before the aria, she is furious that she must change costumes with her servant to win back the Count's love. On the words "consorte crudel" (cruel husband) she assumes the posture of Donna Elvira in *Don Giovanni* — the enraged noblewoman. But when she sings "prima amata" (he loved me before he abused me) she has moved, with the orchestra, into a piano dynamic, and the harmonic questing — we are entering forested, strange territory — assures us that the Countess sings from love and not anger, that she is no opera seria stereotype but a woman whose point of view we must share, as if she were the heroine of a novel. The Countess gives the illusion of musical naturalism: texture of introspection as it really occurs.

And after the first part of the aria she repeats the sublime melody I will avoid describing; repeats it, with one alteration, unutterably poignant. The first time, a rest bisects the phrase. But the second time, the Countess fills in that rest, as if in the midst of her serenity she were growing impulsive and assertive: or as if the deathbed passivity of operatic introspection also allows for instants when nostalgia grows bold and rebellious. We take the Countess to be *one state, never changing,* but then her aria includes a liquid unpredictable moment, and we realize we have underestimated her, and have underestimated our own ability to return with a forgiving liaison to the melody that, the first time around, was prison.

The final section of the aria turns allegro — quick motion — and the Countess exclaims (I paraphrase), "I still have time to change the world!" She gives up her austerity and sings repeatedly "l'ingrato cor" — sounding again like Donna Elvira, focusing on the beloved's ingratitude. Her emphatic attacks and her trill on a D before the cadence make her appear to have acquired, through the medicine of the aria's more dulcet moments, the fortitude to fight for her man, as well as the moral righteousness to accuse him, rather than to ponder the metaphysics of past and present.

But I haven't spoken yet of the uninterrupted sweetness with which Elisabeth Schwarzkopf moves, without haste, through the central melody:

> Dove sono i bei momenti
> di dolcezza e di piacer?
> Dove andaro i giuramenti
> di quel labbro menzogner?
>
> Where are those beautiful moments
> of sweetness and pleasure?
> Where have they gone,
> those vows of a lying lip?

"Dove sono" highlights the soprano's timbre, legato, breath control, and pitch. It is not a showpiece. The soprano is vocally naked: open to humiliation if her taste is less than pure. "Dove sono" is her chance to exhibit fidelity to air, to C major, to a nostalgia permitted to proclaim itself publicly because it is thoroughly socialized.

Mozart is nostalgic for what the Countess represents, as we are nostalgic for the inspiration that filled young Mozart, air he spills back into the Countess's lungs so she can express it to us. And we are so delighted to confront this melody that we are nostalgic for the moment of listening. A quasi-Countess, I sing, "Where has fled the beautiful moment I am now experiencing thanks to your rapturous voice? — a moment I can't repeat because the music moves forward, though thank God you will repeat this melody once more before inexorably advancing to comic entanglement and preoccupation with morality."

A definition (arising from this aria as paradigm) of operatic serenity: melodies and situations that will make the listener, nostalgic for the sensation of being a woman looking inside herself, a woman regretting a fabled, vanished past. The Countess regrets the beautiful moments ("i bei momenti") of her early marriage; listening, we regret the beautiful moments of the so-

prano's performance (as if it were over already), and we regret
the gulf between the contemporary soprano's rendition and the
Mozart aria itself, each performance a bittersweet revisitation of
a lost source. And so we are reminded of our own mournful separation from ways of behaving that are now gone, behaviors we
never liked, such as "boy meets girl" or 'wife forgives husband":
we are riven, suddenly by *our* separation from the Countess,
from this model (who dares to imitate it?) of *a woman enduring the
martyrdom of gender with fortitude.*

Listen to the Countess sing sweetly about events that usually
provoke anger, and learn to forgive history its mutations, domesticity its interruptions. Listen to the Countess, and learn to
observe, celebrate, and *sublimate* your own abjection. Imitate Mozart, famous for his inspiration (he composed quickly and sublimely at an impossibly young age). Singing depends on inspiration: breathing. The Countess *does a Mozart* when she sings —
she does the inspiration trick. She drinks "reality" — foul air —
and transfigures it.

Count Almaviva's "Ecco ridente" (Serenade)

Serenades are songs aware of their "song" nature — dreams in
which you almost wake up because you know you are dreaming.
(Writing these meditations, I feel I am serenading opera itself:
opera, open your window, let me see you, cold beloved on whom
I nurse an unreciprocated crush!) In Rossini's *Il Barbiere di Sivig-
lia* (1816), the first aria is Count Almaviva's; he serenades Rosina,
who is locked in Dr. Bartolo's convent-like palazzo. The Count
plucks a mandolin, which makes him a Lothario, and which also
allies him with the ideology of plucking: secretive conspiratorial
moments in opera are strummed — as are labial moments, when
the harp or another "exotic" instrument brings on a treasured
privacy we are urged to consider feminine. Guitar and pizzicato
strings make his serenade sound real — that is, artificial: even
within the opera's narrative, the Count is genuinely singing.

The aria's purpose is to seduce Rosina (who hasn't yet appeared); the instrument of seduction is the male voice. And so
the voice must be unique. The Count, offering us the floating

timbre of his lyric tenor, convinces us that manhood is just a
caress, not an army; that never until this moment have we understood manhood's intrinsic affability and earnestness; that a
tenor, unlike a baritone, sympathizes with women's secret needs
because his voice, like a woman's, is elevated; that a tenor has
something virgin and unexampled to reveal.

He tells the chorus, "Piano, pianissimo, senza parlar." *Go about
your business without talking.* His serenade — because it is self-con-
sciously "song" — is exempt from this credo of silence. Song, an
arrow, pierces the palazzo's walls — and yet the Count sings because he himself has been wounded:

> Rendi men crudo, oh Dio,
> Lo stral che mi ferì.

> Soften the pain, oh God,
> Of the dart which pierces me.

Here, the phrase is marked "a piacere." The tenor is free to sing
it in the tempo and with the figuration that please him. He is free
to mark his own pleasure. And yet he describes, with showy,
sense-stopping repetitions, a love-wound inflicted by a woman
who hasn't yet appeared, a St. Sebastian gash connected to the
joy that we, Rosina replacements, gain from his high male voice.

In the next section, the tenor abandons rhythmic flexibility
to execute sixteenth notes in disciplined scale patterns, and so
tenor Luigi Alva, as well as the more lachrymose and silken Tito
Schipa (in a 78 from the 1920s), grows briskly businesslike to
cope with the passagework: "Oh, istante d'amore! Felice mo-
mento!" The tenor repeats these words — "instant of love!
happy moment!" — to coloratura. Happy moment of singing!
Instant in which I love displaying my speed and frivolous facility!
Instant of warbling, without object or regret!

Rosina then *does not appear.* We reinterpret his serenade, once
it is over, as a vocal feast served to chorus, audience, and male
servant. It is ostensibly a heterosexual feast, because a present,
palpitating man opens his mouth to invoke a woman. But the
Count's aria is queer as well, because the woman appears not in
person but *in his timbre.* He sings for the pleasure of singing, for
no woman, because he loves to linger in the land of wounds. No
braggart, he is a "sensitive," on display for us. His timbre per-

suades us that maleness is an aubade, the emergence of a hot orange globe, his sweet tone impersonating the feminine *aurora* he
invokes in his opening phrase ("Ecco ridente in cielo / Spunta la
bella *aurora*").

Tenor Tito Schipa's timbre makes me optimistic about maleness: there is nothing sleazy about his restrained rendering of
this serenade. He sings the liaisons between phrases severely rallentando: fermata rest in orchestra lets the tenor linger between
portions of a phrase — adding ornaments, slowing down. And
Schipa unpredictably — in the middle of a phrase! — rises above
the staff on the word "speme." Time, and the orchestra, stop for
this leap.

What are the poetics and politics of a man's rubato? When a
man takes liberties with a phrase — when he sings "at pleasure" — is he bending and stretching the walls of his masculine
identity, becoming ductile and flexible? Or is he becoming Don
Juan: "making a pass" at tempo, taking liberties with the music
as he is free to take liberties with women? I hear Schipa's winning
way of bending time as experimentation, flux, and sexy instability within the borders of a masculinity that usually feigns im-
permeability. When Schipa diminuendos on the high G, the
moment when the largo section of the aria surrenders to allegro,
his focused but small tone sounds "feminine" to me: quickly os-
cillating, nasally earnest, pitched so high within maleness it almost qualifies as an exception — though there's nothing freakish
about his tone. He offers what Western musical conventions encourage us to expect from lyric tenors.

The Count's ardency lacks militancy: voice without the bone,
without the hammer. His is the masculinity of "Ecco!" — of an-
nunciation, exclamation, and surprise. What takes the Count —
and the audience — by storm is not the arrival of Rosina (she
doesn't show up to hear the serenade). We're surprised, rather,
by this new dolce sound entering history: sound of a different maleness, which passes as heterosexual (amorously directed
toward women) but is also self-displaying, given to rallentando
and sudden neurasthenic doubts and vacillations, the tremors of
a rubato that saves the man from the regime of strict tempo. The
Count is trying to wake Rosina up. Instead, he wakes in me (and
in other listeners?) an optimism: I didn't know men could sound
like this, I didn't know masculinity could reveal itself.

Compare the sound of a lyric tenor singing "Ecco ridente" with the sound of Verdi's Otello singing "Esultate!": two male entrances, one comic, one tragic. But "Ecco ridente" isn't simply comic. It offers us the noise of male vanity, male rapture: a man permitted to sound excited. Anywhere outside of the opera house this sound might lead to violence: gaybashing.

The aria is in C major: serene key of "Dove sono." It is early in the opera. It is dawn. It is comedy. We dwell now in the land of stereotype. In the sound of Tito Schipa's rendition of "Ecco ridente," hear not interiority or psychology but the possibility of empathizing with a "nice" man's ardency and sincerity. The Count is voluble; the Count is opening his heart. We either take pity on him or we feel — for the first time in our lives? — that maleness wants our cooperation and participation, that maleness includes us and beckons.

Lucia's Mad Scene (Solitude)

My wedding day, *my* performance, *my* body, *my* voice, all mine, no one can interrupt or stop me: I sing because I want to express my horrid and fascinating loves, but the voice in which I seek my liberation is a body I am forbidden to kiss wholeheartedly, a body divided from itself, a body that doesn't know its meanings and that will die at the end of the scene; and so though I try to use my voice to tell you "I am having an orgasm!" or "Save me from this burning house!" the voice itself is the executioner and the crime and so cannot take sides or utterly embody pleasure and revolutionary ardor. Every time I sing of my pleasure you must listen for a *rip,* like cloth tearing.

Who is Lucia? A performer paid to sing. She likes to make a show, to exaggerate. She is demonstrating how to scream, draw blood, go high, grab attention, startle a crowd, break up family parties and town meetings, wilt, ruin time, defile, delay.

Hearing various divas sing Lucia's mad scene, so central to ideologies of opera and gender, I find it hard to pay attention to the music or the words. I can only pay attention to the voice. (How does this particular diva manage madness?) A woman's *physiological vocal apparatus* is the aria's subject: and the aria intends to prove that her anatomy is tragic. In 1835, Donizetti and Cammarano were mourning the disaster of gender, which is also the tragedy of vocal pleasure.

The marriage between music and words — like the wedding that Lucia hallucinates — is phantasmal. Even when "shallow" practitioners (the nightingale school of Lucias) attempt this set-piece, it stays tragic, unwed: for the scene's "depth" consists in Lucia's body. We experience her anatomy as plot, as narrative, as temporality: a vagina that moves — through musical syntax — somewhere. We listen to Lucia's mad scene for the noises anatomy makes when it aches.

Forced to marry a man she doesn't love, Lucia kills him, and in her bloody nightgown (maybe she is holding a knife) she wanders on stage, where the wedding festivities are still taking place. Her gown is voice-stained. Had Donizetti written this scene a few generations earlier, a castrato might have sung Lucia's part. Blood on her nightgown reinforces a connection between vocal power and self-mutilation — in particular, violence to gender, or gender *as* a prior buried violence. For Lucia to sing, someone (herself?) has had to bleed; some poor paradigmatic soul's gender has had to be disturbed and disrupted for vocal display, a form of tragic catharsis, to occur.

When Lucia comes out, distraught, in her nightgown, Raimondo has already spilled her story, so she enters to hushed, prurient anticipation. Orchestral chords follow the rhythm of Raimondo's portentous exclamation: "Eccola!" "She's here!" Audience pulse quickens. She's adored because she's out of control and murderous. The chorus clears space for her. She is silent, beheld: the chorus says that she looks risen from the dead. Raimondo's "Eccola!" announces a seismic shift in our gender — our erupting joy that the mad scene, structurally the opera's central member (though it pretends to be going haywire), is about to begin.

Throughout the scene she converses with the flute. At her entrance, as in other flute/soprano interchanges in the mad scene, the flute speaks before she does; she responds to its initiatives — a girl provoked into song by aural hallucinations that we, who drink her derangement, share. When we listen to the mad scene, we become Lucia-who-listens, for every phrase she sings responds to a prior phrase in her head.

The flute plays a melody — and she answers, in a stupor, in the middle of her range,

> Il dolce suono
> mi colpì di sua voce!
>
> The sweet sound
> of his voice hits me!

Lucia has knifed Arturo and now in turn she's knifed by her memory of Edgardo's voice. So the mad scene begins with Lucia answering an imaginary male voice: to Lucia, Edgardo sounds like a flute. But the flute is not — except in shape? — a particularly "masculine" instrument. The voice that Lucia produces in echo of the hallucinated fluty Arturo isn't schematically female: Lucia's own association of "flute" with "Edgardo" confounds our map of male versus female timbres and ranges.

Her next phrase also associates male voice with knife and with high pitch: she ascends to a sustained high note (what a gorgeous exposed sound, the hollowness of a grotto or a grave, Callas finds for the G!) on the word "discesa": the sound of his voice *strikes her* to the heart. The flute defines "voice" as the hallucinated dead man you killed and who comes back, unwanted revenant, in your larynx. Thus we swallow — introject — our adversaries.

Fioritura signifies a modicum of sanity, an organized mania: each section of her reverie, thus far, has ended with a trill, an upward extension, or a roulade — an explosion as closure, some outburst to announce that she's done with one thought and wants to move on to the next. If Lucia has mood swings, she (or the musical architecture around her) announces when the swing is about to begin.

"Il fantasma!" she sings, loudly, on a low G-flat, and then for "ne separa" she jumps to the staff's ceiling. She articulates her fright in octave leaps, moving from chest into head register — ascensions that make her seem schizoid and androgynous. Who can contain such rage and still pretend to be "feminine" and vulnerable?

> Ohimè! Sorge il tremendo fantasma
> e ne separa! Ohimè! Ohimè!
> Edgardo, Edgardo! Ah! Il fantasma,

il fantasma ne separa!

Alas! The dreadful phantom arises
and separates us! Alas! Alas!
Edgardo, Edgardo! Ah! The phantom,
the phantom separates us!

What is the specific auditory hallucination that frightens her? The reprise of the love theme — melody she sang by the fountain with beloved Edgardo. (She thinks she wants Edgardo's body but any resurrection of sexual union with him sends her into vocal terror.) The phantom that separates her from Edgardo is the illusion of sexual difference, dooming her to hear him but never become his body. *I'm not Edgardo, I'm not my own past, I'm separated, by a marriage night, from my virgin self.* A cold silver instrument — the flute's reprise — has stolen her subjectivity: the phantom that intrudes, and separates her from her memory of Edgardo, is the flute's numbing repetition, out of context, of her own theme — her "authentic" and spontaneous love degraded into system and motif.

Just now I listened again to Callas's 1953 studio recording of this "il fantasma" passage: I chastise myself for misinterpreting, misrendering. Her timbre's inexpressible loveliness transcends and damns everything I say about this scene. Now I am in Lucia's position — I am trembling, I am saying, "Alas, a phantom separates me from the voice of Lucia!" The phantom is my sexual difference, maleness separating me from embodying Lucia more closely.

Then Lucia imagines — invents — a wedding with Edgardo. She begins by continuing her conversation with the flute. The flute projects the notes of the B-flat major chord — predictably, not playfully — like setting up a trampoline on which a stage victim must jump. Silence; and Lucia sings,

Sparsa è di rose!

It is strewn with roses!

The flute returns again — the same B-flat major chord, higher, and Lucia, unaccompanied, sings

Un'armonia celeste, di', non ascolti?

A celestial harmony, don't you hear it?

Lucia's drama is the listener's: hearing what can't be verified — sound waves set up by one's inmost wound. The mad scene renders the vertigo of self-listening: the fissure between the vocalizing self and the sourceless "ah" that one hears and imitates, producing desire. She sings the reflection or inverse of what she feels. Every phrase Lucia sings denies voice's naturalness and authenticity because each phrase is a vain, flawed imitation ("can't get it right!") of a prior, unrehearsed, unverifiable phrase, condemned as hallucination. Lucia sounds mad because she can't coincide with notes she hears. These uncapturable pipings of a flute are emblems of a past romance, shards of manhood and of gender: the phallus lost or gained when she knifed Arturo in bed.

Lucia grows increasingly jubilant and playacts the wedding ceremony by herself. Coloratura isn't a punishment: it's hydraulic, and powerful, and leads her from a minor-key andante passage, when she passively listens to wedding hymns, to increasingly heartfelt, vigorous cries of "Edgardo! Edgardo!" and then a roulade on the phrase "Oh me felice!" — "Oh, I'm happy!" As in Violetta's "Sempre libera," coloratura signifies joy's explosive force, a pleasure that's socially irresponsible, suicidal, and seemingly directed toward a man though it is really aimed at a phantom and at paying customers. When Callas explodes on "Oh gioia che si sente" — spitting out the pitches — I feel that Lucia has reason to be optimistic, or that, within episodes of alienation (one's own private mad scenes) , there are moments when the joy, though apparently unreasonable, has a motive and a destination; moments when, like the first orgasm I ever had (I've been tempted for pages to say that Lucia's mad scene is a wet dream), we hallucinate that passion has a point, reaches a termination, has rituals only the self alone in her powder room knows. Lucia's mad scene, a ritualized and coherent enactment of how a desiring subject behaves when she thinks she's alone but also knows she's performing, saves queer desire from its reputedly diffuse and suicidal nature.

Lucia wants to make a point. To seem socialized, formal, religious, she induces orchestral chords that lead her into a wholly imaginary marriage ceremony. But orange blossoms capitulate to a joy pathetic because we know that solitude is not what Lucia

wants for her body, and because Callas diminuendos on an A
and then an A-flat down to a G and to a new melody, near the
bottom of the soprano's range, a melody that even Joan Sutherland sings with mortuary tone, the sound of Lucia at the end of
her resources, the *real* Lucia, the *authentic* Lucia, not the performer:

> Alfin son tua, alfin sei mio!
> A me ti dona un Dio.
>
> At last I am yours, at last you are mine!
> A god gave you to me.

Callas sings the word "tua" as if it hurt her body, and "mio," two
measures later, smarts even more. Henceforth she will be overtaken by fioritura, culminating in a duet with the flute in which
she goes first — and she will finally join the flute in soul-numb-
ing, soul-restoring unison: but at this moment when Lucia
catches up to the magic phallus, the missing memory, the flute
that is the reverie and the regret, she sounds craziest. She's utterly sublimated into coloratura, away from the Greek-tragic
mode of declamation. Once she enters fioritura we know she's
dead already, and we don't feel sorry for her anymore; we ad-
mire her as a specimen. If the ornamentation were improvised,
not canned, we might feel that Lucia were at last coming to individual life.

In the cabaletta, "Spargi d'amaro pianto," she buries herself.
Here she has a newlywed's smugness. Lucia, once at the mercy of
gender, now coyly collaborates with it. No more meandering. No
more staying out past her vocal curfew. When she sings "Spargi
d'amaro pianto," her staccato attacks and grace notes (Callas
sings them in slow motion) convey a self-curbing gift for living
on pointe.

The second time around, Joan Sutherland ornaments "Spargi
d'amaro pianto" so floridly I think of Madame Tussaud, wax
manners no one remembers: in the nineteenth century, Lucia's
cabaletta might have been terrifying, each mordent the spur of a
separate sadism, roulades that sound like beauty but are really
anger, hurled at an audience unable to anticipate or shield itself.
The last note of Lucia's mad scene, on each of the three recordings I own, is worn down from overplaying, so I can only hear

the pitch of the final high note but not its size or resonance. And this depletion, this lost note, seems a figure for the impossibility of vesting mystery and truth in a vocal climax. The last stretch of the cabaletta, repeating and embellishing old material, seems a drive through the ghost town of gender; we register surprise that the formerly grand stores and hotels have been boarded up for years.

I want Lucia to be a symbol of sexual willfulness, erotic independence, madness Artaud-style (madwomen are wiser and saner than we are); but I always turn off the stereo, after the mad scene, feeling disappointed.

Don José and Micaëla's Duet (Nostalgia)

Listening to the Callas *Carmen*, creaming butter and sugar for a dessert, I am suddenly distracted by a speaking voice. Split-second thought: the neighbor lady is yelling through the window, "Cut down your dogwood tree, it casts too much shade!" Instead, it is Maria Callas's speaking voice: *Eh! compère, que fais-tu là?* ("Hey, friend, what are you up to there?") When spoken words rip through a sung texture, I think the past is burglaring the present.

From the beginning of memory I have wanted a relationship with *Carmen,* and I have presumed, also from the beginning, that it was too late for such a bond. I wanted to return to an early chapter in my life, to a time when I had been intimate with *Carmen:* that period never existed. How could I have believed, at age ten, that my life was already over, that the years of proximity to the "operatic" were forever finished, when they had not even started? The package from Gotham Records that arrived the week before my tenth birthday and waited unopened on the fireplace: was it the boxed set of *Carmen,* whose "Toreador Song" I knew from a grand opera kiddie record, aria that repeated in my head, the tempo promising forward movement — though *Carmen* only means retrieval? The distinctive smell of the Richmond/London *Carmen* sleeves, the way Janine Micheau, the Micaëla of the moment, pronounces the "j" in *José:* where can I place that odor, where deliver and expunge it? As I work in my apartment's kitchen in 1982 (I am always in the middle of cooking when *Carmen* retrieves my body and relocates it), suddenly Micaëla sings to Don José about the village he has left behind, and I stop, afraid to enter the living room where the record is playing, because if I move, the music will mitigate a wound I want to keep intact.

Carmen has just sung to Don José her seductive "Habanera" (gypsy love song, an imitation of a Spanish air); a mezzo, she makes her voice lewd in a manner not often available to opera singers. Then Micaëla, soprano, from Don José's hometown, enters with a message from José's mother: a letter, some money, and . . . a kiss! Micaëla sings the most beautiful melody in the world while repeating words that the ailing mother had pronounced on the church steps: "Go find my José and give him this kiss!" When Micaëla's lips meet José's, he suddenly *sees his mother* — hallucination he enacts by singing a melody no longer in 4/4 time but now 3/4: lilting and truncated. Micaëla joins, claiming she, too, sees the mother; Micaëla is willing to participate in José's delusion, overjoyed to be a go-between and steal a kiss in the process. But he grows distracted and stares at the flower Carmen threw him. Evil sorceress! Requiring once more the tonic of melody, he sings the gorgeous tune that Micaëla delivered like a message from the grave, though he will postpone for another act his engagement with her timbre (it can't compete with Carmen's) and with the virtues the soprano voice represents: one chaste no-tongue kiss, a melody that brims with the forgotten. Micaëla's melody is so voluptuously harp-shaded, it moves so magnanimously from B-flat major to F major and then to D major and, in the transitions, through such a kaleidoscope of diminished chords, way-stations that tug at the heart, that we may feel, listening to Micaëla, nostalgic for the ideology of the soprano voice, and for *created melody* (as opposed to the pseudo-ethnographic "Habanera" Carmen has just sung). Rhythmically, the moment that Micaëla begins to sing her melody is exciting because triplets (instead of eighth notes) alter time, make us abandon binary thinking, rob us of what we thought we knew.

Micaëla repeats the mother's message but converts it into her own soprano. The mother is lovely to the ear only when mediated: if she came on stage and sang to José herself, her melody would not evoke nostalgia, but might threaten the operagoer's pleasure-regime. We love, in Micaëla, the mother's absence — the originary specter replaced and purified, turned into quotation, and into *melody*, the one principle we still believe is transcendent.

Listening to Micaëla, I feel José's nostalgia for heterosexuality. Love for Carmen is so mediated through otherness and violence that it diverges from the heterosexual monogamy that Micaëla represents — a system that has its share of uncanniness, too, because it excavates a lost world from the listener's interior. When she sings, we can experience Don José's nostalgia for heterosexuality, as if we once lived there: Eden we might have stayed in, had we tried, had we decided, had we said "yes" to Micaëla's harps and melody, had we not met Carmen. . . . Nostalgia for heterosexuality: a wish — paradoxical — to possess a body one does *not* typically wish to possess: a wish to stand *inside Don José's silence* and hear the mother's message infuse Micaëla 's soprano frame. The possibility of joining Micaëla and recollecting the past! Better to listen to the recollection than actually to follow Micaëla out of the opera and into a country a few miles north of Bizet's *Carmen,* a province (I see and smell its trees) where Micaëla and the absent mother dwell.

If Micaëla entered my life I might travel backwards in time with her; I might embark on the voyage of retrieval she promises the listener. Or I might ask her if she prefers women, if she courts me only because she knows I'll refuse her, if the hospital purity of her timbre expresses *her chosen or innate immunity to masculine tones.* Maybe Micaëla's first love is the mother she impersonates, whose steadfastness she celebrates, whose kisses she receives and passes on.

Dido's "When I am laid in earth" (Renunciation)

Death can have a "queer" (self-involved, self-reflexive, camp, matte, sentimental, quaint) rather than a "Greek" (tragic, self-denying, absolving, dignified, authentic) flavor — particularly when it is staged, or suicidal, or when the dying lady speaks her last words to a girlfriend: as in Dido's lament, from Henry Purcell's *Dido and Aeneas* (1680), composed for Mr. Josias Priest's Boarding-School at Chelsey for Young Gentlewomen, a three-act opera that lasts only one hour.

Dido, alone on stage with her companion Belinda, moves, in monody, with drooping accents, downward: "Thy hand, Belinda; darkness shades me: On thy bosom let me rest." The harmonies shift beneath Dido's vocal body, unsettling her. When Dido's lament begins, we are allowed to think, "At last I've found a decorous, contained way to cope with immensities! I've found a position for my grief, somewhere between caricature and the Elgin Marbles!" Dido's Samothracian lament wards off the toxin of "depth." The queen sings:

> When I am laid, am laid in earth,
> may my wrongs create
> no trouble, no trouble in thy breast.

First she moves upward on "when I am laid," carving *mobility* and *destination*, however glacial, from a grief that may have otherwise lacked a future: but then she turns into a frieze again, she gets stuck (broken record), "am laid — am laid" (hysterical tic, the double meaning of "laid" — getting laid — intruding, anachronistically), and she slides down a half-scale to the word "earth"; on "trouble" she appoggiaturas her body downward a fifth, signifying she *wants* trouble to be made, she wants Belinda and the audience of schoolgirls to weep forever because Queen Dido is gone from this world.

Monteverdi's Orfeo repeated "rendetemi" (restore to me), and Dido repeats "remember me": "remember me" first on a D, then again, repeated, on a D, then she sighs ("ah," an appoggiatura, I am taking my time, protracting my dying, turning it into a gorgeous cortège), and moves, for another "remember me," to a high G: REMEMBER ME! And on Flagstad's recording, she repeats the "remember me" section once more, making it difficult for this listener ever to forget Dido's death.

One kind of self-pity is gay or girlish: another is spartan and refined, has the fragrance of catharsis, appears restrained and makes huge points about civilization, and so can pretend to emerge, fat with homilies, straight from dominant culture. Lear and Brutus knew the manly ways of exhibiting sorrow. Dido's grief can *almost* be said to "pass," to transcend playacting, to acquire Attic and Elizabethan dimensions, rather than to reek of the carnival and the women's room.

Dido's grief — her renunciation of life, her display of death-wish in front of the dumbstruck Belinda — is queer because it is equally stiff and supple. She is stone as she sings: nothing genuine, no plasticity. But on the last high G "remember me!" we believe that Flagstad or Dido or some woman existing between the diva and her character *wants to be remembered,* and we believe in Belinda, standing there, loyal from the very beginning, nothing better to do in Carthage than hold the Queen's hand . . . and our listening body's suspension between farce and tragedy, between stillness and plasticity, as if the statue were about to breathe and speak, is camp, and it is operatic.

The opera lasts barely an hour. The entire tragedy seems a scene carved on a snuffbox: Purcell and Tate make womanly tragedy miniature enough to fit the bloomer confines of a young girl's vocal body — the lines lying low, abjuring floridity. *Dido and Aeneas* foreshortens and domesticates tragedy, makes it "cute," the girl-body proportions focusing Dido's fate as a magnifying-glass takes a sun-ray and makes a scrap of paper — or the civilization-upholding fiction of a "queen" *in extremis* — turn to flame.

Dido has a hard time expressing herself (coming out). In her first aria she said, "Ah, ah, ah, Belinda, I am prest with torment not to be confest," and when practical, nosy Belinda countered, "Grief increases by concealing," Dido sang, "Mine admits of no revealing." At the beginning, Belinda extorts an erotic secret from the Queen; by the end, Dido adores confessing, and bends Belinda's ear. When Dido reaches the realm of *sung plangency,* of *stylized lament,* we are happy that at last she has earned the right to confess, that buried sadness has wormed its way out of her queen-stiff body. And so "lament" or "gravity" or "pathos" — these poker-faced, respectable modes — grow lavender, overcast with values that musical culture discountenances, pretending that opera is austere and mature.

The opera's message: confine your laments to the closet. Your voice, echoing against the walls, will resemble a witch's "ho ho ho." At the brink of suicide, you'll have won the right to lament.

A girl will hold your hand, and listen. Your queer psychic economy will have earned you just an aria, just the right, in the name of art and self-restraint, to expel your soul in front of amazed witnesses, schoolgirls who crave your scapegoat's part because, though the scariest, it is also the flashiest.

The Death of Mimì (Mourning)

Even before AIDS I listened to death scenes so that I might identify with the dying woman and the bereft man, so that I might locate "sentimentality" in my body, so that, watching Mimì die of TB, I might stage a departure inside myself and experience, by surviving Mimì's death, the revival of certain extravagant and queer emotions I would later dismiss and keep secret, never explaining the power or coherence of these subjective states evoked by melodrama. We should call by its proper name the pity and terror we feel when an opera mauls us, suffocates us with sentiment, makes no reasoned dramaturgical claim. Not camp, not bathos, not sentimentality: dignify queer emotion by saying *catharsis,* even if opera induces the wish, condemned as effeminate, never to reassemble the socialized self, but instead to remain in tears forever, to stay where Puccini's *La Bohème* (1896) places us. Aren't our own wishes, small and poor, given voice as Mimì adjusts her tubercular body on the couch?

For a self-pitying entrance, everyone must anticipate you, so when you finally arrive, you don't have to work — you merely cough, or sigh, or smile. Mimì can't enter unless a harbinger — another woman — has cleared orchestral and emotional space; and so Musetta enters Rodolfo's garret and with choked voice announces that sick Mimì is just now climbing the stairs to die. Jan Peerce — Rodolfo on the Toscanini recording — cries "Ah!" with cantorial wail as Mimì appears, and the orchestra resumes her theme, "*Mi* chiamano *Mimì.*" Mi Mi is the mirror woman, she who knows but also questions her name, who lives to address herself, to designate or denote her emotions: the self-regarding subject, the narcissist. Mimì borrows back her own melody from the orchestra to ask, "Mi vuoi qui con te?" ("Do you want me here with you?"): rhetorical question, because Rodolfo responds, "Ah! mia Mimì, sempre! sempre!" ("always, always!").

Mimì doesn't know — or doesn't admit — that she is dying; Rodolfo seems sublimely generous to feign "always" when perhaps he has more precise information about her illness. The melody signifies Mimì's deluded sense of "sempre," and Rodolfo, who occupies the melody's climax, thus cooperates with the orchestra's reign of deception: not telling Mimì she is dying — so we can pretend, in the audience, that *we* don't know, so we can surprise ourselves with pleasure when she finally dies. Hearing *La Bohème*, are you willingly seduced, each time, into imagining that Rodolfo and Mimì's shared melody means eternity?

For Mimì's death to forge in our self-loathing breast a new, nightingale-quick worldview, there must be onstage voyeurs and sympathizers: the other bohemians — Schaunard, Colline, Musetta, Marcello — who have no lives of their own, who are utterly abject to the cult of Mimì. Her suffering and vindication depend on this stadium of glances: Rodolfo watches her, and the others watch Rodolfo, so that he, too, becomes a Mimì figure, a public wound.

The bohemians exit, leaving the lovers alone: the theme of male cavorting delivers itself into the hands of the first act's love-duet theme, which occurred in Rodolfo's "I'm a poet and your hands are cold" aria (I write, you freeze). At this moment in the Franco Zeffirelli production, Mimì reaches her hands out to supplicate Rodolfo, who is at the window, his back turned — his bachelor preoccupation leaving Mimì alone with the love theme's reiteration of her impossible, insatiable desire, the orchestra's suddenly dolcissimo graduation from D major to C major opening our hearts. She resembles the listener: unable to begin the duet, passively listening to a reprise of what was once her property. But finally Rodolfo makes his way to Mimì's arms, and *con grande espressione,* she begins a C-minor funeral-march utterance accompanied by orchestral footsteps, quarter notes, no rhythmic motion beyond these heartbeats that give Mimì's proclamation the spaciousness that comes with depression, forgiveness, and bodily injury:

> Ho tante cose che ti voglio dire,
> o una sola, ma grande come il mare . . .
>
> I have many things I want to tell you,
> or just one, but it is immense as the sea . . .

The immense wordless "ocean" she summons is our tendency to drown in *La Bohème* and in Mimì's death; a melodramatic identification opens, wet and unnameable, in the collective body of opera listeners.

It seems again and again that Mimì has arrived at her last moment, but Puccini delays it. She says "la mia cuffietta, la mia cuffietta!" ("my bonnet, my bonnet!") without accompaniment and then rises to an E (still unaccompanied) and then makes it to an F, like health, for B-flat major mirage (harps in the background) and *this, this* is her last moment? Do you remember the first time we met? she asks Rodolfo. Woodwinds have more responsibility for melody than she does — as if the orchestra were mimicking her past so she could observe it for the first time and figure out who she has been and will become.

Her final words are sung to background fragments of "Che gelida manina": the best moment in her life was when Rodolfo noticed that her hands were cold.

> Quì amor . . . sempre con te! . . .
> Le mani . . . al caldo . . . e . . . dormire . . .
>
> Here, my love . . . always with you! . . .
> The hands . . . in the warm . . . and . . . going to sleep . . .

Licia Albanese sings these last phrases pallid and fatigued. Renata Tebaldi clings to the notes, sliding downpitch, as if she were hanging off a high ledge, fingers gripping the uncertain stone.

Rodolfo doesn't know that Mimì is dead (he's staring out the window again, in the Met production); he's self-absorbed, or, clothed in lover's immunity, he can't be penetrated by bad news. The penultimate gesture of the opera: how can we keep this secret from Rodolfo? But finally — in speech, not song — he says, "Che vuol dire, quell'andare e venire . . . quel guardarmi così . . ." ("What did you say, what's this coming and going? why look at me like this?") and then, after a fateful pause —

C-sharp minor chords, quarter-note heartbeats, the same rhythm that accompanied Mimì's "Sono andati," give backbone to his almost embarrassing cry, "Mimì," at the top of his range: our newest diversion is observing the man weep and bleat a high G-sharp "Mimì!" We hear, in the background, the music that accompanied Mimì's statement "I have so many things I want to tell you, or just one, but it is immense as the sea, profound and infinite as the sea . . ." and the music is nautical and shimmery, like Debussy's *La Mer*, particularly after Rodolfo stops crying. Rodolfo will be unhappy for many more years, and so will we. When the orchestra repeats Mimi's "my love for you is immense as the sea," the strings seem her spirit-messengers telling us, from heaven or hell, *to batten on my death scene, to thrive on what can't be summarized or spoken.* The music, at the conclusion, narrates and justifies our own tears, and hides this otherwise embarrassing expenditure in a social context — operagoing. Protocol determines that the performance will end and that, unable to find exact words to describe or pass on the strange experience, we will dismiss it, underestimating melodrama's power to graft the solitary listener to a collectivity of mourners.

LEONARD MICHAELS

The Zipper

FROM THE THREEPENNY REVIEW

"A man goes to bed with Rita Hayworth and wakes up with me."
— RITA HAYWORTH (b. Margarita Carmen Cansino, 1918)

"My mistress' eyes are nothing like the sun."
— WILLIAM SHAKESPEARE

RITA HAYWORTH stars in *Gilda,* but she isn't seen for the first fifteen minutes, while the friendship of two men, played by George Macready and Glenn Ford, is established. Macready saves Ford from being robbed on the docks of Buenos Aires, then hires Ford to manage a gambling casino owned by Macready. They become trusting, affectionate pals in a nightlife society where women are marginal. Then Macready leaves on a business trip to the "interior." When Macready returns, Ford hurries to Macready's mansion and he is surprised to hear about a woman whom Macready just met and married. The woman is heard singing, a muted voice in the interior distance, in a bedroom, in the depths of Macready's mansion. Macready leads Ford toward the singing, into the bedroom, to meet the woman, and — cut — Rita Hayworth lifts her face to look into the camera and see who is there. In this gesture, with all the magic of the word, Rita Hayworth "appears." She is bathed in light, seems even to exude it like a personal quality, like her wavy hair, her voice, and the flow of her body when walking or dancing.

She looks into the camera, into me, my interior, and I see that the friendship of Macready and Ford is in trouble, for this is the

beautiful face of betrayal, jealousy, murder, suicide, war. It is the
face of love from Homer to Shakespeare to the 1940s.

Like other actresses of her day, Rita Hayworth had mythic
power, and could carry a movie without a male star. I thought
she carried *Gilda* despite George Macready and Glenn Ford. To
my view, they were of slightly repulsive dramatic interest, but I
was about thirteen when I saw the movie. I took it as seriously as
life. How could Rita Hayworth get involved with guys like that?

Macready, playing a Nazi agent who lives in Argentina, walks
rigidly erect, carrying a sword cane. He looks frosty, pock-
marked, and desiccated, like the surface of the moon. There is
something priestly about him, a lofty, ascetic air. Ford, playing a
low-life hustler who cheats at cards and dice, has a soft, dark,
sensuous look, sensitive rather than intelligent. He smiles and
wiggles around Macready in a flirty way. Wiggly and Rigid form
a love triangle with Rita Hayworth, very degrading to her, since
she is way out of their league, but then she is repeatedly humili-
ated in the movie. She seems to ask for it, even to need it badly;
once, she actually crawls at Ford's feet. Humiliation, essential
plot matter in Hollywood and novels, is probably basic to fiction
generally. Even the cherished story *Alice in Wonderland,* where a
girl falls into a hole and is then repeatedly insulted in mind and
body, has to do with humiliation. When I saw *Gilda,* I didn't wonder if there was a universal need for such subterranean experience.

Much dramatic tension is created when neither Rita Hayworth
nor Ford tells Macready — who is made suspicious by their
instantaneous, mutual hostility — that they already know each
other and were once lovers. Not telling Macready, they betray
him. Ford thinks he is loyal to Macready, protecting his peace of
mind, etc., and he is angry at the intrusion of Rita Hayworth into
his paradisal friendship. He says, in a voice-over after Macready
presents him to her, that he wanted to hit her, and he also
wanted to hit Macready. Ford is bitterly frustrated and confused.
I disliked him, but I suffered his anguish.

Trying not to succumb to Rita Hayworth's charms, Ford becomes increasingly self-righteous and more rigid than Macready. There is an excruciating moment when Macready, concerned not to look like a jealous husband, tells Ford to pull Rita

Hayworth away as she dances with another man in Macready's casino. But she will not only dance with other men, she will also go out with them. She doesn't love Macready; she fears him, and yet she makes him jealous of Ford, just as she makes Ford jealous of her and other men. It emerges that her licentious bitchery means only that she loves Ford; he loves her, too. They are trapped in a viciously delicious game of mutual detestation which becomes the main plot. It complicates, in a feminine way, through flamboyant gestures and shows of feeling. The subplot, full of male violence — guns, fistfights, crime, war — is turgid and easy to forget. You might say the movie is sexually structured, the woman (feeling) on top.

Rita Hayworth, with her amazing blond light in this dark movie (where almost everything happens in rooms, and even the outdoors seems indoors), suggests that dark and light are Manichean opposites — dark is evil, light is good. Gray represents confusion of good and evil. I certainly didn't think this when I saw the movie in the Loew's theater on Canal Street, in the Lower East Side of Manhattan. I didn't think anything. I felt the meaning of things, especially the morally murky weight of the gray-lighted bedroom scene where Rita Hayworth asks Macready to unzip her dress as she lies on a bed. She says more than once that she has trouble with zippers, a helpless girl imprisoned in the dress of a grownup. Zippers, a major erotic trope of forties movies, represented a man's access to a woman's body, despite her invisible metal teeth.

I didn't want Macready to unzipper Rita Hayworth's dress. I didn't want Macready to touch her, though she is married to him, and she herself invites physical intimacy. Macready has told Ford he is "crazy about her," so his heart is in the right place. Nevertheless, I didn't want him to touch Rita Hayworth. I knew he doesn't really love her; doesn't even feel desire or lust, only a sickening idea of possession, and a mysterious need for betrayal. Why else would he hire Ford, a known cheater, as his most trusted assistant? and why else would Macready marry a woman — even Rita Hayworth — he has known only one day?

Macready flaunts his frightening sword cane, which he calls his "friend," but he moves in a delirium of masochistic self-destruction, and he is finally stabbed in the back by his "friend," literally the cane, metaphorically Ford. Macready gets what he deserves, which is what he wants, including sexual betrayal by Ford. Despite Ford's furious resistance to her, Ford gets Rita Hayworth, which is what she wants. Everything seems to work out, to balance and close, but not for me. I left the movie haunted by images of Rita Hayworth, yearning for her.

She had so much beauty and vitality that I assumed she would recover from what Macready did after unzippering her dress. Whatever it was, it wasn't good, but I supposed it happened a lot in Hollywood, where men go about touching women without feeling love, and — utterly unbearable — there are women who want to be Macreadied. Thus: in the religioso movie darkness, I saw Rita Hayworth request her own humiliation by the ascetic, priestly, frightening Macready. Zip. She is sacrificed and apotheosized. I had to remind myself that *Gilda* is a movie, not real life, and George Macready is a fine actor; also, probably, a nice guy.

No use.

The creep touched her.

I understood that real life is this way.

Nothing would be the same for me again.

I wanted to forget the scene, but it had happened as if to me, and was now fixed in my personal history, more indelibly than World War II. Only an instant of zipper business, yet it colored my love for Rita Hayworth with pity and grief. She lay there, utterly still and vulnerable, and Macready leaned over her the way kids play doctor, an eerily erotic game.

Seeing this was like a criminal privilege, though I was only sitting in a movie theater, doing nothing but looking. But I looked. I didn't shut my eyes. Unspeakable apprehensions — pleasure? — were aroused in me, in my head or heart, that secret, interior, moral theater (as opposed to the public showplace, the Loew's Canal) where movies dreamily transpire, differently for each of us. I disapproved of the sensations, the so-called pleasure, but pleasure and disapproval feed on each other. Rita Hayworth will be all right in the morning, I told myself. It won't matter what Macready did, though it was shameful and sad. What I felt was, perhaps, felt by millions.

Today, these feelings are considered sentimental; quaint.

They have lost force and spontaneity. We still have them, maybe, but they no longer have us. Macready did it to Rita Hayworth. So? He didn't rape her. The scene ended. I didn't have to watch Macready actually do anything, not that it would have been possible to film Macready in bed, doing things to Rita Hayworth, without destroying the movie. The remake of *Gilda* will, of course, show Macready doing everything, but it must be remembered that *Gilda* was released when feelings — like clothing styles, popular dances, car designs — were appreciated differently from today. Perhaps feelings as such had a far higher value. Movies didn't have to show naked bodies, fucking, paraphilia, or graphic mutilation and bloody murder. Techniques of suggestion were cultivated — the zipper, for example. Less was more except in regard to words. There were long scenes brilliant with words. We didn't so much use our eyes, like roots digging into visible physical bodies for the nourishment of meanest sensation. The ear, more sensuous than sensual, received the interior life of persons, as opposed to what is sucked up by the salacious eyeball.

Later in the movie, Rita Hayworth asks again for help with her zipper, during a nightclub routine, as she does a striptease dance. Several men hurry to oblige and help her become naked. Ford notices, has a tizzy, stops things from going too far. He slaps her. His hand doesn't wither and rot. Not only is there injustice, there is no justice. I feel so sorry for her, not to mention myself, poor kid, having to grow up, to know such things. Rita Hayworth is never seen disrobed in the movie, though it is threatened more than once. The atmosphere of dark repression and mysterious forces — the mood or feeling of the movie — might be destroyed by the revelation of her body. It scared me as she began her striptease dance in the nightclub. I didn't want everybody to see her body, or even to see that Rita Hayworth had a body. (The length of her beautiful left leg — I nearly died — is fleetingly exposed by a slit in her dress, as she dances.)

Two years later, I had sex for the first time, and I was taken by a weird sorrow riding home alone in the subway, as visceral odors lifted from my hands, reminding me that I'd fallen a few hours ago with my girlfriend — both of us virgins — from Heights of Desire, into bodies. (Religious movements, west and east, have cultivated a practice of dreamily disembodied, extended, nonorgasmic sex, as described in John Donne's poem "The Ecstasy.")

In plain sight of Ford, who is obliged by his job to watch her, Rita Hayworth flirts with other men and says, "If I were a ranch, they'd call me the Bar-Nothing." She thus tortures Ford, showing him — in the desires of other men — the body he can't let himself have. Ford watches. He tries to seem angry, then blurts out that Rita Hayworth can do whatever she pleases. It doesn't matter to him. He says he will personally deliver Rita Hayworth to her other men, then pick her up like "laundry" and return her to Macready. In effect, everything Rita Hayworth does with other men will be determined and controlled by Ford. Impassioned and irrational, Ford doesn't know what he means.

My moral notions, already disturbed, were further disturbed — the hero talks like this? I was being introduced to deep stuff, subterranean forces, years before I understood what was happening to me, or maybe the world in the forties. It had to do with sex — hardly anything doesn't — but I didn't know about sex. I believed something more important was at stake. I saw Bad presenting itself — in the form of pleasure — as entertainment; and I was being made to know that I was susceptible to the pleasure of Bad, if for no other reason than that Bad was in me, like Gog and Magog.

Was the experience indeed pleasure, not merely a strong sensation, like the electrical excitement of an idea, or the effect of a novelty, or a demonic, masturbatory fantasy? If it was a real feeling, could I be violated by it, my own real feeling? Could it happen to anyone? If so, could anyone ever be a good person?

I continued to wonder, without words to analyze or describe it, about the distinction — in real life — between pleasure and its innumerable imitations. Saint Augustine says, "The love of this world is fornication against God," and that's that. For me, the question was, if I felt something I believed was bad, but it felt good, would I want to fornicate against God again and again? and would I then despise other pleasures, assuming other pleasures remained to me? Had Macready unzipped me, too? In Flannery O'Connor's masterpiece, "A Good Man Is Hard to

Find," a mystical murderer says, "It's no real pleasure in life." I wondered about real pleasure. What is it?

Ford's antiheroic, homoerotic hysteria, basic to the dramatic effect in *Gilda,* is virtually explicit when Rita Hayworth suggests that a psychiatrist can tell Ford that he likes the idea of Rita Hayworth as "laundry," or dirty — that is, of her doing things with other men. I didn't understand this in feeling or thought. Is sexual infidelity — deserving of death in the colorful Mediterranean community I came from — what Ford likes? I didn't see his angry, tyrannical show of controlling power as a refusal to acknowledge that he is the hapless creature of dark impulses. Rita Hayworth understands what's going on in Ford, but Ford never gains understanding of himself. Instead, he becomes sadistically determined to punish Rita Hayworth for his inadmissible need to see her do what he likes her to do.

Gilda — written by a woman, starring a woman, produced by a woman — suggests that women know better than men what men are looking at when men look at women. They know that such looking — a function of blindness — is not seeing. In effect, Rita Hayworth exists fantastically for Macready and Ford within the so-called "male gaze." She is created by their looking, a form of ideological hypnosis, or blindness, or stupidity, perhaps crucial to the perpetuation of human society as it presently exists. In the movie, the male gaze keeps two men fixated on a woman rather than each other. Outside the movie, in real life, Rita Hayworth was the fixation of millions of men in the armed services, their favorite "pinup girl." An erotic icon, she kept our boys straight.

In *Gilda,* Rita Hayworth famously sings one song several times. (I later found out her voice is dubbed; also, her hair is dyed, her hairline is fake, her name is Margarita.) The refrain of her song is "Put the blame on Mame, boys." Mame (Freudian pun intended) is responsible for cataclysmic occurrences — the Chicago fire, a terrible snowstorm, etc. (She's hot, the city burns; she's cold, "for seven days they shovelled snow.") The song ironically implies that boys, who are exquisitely tortured by her capricious dominatrixiness, want to imagine that Mame has tremendous, annihilating power. I could see the amusement in Rita Hayworth's eyes as she pretends to sing, and I loved her for that, her peculiar quality of spirit. Not quite playing the role, she is more real, nearly accessible, more heartbreaking.

The audience learns that Ford abandoned her in the "interior" when he ran out of money, before the movie begins. To express the audience's contempt for him, the attendant in the men's room of Macready's gambling casino, a comic philosophical figure, lowly and godlike, twice calls Ford a "peasant." Ford lacks aristocratic sensibility, or class. But Rita Hayworth gives him an opportunity to transcend himself by choosing her over his career as Macready's thing. He doesn't choose her until the end of the movie, when he supposes Macready is dead. Ford thus remains a peasant, or, at best, a grubby careerist who takes his work more seriously than love. The movie ends. Poor Rita Hayworth goes off with Ford. A grim winter night, streetlights, traffic — the shock of the real — awaited me.

I went down Madison Street, passing under the Manhattan Bridge, then turning left on Market Street, walking toward the East River, until I came to Monroe Street and turned right. These directions, these streets, restored me to my life. I passed the tenements with their Italian grocery stores and candy stores, and I passed my old elementary school, a huge grim soot-dark Victorian building, P.S. 177. From the church of Saint Joseph, at the corner of Cherry and Market streets, I heard a bell tolling the hour. The church stood opposite our first-floor apartment in a building called Knickerbocker Village. Walking down Monroe Street, I approached the wavering light of Friday night prayer candles in our kitchen window. The shadow of my mother, against the window shade, moved from refrigerator to stove. Everything as it should be. Italian ladies with shopping bags and baby carriages. Italian kids sitting on the stoops of their tenements. This was real. Too different — like a blond woman who might bring the solidity and value of this neighborhood into question — wasn't good.

The darkness of the movie, like a darkness inside me, contained nothing real, but there was a faint glow of *Gilda* within it, and I felt tumultuous yearning for Rita Hayworth — the woman, not the actress. I yearned to bring her home, where she would descend, or lovingly condescend, to sweet reconciliation with the ordinariness of my life, even its banality and boredom, which I believed was good. The good. My mother, cooking good dinner in the small but good kitchen of our three-room apartment, would be embarrassed. She would apologize to bad Rita

Hayworth for not having prepared a more sumptuous dinner, but I hadn't given any warning. "Do you like borscht? It's good. Do you know, Miss Hayworth, the good doctor who delivered your bad baby is my good cousin from Canada? When he told me that he delivered your bad baby, I almost fainted. Maybe you remember him. Tall. Curly hair."

It was like this for me, in a day when love was praised and much desired, even the terrible anguish it was known to inflict. As for Rita Hayworth — dream of heroes, three husbands, millions of servicemen — she was love, catastrophic, wild, impossible to domesticate. So much of her life was public, spectacular imagery that it is hard to suppose she also had a real life, or to suppose that her feelings about Rita Hayworth were not the same as ours.

DAVID RIEFF

Victims, All?

FROM HARPER'S MAGAZINE

IMAGINE A COUNTRY in which millions of apparently successful people nonetheless have come to believe fervently that they are really lost souls — a country where countless adults allude matter-of-factly to their "inner children," who, they say, lie wounded and in desperate need of relief within the wreckage of their grown-up selves. Imagine the celebrities and opinion-makers among these people talking nightly on TV and weekly in the magazines not about their triumphs but about their victimization, not about their power and fame but about their addictions and childhood persecutions.

Imagine that this belief in abused "inner children" dragging down grown-up men and women has become so widespread as to exert considerable influence over the policies of such supposedly practical bodies as corporations, public hospitals, and boards of education — which, in turn, have taken to acting as if the greatest threat facing their various constituencies is a nexus of addictions and other self-destructive "behaviors," ranging from alcoholism and drug addiction to the more nebulous, if satisfyingly all-encompassing, category of "codependency," a term meaning, in essence, any reliance for one's sense of self on the opinion of someone else, someone more often than not plagued by his or her own addiction. One would be imagining a place, then, where nearly *everyone* is identified — is identifying himself or herself — as some sort of psychological cripple.

In this country, it is taken for granted that no blame for these addictions or dependencies can be assigned to those who exhibit them. Terms such as "character," "weakness," and "individual responsibility" are no longer deemed appropriate. Those who drink too much, take drugs, or destroy themselves (and their co-dependents) in other ways suffer either from a disease (like alcoholism) or from difficulties that are the direct, ineluctable result of the faulty upbringing to which they were subjected as children.

A desperate creed, and yet this country is not — as, upon hearing it, an outsider might have reason to suppose — on anything approaching its last legs. It has neither been bombed by fighter aircraft so technologically advanced as to be undetectable to its air defenses nor has its morale been unhinged by the rigors of prolonged triple-digit inflation, an austerity program imposed by the World Bank, the emigration of its skilled professionals, or intercommunal savagery. To the contrary, here is a country that, although scarcely without its difficulties, remains one of the richest countries on earth, indeed one of the richest places the world has ever known.

There is even a good argument to be made that the most salient thing about this country is not its apprehension of decline but, rather, how many people from all over the less favored reaches of the globe seem willing to risk anything to pull up stakes and immigrate here — and, having arrived, to fill with reasonably good grace all those dirty, humiliating, low-paying jobs that native-born workers have grown unwilling to perform.

In any event, those drawn to the idea of their wounded "inner child" are doing pretty well. Many have life stories that hew to what has long been the country's favorite narrative about itself: rags to riches. But now there has developed a new narrative: from addiction, through discovery of the "inner child," to recovery. In this country, this is the story men and women are increasingly telling themselves and one another. The country is the United States of America, circa 1991.

Most public-minded Americans would agree that there is a crucial debate going on just now, the resolution of which will have a deep impact on the character of our society. I am referring to the debate over "political correctness." President Bush, perhaps because he has always had a keen eye for inflammatory domestic symbols, has joined the chorus of voices that have dubbed the "P.C./multiculturalism" debate the most significant domestic argument about ideas in decades. At the same time, like the professors and pundits on both sides of the issue, he has been silent about the meaning of that much larger and, in terms of money and mass appeal, more influential enthusiasm that is usually referred to as the twelve-step, or recovery, movement.

This is not to underestimate the importance of political correctness. Certainly, on university campuses, however vociferously and disingenuously the militants themselves continue to deny it, the teaching of the humanities has largely been hijacked, replaced by the factitious cant of deconstructionism and Third World apologetics, or, as its proponents, with their flawlessly tin ears, prefer to call it these days, "postcoloniality." Yet the fact remains that for every literature department that has been taken over by one or another of the vying ethnic and intellectual particularisms that pass for thinking in the contemporary academy, there are likely to be at least two new books preaching the message of recovery edging their way onto the national best-seller lists, not to mention the innumerable twelve-step chapters being formed every month in cities and suburbs all over the country.

Nevertheless, for intelligent Americans with no direct experience of these groups, the recovery movement is news from the fringe, trivial and evanescent. And it is a safe bet that books bearing such titles as *Healing the Child Within; Lost in the Shuffle: The Co-dependent Reality; The Road Less Traveled; Children of Trauma: Rediscovering Your Discarded Self;* and *Choice-Making for Co-dependents, Adult Children and Spirituality Seekers* will never be held up by some Republican officeholder caught in a tight race against a liberal challenger the way the works of leading radical multiculturalists are likely to be during the 1992 campaign. Nor are authors like John Bradshaw, Robert Subby, Scott Peck, Sharon Wegscheider-Cruse, or Ann Denis likely to find themselves excoriated as threats to Western civilization.

On the face of things, however, it is by no means immediately obvious why this should be so. Indeed, the claims that the recovery movement routinely makes for itself seem far more radical and infinitely more destabilizing of Establishment values than even the most picturesque pronouncements of the campus radicals. When, for example, John Bradshaw, one of the recovery movement's leading figures, insists that "soul-murder is the basic problem in the world today," and then goes on to assert that everything about the way people live in modern America — not their life-style so much as their "death style," as Bradshaw puts it — confirms its essentially pathological character, he is going a great deal further than those who content themselves with demonstrating for the transformation of university humanities curricula.

Even when it comes to those assumptions that the recovery movement shares with radical multiculturalism, it is almost invariably within the context of recovery that they are presented in their most extreme form. Both movements deny the value of any important distinction between the personal and the political; but where the multiculturalists, however much their politics too may be based on feelings, at least try to hold on to certain political categories, the recovery people are interested only in their subjective selves. When *they* say the personal is the political, they really mean it.

That the recovery psychotherapists are more radical than the academic multiculturalists becomes most clear when one examines the politics of victimhood, a centerpiece of both movements. In P.C. circles, this idea is inherently self-limiting in the sense that if the concept of oppression is to make any kind of sense, the situation of the various groups of victims — be they blacks, Hispanics, women, or gays — must be opposed to that of an oppressor group — these days, straight white males. Proponents of recovery do not think in group terms. They claim that virtually everyone in the country is, in some essential sense, a victim — a victim, mostly, of abusive parents. Moreover, the recovery advocates say they have the statistics to back up this sweeping assertion. "What we're hearing from experts," John Bradshaw confidently told an interviewer not long ago, "is that approximately 96 percent of the families in this country are dysfunctional to one degree or another."

Small wonder, then, that for the recovery movement only a complete transformation of American society will do. Unlike the demands made by even the most extreme multiculturalists, which mostly boil down, for all the apocalyptic verbiage in which

they come wrapped, to calls for various sorts of linguistic affirmative action, the goals of the recovery movement appear to be
authentically millennial. Even the gravest of the specific ills the
movement wants to remedy — the physiological and psychological addictions, as well as what, more broadly, recovery writers
often characterize as "chronic inner pain" — are no more than
symptoms of the larger spiritual crisis, and their redress is only
the first step toward some larger spiritual awakening. As Bradshaw has put it, "I believe there are moments of great readiness
in collective human consciousness . . . I think if we were to use a
new Jungian archetype to characterize our time it would be the
wounded child . . . and so if we change parent-child relationships, we can change history."

It is, perhaps, the use of this sort of pop-psychological language
that has led American intellectuals and academics to underestimate the recovery movement. There is nothing new about recovery except the packaging, they tend to say, insisting that the
search for "inner children" and such is only the latest in that long
series of enthusiasms for self-improvement to which Americans
have been drawn since at least the middle of the nineteenth century. They admit that Bradshaw's books sell millions of copies
but go on to remind you that neither the turn-of-the-century
French psychotherapist Emile Coué nor Aimee Semple Mc-
Pherson, whose revivals attracted thousands in the 1920s, did too
badly either.
    There is no denying that the "self-help" ethos is anything but
new. Indeed, few Americans, no matter how European they may
fancy themselves to be, live untouched by the conviction that
they can change almost anything about themselves if they really
want to do so. For Americans, self-creation has from the beginning been the essential act. The great American stories, from
James Fenimore Cooper to Philip Roth, are about busting free,
finding some way of shucking off the bonds of family and tradition, not so much with the purpose of winning the freedom to *be*
oneself as out of the conviction that only the act of lighting out
for the territories ensures that one will ever *become* oneself.
    This old myth of the frontier is part of the story, of course. If
spiritual quests have always been described as journeys, rarely

has the spatial element had such resonance as in the American version. When the recovery writer Sharon Wegscheider-Cruse calls one of her books *Learning to Love Yourself: Finding Your Self-Worth,* the echoes of the California state motto, born of the Gold Rush — Eureka ("I Have Found It") — are still audible. But even the noise of those spiritual covered wagons is, in the end, less compelling than another entrenched American idea, that of "know-how." The point of all these self-help books — of the entire recovery movement — is to give someone interested the *means* to recover. The very phrase "twelve-step program" is telling enough, as is the frequency with which a successful recovery book is soon accompanied by a "workbook" of some kind. Thus, John Bradshaw writes a book on the "inner child," but just down the shelf from it in most bookstores is Cathryn L. Taylor's *Inner Child Workbook: What to Do with Your Past When It Just Won't Go Away.* Sometimes the same author produces both works. Melody Beattie's *Codependent No More* sold almost 2 million copies when it appeared in 1987. Three years later, Ms. Beattie was back on the best-seller list with *Codependents' Guide to the Twelve Steps.*

It seems that given the proper tools, success is all but a sure thing. The recovery gurus may occasionally pause to insist that "working a program," to use the argot of the movement, can be a grueling business. But for the most part, the tone is relentlessly upbeat. In the section of his book *Lost in the Shuffle* called "Recovery Hints and Reminders," Robert Subby writes of the year or two he expects it will take an addict to kick his or her habit. "These will not be years spent in drudgery and self-denial, but they will be years filled with learning a new way of life, building healthy relationships and laying the foundation for self-actualization." The tone is so artisanal that one wonders how Dr. Subby resisted the urge to just come out and say *pouring* the foundation. But when the promise is self-transformation, getting off dope or booze, no matter how essential, must indeed come to seem like little more than a kind of karmic renovation project.

And it is striking to what degree the American embrace of the how-to and the American apprehension of the psychological can be reconciled within the context of the idea of recovery. Alienated we may be, but whether it's on the floor of the health club or in one of John Bradshaw's codependency workshops, where people pay hundreds of dollars a day to interact with their "inner children," often represented by toy animals they hold in their hands — frogs, usually, or teddy bears — it's all in the know-how.

The direct antecedent of all the twelve-step groups is not hard to identify. As almost every recovery writer makes clear, the movement derives its method and its inspiration from Alcoholics Anonymous. Many recovery books begin with impassioned accounts of their authors' alcoholism and their eventual discovery of the twelve steps through which they found a way out of their misery at a moment when they were convinced that all was lost. To understand how addiction and recovery have become our central metaphors — addicted to cocaine, the wrong kind of men, TV, gas guzzlers; recovering from too much sex, too little leisure, welfare dependency, the Vietnam syndrome — one first needs to look at AA.

Certainly it would be difficult, in any event, to overstate the influence that AA has exerted over mainstream American life since its formation in the 1930s, the outgrowth of a chance encounter in Akron, Ohio — every AA member learns this story; it is the organization's Genesis — between Bill Wilson, a stockbroker from New York City who had recently stopped drinking but was desperately afraid that he was on the verge of taking it up again, and the alcoholic Akron physician Bob Smith, who lives on in AA lore as Doctor Bob, a man who had tried everything but had never succeeded in remaining sober for very long. Not only has the so-called Big Book of the organization sold millions of copies since its first edition was published in 1939, but the millions of members who have belonged to AA over the decades have been followed by millions more who have been to at least one AA meeting sometime in their lives.

In retrospect, AA at its founding seemed like one of the responses offered by a white, Protestant, small-town America despondent over the failure of Prohibition. Passed in 1919, the Volstead Act was ignominiously repealed in 1933, and with its passing went any serious hope of legally mandated temperance. Of course, AA was no more a conscious expression of these changed circumstances than the turning inward that art historians discern in Biedermeier furniture was a thought-out response to the failure of political liberalism in Central Europe in the early nineteenth century. That said, like Biedermeier, AA can be partly understood as such a turning inward. Instead of political action, AA followed its spiritual progenitor, the early-twentieth-century Oxford Group, in preaching a species of personalized moral rearmament. Individual AA members would accomplish what political action had failed to: they'd do away with booze. In the process, a "social problem" was transformed into a "disease" over which alcoholics insisted they had no control.

It is interesting that so many of the recovery advocates speak of their own political involvement during the 1960s. Indeed, some write of that period so nostalgically that it is hard not to feel they are looking for their "inner decade" as much as their "inner children." "For me," writes Lucia Capacchióne, author of *Recovery of Your Inner Child,* "the sixties were about marriage, family, and artistic achievement. On the larger level they were also about human rights, and I helped fight Johnson's War on Poverty as a Head Start director. By the decade's end, the Women's Movement was fully launched. Like many of my sisters, I was juggling a number of roles, i.e., wife, mother, artist, and educator. Then, one day, the bottom dropped out as the seventies began . . ."

To the followers of recovery, the lesson of their activism during the sixties is that those political involvements were either, as Bradshaw once put it, "not genuine . . . a mood-altering trip" — in other words, yet another form of codependency, this time on revolution — or else simply premature. Most would angrily deny that their absorption in what they sometimes call "ego work" represents any abdication of social responsibility. "You can't go to work in the social order unless you've healed the wound (of your inner child)," Bradshaw has said.

Of course, many of these ideas were commonplace in the sixties as well. What else, when all is said and done, is all this talk in recovery circles about the primacy of the emotional over the rational, the instinctual over the repressed, and the spontaneous over the deliberate, if not a New Age gloss on the wilder assertions of a Wilhelm Reich or an R. D. Laing — the transliteration into Middle American terms of that catchphrase of May '68, "the imagination to power"? But whereas in the now much-maligned sixties there was always at least a tension between the impulse to heal oneself and the impulse to heal the world, the recovery movement is in no doubt as to which choice is the right one. In recovery, one returns not to first principles but to the "inner child," the most private self. In this, recovery is fully the product less of the decade during which many of its adherents were young than of the Reaganite eighties. When John Bradshaw replies to a question from an interviewer about how he sees the obligations adults owe their aging parents by declaring flatly that "we didn't come into this world to take care of Mom and Dad," he is, wittingly or not, recapitulating the Reagan-Bush approach when confronted by the problems of the frail and vulnerable in American society. The message, whether psychological or political, is that there are no civic, no social obligations, only private ones.

It will be obvious that Bradshaw is not a man to shrink from extremes. For him, not only are the personal and the political one and the same, but so are the historical and the psychological. Borrowing liberally from the work of the Swiss child psychoanalyst Alice Miller, he argues that Nazism was the direct result of Hitler's having been abused as a child. Hitler, too, it would seem, was a victim. "Hitler," Bradshaw writes, "was re-enacting his own childhood, using millions of innocent Jews as his scapegoats." Small wonder, then, that Bradshaw and those who accept his arguments believe that recovery work is far more important than any more conventional social activism. As Bradshaw puts it, "Hitler and black [sic] Nazism are a cruel caricature of what can happen in modern Western society if we do not stop promoting and proliferating family rules that kill the souls of human beings."

More than anything else, it is this bleak, totalizing view of the world that distinguishes the message of most recovery books from that contained in the other self-help volumes with which they share space on bookstore shelves and best-seller lists. The message is not Coué's "every day, in every way, I'm getting better and better," or Norman Vincent Peale's "power of positive thinking," or even Eric Berne's rather more tentative "I'm okay, you're okay." These authors offered little direct criticism of society in those books. Contrast their messages with John Bradshaw's unyielding assertion that "our family life is killing the souls of human beings" and his recommendation that since "most families are dysfunctional because our rules for normalcy are dysfunctional . . . the important issue is to find out what species of flawed relating your family specialized in. Once you know what happened to you, you can do something about it."

And the one thing that all the recovery writers insist upon is that whether an individual remembers it or not, *something did happen.* According to Dr. Charles Whitfield, one of the most successful recovery writers, only between 5 and 20 percent of Americans grew up "with a healthy amount and quality of love, guidance and other nurturing. . . ." The rest — and, unsurprisingly, most recovery writers favor Dr. Whitfield's lower figure for those raised in healthy homes — did not receive anywhere near enough of the aforementioned psychic nutrients to successfully "form consistently healthy relationships, and to feel good about themselves and what they do." If the result is not a substance addiction like drink or drugs, it is likely to be a "process" addiction taking the form of either too much interest in some activity or too much reliance on some other person or thing for an individual's sense of identity — the dreaded codependency.

In their book *Adult Children: The Secrets of Dysfunctional Families,* John and Linda Friel provide a list of recovery groups — an incomplete list, they advise — that maps (or begins to) the contours of contemporary American addiction and victimhood. Beginning with AA, the Friels go on to note Al-Anon (the organization founded as a sort of ladies' auxiliary to AA, in the period when it was all male, to help the wives — later, more ecumenically, any loved one — of alcoholics), Alateen, Al-Atot, Narcotics Anonymous, Cocaine Anonymous, Overeaters Anonymous, Bulimics/ Anorexics Anonymous, Sexaholics Anonymous, Sex Addicts Anonymous (the recovery movement is full of mysteriously fine distinctions), Adult Children Anonymous, Adult Children of Alcoholics, Gamblers Anonymous, Spenders Anonymous, Smokers Anonymous, Debtors Anonymous, Fundamentalists Anonymous, Parents Anonymous, Child Abusers Anonymous, Workaholics Anonymous, Shoplifters Anonymous, Pills Anonymous, and Emotions Anonymous.

Whew! And, of course, such a list is infinitely expandable. For if there is really not all that much difference between working too hard and abusing your children (and the Friels' decision to place them side by side suggests that in the recovery context, there really isn't), then any conduct that can be engaged in enthusiastically, never mind compulsively — from stamp collecting to the missionary position — would be one around which a recovery group could presumably be organized.

And new categories are indeed cropping up all the time. The biggest growth sector seems to have been in the codependency area. Cocaine Anonymous has begot Co-Anon; Narcotics Anonymous, Nar-Anon; Overeaters Anonymous, a slim O-Anon; and Sex Addicts Anonymous, Co-Sa. But there are plenty of wholly new addictions to recover from as well, including at their different ends of the tragedy scale Incest Survivors Anonymous, which is ghastly and self-explanatory, and Recovering Couples Anonymous, which is mysterious and turns out to mean a kind of group family therapy in which couples can figure out how to stay together. As Melody Beattie puts it in her *Codependents' Guide to the Twelve Steps,* the goal of RCA is "mutual interdependence," which, it seems, is not to be confused with codependency. The list goes on and on, and it is clear that the next decade will give rise to any number of new subsets of the victimized, the impaired, and the addicted.

It is interesting to chart just how a new group of victims is located. To take but one example, in 1983 Janet Geringer Woititz wrote a book called *Adult Children of Alcoholics.* It was turned down by most mainstream publishers and at first was sold almost entirely by mail order. Within four years, however, Woititz's book had not only gotten onto the *New York Times* best-seller list, eventually selling more than 2 million copies, but had spawned a movement, the National Association for Children of Alcoholics, a magazine, *Changes,* and a whole new category within that larger grouping that Herbert Gravitz and Julie Bowden, authors of *Recovery: A Guide for Adult Children of Alcoholics,* call the 96 percent of the population who are "children of trauma." But after the magazine and the movement and the database, could the spin-off be far behind? Of course not. In 1988, Ann Smith, the director of a Pennsylvania family-services clinic, published *Grandchildren of Alcoholics: Another Generation of Co-dependency.*

"My apologies," she writes, "'for introducing another 'label.' I know of no other way to bring this group of people out of hiding and into recovery."

Here I must declare an interest. Being the adult grandchild of an alcoholic — one is not supposed to hide these facts in the land of the free and the home of the autobiography — I naturally scrutinized Ms. Smith's book with particular care. But while it is never safe to underestimate the power of repression, I must report that I just don't see it. I was surprised to learn that the first characteristic Ms. Smith identifies in people like me is a "distorted family image." This turns out to mean "seeing only the good in [one's family]." Now, this is not a trait associated with either my family or, I would submit, that of many other writers. Oh well. The second category is "'self-blaming." It may be old-fashioned to say this, but would that it were so. The rest of Ms. Smith's list is scarcely more revealing. I had been "outed," it seemed, for no purpose. Indeed, I have been more shaken up by a trip to a Broadway fortune-teller.

Of course, it may be that I simply do not know which addiction or codependency I have. There are, after all, so many to choose from. This is presumably why so many of the recovery books on the market include endless questionnaires and checklists through which the reader can take a reading on his or her emotional situation. The categories are, to put it charitably, broadly phrased. In *Bradshaw On: The Family*, for example, the author offers a checklist for what he calls "adult children of dysfunctional families"; i.e., his readers, not to say the American people as a whole. "See if you identify yourself in several of the following traits," he writes. "If you do, it's likely that you are co-dependent and are carrying your family dysfunction." These traits turn out to include such harmless aspects of temperament as "inveterate" dreaming and keeping "secrets." There is even the fearsome trait "'avoids depression through activity," which, particularly if one is prey to severe depression, hardly seems like such a bad idea.

Dr. Charles Whitfield's "Recovery Potential Survey" in his *Healing the Child Within* is, if anything, even more all-encompassing. Indeed, it is hard to see how, given the way Dr. Whitfield has defined childhood trauma, *any* reader could feel exempt. The questions in the survey range from relatively benign queries like "Do you seek approval and affirmation?" through the more ominous "Do you respond with anxiety to authority figures and angry people?" (here one wants to ask, with or without a firearm in their hands?) to the merely bathetic, as in that old self-help standby "Do you find it difficult to express your emotions?" And, of course, the whole thing is rigged. It turns out that in Dr. Whitfield's system of grading, even one answer of "occasionally" (never mind "often" or "usually") means that the respondent stands in considerable need of having his or her inner child tended to. And just to make sure that those who have not admitted to any such feelings aren't let off the hook, Dr. Whitfield is quick to point out that if the reader answers "mostly 'Never,' you may not be aware of some of your feelings." Checkmate.

For people like Whitfield and the other recovery writers to insist that we are all victims is pretty much the same thing as asserting that no one is a victim. Either way, the civic voice is muffled, if not blotted out; it is up to you or to me, but not we. Of course, such an outbreak of self-pity among the affluent classes as recovery has spawned all but ensures that the real victims in American society — those who will never be affluent enough or have enough free time to work it out with their "inner children" — will not get the attention that is the necessary first step to any improvement in *their* lives.

Meanwhile, resources as well as attention are lavished on "inner children." Bradshaw writes in *Homecoming: Reclaiming and Championing Your Inner Child* that he found he had to balance the demands of his new celebrity with his obligations to his "inner child" and so "chose some things that my inner child likes. For the last few years, we always fly first class."

The recovery writers insist that nearly everyone in the United States has been the victim of some instance of child abuse. One would think that if a term like "child abuse" is to have any real meaning, it must be limited to some variant of sexual violation or battery. The recovery movement would have it otherwise. They talk of mental abuse, of parents abusing their children by "invalidating their experiences," even of abusers who thwart "the child's spirituality," to quote Charles Whitfield. So much for life in its full, honest imperfection.

In recovery workshops, as well as at home in the living room, recovery workbooks opened, people are encouraged to try to get in touch with that "inner child" and discern, through a dialogue with it,whether they were abused: "memory work," it is called. One might reasonably ask if someone moved to do such memory work were not, in some way, predisposed to uncover evidence of abuse — some explanation of their addiction or emotional un-happiness. But this is not a question to be entertained. Steven Farmer writes in his book *Adult Children of Abusive Parents,* "No matter how abuse is defined or what other people think, you are the ultimate judge: If you think you were abused, you were. If you're not sure, you probably were."

What matters is the story that you arrive at. Thus, to imagine is to make it so, or, as the title of an anthology of postwar American women writers would have it, "We are the stories we tell." Bradshaw's story is, as he says in *Homecoming,* that we are "divine infants in exile," a nation of E.T.s desperate to come home. And it seems that increasing numbers of Americans are beginning to agree with him.

But *are* we the stories we tell? During the period that I was reading little but recovery books, I kept remembering an en-counter I had seen once on television between reporters and the grieving father of one of the passengers killed when Sikh terror-ists blew up an Air India flight over the Irish Sea in 1985. The weeping father had been shown coming out of the makeshift morgue that the Irish police had set up in a small coastal village, and no sooner had he done so than he was surrounded by the hacks, who bombarded him with questions. "What are you going to do?" one called out. To which, with astonishing dignity, the man replied simply, "Do? What do you expect me to do in this dirty world?"

The point that he was trying to make through his sobs was pre-cisely the one that the recovery movement is most anxious to deny. Life may be whatever story you invent in a Bradshaw sem-inar, but only very affluent, very cut-off people could persuade themselves, at least once they have "returned home," that this is really the way things are. A quick way of seeing just how specific the recovery idea is to prosperous Americans in the late twentieth century is to think how preposterous it would seem not only to a man whose daughter had just been killed by a terrorist bomb, or someone who was hungry, but to someone, anyone, in Croatia, the Soviet Union, or South Africa. It is a safe bet that they are more worried about what will befall their real children than what has befallen their inner children. It is a measure of the continued economic success of the United States that so many of its citizens could be so buffered from the real harshness of the world that they can spend their time anatomizing the state of their own feelings and speculating, often deep into middle age, about whether or not their parents always behaved as well as they should have.

In most of the world, though, people's thoughts are elsewhere. Beyond our innocent shores, it is understood that the past is not always knowable and never recuperable, that there is sometimes nothing to be done, and that reality conforms neither to our desires nor to our schemes, psychic or material. There is chance, and fate, and tragedy.

Of course, it is true that there is a group within the population who often do not know this or believe it. We call them children, and while we may envy them their ignorance, and their belief in the potency of their own wishes, we know that they are under a false impression. We also know, or should, that however much we may feel nostalgia for our childhood, there is no going back, no reprieve from adulthood, which is to say from consciousness. That is the splendor and misery of being an adult, a condition from which we should not want to and, more to the point, cannot recover.

Look Away, Dixie Land

FROM THE NEW YORK REVIEW OF BOOKS

1

"OAKLAND CEMETERY hasn't changed much in the hundred and thirty-odd years it has sheltered Atlanta's favored dead," writes the contemporary Atlanta novelist Anne Rivers Siddons, in her novel *Peachtree Road*. "Our crowd has always been in and out of Oakland almost as frequently and as easily as we enter and leave our homes and clubs. . . . Lucy always swore that it was here that she and Red Chastain first made love, on top of Margaret Mitchell's grave."

Fifty-five years after its 1936 publication, *GWTW* remains a cult novel of the American Civil War, and its author, Margaret Mitchell, a local Atlanta deity. An instant best-seller on publication, the novel has an amorphous quality, like a ghost unobstructed by doors and walls, that allowed it to be interpreted to nearly any purpose by nearly any of its nonblack readers. During the war, it was popular in Britain, presumably as a picture of a courageous and embattled people; it was equally popular among the Axis powers, presumably for its picture of a master race defending civilization. A wartime pirated edition was immensely popular in Japan, and the story was eventually adapted as an all-female musical revue in Tokyo. Polish resistance fighters read it avidly, as did Eva Braun, who listed Margaret Mitchell as one of her two favorite authors.

To date, the book has sold 28 million copies, second only to the Bible, and is available in at least thirty countries. The book's life was extended, too, through the equally popular David Selznick film of 1939, and through having become a cultural toy not unlike Walt Disney's Mickey Mouse, although Tara has not matched the wealth of the magic kingdom. It is tempting to see Mickey as a spokesman for the playfulness, the fun, of commerce, while Scarlett and Rhett represent commerce as a kind of eroticism. There are *Gone With the Wind* perfumes exhorting us to "feel their passion," *GWTW* chess sets with pieces modeled after Clark Gable and Vivien Leigh, and costume dolls of Scarlett O'Hara, an odd example of an ironic current in the American toy industry, conjuring a picture of little girls playing with the image of a murderess who despised her two eldest children. There are lithographs, posters, and collector's plates. And now there is a sequel, written by a romance novelist under the guidance of the Mitchell estate, and a lengthy biography of Mitchell herself, written by a history professor named Darden Asbury Pyron, who shares Mitchell's southern roots and has previously edited a collection of critical essays on *Gone With the Wind* titled *Recastings.*

Gone With the Wind was from the outset an arena for critical and historical conflicts. The contradiction between its popular success and critical rejection by the most influential critics of its day, a failure that increasingly embittered Margaret Mitchell, dramatized the characteristic aesthetic irony of the United States: how can it be that if majority rule democracy represents supreme political judgment, that degree of readership does not also represent ultimate artistic judgment? And what is the nature and meaning of popular success when many African American thinkers, including James Baldwin and Malcolm X, have found *Gone With the Wind* offensive? Critics like Malcolm Cowley, the champion of Faulkner, and Bernard De Voto have argued, on different grounds, that *GWTW* was an artistic failure. Richard Dwyer, in an essay included in Mr. Pyron's collection *Recastings,* argues that "its popularity is the *only* criterion by which *GWTW* is still being judged here and elsewhere."

   Gone With the Wind's role as the central popular account of the white South's political theology continues to be controversial, too. Richard Harwell, editor of a *GWTW* "scrapbook," *Gone With the Wind as Book and Film,* wrote that the novel was "that great desideratum of the UDC [United Daughters of the Confederacy], an unbiased history of the war from the Southern point of view." *GWTW* exemplifies the ongoing arguments over which story of the Civil War South is the true story, fights as bitter as the ones between religious denominations over which sect represented the real Jesus, and as important.

The unresolved aesthetic and historical struggles over the book's value make the title of a 1940 Count Basie recording a shrewd and witty question: "Gone With 'What' Wind?"

Margaret Mitchell was born in 1900, to a well-to-do Atlanta lawyer, Eugene, and his Irish Catholic wife, May Belle. Eugene's family was known in Atlanta when it was still a village called Marthasville; his grandfather was a circuit-riding Methodist minister supposed to have performed the first wedding in the town, while the minister's brother opened Atlanta's first cotton brokerage house in 1843. Eugene Mitchell's father earned a substantial living in real estate speculation in post–Civil War Atlanta, and was the city's mayor pro tem in 1880. It was a family of urban businessmen and politicians, invoking its Confederate service through naming family members for Confederate generals. Margaret Mitchell's maternal family was less orthodox in its southern heritage, since they were Irish Catholics who had preserved their Catholicism in the New World by marrying newly arrived Irish immigrants. Mitchell's mother's side of the family provided the model for Tara, a three-thousand-acre, thirty-five-slave farm in Clayton County, Georgia, known to the family as Rural Home. And Mitchell's land-greedy, argumentative Irish maternal grandmother seems to have provided in part a model for her future heroine, Scarlett O'Hara.

Mitchell's maternal grandfather did well, too, in real estate and local politics, as a member of the Atlanta Police Commission. They were the kind of family who as stockholders in the City Railway Company could send a servant to stop a passing trolley car outside their house until they had finished dressing and were ready to board.

It would be interesting to have some sense of how Mrs. Mitchell's Irishness and Catholicism might have affected her and her children's daily life in Atlanta, a largely Protestant city. Pyron describes the Atlanta police force of the 1880s as substantially Irish, and William Howard Russell, the *London Times* correspondent during the Civil War, was struck by the number of Irishmen in the Union Army, both circumstances that might have invited snubs. Oakland Cemetery, the prestige address for Atlanta's dead, has a separate Irish quarter, "tactfully dedicated to the Hibernian Rifles of our cherished War," writes Anne Rivers Siddons. Pyron tells us that Eugene Mitchell's father was "bitterly opposed" to his marriage to May Belle Stephens, but the objection to the union between two wealthy and prominent families is never fully explained. Could it have been May Belle's Irish Catholicism? Mr. Pyron, disappointingly, does not raise the question.

Mitchell spent her early childhood in a thirteen-room Victorian house; she was a tomboyish girl who loved baseball and horseback riding, and was often dressed as a boy, her mother's response to an early accident when Margaret's skirt caught fire from an open grate.

When she was five, Pyron tells us, she witnessed one of the most violent race riots in regional history, the 1906 Atlanta riots that were reported with mesmerized horror throughout the nation. "White gangs roamed the city searching for victims. . . . When the rumor circulated that 'negro mobs had been formed to burn the town . . . ,' [a Mitchell neighbor] 'went down the street warning every man to get his gun and be ready at a moment's warning.'" Margaret suggested that Eugene Mitchell stand guard with a sword, and he "adopted the suggestion." Twenty years later, Margaret remembered having taken panicked refuge under the bed.

There is a troubling lack of detail in Pyron's account of what must have been a crucial traumatic event in Mitchell's childhood. It was white mobs who, "inflamed by the Democratic party's successful white supremacy election," "looted, plundered, lynched, and murdered." How did the violence of white mobs become translated in Mitchell's neighborhood to town-burning "Negro mobs"? Did Mitchell's family, loyal Democrats with ties to city government, have any role in or view of the inflammatory elections? And what was the little girl told about the danger she was in — did the situation create tension and mistrust between the white family and the black household staff such a family inevitably employed?

Pyron tells us later in the biography that

> Atlanta and its newspapers remained tightly controlled by local elites. . . . [Margaret's] family had known the editors, publishers, and owners of the town's press for decades; they had indeed been owners themselves. Her uncle, Frank Rice, had helped found the *Atlanta Journal,* for example, along with the close family friend, the political boss, Hoke Smith.

One wonders, what were the official accounts of the riots published in the Mitchells' friends' papers? Pyron does not explore these questions, concentrating on Mitchell's personal relations with her immediate family. It is frustrating that he tells us so little about the society she grew up in and her family's part in it.

Mitchell's generation, including Wilbur Cash, author of *The Mind of the South,* William Faulkner, and the Georgia novelist and civil rights activist Lillian Smith, grew up in the heyday of southern lynching. They were surrounded by its rhetoric and by the conviction of their South that states' rights included the right to torture and murder blacks. W. J. Cash and Lillian Smith wrote about lynchers who were figures of local folklore, inspiring fear, awe, and often admiration as men who were free to kill without social, legal, or moral constraint. This was the South of Pitchfork Ben Tillman, James K. Vardaman, the Mitchells' friend Hoke Smith, and Coleman Blease, in which campaign promises included threats of violence against blacks. Coleman Blease boasted of having "planted" the finger of a black lynching victim in his garden. Speeches like these were part of the public political discourse of the South. These men were often the elected officials of Margaret Mitchell's South. Their rhetoric and imagery, its fragments in overheard discussions of the grown-ups, must have formed a part of her childhood memories and impressions.

Another curious obscurity in Mr. Pyron's account of her childhood is any mention of a black nurse who might have cared for Margaret. As Lillian Smith pointed out, this remarkable feature of southern childhood, in which children were brought up by two conflicting mother figures, "powerfully influenced the climate of many Southerners of the dominant class." Mitchell's memories of her nurse would shed some light on the character of her childhood; and there is room for speculation if she was silent on the subject.

Mitchell's first contact with storytelling was through her relatives' accounts of family history and experiences of the Civil War: "I heard so much when I was little about the fighting and the hard times after the war that I firmly believed Mother and Father had been through it all." In an autobiographical sketch, Mitchell wrote with an air of self-mockery, "In fact I heard everything except that the Confederates lost the war. When I was ten years old, it was a violent shock to hear that General Lee had been licked." The knowledge of the South's defeat in the Civil War, her humorous exaggeration aside, pervaded Mitchell's childhood, and even her relations with her family. Her mother, whom Pyron presents convincingly as the important relationship of her life, used images of the Confederate defeat and its consequences to terrorize her daughter into obedience.

Mrs. Mitchell, with the exception of her Catholicism, seems to have been a living summary of the values of a well-to-do southern lady. "Ramrod stiff, her back never touched the back of a chair." She believed that "prompt, vigorous application of the hairbrush" would correct any disciplinary problems a child might present, and addressed Margaret's early shyness through that method. Mitchell's brother remarked that "with Mother rudeness ranked with sins which cried to heaven for vengeance." Her brand of Christian charity appears to have been so aggressive that it would have alarmed Jesus. She worked steadfastly on behalf of the Roman Catholic Church during the worst years of the hysterical outbursts of Georgia Democrat Tom Watson against her religion, attacks extreme enough for him to have been indicted three times (though never convicted) for his vicious 1910 book, *The Roman Catholic Hierarchy.* One wonders how the young Margaret, presumably attending Mass and Sunday classes, reacted to the fierce anti-Catholicism that was becoming an almost institutionalized feature of southern politics during the period.

Mrs. Mitchell was also an ardent suffragette, although the cause of votes for women in the South was often put to dubious political uses, gathering momentum during the very years that southern states were instituting the practices of segregation made legal by the Supreme Court's *Plessy* v. *Ferguson* decision of 1896, and creating the legislative programs that undercut the hard-won right of blacks to vote. Enfranchising women would add to the pool of white voters and would also differentiate white women's social stature more sharply from that of blacks, a group from which they had not been so securely distinguished in pre-war days. "Let women and Negroes alone," said the hero of Beverley Tucker's 1836 plantation novel, *George Balcombe*. "Leave them in their humility, their grateful affection, their self-renouncing loyalty, their subordination of the heart, and let it be your study to become worthy to be the object of these sentiments."

Whether or not Mrs. Mitchell's feminism combined, as many southern women's did, the progressive and the reactionary, she cuts a figure with a bitterly imperious, not to say garbled, view of the world. " 'Don't talk to me about liberation in modern society,' she exclaimed. 'We've got to go back three or four hundred years and treat women as they were treated then.' " In her deathbed letter to her daughter, she conflates "mental," "moral," and "financial success," and she emerges in the Pyron biography as someone whose chief ambition for herself and for her children was to maintain their place in the highest southern caste.

When Margaret threw a tantrum about entering first grade, Mrs. Mitchell drove the little girl to "the ruins of once-proud houses" where

> charming, embroidering, china-painting one-time belles, who, after the war had deprived them of their means, degenerated pitifully. And she told me that my own world was going to explode under me someday, and God help me if I didn't have some weapon to meet the new world.

Mrs. Mitchell's message is not unlike her daughter's future heroine's: "degeneration" is a degeneration of money and caste; the ultimate goal to which feminine education, ambition, and even independence must cleave is the preservation of money and caste. Here too is the underlying bitterness toward men shared by Scarlett O'Hara. Men, after all, had contracted for and failed to provide these women with means. The even more implicit message in taking a child to a decaying neighborhood, the sort of neighborhood that black housing might border on, is that once money and caste erode, once privilege is lost, whites are no better and perhaps even worse than blacks, having fallen so much further.

May Belle Mitchell, paradoxically, did not instill respect for education in her daughter by this tactic, but rather a terror of defeat, and a lifelong inability to tolerate competition so powerful that it was a relief to use the excuse of her mother's death to drop out of college. She wrote to her brother from Smith, "There are so many cleverer and more talented girls than I. If I can't be first, I'd rather be nothing." So she returned to Atlanta, where she knew how to be first.

2

The seething bitterness of defeat was a part not only of southern family life but of its political and sexual psychology. A rage at defeat underlay white supremacist platforms; whites could still be masters with or without slaves; the humiliation of defeat increased the virulence of whites toward blacks, who had, after all, explicitly or implicitly, been on the winning side. The knowledge of defeat added variants to the white terror of interracial sex. The defeated white southern men had begun the war as masters, boasting of their virile invincibility in battle, and failed before the witness of white women to back these boasts up. Part of the emotional logic of segregation was that unlike slavery, it made a world in which black people were nearly invisible; their very existence was unbearable evidence of southern defeat.

The tortuous evasion of the fact of southern defeat was as strenuously carried on in southern literature as in southern life. Thomas Dixon, the white supremacist novelist par excellence of Margaret Mitchell's childhood, was so preoccupied with proving that Lincoln had never really meant to free the slaves that he wrote a novel about Lincoln called *The Southerner*. One would be hard-pressed to come up with a southern novel whose central figure is Robert E. Lee; he is too nakedly a figure of defeat, however heroic. Mitchell's own strategy was to emphasize that her two victorious characters, Rhett and Scarlett, had both never believed in the Confederate cause, and therefore never shared in its defeat, a solution which brilliantly simplified readers', and particularly southern readers', response to them.

Margaret never developed a taste for school, but she loved to read, although she claimed that her mother "just about beat the hide off me for not reading Tolstoy or Thackeray or Jane Austen, but I preferred to be beaten." From age twelve, according to Pyron, "she gave herself over to romances and adventures, dime novels, and cheap thrillers." She was also her neighborhood playwright, producing plays and pageants, dramatizing and acting in her own version of a Thomas Dixon novel about the Ku Klux Klan called *The Traitor: A Story of the Fall of the Invisible Empire.* Dixon's novels about Reconstruction and the knightly glory of the Ku Klux Klan, or "invisible empire," included *The Clansman,* on which D. W. Griffith's well-known and controversial movie *The Birth of a Nation* was based. The Dixon family was a powerful presence in Margaret Mitchell's South. Both Dixon and his brother, A.C., were Baptist ministers; A.C. delivered the commencement address, warning of "the menace of evolution," at W. J. Cash's 1922 graduation from Wake Forest College, while the story of how Thomas Dixon enlisted the help of Woodrow Wilson to quiet the protests of the NAACP (which Dixon called the "Negro Intermarriage Society") over *The Birth of a Nation* is a fascinating one.

Dixon's books were novelizations of the standard white southern view of Reconstruction, celebrating the Klan and almost always containing an obligatory rape of a white woman by a black man. It seems disingenuous of Mr. Pyron to tell us nothing about the plot of the play young Margaret adapted from *The Traitor;* if it offered Dixon's usual convergence of sex and racism, then it would have been highly charged material for a gently bred sixteen-year-old girl to act out.

When *Gone With the Wind* was published, Thomas Dixon wrote Margaret Mitchell a fan letter that Mr. Pyron does not quote. He raved, "You have not only written the greatest story of the South ever put down on paper, you have given the world the Great

American Novel." Mitchell replied with thanks: "I was practically raised on your books and love them very much."[1]

Mrs. Mitchell was ambitious for her daughter to attend college, and enrolled Margaret at Smith. Perhaps as a subtle way of reassuring her family that she still belonged to them, Margaret displayed an intense dislike of the Northeast. "It's a barbarous country," she wrote, "it's only money, money, *money* that counts," perhaps placating her father by repeating this reliable southern cliché. Her brother, however, later wrote freely about the Mitchells' affluence, remembering Margaret's teenage flirtations with the young World War I officers of nearby Camp Gordon: "Margaret could entertain these young men. She had a big house, servants, a car that would hold seven people. . . ." Mitchell was never able to examine the role of privilege in her life, either as obstacle or as opportunity. If anything, she tended to fantasize herself as a pioneer, singlehandedly clearing acreage others were too weak to work. Incredibly, when she returned permanently to Atlanta after two semesters at Smith, she described herself as entering "an unknown country where I knew no one except Dad and Steve and had to make my own way."

At Smith, she renounced "the religious Catholic code under which I had been brought up," and "abandoned the church entirely after returning to Atlanta," although she seems to have left no record that would help explain her reasons for doing so; these must have been complex, given that her childhood coincided with the anti-Catholic politics of Tom Watson. She witnessed too, during the period of writing *Gone With the Wind*, the region-wide, virulent, highly publicized attacks on Al Smith as a Catholic that helped defeat him in his 1928 campaign for the presidency against Herbert Hoover. A friend remembered, "She used to talk about the Catholics the same way some people talk about New York Jews," but there is nothing concrete to explain such hostility.

Mitchell's dislike of the North was increased by her rage at having to share a history class with a black student. She de-

---

1. *Margaret Mitchell's "Gone With the Wind" Letters: 1936–1949*, edited by Richard B. Harwell (Macmillan, 1976).

manded a transfer from the teacher, who refused to grant it; Mitchell managed to wangle the transfer finally from the college administration. Mitchell remembered twenty years afterward confronting the Yankee teacher and accusing her in the standard southern way of knowing nothing about the real lives of blacks: "She wanted to know if Miss Ware 'had ever undressed and nursed a Negro woman or sat on a drunk Negro man's head to keep him from being shot by the police.'" The speech seems more revealing to me than it does apparently to Mr. Pyron, who quotes it without comment. But it is a striking example of the duplicity of southern paternalism and charity giving, of the moral slavery of obligation demanded in return. It could have come straight out of Thomas Dixon's novel *The Clansman,* in which blacks like "Old Aleck" are castigated for running away from whites "who saved him from burning to death when he was a boy!" The other striking feature of Mitchell's remark is its unmistakably sexual imagery, the bizarre conflation of sexuality and power that is central to racism. Negro men of the 1920s may well have been far more likely to survive the police if white girls did not sit on their heads in public.

At Smith, too, other elements of her preoccupation with sex as power began to emerge. There is something sadistic in her pleasure in refusing even the most noncommittal physical encounter. Of a man she refused to kiss, she wrote, "I knew as he bent to kiss my hand, that I was mistress of this last situation. . . ." To the same man, she wrote challengingly, "I've drawn a line that men can't pass except by force." The idea of rape surfaces in repeated references throughout the rest of her life. "John," she wrote to her husband's sister, "never tried to rape me."

Mitchell returned to Atlanta to keep house for her father and brother more as an excuse to leave school than out of domestic necessity. Despite the cook and the chauffeur-handyman, she found housekeeping exhausting.

> The butler, who thought he was merely for ornamental purposes, received the shock of his youthful career when I walked in Monday, coupling my "Hello folks," with "Wash the windows, wax the floors, polish the furniture." After two days of labor (both for me and him — it was hard work making him work!) he privately thought I was the meanest white woman God ever made.

"Such tasks," writes Pyron, "proved to be only more examples of the numberless obligations that fragmented her days, frayed her nerves, and drained her strength." "The next year actually increased the pace," he writes solemnly. "She debuted."

Mitchell's return to Atlanta also coincided with the onset of a lifetime of ambiguous physical suffering, some of it due to a steady occurrence of the accidents for which she was a magnet, and some of it due to hypochondriacal fantasy. At the end of her debut year, for instance, she summered largely in the local hospital, being treated for an undiagnosed illness whose cause was, according to her, that "just about everything below my waistline was out of place."

After a contretemps with the local Junior League, possibly over a too daring apache dance she performed at a charity event, Margaret became involved with a pair of roommates, both of whom she married, one after the other. The first husband, Red Upshaw, was a rough alcoholic ne'er-do-well; the second husband, John Marsh, a phlegmatic mama's boy who seems to have had some features in common with the plodding "old-maidish" Frank Kennedy character who is Scarlett O'Hara's second husband. Upshaw, Mitchell, and Marsh were a strange threesome — Marsh was his rival's best man, writing an almost comically Oedipal letter to his mother after the wedding: "Dearest Mother, there were many times when I wanted you terribly. No one else could have taken your place. . . . We're all children even when we grow up, and we don't want nobody else but our mothers some times."

Mitchell's marriage to Upshaw lasted ten months; Upshaw had failed even at bootlegging and had also behaved violently to his wife, culminating in a punch in the face mentioned in the divorce suit. In the aftermath of her separation from Upshaw, Mitchell went to work for the Sunday magazine of the *Atlanta Journal*. Mitchell herself saw this part of her life history as a step of heroic unconventionality: "I stopped being a nice girl and became a reporter," she wrote, and described herself as "a product of that era when city editors kept long-handled polo mallets beside their desks just to shatter the skulls of applicants for jobs." While Mitchell's work at the *Journal* certainly represented daring and rebellion to her, her account of her *Journal* work obscures the fact that she worked as a features writer on the Sunday maga-

zine, where, Pyron mentions, "almost all the staffers . . . were fe-
males; all the writers were."

She not only obscures but doesn't acknowledge another relevant fact; the *Atlanta Journal* was founded by the close Mitchell
family friend Hoke Smith and by Mitchell's uncle. It is hard to
imagine that being a niece of the founder, as well as the wealthy
debutante daughter of a prominent family, would have had no
bearing on her hiring, which is not to say that she was not a talented features writer. As Pyron points out, "She possessed a
great sense of good leads." The opening sentence of *Gone With
the Wind* was probably the most perfect lead she ever wrote. With
the keen sense of the pictorial that journalists in particular cultivated in those pretelevision days, the control of pace that Mitchell learned responding to deadlines and word limits, the smooth
vocabulary purged of any complication, and an expert way with
the well-timed anecdote, the prose style and structure of *Gone
With the Wind* are descended from the style of features journalism.

At the *Journal,* Mitchell wrote features on such subjects as her-
oines of Georgia history, summer camps, and debutantes. Some
of her newspaper work gives a helpful glimpse of the upper-class
southern life of the twenties that H. L. Mencken had mocked in
his famous article "The Sahara of the Bozart." In a piece on the
adventures of Georgia debutantes on the Grand Tour, Mitchell
records their responses to Europe and Egypt: "Oxford isn't a bit
like Tech or Georgia," one says. And another describes the guide
on their visit to Egypt: "Although he was a little too dark to be
romantic, he had wonderful manners. . . . We didn't waste any
time on Tutankhamen. We couldn't be bothered." The girls
drove "at top speed through the streets of Jerusalem" and gig-
gled at the "Eastern women" who watched them "in horrified
awe as we tore around in the car, . . . honking the horn. . . .
We certainly had the right of way in the Holy Land." Interestingly, Pyron asserts, "These bumptious, unpretentious provincial belles actually represented something close to the models
that the author herself admired." What comes through here,
though, is hardly unpretentiousness, but the blindness of a provincial ruling class, whose inability to perceive life on other terms
than its own is a point of pride, a demonstration of power.

Mitchell shared in the concerns of the post–World War I flapper generation, though characteristically her approach to these issues seems personal to the point of egocentricity: "Could a girl be virtuous and bob her hair? Could she have a home and husband and children and a job too? Should she roll her stockings, park her corsets, be allowed a latch key?" Her newspaper work seems not to have taken her outside her milieu, judging from the number of pieces she wrote about debutantes. She seems not to have taken any notice of events like the Scopes trial, though she was a working journalist in 1925, and the southern newspapers were full of debate about an event that dramatically polarized the region. The tone of her relatively brief time as a journalist (four years) is, like her apache dance, less one of considered rebellion than that of a madcap society girl, following the iron butterfly of her will.

John Marsh, the rival of Mitchell's ex-husband, resurfaced during this period; they seem to have been fatally compatible. Mitchell, Pyron tells us, was "repulsed" by sex, and Marsh found "certain aspects of the [marriage] relationship . . . distasteful." They agreed, however, to marry on Valentine's Day of 1925, which produced an episode out of Freud by the Marx Brothers. The day after John informed his mother of the engagement, he got sick, oddly enough with symptoms described in a recent article of Mitchell's. He had to be hospitalized, and "reached his lowest ebb on February 14." After two months of hospitalization and convalescence he recovered enough to go through with the wedding, though he appears to have slept through most of the marriage while Mitchell amused herself looking over her collection of pornography, including picture postcards from Paris. Mitchell remarked, "I have to put him to bed around nine thirty except on the one night a week when we go out and hardly see him any other time."

Not to be outdone, Mitchell herself got sick, nine significant months after the marriage, perhaps when she, who felt ambivalent to the point of hostility toward children, began to feel pressured by social expectations that she would have a baby. She was sick, she believed, because "a mysterious spring of corruption poisoned her whole body, and this toxic fountain became the source of . . . ailments . . . that plagued her in these years."

Mitchell's marriage thereafter is the story of husband and wife alternating ailments and furiously repudiating doctors who frustratedly suggested their sufferings had "nervous" origins.

Mitchell left the paper when she married, and used her leisure to write. During 1926, she wrote a draft of a jazz age novel and a southern gothic novella with "a hint of miscegenation," according to her private secretary, Margaret Baugh, who recorded her memories of both stories in 1963. Mr. Pyron accepts Baugh's memory of the first story, but seems at pains to refute her memory of anything to do with " 'Ropa Carmagin"; Mitchell's lost story, he tells us, was a reworking of a story told her by an Alabaman "without anything to do with race or miscegenation. . . . Mitchell had her obsessions, but they did not include this category of folk." It is not clear from the biography whether or not " 'Ropa Carmagin" was destroyed by Mitchell's brother's order, as the jazz age novel was.

Mr. Pyron, in any case, seems too insistent on this point; he can only say with strict truth that there are two memories of the story, one mentioning miscegenation, one not. Nor can he say so absolutely that Mitchell had no interest in the subject of miscegenation, since her papers have been preserved so selectively, and since the subject does figure in *Gone With the Wind.* Her brother, Stephens Mitchell, as Pyron himself points out, was burning papers until "the early sixties"; indeed the original draft of *Gone With the Wind* was burned. It seems manipulative of Mr. Pyron to accept the secretary's memory in one case but not the other, and to guide us so hastily away from the subject.

In 1926, Mitchell began writing *Gone With the Wind.* It is difficult to establish much about her process of writing it, or the time it took her, since Mitchell kept her book hidden from nearly everyone in her circle until it was published, and after publication she circulated, as Pyron points out, "the most various chronologies and origins of her novel." The time she claimed to have spent in writing the book lengthened, it seems, in proportion to the consistency with which critics dismissed it as important literature. During the early years following its publication, she said that it was the work of three years, and could have been finished in one under better circumstances, but by 1942, "she now presented the decade-long labor as a fact." It was so characteristic of Mitchell to change her story to suit her mood and her listener that she presents a biographer with particular problems; unless there is substantial external corroboration, we can never be sure that Mitchell is telling the truth. She handled inquiries about her work as she did personal relations, with the traditional belle's opportunism; one friend describes her social character: "As soon as Peggy could discover or imagine the trend of one's secret wish as regarded one's self, she played up to it quite openly and laid on the flattering picture."

3

The stories of Macmillan's discovery of *Gone With the Wind* — Mitchell's last-minute delivery of the manuscript to a publisher scouting the South for fiction, the change of the heroine's name from Pansy to the more glamorous Scarlett, the title's metamorphosis from *Tomorrow Is Another Day* to *Gone With the Wind* — are familiar. *Gone With the Wind,* with its enormous sales, record-breaking movie rights fee, and publicity spin-offs, became an industry for Mitchell and her family. The rest of Mitchell's professional life was spent on *Gone With the Wind* business; there were foreign rights and contract disputes, while the rest of her writing time was absorbed by her insistence on sending personal replies to the countless letters she received. She told Lillian Smith in 1936, during an interview before publication, that she hoped the Lord would protect her from writing another book, and she assisted him in answering her prayer.

Pyron also takes us over the old Hollywood ground: the public casting of Gable, the highly publicized search for Scarlett, the patchwork script, to which F. Scott Fitzgerald, who felt "a certain pity for those who consider it [the novel] the supreme achievement of the human mind," contributed a minor scene or two.

Here is Margaret Mitchell railing with tart charm against the columns the producer added to Tara, which should have "looked nice and ugly like Alex Stephens' Liberty Hall." Mitchell was, as usual, having it both ways; she did after all take a farm called Rural Home and give it the name "Tara," the home of the legendary kings of Ireland.

Pyron describes the maniacal excitement of Atlanta over the

1939 movie premiere; Clark Gable's arrival eclipsed reports of Hitler's ongoing war in Europe. Antiaircraft spotlights were installed by army technicians to light the stars' arrival at the premiere. "This triumph blotted out the stigma of Appomattox," writes Pyron.

It was Margaret Mitchell's moment of maximum lionization. When Gable appeared at the theater, he reminded the crowd, "This night should belong to Margaret Mitchell." What Pyron does not tell us is that the black stars were not invited to the premiere, against David Selznick's protests. His representative in Atlanta persuaded him that it would be embarrassing to have to house the black actors in blacks-only hotels, and that their presence "might cause comment and might be a handle someone could seize and use as a club." The programs distributed in the South deleted the picture of Hattie McDaniel that the northern programs retained.

Pyron lavishes his account of the premiere with details of Mitchell's clothes — white velvet evening coat, pink tulle gown, and her speech, following the emcee's fervent "God bless our little Peggy Marsh," in which she thanked the taxi drivers, the Junior League, the bankers, and filling station attendants — "What could I have done — and my Scarlett — without their kindness and their helpfulness!" "It was classic Mitchell generosity," writes Pyron.

What he does not tell us about were the painful and vitriolic divisions of black opinion over *Gone With the Wind:* was it a bone with meat on it or was it a bone stripped bare? The whites-only Junior League ball Mitchell and the movie stars made their way to after the premiere was attended by another famous Atlantan. Martin Luther King, Senior, was present, since his own Ebenezer church choir, dressed in "Mammy" costumes, serenaded the all-white audience under the direction of Mrs. King. Martin Luther King, Junior, ten years old, was sitting on the stage in pickaninny costume. It seems remarkable that Mr. Pyron does not add to his account of the *Gone With the Wind* premiere that the greatest black emancipator since the Civil War attended, dressed as a slave, what was probably the gaudiest celebration of white supremacy in the twentieth-century South. Martin Luther King, Senior, was severely censured by the Atlanta Baptist Ministers' Union for his decision to participate in the event.

Pyron does not touch on the racial issues that making *Gone With the Wind* presented. While he describes the outrage of Mrs. Dolly Lamar Lunceford, president of the United Daughters of the Confederacy, over foreigners playing southerners, he does not describe the negotiations of the NAACP with Selznick over the use of the word "nigger" in the script, or the proposals of various black activists that a black adviser be employed as consultant, as two white advisers, one northern, one southern, were. Walter White, the executive secretary of the NAACP, wrote David Selznick to suggest that the filmmakers read W. E. B. Du Bois's *Black Reconstruction,* a wonderfully ironic suggestion, since the historical substructure of Mitchell's novel had its foundation in the accepted white southern view of Reconstruction. It was the second time Du Bois's scholarship had been brought to the attention of a filmmaker; D. W. Griffith had offered a reward to anyone who could prove historical errors in *The Birth of a Nation,* but refused to pay the African American scholars who accepted his challenge.

Selznick, to his honor, struggled to "make the Negro come out on the right side of the ledger." "I feel so keenly," he wrote, "about what is happening to the Jews of the world that I cannot help but sympathize with the Negroes and their fears. . . ." While Selznick did substitute the word "darky" for "nigger" and substitute a white for the black man who attempts to rape Scarlett in the novel, the bulk of his changes — ridding the film of explicit references to the KKK and excising the book's contemptuous speeches about "free niggers" — had the effect less of presenting a more accurate view of history than of removing any traces of white enslavement of and violence toward blacks. For all Selznick's good intentions, the movie portrayal of blacks extended the astonishing sleight-of-hand of the book, which presented a picture of slavery that made it seem almost perfectly voluntary on the part of blacks, not to mention positively virtuous.

Fame brought Mitchell a corrosive blessing; she could never face the prospect of writing another book, a hard fate for a writer, while the attention given the book made more public its failure among serious reviewers, a failure she attributed to the influence of left-wing critics. She was bitterly defensive in identifying criti-

cism of *Gone With the Wind* with leftist politics; in 1936, she wrote
to the southern Civil War novelist Stark Young,

> I would be upset and mortified if the Left Wingers liked the book. I'd
> have to do so much explaining to family and friends if the aesthetes
> and radicals of literature liked it. Why should they like it or like the
> type of mind behind the writing of it? Everything about the book and
> the mind are abhorrent to all they believe in. One and all they have
> savaged me and given me great pleasure.

Political liberalism and its connection to the criticism of *Gone
With the Wind* seemed to preoccupy Mitchell increasingly in her
late years. Her own politics were impeccably right-wing, and she
supported the notoriously racist Georgia governor Herman Tal-
madge, kept "Red" files on other southerners, including the social worker Katherine DuPre Lumpkin and the novelist Lillian
Smith, and grew obsessively concerned with attacks on *Gone With
the Wind* in Communist journals. "Between 1936 and 1944, no
journals in the United States paid as much consistent attention to
Mitchell's novel and its cinematic avatar as *New Masses* and the
Daily Worker," writes Pyron. And these journals probably had few
readers as avid as Margaret Mitchell, who believed their "ultra
radical statements about 'Gone With the Wind' and the South . . .
by 1946 were appearing [in] magazines heretofore considered
conservative."

Her last years were a welter of bitter politics and hypersensitiv-
ity to anyone she felt failed to do justice to GWTW, critically or
financially (she hounded a Dutch publisher on a rights matter
throughout the entire Nazi occupation of Holland), and the
usual fights with doctors. Mitchell's handling of a prominent car-
diologist who advised her husband to stop smoking and exercise
regularly after a heart attack is noteworthy for its characteristic
combination of fantasy and aggression. She indignantly fired the
doctor, and put her husband to bed for virtually two years, feed-
ing him "spoonbread for breakfast, apple pie for lunch, caramel
pie and peppermint ice cream for supper." He never again, after
this regime, returned to work or normal life. Four years after
Marsh's heart attack, in August 1949, Mitchell was struck by a
speeding taxicab and died in an Atlanta hospital, killed by the
last of the series of accidents that had begun in childhood and
recurred throughout her life.

Mr. Pyron's biography is courageous in its revelations of some aspects of Margaret Mitchell's life while programmatically evasive toward others. It cannot have been easy for a champion of *Gone With the Wind* to have recorded in much greater detail than in previous biographies Mitchell's troubled sexuality, her hypochondria, and the near fanaticism of her right-wing politics, or the neurotic degree to which personal fantasy governed her life. Mr. Pyron has effectively corrected the public image so carefully cultivated in her lifetime of the author as an ordinary housewife.

His unfortunate occasional attempts at novelizing scenes of Mitchell's life and a florid, sometimes pompous prose style, reminiscent of the intensely oratorical American Abimelech V. Oover in Beerbohm's *Zuleika Dobson,* undercut somewhat impressions of his frankness. His habit of referring to the young Margaret Mitchell as "the child" in hushed tones is offputting, while his must be one of the very few biographies published in the late twentieth century that calls an American teenager a "maid."

The stunning length devoted to the short-lived author of a single book is testimony to Pyron's ambition on behalf of Margaret Mitchell and her novel, as is the elaborate critical account he gives of *Gone With the Wind.* In order to make his case for the novel, Mr. Pyron must struggle to present it as offering radically innovative views of its period, a novel almost exclusively concerned with "the burden of contradiction" that "was a woman's life." Mr. Pyron's view of the book, like his account of Margaret Mitchell's life, is based on his presentation of her novel as essentially a domestic story; "the larger purpose of her novel," he tells us, was "to write *women's* history." But this claim gives us an incomplete, evasive, and ultimately specious view of the novel, as Mr. Pyron's reduction of Mitchell's childhood to essentially the history of one relationship, Margaret's and her mother's, gives us only the most partial understanding of who she was or the period she grew up in, the pervasive intensity of its legally sanctioned racism, and the incalculable pressures on whites who questioned that racism, threats that were not only social but intimate.

We can imagine the pressures on whites who rebelled through the plot of another popular novel, *The Godfather,* in which the hero has to embrace criminal life or lose his family's love and respect. The Atlanta of Pyron's biography is largely confined to the interior of Mitchell's houses and the Piedmont Driving Club, in order to facilitate his effort to portray a woman who lived an essentially conventional upper-class southern life as a rebel, and in order to elude the difficulties of making a case for a whites-only novel as a work of art. If *Gone With the Wind* is primarily about what is now fashionably called gender issues, then we must draw the strange conclusion that there are no black women.

In *Gone With the Wind,* Pyron tells us, "race and politics and their Reconstruction moral are quite irrelevant, constituting no more than a backdrop for the real story — Scarlett O'Hara's struggle against the confines of Southern womanhood." "Slavery as a social or economic system hardly exists in the novel," though Mitchell expends many pages in her Reconstruction section praising it as a better way of life for blacks than freedom. Nor can we find in the world of the southern household any safety from racial issues. "Slavery," wrote South Carolinian William Henry Trescott before the Civil War, "informs all our modes of life, all our habits of thought, lies at the basis of our social existence, and of our political faith." Slavery and racism underlay every aspect of southern life from social behavior to philosophical thinking to erotic love. White assumptions about blacks permeated colloquial southern speech, apparent even in the ordinary conversation of Mitchell's daily life: she describes John Marsh as sleeping more "'than any white boy I ever saw," and when Marsh seeks a metaphor for working hard, what comes to mind is "I was sweating like four niggers."

It is hopeless to retreat from the problem of racism to Mitchell's personal and Scarlett's fictional struggles against the role of the "icon" the "Southern Lady," a figure utterly entangled with the practice of slavery. We can look at Scarlett's own definition of southern ladyhood: "She knew she would never feel like a lady again . . . until black hands and not white took the cotton from Tara." And when does Rhett cease to be a renegade and prove himself the lady's counterpart, the traditional southern gentleman? In his words, "I'll frankly admit . . . I did kill the nigger. He was uppity to a lady, and what else could a Southern gentleman do?"

In addition, Scarlett is no rebel; her only protest against the absolute power of the southern patriarch, a power so absolute that the Alabama Supreme Court could not define any limit for it, is that she is not a patriarch. Her rebellion is over the degree of her personal power, not over the nature of that power, her quarrel only over exchanging one role for another, more powerful one in a system she thoroughly accepts. How does Scarlett escape the confines of southern womanhood? By embracing for herself the absolute power of southern manhood.

Pyron has claimed that criticisms of *Gone With the Wind* as a novel that is an apology for racism are criticisms on "cultural" or "sociological," not strictly "literary," grounds. But racism is an imaginative as well as an ethical failure; Mitchell's failure to imagine black people as fully human is a devastating artistic failure, although it mirrors her culture's failure to do so; and that failure falsifies her view of the relationships she describes while it overtly distorts her book's picture of the past. Mitchell has not an ambiguous perception of reality but a demonstrably false one. There is a point at which the intersection of imagination and moral life becomes inevitable, since the faculty of imagination is one of the elements that make moral life possible. And there is a point of inevitable intersection between literature and culture, since the stories people believe about what happened in the past will often govern the way they lead their lives.

4

Gone With the Wind was the culmination of a line of polemic southern fiction that preceded the war, gained momentum after the publication of *Uncle Tom's Cabin* through proslavery novels like *The Planter's Northern Bride,* and was carried on even more fervently after Reconstruction by writers like Thomas Nelson Page and Thomas Dixon. It was a missionary literature, pleading the Confederate cause in antebellum years and insistently continuing the war by other means when it was lost. Thomas Nelson Page wrote in his 1898 novel, *Red Rock,* "It was for lack of literature that [the South] was left behind in the great race for outside support, and that in the supreme moment of her existence, she found herself arraigned at the bar of the world without an advocate and without a defense." Thomas Dixon's works had the same underlying intention; he said exultantly of *The Birth of a Nation,* the 1915 movie based on his novel, that "every man who comes out of one of our theatres is a Southern partisan for life." Some of the elements of the southern literature of advocacy vary, but the basic propositions of the creed remained unchanged: the uncritical certainty of the justice of the Confederate cause, the belief that the South had created a superior civilization that flowered in the antebellum past, and the conviction that black people were inferior to white people and needed to be ruled by them.

These elements of the advocacy school of fiction stayed continuous from Page's Cavalier mansions to Mitchell's lusty red clay country, whether the blacks were worshipful peasants, as in Stark Young's 1934 *So Red the Rose:* "Valette had a way of ordering the servants like a young tyrant, and the Negroes adored her for it," or "autocrats of the kitchen" like Mitchell's Mammy and Uncle Peter. In each case, the atmosphere is different; Thomas Nelson Page's books have the earnest flavor of tracts, while Stark Young's novel is a haughty guide to good manners for the uncouth, and *Gone With the Wind* has more in common with the vernacular of advertising. Scarlett is like something out of a perfume ad; a tempestuous, photogenic heroine, a "wild mad night," almost photographic scene-setting, a realism of decor that, as advertising has recognized, is often the most successful way of promoting fantasy. And it is as fantasy rather than literature that *Gone With the Wind* was so readily embraced by readers.

Stephen Vincent Benét inadvertently struck home when he wrote that it reminded him of his childhood experiences of reading. An Atlanta newspaperwoman wrote of it when it was published, "I don't know whether *Gone With the Wind* is a true picture of the South of those days. But I do know that it is a true picture of the picture of those days that I had gotten when a child." *Gone With the Wind* is a kind of macabre children's book, with its toylike stereotypes, its universe of people who are good when they do as they are told and bad when they don't, its handling of facts and human beings as no more than components of a single will. With its primitive and unexamined fantasies and beliefs transferred intact onto the page, it offers a child's interpretation of history; it is a bedtime story for the white South.

*

Mitchell's family were in a sense official custodians of southern history; her father was president of the Atlanta Historical Society, her brother edited a local history journal, and she described her mother as "an authority on Southern history." Were there black members of the Atlanta Historical Society during Mitchell's lifetime? Almòst certainly not. That Mitchell set out to write a historical novel suggests how conscious she was of this family legacy, and her much publicized preoccupation with verifying historical detail reinforces the impression. But as any editor will testify, fact-checking is not quite the same task as research. Mitchell wrote a somnambulist's historical novel; she seems to be unconscious of the meaning of many of the details she so carefully verified, and as in a dream, contradictory fragments are set side by side without examination in her book, while the reader of *Gone With the Wind* is supposed to dream his way past these contradictions, to think about them tomorrow. Does no one notice that Rhett, supposedly a figure of romance, is a murderer of black men? Does no one notice that Tony Fontaine, the flower of Clayton County youth, kills a black man, naturally for making a sexual approach to a white woman? And what is the invincible Scarlett's response to this? " 'What can we do with devils who'd hang a nice boy like Tony just for killing a drunken buck and a scoundrelly Scallawag to protect his women folks? . . . There were thousands of women like her, all over the South, who were frightened and helpless."

This passage slips past in its unconscious confidence that it will occur to no one that black women stood in far greater need of protection from white men, who exercised a complete sexual tyranny. And the reader drowsing over his julep can also be relied on not to register the odd notion that the central establishing act of gentlemanly white virility is murder — for Tony Fontaine, for Rhett, and Ashley, and even Frank Kennedy, Scarlett's effeminate second husband. Here Tony recounts a killing to Frank: " 'No, by God, I cut him to ribbons.' 'Good,' said Frank casually. 'I never liked the fellow.' Scarlett looked at him. This was not the meek Frank she knew. . . . There was an air about him that was crisp and cool. . . . He was a man." And when Scarlett discovers that Frank and Ashley have set out to lynch the men she encountered on the Shantytown Road, she is told, "Mr. Kennedy is in the Klan and Ashley, too, and all the men we know. . . . They are men, aren't they? And white men and Southerners." Scarlett, too, has entered into this fraternity of murder by killing a marauding Yankee soldier.

Mitchell seems almost thematically unaware of the significance of even the details she records of daily life. In a novel partly set on a plantation, we are shown only one Tara servant who is married and has a child; incredible from many perspectives, including the fact that black children were salable commodities on plantations. In chapter one, the Tarleton twins' servant Jeems tells his masters, "Ah heap rather de paterrollers git me dan Mis Beetriss when she in a state," a single minimizing reference to the patrols funded by plantation owners to capture runaway slaves. One of the many reasons it was important to keep slaves illiterate was that they would not be able to write out passes for themselves to show the patrols.

Even a simple detail of costume in the novel reveals an ignorance on Mitchell's part that approaches brutality. In the famous scene after the birth of Scarlett and Rhett's daughter, Mammy celebrates by wearing a red petticoat Rhett has given her as a present, in a scene intended to show the teasing affection and warmth that existed between blacks and whites. The scene takes on a different contour if we look closely at the petticoat. Black women, of course, couldn't wear hoops — they had to be mobile to fetch and carry, and hoops were costly. A slave remembers, "De white women wore hoops skirts but I neber seed a black woman wid one on. Dey jes starched their petticoats an' made their dresses stand out like hoops under dem."

Details like these help us see how impossible it is in novels about the South to isolate one element of southern life, such as the lives of white southern women, and declare it to be a zone free of the consequences of slavery; the enslavement of blacks was not only an inescapable reality of southern life, but became, even more defensively as the institution was challenged, a central feature of southern values. Its shadow was everywhere; Mitchell was helpless to keep it out of even the affair between Rhett and Scarlett, which has inexplicably been taken for a love story, when it is almost entirely expressed through the imagery of slave and master. Although human beings can sustain an astonishing level of contradiction, it seems useful to point out yet again that the central sexual act of this love story is a rape; in fact, it is sex used punitively, as punishment for Scarlett's infidelity. And Scarlett's response to this romantic night in which Rhett "had humbled her, hurt her, used her brutally"? She feels "passion . . . as dizzy sweet as the cold hate when she had shot the Yankee. . . . She could hold the whip over [Rhett's] insolent black head. . . . From now on she had him where she wanted him . . . where she could make him jump through any hoops she cared to hold." Isn't it romantic?

Gone With the Wind is a historical novel which exists to obscure and conceal the reality of the past. It has less claim to being a classic than Atlanta's other most popular product, Coca-Cola. If Mitchell had a genius, it was genius for omission, operating even in her choice of the title *Gone With the Wind*. It is the last half of a line from an Ernest Dowson poem — the full line reads, "I have forgot much, Cynara! Gone with the wind!"

Although *Gone With the Wind* has been praised by Pyron, among others, for the innovation of the realism with which it supposedly presents the frontier quality of plantation life of the southern interior, a far more powerful work of realism which presents a much less glamorous picture of plantation life was published and won a Pulitzer Prize in 1931, pre-dating *Gone With the Wind* by five years. Curiously, Margaret Mitchell appears not to have read T. S. Stribling's *The Forge*. But Mr. Pyron's biography also indicates that she made no comment during her lifetime about any book by William Faulkner, the preeminent southern novelist whose publication history spans Mitchell's entire adult writing life and whose *Absalom! Absalom!* was published in the same year as *Gone With the Wind*. The Tennessee-born Stribling's novel is a remarkable work of realism of the Dreiser school. Dreiser himself wrote that it "is the only novel of all those attempting to cover either the Southern or Northern point of view, that I think worth a straw . . . it is fair to life and to the individual in the South who found himself placed as he was at that time. Really, it is a beautiful book — dramatic, amusing, sorrowful, true."[2]

Stribling's fictional plantation is not named Tara; it is called "Old man Jimmie Vaiden's home . . . half a house and half a

2. T. S. Stribling, *The Forge* (University of Alabama Press, 1985), p. x.

fort." Vaiden has risen from the trade of blacksmith to the dignity of a landed man, and Stribling gives a scrupulous picture of the plantation life of the interior South, the town general store, the small-scale brawls, the range of opinion about the practicality of secession, the crudity of its amusements. When news of Fort Sumter reaches Vaiden's neighborhood, the boys celebrate by shooting at iron anvils and enjoying their noise in the same spirit in which they now rush for their car horns on New Year's Eve.

Faulkner's powerful exploration of the consequences of southern life reveals the racking double life that racism imposes on blacks and whites, but at times can make racism seem a matter more of inner life. Stribling's novel shows us, without melodrama, slavery as an integral part of domestic life; it is a world of casual arbitrary power over the lives and deaths of human beings, where men and women are material sold in as quotidian a way as dress lengths, where the sale of someone's black husband or wife may be financing the preparation for a white relative's wedding. It is the breathtaking ordinariness of slavery as Stribling narrates it that is more shocking than acts of deliberate and calculated cruelty that have sometimes made enslavement seem the work of a few insane perverts. Stribling's pleasant, attractive white heroine is capable of impulsive acts of generosity toward the attractive, pleasant slave girl who neither realizes is her half-sister, but while Marcia is happy to lend a pretty dress to Grace, she is outraged when she is ordered to put on the dress "after a nigger's had it on!"

Stribling's black characters are seen through the multiple unstable relationships they had to the world of the white masters. Stribling is not afraid to write a scene in which a slave encounters the patrol without a pass, to let us see how danger, oppression, and duplicity were part of daily life, as the slave expresses his joy to the white patrol over the Confederate victory at Manassas, and later, in the quarters, tells the other slaves of his despair over the outcome of the battle. The steady, determined documentary intention Stribling brings to his account of southern life of this period exposes the domineering insistence of Mitchell's selectivity in her treatment of the era. None of the real artist's delicate, patient, risky effort to explore the relationship of what he imagines to external reality is practiced.

In Mitchell's novel, the imagination is employed not for the purposes of creation but as an extension of her will. Margaret Mitchell's approach to the problems of human relationships, of history, to the external world, is to create a counterworld in which things are what she says they are. *Gone With the Wind* gives us frightening and useful insights into the operations of imagination corrupted by power, and into the processes through which white fantasies about black people were enacted as legislation.

Now, with the blessing of the Mitchell estate, we can tote the weary load of a sequel, written by the romance novelist Alexandra Ripley. An enterprising computer, possibly the audience most suited to Ripley's novel, has determined that it has a fourth-grade reading level, as opposed to the original novel's fifth-grade reading level.

Communism evolved an official fiction in which novels were interchangeable; official ideology made possible the novel without an author. Late capitalism seems to have developed a novel whose only content is its own publicity. Ripley's book is nothing more than a promotion for a novel she didn't write; Scarlett, Rhett, and other characters recycled from Mitchell's novel show up in the sequel like guests on TV talk shows, flogging their forthcoming movies, or in this case their appearance in Ripley's novel.

Scarlett, the product of the land of the fee and the home of the slave, is excruciatingly dull. Otherwise its effect alternates between the comic and the pitiful. It is pitiful to witness the tiny gnat of Ms. Ripley's imagination beating against the impenetrable glass of fiction, but what she has done with the figures of Rhett and Scarlett is almost compulsively comic.

The plot of the novel is very simple; it consists almost entirely of shopping. After Melanie's funeral, Scarlett follows Rhett to Charleston, where he has retreated to the company of the mother he "worships," Ripley tells us approvingly. In Charleston, Scarlett makes friends with Rhett's mother; they shop together. Rhett, that former master of the theatrically burning gaze, has changed. Ripley's Rhett takes Scarlett sailing and points out dolphins, saying, "I always think they're smiling, and I always smile back. I love dolphins, always have."

A storm forces Rhett and Scarlett to a beach, where they engage in an impulsive act of sex, of "swirling, spiraling rapture" that brought nothing to mind so vividly as the name of an old recipe: Shrimps Aflame.

Even sex is a form of shopping in Ripley's novel, since its sole purpose is to acquire Rhett. At any rate, the couple quarrel, and Scarlett visits Savannah, where she goes shopping. She returns to her ancestral Ireland, where she acquires land and another child by Rhett from their beach rapture. She also hires a decorator for her country house, who does the child's room with a "frieze of alphabet animal paintings" and "child-size chairs and tables." She and Rhett are eventually reconciled, a reunion which doubtless increases their purchasing power.

Far more important than anything else Alexandra Ripley has written is the contract she signed with the Mitchell estate not to include miscegenation in her sequel. Her agent, Robert Gottlieb, clarified the agreement for *New York Post* reporters by explaining "that falls under the category of bizarre sexual behavior." The contractual acceptance of this literary Nuremberg law is shocking, but so is the phlegmatic public response. What would have been the response if a neo-Nazi novelist had signed a major book contract on the basis of excluding any romance between Jews and Germans? Or a black novelist had agreed to exclude sexual relationships between blacks and Jews?

The taboo against interracial sex remains central to white and black racism, partly because interracial sex represents to racists a relinquishing of power, an acceptance of the common humanity of the partners. It is a marvelous irony that being human is the greatest terror of all. Given the treacherous complexities of the history of blacks and whites in relation to each other, and given the pressures exerted on interracial lovers by both whites and blacks, interracial romance is always a matter of emotional intricacy, and at times of heroic love. It is a paradoxical spectacle to see this display of contempt for human love by a writer whose trade is the romance novel. It is also a paradoxical spectacle to see that a novel in which shopping is the principal erotic experience is not considered sexually bizarre.

Alexandra Ripley, the Mitchell heirs, and the publishers who cooperated with this agreement are still whistling Dixie, that defunct national anthem whose message to its followers is still "Look away, look away."

GEORGE W. S. TROW

Needs

FROM THE NEW YORKER

FIRST, WHAT I need you to do is give me permission to drive you completely insane by using the word "need" in places where another word, like "want" or "order," would be more "honest." We're going to be doing this (with your permission, of course — but we need you to give your permission) in phrases such as *I* (or *we* — the editorial "we") *need you to do this* and *we need you to do that.* Also, as part of this process, I need you to totally accept and validate the phrase *we need for you* . . . to do this or that, even if that phrase makes you want to stand up and hit me. I need for you to do it. That's it. That's all there is to it. If it were just a matter of what I *wanted* — hey, it would be different. In this case, my needs are involved, and I just can't back down. So bear with me, because I also need for you to initial where I reserve the right to use the repulsive phrase *what you need to do is.*

I want you to get to know me, O.K.? I (we) am (are) not comfortable thinking of myself (ourself) as a person who ruthlessly and rudely demands things of persons like yourself. When I (we) shove a rental-car agreement in front of you, I (we) want (need for) you to have the feeling that life is a matter of:

    1. Fine Options
and
    2. Splendid Choices.

At the same time, I (we) need for you to do very specific things — things so specific you would never dream them up in one million years. So why not accept a little guidance?

*

You are now ready to check in with our Guidance Department. Ready? Now you need to read and understand why you have to sign, date, and initial the paragraph beginning "other word choices — surrendering the right to require the use of."

☐Other Word Choices — Surrendering The
Right To Require The Use Of.

We need for you to sign this paragraph. Right now. Just do it. That's the Nike ad. "Just do it." Remember the handsome young athlete running through the decayed city? Think about him, how he's running and running and not asking a single question. We need for you to think about that, how *he* isn't asking any questions — just running and running — and then we need you to sign.

X _____
                  Signature

Thanks! O.K. We're out of novice level now, and you did great. But you didn't date it. What you need to do — oh, there he is, that runner! He's better-looking than ever! Look at those muscles! How does he get such a great body, living where he does, where the poor people live? Tempts you to ask questions, doesn't it? But *he's* not asking questions. *Doesn't have the time,* what with his TV work, etc. Guess *you* aren't going to bother with the old read-for-detail drag-o-rama, what with your high ambitions and goals — for the fulfillment of which there is barely time! And you already at a level where you breathe and hold down a job! Whew! Am I impressed! But before we can process your application we need for you to give us a thousand dollars. O.K. Thank you. You're great! But, uh, this thousand dollars is in *dollars.* We need to have you transfer that to *Swiss* dollars — which they call "*francs*" in one of the quaint *patois* they use over there in Switzerland. We need for you to do that, and while you are asking your financial institution to handle the foreign-exchange problem, we need for you to write a short essay on the Swiss — their historic neutrality, their cleanliness, and so on. THAT'S THE ESSAY QUESTION. THEN THERE ARE SOME MULTIPLE CHOICE.

What you need to do is take the essay question home with you, bring it in tomorrow, and do the multiple choice now. Actually, there's only one multiple choice. By the way, are you sure you want to decline collision? Now here's your question.

The word "patois" indicates:

(a) Provincial speech — as found, for instance, in backward, rural areas
(b) Substandard housing
(c) A big patio

O.K. Now you are at our highest level. What you did so far is fine, but you should know that in some states insurance coverage isn't what it should be, because lax regulators have let the whole thing go down the drain, so as a service to you we've made the optional coverage automatic. If you don't want the optional protection, we need for you to swear before a federal court judge bad, because then you've missed the point. We need for you to try harder to get the point so we can release the steaming hot dinner and the delicious frozen Margarita to your custody. We need for you to watch *48 Hours* for forty-eight hours. That usually does the trick in problem cases. The overtime is five dollars and twenty-two cents. We need for you to consider if it shouldn't have more of a multicultural aspect. Are you sure you want to decline the collision? Think it over. I'll be waiting on the big patio.

JOHN UPDIKE

First Things First

FROM ART & ANTIQUES

SIFTING THROUGH my recently dead mother's possessions, I encountered more than one object — a chunky magnifying glass, a small copper ashtray still darkened by my father's cigarette ashes, a thick pale-green ceramic candlestick, its handles akimbo like an angry woman's arms — which reawakened in my nervous system an infantile sense of largeness, of a numbly grasped ominousness, like statues of gods viewed in smoky caves. Items of inexpensive mass manufacture, they had been left behind by the evolutions of style and of manufacturing economy. Their old-fashionedness related to the thirties and the forties, decades entirely historical to most of the world's living population but as intimately real to me, a man not yet old, as my own pillow. The era's substances — the kitchen tables covered in oilcloth, the slate sinks, the wooden iceboxes, the square soaps, the toys of real rubber and lead — cradled my growing awareness and formed material expectations which modern plastics and brittle "white metal" inevitably disappoint; the evidence of my senses proposes, over a lifetime, a world increasingly lightweight, odorless, gimcrack, and flimsy, where grotesquely inflated money is traded for pathetically shoddy goods. Real fur was guiltlessly abundant in that primitive world of the thirties, and one of my mother's old coats, found at the back of a closet, unworn for decades, was trimmed with a collar of red-brown fox fur, each hair tipped with black. I stared at the texture wondering why it spoke to me so strongly, in the smoky cave of lost time, and realized that this fur had been habitually close to my face, its details pressed sharply into my passive infant awareness. My mother, not dead but alive and young and fashionable, was carrying me against her shoulder.

The photographic genius of Edward Steichen has captured, at his daughter Mary's behest, the primal frontality and awesome scale of those simple things that dawn, so metaphysically laden with wordless meaning, upon the child's consciousness. The basic equipment of life is quite conservative in design, and of these objects photographed in 1930, two years before my birth, few will be utterly strange to a child of today. The teddy bear, for example, is a bit more disheveled in his fur, and probably harder in his body, than the boneless Dacron-furred contemporary teddies, which seem designed more as throw pillows than as sturdy companions for a child. My bear, with tawny blond hair and limbs that moved on stiffish little swivels, was called Bruno. His two-tone brown eyes came out on long pins like hatpins, and one of them got lost, so he was disturbingly one-eyed. Cruelly, tenderly, I would remove his surviving eye, study his blind blond socket, and then with a lordly compassion reinsert the bright hatpin, restoring helpless Bruno's sight.

Destruction, aggression, and investigation are hard to distinguish in an infant's gropings toward reality. Recently I watched my youngest grandson cope with a present I had given him for his first birthday. It was a set of French bells mounted in a circle that could be spun, the bells colored like a rainbow and numbered so that tunes could be picked out with the mallet provided. Pealing glissandos could be produced by spinning the circle and letting the mallet caress the bells as they flashed by, their rainbow merged into a glittering gray. A toy, certainly, to appeal to a Francophile grandfather of arrested musical development. The one-year-old quickly discovered that the bells, struck with a fisted mallet, responded with a noise, and that his towering audience of parental figures approved. Very intelligently, I thought, he figured out that the full circular set, struck glancingly by his hand, would spin, but that when the toy lay upside down on the floor the same effect was impossible to produce. His attempt to imitate the glissando we demonstrated was frustrated by his inability to hold the mallet lightly enough. His further experiments were so hard to distinguish from a destructive assault that we temporarily separated the boy and the toy.

The ageless charm of blocks, surely, is their susceptibility to being knocked down and reassembled, their unblaming accommodation of those cycles of construction and deconstruction whereby the young child expresses his ambivalence toward the world that so imposingly surrounds him. His or her impulse to snuggle Bruno has a companion itch to kill, to remove irritating obstacles from a horizon crowded with frustrations and challenges. Among the striking qualities of Steichen's solemn photographs of common things is their *menace* — the giant-faced alarm clock, the hot-water faucet with its scalding long nose.

To a very young child, a home holds cheerful, sunlit patches and pockets of mystery and magic. The area around our upright piano, for instance, in its seldom-visited "piano room," was charged with a sinister electricity for me, even before the painful lessons and music books, the big flat books haunted by spidery images of Mozart with his white pigtail and Moussorgsky with his bleary hang-dog eyes. On top of the piano lay a nest of curiosities — a faded red runner of mazy Oriental design, a chocolate-brown metal box containing unreadable and momentous documents, and a little brass tiger, its stripes incised, its mouth snarling, and the underside stamped CHINA. All these are now in my possession, and have not lost their cloudy old largeness and potency, their fuzz of significance. Through their curious quiddity, my own existence — its final unknowableness, its mortality — began to gather specifics.

The Steichens' little book, entitled *The First Picture Book*, was not a great success and has languished out of print during most of the sixty years since its publication. The reasons for this neglect are harder to descry than the reasons why it seems so worth reprinting now. Deciphering the shadows and highlights and foreshortening of a photograph takes some optical sophistication. A child's own drawings embody less visual appearances than *ideas:* sky is blue and at the top of the paper, grass is green and at the bottom, men and women are upright stalks in between, sprouting wavery limbs. Illustrations by a graphic artist, however skilled, also embody notational ideas, chiefly in the all-important outlines, which do not exist in nature. A drawing in its very texture comfortingly declares the intervention of a human mind, eye, and hand; a photograph, however controlled, has something of nature's own brute opacity. It can possess, too, a troubling duplicity, a *trompe-l'oeil* uncertainty: a child's senses do not instinctively sort out images from things themselves. The conventions whereby the photographer's art is comprehended and appreciated are, like those of cinema-viewing, more recently established than those of drawing and painting and, being bound up with a changing technology, less instinctive. Also, children and their parents may have felt, with a world of gaudily colored children's books to choose from in 1930, photography's black-and-white rather dreary.

Whereas we respond, in 1991, to Steichen's photography, even in this narrow project, as an art in a heroic exploratory stage. Improvements in film sensitivity, lighting equipment, and focus capabilities made possible for photographers of the 1910s and 1920s a range of formal experiments comparable to those in easel painting from cubism on. The two arts mutually excited each other, painting to an extent being freed from its representational duties by the arrival of photography, and photography in turn goaded by avant-garde painting into attempting abstract and expressionistic effects. Steichen, a photographer since the age of sixteen, returned from his service in World War I still with painterly ambitions. At his home in Voulangis, France, he executed a series of geometric paintings as illustrations for a children's book (never published) and another set of paintings based upon the Chinese symbols of yin and yang. Then, in 1921, renouncing his efforts to become a painter and burning all his canvases, he embarked upon his famous series of over a thousand photographs of a white teacup and saucer, with minute adjustments of shadow and background. Still life, including bodies and landscapes photographed as still life, purified of anecdotal interest, was the dominant mode of twenties photography, in the work of such masters as Steichen, Edward Weston, Alfred Stieglitz, Paul Strand, and Charles Sheeler; the luminous precision and monumental stillness of their images still represent, for many, the essence of art photography. By the 1930s, Henri Cartier-Bresson and others would leave the studio entirely behind, pursuing with fast film and hand-held cameras the fleeting pictorial moment in the life of the streets, in a world where social and political issues had become newly urgent.

The images of the Steichens' *First Picture Book* savor of an art still seeking a classic repose and absolute definition, in objects sometimes posed on a velvety black background and always in a frame of strict selectiveness. Nothing is present by accident, not even the marks in the sand surrounding the beach toys. The few surviving negatives indicate the tonal richness and range of grays lost to the period's halftone photogravure; even so, we can clearly see the weave of the tablecloth, the seams of the rubber ball, the alarming jungle of the grassy lawn. The perspectives, chosen for maximum clarity, sometimes lift the child up, over his breakfast toast and silver mug of milk, in a way that suggests aerial photography, with which Steichen had become familiar in wartime. The blocks and toy trains are set out with an ideal orderliness that reminds us of the unforgiving rows and jutting planes of fascist imagery. This is a no-nonsense baby's world: the preface sternly warns us, "Fanciful tales or pictures having for a basis nothing the baby knows may lead to a later inability to distinguish between fact and fancy."

But fact blends into fancy. A few sentences earlier, Mary Steichen Martin states that "to a baby everything is 'wonder-full,' " and so it might be said that for a photographer all visual appearances are opportunities for wonder and study. A photograph's quick and exact rendition of the gradations of light caught in its lens still strikes us as a miracle, a nullification of time's blurring, eroding flow. Steichen's own statements about photography, like his industrious and eminently practical explorations of the medium, avoid the high-flown. "Photography," he wrote, "renders service with a precision well beyond the scope of any other visual means." This capacity for precision, to see better than the human eye, enlarges and renews our visual universe, from the revelation of microscopic forms by the magnifying lens to the discovery of pure forms in a cabbage as photographed by Edward Weston or a rock face by Paul Caponigro. Much as manual work develops calluses, quotidian living inculcates a certain imperviousness, and we walk through our days wastefully ignorant of what we are seeing. In its innocent clarity a child's eye approximates the camera's fine-ground, unprejudiced lens. In his 1963 *Life in Photography,* Steichen gives a typically factual account of this project:

"In 1930, my daughter Mary, now grownup and married, came to me with a proposition. She said she felt the need of some kind of book to interest her small children in pictures. . . . I made realistic still-life photographs of the objects that a small child could recognize as part of his life. One was a picture of a washstand with a toothbrush set in a glass. After the book was published, a letter came from a mother telling us that, when her child came to this picture, he stopped, making the gesture of taking the brush out of the glass, and then simulated the movement of brushing his teeth. He ended the performance by spitting into the washbasin in the picture!"

Though few adult connoisseurs will make this moist mistake, we do like the purposeful, unironical realism of these photographs, their minimalism. The camera sees so much, a little is often plenty. The single apple, banana, and twig of grapes on their plate, on the checked tablecloth, have the heavy edibility of an entire heaped sideboard by Chardin. Miles of sand beckon in a few square feet, and a whole table seems to gleam in a single setting of silver, so vivid is its sheen, so immaculate its expectancy. Steichen's still unfolding pleasure in the powers of his technical equipment gives his little subjects the gravity and power of a child's first impressions. The lighting is hot and vertical, like that of thirties movies, whose actors and actresses move in their white gowns and black tuxedos through a synthetic indoors with the sharp-shadowed glamour of Steichen's celebrity portraits for *Vanity Fair*. When, toward the end of this decade, the sense of exploration left Steichen's commercial studio work — his well-paid fashion and advertising photography — he closed up shop, and retired at the age of fifty-nine to explore the real sun of the West and the new-opened possibilities of Kodachrome color film. But the dew of artistic adventure still glistens in these attentive, larger-than-life images. Photography, for all its contemporary abundance, still plays a minor part in the vast world of children's illustrated literature. The Steichens' charming experiment stands almost alone, at the gate of a path not taken, though well-mapped by theory and brilliantly lit by a master's practice. We can see *The First Picture Book* for the treasure it is — a collection of glowing archetypes, a magic book of signs, a wordless primer of "first affections."

JOHN UPDIKE

The Mystery of Mickey Mouse

FROM ART & ANTIQUES

IT'S ALL in the ears. When Mickey Mouse was born, in 1927, the world of early cartoon animation was filled with two-legged zoomorphic humanoids, whose strange half-black faces were distinguished one from another chiefly by the ears. Felix the Cat had pointed triangular ears and Oswald the Rabbit — Walt Disney's first successful cartoon creation, which he abandoned when his New York distributor, Charles Mintz, attempted to swindle him — had long floppy ears, with a few notches in the end to suggest fur. Disney's Oswald films, and the Alice animations that preceded them, had mice in them, with linear limbs, wiry tails, and ears that are oblong, not yet round. On the way back to California from New York by train, having left Oswald enmeshed for good in the machinations of Mr. Mintz, Walt and his wife Lillian invented another character based — the genesis legend claims — on the tame field mice that used to wander into Disney's old studio in Kansas City. His first thought was to call the mouse Mortimer; Lillian proposed instead the less pretentious name Mickey. Somewhere between Chicago and Los Angeles, the young couple concocted the plot of Mickey's first cartoon short, *Plane Crazy,* costarring Minnie and capitalizing on 1927's Lindbergh craze. The next short produced by Disney's fledgling studio — which included, besides himself and Lillian, his brother Roy and his old Kansas City associate Ub Iwerks — was *Gallopin' Gaucho,* and introduced a fat and wicked cat who did not yet wear the prosthesis that would give him his name of Pegleg Pete. The third short, *Steamboat Willie,* incorporated that brand-new novelty a sound track, and was released first, in 1928. Mickey Mouse entered history, as the most persistent and pervasive figment of American popular culture in this century.

His ears are two solid black circles, no matter the angle at which he holds his head. Three-dimensional images of Mickey Mouse — toy dolls, or the papier-mâché heads the grotesque Disneyland Mickeys wear — make us uneasy, since the ears inevitably exist edgewise as well as frontally. These ears properly belong not to three-dimensional space but to an ideal realm of notation, of symbolization, of cartoon resilience and indestructibility. In drawings, when Mickey is in profile, one ear is at the back of his head like a spherical ponytail, or like a secondary bubble in a computer-generated Mandelbrot set. We accept it, as we accepted Li'l Abner's hair always being parted on the side facing the viewer. A surreal optical consistency is part of the cartoon world, halfway between our world and the plane of pure signs, of alphabets and trademarks.

In the sixty-four years since Mickey Mouse's image was promulgated, the ears, though a bit more organically irregular and flexible than the classic 1930s appendages, have not been essentially modified. Many other modifications have, however, overtaken that first crude cartoon, born of an era of starker stylizations. White gloves, like the gloves worn in minstrel shows, appeared after those first, to cover the black hands. The infantile bare chest and shorts with two buttons were phased out in the forties. The eyes have undergone a number of changes, most drastically in the late thirties, when, some historians mistakenly claim, they acquired pupils. Not so: the old eyes, the black oblongs that acquired a nick of reflection in the sides, *were* the pupils; the eye whites filled the entire space beneath Mickey's cap of black, its widow's peak marking the division between these enormous oculi. This can be seen clearly in the face of the classic Minnie; when she bats her eyelids, their lashed shades cover over the full width of what might be thought to be her brow. But all the old animated animals were built this way from Felix the Cat on; Felix had lower lids, and the Mickey of *Plane Crazy* also. So it was an evolutionary misstep that, beginning in 1938, replaced the shiny black pupils with entire oval eyes, containing pupils of their own. No such mutation has overtaken Pluto, Goofy, or

Donald Duck. The change brought Mickey closer to us humans, but also took away something of his vitality, his alertness, his bug-eyed cartoon readiness for adventure. It made him less abstract, less iconic, more merely cute and dwarfish. The original Mickey, as he scuttles and bounces through those early animated shorts, was angular and wiry, with much of the impudence and desperation of a true rodent. He was gradually rounded to the proportions of a child, a regression sealed by his fifties manifestation as the genius of the children's television show *The Mickey Mouse Club,* with its live Mouseketeers. Most of the artists who depict Mickey today, though too young to have grown up, as I did, with his old form, have instinctively reverted to it; it is the bare-chested basic Mickey, with his yellow shoes and oval buttons on his shorts, who is the icon, beside whom his modified later version is a mere mousy trousered pipsqueak.

His first, iconic manifestation had something of Chaplin to it; he was the little guy, just over the border of the respectable. His circular ears, like two minimal cents, bespeak the smallest economic unit, the overlookable democratic man. His name has passed into the language as a byword for the small, the weak — a "Mickey Mouse operation" means an undercapitalized company or minor surgery. Children of my generation — wearing our Mickey Mouse watches, prying pennies from our Mickey Mouse piggy banks (I won one in a third-grade spelling bee, my first intellectual triumph), following his running combat with Pegleg Pete in the daily funnies, going to the local movie-house movies every Saturday afternoon and cheering when his smiling visage burst onto the screen to introduce a cartoon — felt Mickey was one of us, a bridge to the adult world of which Donald Duck was, for all of his childish sailor suit, an irascible, tyrannical member. Mickey didn't seek trouble, and he didn't complain; he rolled with the punches, and surprised himself as much as us when, as in *The Little Tailor,* he showed warrior resourcefulness and won, once again, a blushing kiss from dear, all but identical Minnie. His minimal, decent nature meant that he would yield, in the Disney animated cartoons, the starring role to combative, sputtering Donald Duck and even to Goofy, with his "gawshes" and Gary Cooper–like gawkiness. But for an occasional comeback like the "Sorcerer's Apprentice" episode of *Fantasia,* and last year's rather souped-up *The Prince and the Pauper*, Mickey was through as a star by 1940. But as with Marilyn Monroe when her career was over, his life as an icon gathered strength. The America that is not symbolized by that imperial Yankee Uncle Sam is symbolized by Mickey Mouse. He is America as it feels to itself — plucky, put-on, inventive, resilient, good-natured, game.

Like America, Mickey has a lot of black blood. This fact was revealed to me in conversation by Saul Steinberg, who, in attempting to depict the racially mixed reality of New York streets for the supersensitive and race-blind *New Yorker* of the sixties and seventies, hit upon scribbling numerous Mickeys as a way of representing what was jauntily and scruffily and unignorably there. From just the way Mickey swings along in his classic, trademark pose, one three-fingered gloved hand held on high, he is jiving. Along with round black ears and yellow shoes, Mickey has soul. Looking back to such early animations as the early Looney Tunes' Bosko and Honey series (1930–36) and the Arab figures in Disney's own *Mickey in Arabia* of 1932, we see that blacks were drawn much like cartoon animals, with round button noses and great white eyes creating the double arch of the curious peaked skullcaps. Cartoon characters' rubberiness, their jazziness, their cheerful buoyance and idleness, all chimed with popular images of African Americans, earlier embodied in minstrel shows and in Joel Chandler Harris's tales of Uncle Remus, which Disney was to make into an animated feature, *Song of the South*, in 1946.

Up to 1950, animated cartoons, like films in general, contained caricatures of blacks that would be unacceptable now; in fact, *Song of the South* raised objections from the NAACP when it was released. In recent reissues of *Fantasia*, two Nubian centaurettes and a pickaninny centaurette who shines the others' hooves have been edited out. Not even the superb crows section of *Dumbo* would be made now. But there is a sense in which all animated cartoon characters are more or less black. Steven Spielberg's hectic tribute to animation, *Who Framed Roger Rabbit?*, has them all, from the singing trees of Silly Symphonies to Daffy Duck and Woody Woodpecker, living in a Los Angeles ghetto, Toonville. As blacks were second-class citizens with entertaining qualities, so the animated shorts were second-class movies, with unreal actors who mocked and illuminated from underneath the real world, the live-actor cinema. Of course, even in a ghetto there are class distinctions. Porky Pig and Bugs Bunny have homes that they tend and defend, whereas Mickey started out, like those other raffish stick figures and dancing blots from the twenties, as a free spirit, a wanderer. As Richard Schickel has pointed out, "The locales of his adventures throughout the 1930s ranged from the South Seas to the Alps to the deserts of Africa. He was, at various times, a gaucho, teamster, explorer, swimmer, cowboy, fireman, convict, pioneer, taxi driver, castaway, fisherman, cyclist, Arab, football player, inventor, jockey, storekeeper, camper, sailor, Gulliver, boxer," and so forth. He was, in short, a rootless vaudevillian who would play any part that the bosses at Disney Studios assigned him. And though the comic strip, which still persists, has fitted him with all of a white man's household comforts and headaches, it is as an unencumbered drifter whistling along on the road of hard knocks, ready for whatever adventure waits at the next turning, that he lives in our minds.

Cartoon characters have soul as Carl Jung defined it in his *Archetypes and the Collective Unconscious:* "soul is a life-giving demon who plays his elfin game above and below human existence." Without the "leaping and twinkling of the soul," Jung says, "man would rot away in his greatest passion, idleness." The Mickey Mouse of the thirties shorts was a whirlwind of activity, with a host of unsuspected skills and a reluctant heroism that rose to every occasion. Like Chaplin and Douglas Fairbanks and Fred Astaire, he acted out our fantasies of endless nimbleness, of perfect weightlessness. Yet withal, there was nothing aggressive or self-promoting about him, as there was about Popeye. Disney, interviewed in the thirties, said, "Sometimes I've tried to figure out why Mickey appealed to the whole world. Everybody's tried to figure it out. So far as I know, nobody has. He's a pretty nice fellow who never does anybody any harm, who gets into scrapes through no fault of his own, but always manages to come up grinning." This was perhaps Disney's image of himself: for twenty years he did Mickey's voice in the films, and would often say, "There's a lot of the Mouse in me." Mickey was a character created with his own pen, and nurtured on Disney's memories

of his mouse-ridden Kansas City studio and of the Missouri
farm where his struggling father tried for a time to make a living. Walt's humble, scrambling beginnings remained embodied
in the mouse, whom the Nazis, in a fury against the Mickey-
inspired Allied legions (the Allied code word on D-Day was
"Mickey Mouse"), called "the most miserable ideal ever revealed
. . . mice are dirty."

But was Disney, like Mickey, just "a pretty nice fellow"? He was
until crossed in his driving perfectionism, his Napoleonic capacity to marshal men and take risks in the service of an artistic and
entrepreneurial vision. He was one of those great Americans,
like Edison and Henry Ford, who invented themselves in terms
of a new technology. The technology — in Disney's case, film animation — would have been there anyway, but only a few driven
men seized the full possibilities and made empires. In the dozen
years between *Steamboat Willie* and *Fantasia*, the Disney studios
took the art of animation to heights of ambition and accomplishment it would never have reached otherwise, and Disney's personal zeal was the animating force. He created an empire of the
mind, and its emperor was Mickey Mouse.

The thirties were Mickey's conquering decade. His image cir-
cled the globe. In Africa, tribesmen painfully had tiny mosaic
Mickey Mouses inset into their front teeth, and a South African
tribe refused to buy soap unless the cakes were embossed with
Mickey's image, and a revolt of some native bearers was quelled
when the safari masters projected some Mickey Mouse cartoons
for them. Nor were the high and mighty immune to Mickey's el-
emental appeal — King George V and Franklin Roosevelt insisted that all film showings they attended include a dose of
Mickey Mouse. But other popular phantoms, like Felix the Cat,
have faded, where Mickey has settled into the national collective
consciousness. The television program revived him for my children's generation, and the theme parks make him live for my
grandchildren's. Yet survival cannot be imposed through weight
of publicity; Mickey's persistence springs from something un-
hyped, something timeless in the image that has allowed it to pass
in status from a fad to an icon.

To take a bite out of our imaginations, an icon must be simple.
The ears, the wiggly tail, the red shorts, give us a Mickey. Donald

Duck and Goofy, Bugs Bunny and Woody Woodpecker are inextricably bound up with the draftsmanship of the artists who make them move and squawk, but Mickey floats free. It was Claes Oldenburg's pop art that first alerted me to the fact that Mickey Mouse had passed out of the realm of commercially generated image into that of artifact. A new Disney gadget, advertised on television, is a camera-like box that spouts bubbles when a key is turned; the key consists of three circles, two mounted on a larger one, and the image is unmistakably Mickey. Like yin and yang, like the Christian cross and the star of Israel, Mickey can be seen everywhere — a sign, a rune, a hieroglyphic trace of a secret power, an electricity we want to plug into. Like totem poles, like African masks, Mickey stands at that intersection of abstraction and representation where magic connects.

Usually cartoon figures do not age, and yet their audience does age, as generation succeeds generation, so that a weight of allusion and sentimental reference increases. To the movie audiences of the early thirties, Mickey Mouse was a piping-voiced live wire, the latest thing in entertainment; by the time of *Fantasia* he was already a sentimental figure, welcomed back. *The Mickey Mouse Club*, with its slightly melancholy pack leader, Jimmie Dodd, created a Mickey more removed and marginal than in his first incarnation. The generation that watched it grew up into the rebels of the sixties, to whom Mickey became camp, a symbol of U.S. cultural fast food, with a touch of the old rodent raffishness. Politically, Walt, stung by the studio strike of 1940, moved to the right, but Mickey remains one of the thirties proletariat, not uncomfortable in the cartoon-rickety, cheerfully verminous crash pads of the counterculture. At the Florida and California theme parks, Mickey manifests himself as a short real person wearing an awkward giant head, costumed as a ringmaster; he is in danger, in these nineties, of seeming not merely venerable kitsch but part of the great trash problem, one more piece of visual litter being moved back and forth by the bulldozers of consumerism.

But never fear, his basic goodness will shine through. Beyond recall, perhaps, is the simple love felt by us of the generation that grew up with him. He was five years my senior and felt like a playmate. I remember crying when the local newspaper, cutting

down its comic pages to help us win World War II, eliminated the
Mickey Mouse strip. I was old enough, nine or ten, to write an
angry letter to the editor. In fact, the strips had been eliminated
by the votes of a readership poll, and my indignation and sorrow
stemmed from my incredulous realization that not everybody
loved Mickey Mouse as I did. In an account of my boyhood written over thirty years ago, "The Dogwood Tree," I find these sentences concerning another boy, a rival: "When we both collected
Big Little Books, he outbid me for my supreme find (in the attic
of a third boy), the first Mickey Mouse. I can still see that book. I
wanted it so badly, its paper tan with age and its drawings done
in Disney's primitive style, when Mickey's black chest is naked
like a child's and his eyes are two nicked oblongs." And I once
tried to write a short story called "A Sensation of Mickey Mouse,"
trying to superimpose on adult experience, as a shiver-inducing
revenant, that indescribable childhood sensation — a rubbery
taste, a licorice smell, a feeling of supernatural clarity and close-
in excitation that Mickey Mouse gave me, and gives me, much
dimmed by the years, still. He is a "genius" in the primary dictionary sense of "an attendant spirit," with his vulnerable bare black
chest, his touchingly big yellow shoes, the mysterious place at the
back of his shorts where his tail came out, the little cleft cushion
of a tongue, red as a valentine and glossy as candy, always peeping through the catenary curves of his undiscourageable smile.
Not to mention his ears.

GORE VIDAL

Lincoln Up Close

FROM THE NEW YORK REVIEW OF BOOKS

ONCE, AT THE Library of Congress in Washington, I was shown
the contents of Lincoln's pockets on the night that he was shot at
Ford's Theater. There was a Confederate bank note, perhaps acquired during the president's recent excursion to the fallen capital, Richmond; a pocket knife; a couple of newspaper cuttings
(good notices for his administration); and two pairs of spectacles.
It was eerie to hold in one's hand what looked to be the same
spectacles that he wore as he was photographed reading the Second Inaugural Address, the month before his murder. One of
the wire "legs" of the spectacles had broken off and someone,
presumably Lincoln himself, had clumsily repaired it with a
piece of darning wool. I tried on the glasses: he was indeed far-
sighted, and what must have been to him the clearly printed lines
"let us strive on to finish the work we are in; to bind up the nation's wounds" was to my myopic eyes a gray quartzlike blur.

   Next I was shown the Bible which the president had kissed as
he swore his second oath to preserve, protect, and defend the
Constitution of the United States; the oath that he often used, in
lieu of less spiritual argument, to justify the war that he had
fought to preserve the Union. The Bible is small and beautifully
bound. To the consternation of the custodian, I opened the
book. The pages were as bright and clear as the day they were
printed; in fact, they stuck together in such a way as to suggest
that no one had ever even riffled them. Obviously the book had
been sent for at the last moment; then given away, to become a
treasured relic.

Although Lincoln belonged to no Christian church, he did speak of the "Almighty" more and more often as the war progressed. During the congressional election of 1846, Lincoln had been charged with "infidelity" to Christianity. At the time, he made a rather lawyerly response. To placate those who insist that presidents must be devout monotheists (preferably Christian and Protestant), Lincoln allowed that he himself could never support "a man for office, whom I knew to be an open enemy of, and scoffer at, religion." The key word, of course, is "open." As usual, Lincoln does not lie — something that the Jesuits maintain no wise man does — but he shifts the argument to his own advantage and gets himself off the atheistical hook much as Thomas Jefferson had done almost a century earlier.

Last, I was shown a life mask, made shortly before the murder. The hair on the head has been tightly covered over, the whiskers greased. When the sculptor Saint-Gaudens first saw it, he thought it was a *death* mask, so worn and remote is the face. I was most startled by the smallness of the head. In photographs, with hair and beard, the head had seemed in correct proportion to Lincoln's great height. But this vulpine little face seems strangely vulnerable. The cheeks are sunken in. The nose is sharper than in the photographs, and the lines about the wide thin mouth are deep. With eyes shut, he looks to be a small man, in rehearsal for his death.

Those who knew Lincoln always thought it a pity that there was never a photograph of him truly smiling. A non-user of tobacco, he had splendid teeth for that era, and he liked to laugh, and when he did, Philip Hone noted, the tip of his nose moved like a tapir's.

Gertrude Stein used to say that U. S. Grant had the finest American prose style. The general was certainly among our best writers, but he lacked music (Gertrude lacked it too, but she did have rhythm). Lincoln deployed the plain style as masterfully as Grant; and he does have music. In fact, there is now little argument that Lincoln is one of the great masters of prose in our language, and the only surprising aspect of so demonstrable a fact is that there are those who still affect surprise. Partly this is due to the Education Mafia that has taken over what little culture the

United States has, and partly to the sort of cranks who maintain that since Shakespeare had little Latin and less Greek and did not keep company with kings, he could never have written so brilliantly of kings and courts, and so not he but some great lord wrote the plays in his name.

For all practical purposes, Lincoln had no formal education. But he studied law, which meant not only reading Blackstone (according to Jeremy Bentham, a writer "cold, reserved and wary, exhibiting a frigid pride") but brooding over words in themselves and in combination. In those days, most good lawyers, like good generals, wrote good prose; if they were not precisely understood, a case or a battle might be lost.

William Herndon was Lincoln's law partner in Springfield, Illinois, from 1844 to February 18, 1861, when Lincoln went to Washington to be inaugurated president. Herndon is the principal source for Lincoln's pre-presidential life. He is a constant embarrassment to Lincoln scholars because they must rely on him, yet since Lincoln is the national deity, they must omit a great deal of Herndon's testimony about Lincoln. For one thing, Lincoln was something of a manic-depressive, to use current jargon. In fact, there was a time when, according to Herndon, Lincoln was *"as 'crazy as a loon' in this city in 1841."* Since this sort of detail does not suit the history departments, it is usually omitted or glossed over, or poor Herndon is accused of telling lies.

The Lincoln of the hagiographers is forever serene and noble, in defeat as well as in victory. With perfect hindsight, they maintain that it was immediately apparent that the Lincoln-Douglas contest had opened wide the gates of political opportunity for Lincoln. Actually, after Lincoln's defeat by Douglas for the U.S. Senate, he was pretty loonlike for a time; and he thought that the gates of political opportunity had slammed shut for him. Lincoln's friend Henry C. Whitney, in a letter to Herndon, wrote:

> I shall never forget the day — January 6, 1859 — I went to your office and found Lincoln there alone. He appeared to be somewhat dejected — in fact I never saw a man so depressed. I tried to rally his drooping spirits . . . but with ill success. He was simply steeped in gloom. For a time he was silent . . . blurting out as he sank down: "Well, whatever happens I expect everyone to desert me now, but Billy Herndon."

*

Despite the busyness of the Lincoln priests, the rest of us can still discern the real Lincoln by entering his mind through what he wrote, a seductive business, by and large, particularly when he shows us unexpected views of the familiar. Incidentally, to read Lincoln's letters in holograph is revelatory; the writing changes dramatically with his mood. In the eloquent, thought-out letters to mourners for the dead, he writes a clear firm hand. When the governor of Massachussetts, John A. Andrew, in the summer of 1862 wrote that he could not send troops because his paymasters were incapable of "quick work," Lincoln replied, "Please say to these gentlemen that if they do not work quickly I will make quick work of them. In the name of all that is reasonable, how long does it take to pay a couple of regiments?" The words tumble from Lincoln's pen in uneven rows upon the page, and one senses not only his fury but his terror that the city of Washington might soon fall to the rebels.

Since 1920 no American president has written his state speeches; lately, many of our presidents seem to experience some difficulty in reading aloud what others have written for them to say. But until Woodrow Wilson suffered a stroke, it was assumed that the chief task of the first magistrate was to report to the American people, in their Congress assembled, upon the state of the union. The president was elected not only to execute the laws but to communicate to the people his vision of the prospect before us. As a reporter to the people, Lincoln surpassed all presidents. Even in his youthful letters and speeches, he is already himself. The prose is austere and sharp; there are few adjectives and adverbs; and then, suddenly, sparks of humor.

Fellow Citizens — It will be but a very few words that I shall undertake to say. I was born in Kentucky, raised in Indiana and lived in Illinois. And now I am here, where it is my business to care equally for the good people of all the States. . . . There are but few views or aspects of this great war upon which I have not said or written something whereby my own opinions might be known. But there is one — the recent attempts of our erring brethren, as they are sometimes called — to employ the negro to fight for them. I have neither written nor made a speech on that subject, because that was their business, not mine; and if I had a wish upon the subject I had not the power to introduce it, or make it effective. The great question with them was, whether the negro, being put into the army, would fight for them. I do not know, and therefore cannot decide. They ought to know better than we. I have in my lifetime heard many arguments why the negroes ought to be slaves; but if they fight for those who would keep them in slavery it will be a better argument than any I have yet heard. He who will fight for that ought to be a slave. They have concluded at last to take one out of four of the slaves, and put them in the army; and that one out of the four who will fight to keep the others in slavery ought to be a slave himself unless he is killed in a fight. While I have often said that all men ought to be free, yet I would allow those colored persons to be slaves who want to be; and next to them those white persons who argue in favor of making other people slaves. I am in favor of giving an opportunity to such white men to try it on for themselves.

Also, as a lawyer on circuit, Lincoln was something of a stand-up comedian, able to keep an audience laughing for hours as he appeared to improvise his stories; actually, he claimed no originality as "I am a re-tailer."

Lincoln did not depend very much on others for help when it came to the writing of the great papers. Secretary of State William Seward gave him a line or two for the coda of the First Inaugural Address, while the poetry of Shakespeare and the prose of the King James version of the Bible were so much in Lincoln's blood that he occasionally slipped into iambic pentameter.

The Annual Message to Congress, December 1, 1862, has echoes of Shakespeare's *Julius Caesar* and *Macbeth* (ominously, Lincoln's favorite play):

We can not escape history. We of this Congress and this administration will be remembered in spite of ourselves. No personal significance, or insignificance, can spare one or another of us. The fiery trial through which we pass will light us down, in honor or dishonor, to the latest generation.

A few years earlier, at Brown University, Lincoln's young secretary, John Hay, wrote a valedictory poem. Of his class's common memories, "Our hearts shall bear them safe through life's commotion / Their fading gleam shall light us to our graves." But of course, Macbeth had said long before Hay, "And all our yesterdays have lighted fools / The way to dusty death."

Of Lincoln's contemporaries, William Herndon has given us the best close-up view of the man that he had shared an office with for seventeen years. "He was the most continuous and severest thinker in America. He read but little and that for an end. Politics were his Heaven, and his Hades metaphysics." As for the notion that Lincoln was a gentle, humble, holy man, even John Hay felt obliged to note that "no great man was ever modest. It was [Lincoln's] intellectual arrogance and unconscious assumption of superiority that men like Chase and Sumner could never forgive." Along with so much ambition and secretiveness of nature, Lincoln also had an impish sense of humor; he liked to read aloud comic writers like Petroleum V. Nasby, and he told comic stories to divert, if not others, himself from the ongoing tragedy at whose center he was.

What was it like to be in the audience when Lincoln made a speech? What did he really look like? What did he sound like? To the first question we have the photographs; but they are motionless. He was six feet four, "more or less stoop-shouldered," wrote Herndon. "He was very tall, thin, and gaunt. . . . When he first began speaking, he was shrill, squeaking, piping, unpleasant; his general look, his form, his pose, the color of flesh, wrinkled and dry, his sensitiveness, and his momentary diffidence, everything seemed to be against him." Then, "he gently and gradually warmed up . . . voice became harmonious, melodious, musical, if you please, with face somewhat aglow. . . . Lincoln's gray eyes would flash fire when speaking against slavery or spoke volumes of hope and love when speaking of liberty, justice and the progress of mankind."

Of Lincoln's politics, Herndon wrote, he "was a conscientious conservative; he believed in Law and Order. See his speech before Springfield Lyceum in 1838." This speech is indeed a key to Lincoln's character, for it is here that he speaks of the nature of ambition and how, in a republic that was already founded, a tyrant might be tempted to reorder the state in his own image. At the end Lincoln himself did just that. There is a kind of terrible Miltonian majesty in his address to the doubtless puzzled young men of the Springfield Lyceum. In effect, their twenty-nine-year-old contemporary was saying that for the ambitious man, it is better to reign in hell than serve in heaven.

In the end, whether or not Lincoln's personal ambition undid him and the nation is immaterial. He took a divided house and

jammed it back together. He was always a pro-Union man. As for
slavery, he was averse, rather than adverse, to the institution but
no Abolitionist. Lincoln's eulogy on Henry Clay (July 6, 1852) is
to the point. Of Clay, Lincoln wrote,

> As a politician or statesman, no one was so habitually careful to avoid
> all sectional ground. Whatever he did, he did for the whole country.
> . . . Feeling as he did, and as the truth surely is, that the world's best
> hope depended on the continued union of the States, he was ever jeal-
> ous of, and watchful for, whatever might have the slightest tendency
> to separate them.

He supports Clay's policy of colonizing the blacks elsewhere; today any mention of Lincoln's partiality for this scheme amuses
black historians and makes many of the white ones deal economically with the truth.

Eight years later, the eulogist, now the president, promptly
made war on those states that had chosen to depart the Union on
the same high moral ground that Lincoln himself had so elo-
quently stated at the time of the Mexican War in 1848: "Any people anywhere, being inclined and having the power, have the
right to rise up, and shake off the existing government, and form
a new one that suits them better." Lawyer Lincoln would probably have said, rather bleakly, that the key phrase here was "and
having the power." The Confederacy did not have the power; six
hundred thousand men died in the next four years; and the
Confederacy was smashed and Lincoln was murdered.

In a sense, we have had three republics. The first, a loose con-
federation of former British colonies, lasted from 1776 to 1789,
when the first Congress under the Constitution met. The second
republic ended April 9, 1865, with the South's surrender. In due
course Lincoln's third republic was transformed (inevitably?)
into the national security state where we have been locked up for
forty years. A fourth republic might be nice.

In any event, for better or worse, we still live in the divided
house that Lincoln cobbled together for us, and it is always useful
to get to know through his writing not the god of the establish-
ment-priests but a literary genius who was called upon to live,
rather than merely to write, a high tragedy. I can think of no one
in literary or political history quite like this essential American
writer.

Biographical Notes

ANNE CARSON is a professor of ancient Greek and Latin at McGill University in Montreal. She is currently working on a volume of essays entitled *I Can Swim Like the Others: Three Essays in the Anthropology of Water* and is also training to paint volcanoes. Her book *Short Talks* is to be published by Brick in 1992.

JOAN DIDION has written four novels, the most recent of which is *Democracy*, and several books of essays and reporting, including *Slouching Towards Bethlehem*, *The White Album*, *Salvador*, and *Miami*. She contributes to the *New York Review of Books* and *The New Yorker*. Her most recent collection of essays is *After Henry*.

E. L. DOCTOROW is the author of *Lives of the Poets: Six Stories and a Novella* and the novels *The Book of Daniel*, *Ragtime*, *World's Fair*, *Loon Lake*, and *Billy Bathgate*. A new novel will be published in the spring of 1993.

RONALD DWORKIN is the professor of jurisprudence at Oxford University and a professor of law at New York University. He has written a number of articles and books on philosophy, politics, and law, including *Taking Rights Seriously* and *Law's Empire*. He is completing a book about abortion and euthanasia, to be published by Knopf.

STANLEY ELKIN is Merle King Professor of Modern Letters at Washington University in St. Louis. A member of the American Academy and Institute of Arts and Letters, he has published a dozen works of fiction, including *The MacGuffin*, *The Living End*, *The Dick Gibson Show*, *The Franchiser*, *The Magic Kingdom*, and *George Mills*, which won the 1982 National Book Critics Circle Award. A collection of his essays, *Pieces of Soap*, was published by Simon & Schuster this year.

Philip Fisher is a professor of English at Harvard and has written on literature and art. His most recent book, *Making and Effacing Art*, sets out a theory of modern painting and of the institutions of modern art. He is at work on a book on the passions, especially anger, fear, grief, and wonder, in relation to modern vocabularies of moods, feelings, and emotions. The essay on Hamlet printed here draws on this larger project.

William H. Gass is the author of seven books of fiction and nonfiction, including *Omensetter's Luck*, *In the Heart of the Heart of the Country*, *On Being Blue*, and *The World Within the Word*. He is the David May Distinguished University Professor in the Humanities and director of the International Writers Center at Washington University in St. Louis. His most recent collection of essays, *Habitations of the Word*, won the 1986 National Book Critics Circle Award for criticism. He has just completed a novel, *The Tunnel*.

Adam Gopnik is an editor and staff writer at *The New Yorker*. He is a regular contributor to "Notes and Comment" and "The Talk of the Town," and since 1988 has also been the magazine's art critic. If he could find the time this year, he would like to try to finish a book of short biographies of American artists, a novel about how people get into debt, another book about a modern house in Paris, and a children's story about a penguin who escapes from the Central Park Zoo. He doubts that he will.

John Guillory is a professor of English at Johns Hopkins University and the author of *Poetic Authority: Spenser, Milton, and Literary History* as well as essays on topics in Renaissance literature. He has just completed a book on the current debate about the university curriculum, entitled *Cultural Capital: The Problem of Literary Canon Formation*, to be published by the University of Chicago Press in the spring of 1993.

Elizabeth Hardwick is the author of three novels, the most recent of which is *Sleepless Nights*, and three volumes of essays, the most recent of which is *Bartleby in Manhattan*. Stories and essays have appeared in all the leading magazines, especially *The New York Review of Books*, which she helped found and where she is at present the advisory editor.

Vicki Hearne is the author of two volumes of poetry, *Nervous Horses* and *In the Absence of Horses*, and two books of essays, *Adam's Task: Calling Animals by Name* and *Bandit: Dossier of a Dangerous Dog*. An active professional dog trainer, she is at Yale University. Her forthcoming collection of prose will be called, and is about, *Animal Happiness*.

JAMAICA KINCAID is the author of *Annie John, A Small Place,* and *Lucy.* Her first book, *At the Bottom of the River,* received the Morton Dauwen Zabel Award of the American Academy and Institute of Arts and Letters, and her stories have appeared in *The New Yorker, Rolling Stone,* and *Paris Review.* She was born in and remains a citizen of Antigua, an island in the Caribbean, and lives with her husband, her daughter, and her son in Vermont.

WAYNE KOESTENBAUM is the author of *Ode to Anna Moffo and Other Poems* and *Double Talk: The Erotics of Male Literary Collaboration.* His new book, *The Queen's Throat: Opera, and the Mystery of Desire, Homosexuality,* which includes the essay in this volume, will be published by Poseidon in the winter of 1993. He is completing a second collection of poems, to be published by Persea. He teaches English at Yale.

LEONARD MICHAELS is the author of two story collections, *Going Places* and *I Would Have Saved Them If I Could,* and a novel, *The Men's Club.* He has received an award from the American Academy and Institute of Arts and Letters, a Guggenheim Fellowship, and various awards for his short stories, several of which have appeared in the O. Henry Prize collections. His work has been translated into a dozen languages. His most recent book, largely autobiographical, is *Shuffle.* Forthcoming in the fall of 1992 is *Sylvia,* a novel based on his first marriage.

DAVID RIEFF is the author of *Going to Miami: Exiles, Tourists, and Refugees in the New America* and *Los Angeles: Capital of the Third World.* His essays have appeared in *Harper's, Esquire,* the *Times Literary Supplement,* and *Salmagundi.* His next book, *The Exile: Cuba in the Heart of Miami,* will be published in the spring of 1993.

PATRICIA STORACE is the author of a book of poems, *Heredity.* Her poems have appeared in *The Best American Poetry* and her essays in *The New York Review of Books, Newsday,* and *Condé Nast Traveler,* among other publications. She is currently working on a book about modern Greece, to be published by Pantheon.

GEORGE W. S. TROW is the author of "Within the Context of No Context," an attempt to make sense of media civilization in terms of autobiography and classic social history. This effort continues in a work in progress so far entitled *The Goddess Loves the Sailor.* He is also the author of *Bullies,* a collection of satiric stories, and *The City in the Mist,* a novel. In 1985 he was awarded the Jean Stein Prize by the American Academy and Institute of Arts and Letters. He is on the staff of *The New Yorker.* Long ago, he was a founding editor of *National Lampoon.*

JOHN UPDIKE was born in 1932 in Shillington, Pennsylvania. After graduation from Harvard in 1954 and a year at an English art school, he worked for two years for *The New Yorker*'s "Talk of the Town" department. Since 1957 he has lived in Massachusetts as a free-lance writer. His most recent book was a collection of his essays and criticism, *Odd Jobs,* and out this fall will be a new novel, *Memories of the Ford Administration.*

GORE VIDAL was born in West Point and is the author of twenty-two novels, including the American chronicle *(Burr, Lincoln, 1876, Empire, Hollywood, Washington, D.C.),* five plays, and six collections of essays, of which *The Second American Revolution* won the National Book Critics Circle Award for criticism in 1982. *Live from Golgotha,* a novel, and *Screening History,* essays, will be published in 1992.

Notable Essays of 1991

SELECTED BY ROBERT ATWAN

DAVID ABRAM
The Ecology of Magic. *Orion*, Summer.

ROGER ANGELL
Homeric Tales. *The New Yorker*, May 27.

TED ANTON
Dream Book. *Latino Studies Journal*, May.

JAMES AXTELL
The Making of a Scholar-Athlete. *Virginia Quarterly Review*, Winter.

EVE BABITZ
Jim Morrison Is Dead and Living in Hollywood. *Esquire*, March.

ELLIOT BAKER
The Road Not Taken. *GQ*, September.

NICHOLSON BAKER
Exchange. *The Atlantic Monthly*, April.

STANISLAW BARANCZAK
Memory: Lost, Retrieved, Abused, Defended. *Columbia*, Fall.

SUSAN BERGMAN
Three Daughters. *North American Review*, March.

SVEN BIRKERTS
Into the Electronic Millennium. *Boston Review*, October.

ROBERT BOYERS
Culture and the Intellectual at the Height of the Time. *TriQuarterly 80*.

ROSEMARY BRAY
Taking Sides Against Ourselves. *New York Times Magazine*, November 17.

BREYTEN BREYTENBACH
The Long March from Hearth to Heart. *Social Research*, Spring.

HAROLD BRODKEY
The Animal Life of Ideas. *XXIst Century*, Winter.

COLETTE BROOKS
The Speed of Light. *Georgia Review*, Summer.

CATHERINE SAVAGE BROSMAN
On Husbandry. *Sewanee Review,*
Spring.

ROSELLEN BROWN
Donald Barthelme: A Preliminary Account. *South Atlantic Quarterly,* Summer.

STEPHEN T. BUTTERFIELD
Of Lineage and Love. *The Sun,* May.

ALLISON CADBURY
The Ikon Carver. *Georgia Review,*
Summer.

TERRY CAESAR
On Teaching at a Second-Rate University. *South Atlantic Quarterly,*
Summer.

ROBERT CANTWELL
Of Kings' Treasuries. *New England
Review,* Fall.

KELLY CHERRY
Nightwork. *Gettysburg Review,* Winter.

JUDITH ORTIZ COFER
Advanced Biology. *Missouri Review,*
Vol. 14, No. 2.

JAMES CONAWAY
Absences. *Harper's Magazine,* June.

BERNARD COOPER
A Clack of Tiny Sparks: Remembrances of a Gay Boyhood. *Harper's
Magazine,* January.

ROBERT DARNTON
Adventures of a Germanophobe. *Wilson Quarterly,* Summer.

W. S. DI PIERO
On the Greatness of the Less than

Perfect: A Miscellany. *Epoch,* Vol.
40, No. 2.

WAYNE DODD
Fellowship. *Georgia Review,* Winter.

ANDRE DUBUS
Husbands. *Epoch,* Vol. 40, No. 1.

GERALD EARLY
Life with Daughters or the Cakewalk
with Shirley Temple. *Hungry Mind
Review,* Winter.

LARS EIGHNER
On Dumpster Diving. *Threepenny Review,* Fall.

JEAN BETHKE ELSHTAIN
The Victim Syndrome. *Society,* May/
June.

JOSEPH EPSTEIN
Time on My Hands, Me in My Arms.
American Scholar, Autumn.
The Academic Zoo: Theory — in
Practice. *Hudson Review,* Spring.

LESLIE EPSTEIN
Civility and Its Discontents. *The American Prospect,* Summer.

ROBERT FINCH
Being at Two with Nature. *Georgia
Review,* Spring.

STEPHEN FRIED
My Last Paper for Nora. *Philadelphia,*
May.

NEAL GABLER
Now Playing: Real Life, the Movie.
New York Times, October 20.

PHILIP GARRISON
Where Pigs Can See the Wind. *North-*

west Review, Vol. 28, No. 3/Vol. 29, No. 1.

Burning What We Weave. *Puerto del Sol,* Spring.

HENRY LOUIS GATES, JR.
"Authenticity," or the Lesson of Little Tree. *New York Times Book Review,* November 24.

THOMAS GAVIN
The Truth Beyond Facts: Journalism and Literature. *Georgia Review,* Spring.

DANA GIOIA
Can Poetry Matter? *The Atlantic Monthly,* May.

TOD GITLIN
On Being Sound-Bitten. *Boston Review,* December.

ALBERT GOLDBARTH
Both Definitions of Save. *Iowa Review,* Vol. 21, No. 1.

MARY GOLDEN
Bluelight. *Northwest Review,* Vol. 19, No. 2.

ALBERT GOLDMAN
Memphis to Memphis. *Conjunctions,* No. 16.

RICHARD GOLDSTEIN
The New Anti-Semitism: A Geshrei. *Village Voice,* October 1.

NADINE GORDIMER
Three in a Bed. *New Republic,* November 18.

STEPHEN JAY GOULD
Opus 200. *Natural History,* August.
Fall in the House of Usher. *Natural History,* November.

ALVIN GREENBERG
Voices. *Antioch Review,* Fall.

STEPHEN GREENBLATT
Story-Telling. *Threepenny Review,* Winter.

ALLAN GURGANUS
The Ramada Inn at Shiloh. *Granta,* No. 35.

C. W. GUSEWELLE
The Year I Was Young. *Missouri Review,* Vol. 14, No. 3.

RACHEL HADAS
Visiting Schools. *Partisan Review,* No. 4.

JOHN HAINES
Early Sorrow. *Ohio Review,* No. 47.

DONALD HALL
Purpose, Blame, and Fire. *Harper's Magazine,* May.

SUE HALPERN
In Solitude, for Company. *Antaeus,* Autumn.

PETE HAMILL
Maybe I'm Dying. *Esquire,* January.

DANIEL R. HARRIS
Effeminacy. *Michigan Quarterly Review,* Winter.
What Is the Politically Correct? *Salmagundi,* Spring/Summer.

STEVE HARVEY
The Nuclear Family. *Shenandoah,* Fall.

LINDA HASSELSTROM
Lettuce Bouquets for a Dry Country. *Iowa Woman,* Spring.
Vultures. *Northern Lights,* Winter.

LARRY HEINEMANN
Syndromes. *Harper's Magazine,* July.

DAVID HELLERSTEIN
A Complete Theory of Ghosts. *North American Review,* June.

RICHARD HILL
Ain't No Cure for the Big Chill Blues. *American Voice,* Winter.

GERTRUDE HIMMELFARB
Of Heroes, Villains, and Valets. *Commentary,* June.

EDWARD HOAGLAND
Passing Views. *Harper's Magazine,* January.

ELIZABETH HOLMES
Staying Apart. *North Dakota Quarterly,* Winter.

PAUL HORGAN
To Meet Mr. Eliot: Three Glimpses. *American Scholar,* Summer.

IRVING HOWE
The Value of the Canon. *New Republic,* February 18.

PAT C. HOY II
The Spirit Was Willing and So Was the Flesh. *Agni Review,* No. 33. Soldiering. *Sewanee Review,* Spring.

VALERIE HURLEY
Riders on the Earth. *Missouri Review,* Vol. 14, No. 1.

EDWARD IWATA
Race Without Face. *San Francisco Focus,* May.

DENIS JOHNSON
Knockin' on Heaven's Door. *Esquire,* April.

TERESA JORDAN
Legends. *Lear's,* March.

LAURA KALPAKIAN
Of Time and the Flood Channel. *Ohio Review,* No. 41.

MICHAEL KELLY
Being There. *GQ,* June.

RICHARD M. KETCHUM
Memory as History. *American Heritage,* November.

JAMES KILGO
Mountain Spirits. *Sewanee Review,* Summer.

ROGER KIMBALL
The MLA in Chicago. *New Criterion,* February.

JUDITH KITCHEN
Research. *Prairie Schooner,* Fall.

WILLIAM KITTREDGE
White People in Paradise. *Esquire,* December.

CARL H. KLAUS
Montaigne on His Essays: Towards a Poetics of the Self. *Iowa Review,* Winter.

JANE KRAMER
Letter from Europe. *The New Yorker,* January 14.

LEONARD KRIEGEL
Freezing Flesh. *Gettysburg Review,* Winter.
Summer Dreams. *Sewanee Review,* Spring.

CHRISTOPHER LASCH
The New Age Movement: No Effort, No Truth, No Solutions. *New Oxford Review*, April.

SYDNEY LEA
A Winter Grouse. *Virginia Quarterly Review*, Winter.

DAVID LEHMAN
The End of the Word. *Gettysburg Review*, Winter.

SAMUEL LIPMAN
Tennis Days. *American Scholar*, Autumn.

PHILLIP LOPATE
The Dead Father: A Remembrance of Donald Barthelme. *Threepenny Review*, Summer.

NORMAN MAILER
How the Wimp Won the War. *Vanity Fair*, May.

THOMAS MALLON
Rodeo. *Yale Review*, No. 79.

MANNING MARABLE
Black America in Search of Itself. *Progressive*, November.

PAUL MARIANI
Beginnings. *Gettysburg Review*, Summer.

PETER MARIN
Born to Lose: The Prejudice Against Men. *The Nation*, July 8.

JERRY MARTIEN
In the Land of Loose Money. *Raritan*, Winter.

MICHAEL MARTONE
Correctionville, Iowa. *North American Review*, December.

FRANCES MAYES
Whatever Was Hidden. *American Scholar*, Summer.

KENNETH A. McCLANE
Keep on Keeping on. *Northwest Review*, Vol. 28, No. 3/Vol. 29, No. 1.

THOMAS McGUANE
The F-Word. *Esquire*, December.

LOUIS MENAND
What Are Universities For? *Harper's Magazine*, December.

W. S. MERWIN
Inez. *XXIst Century*, Winter.

JANE MILLER
Madonna. *Ploughshares*, Winter.

ADALAIDE MORRIS
Cuttings. *Sonora Review*, Winter.

JOHN MORRISON
Is Feminism Hurting Gay Men? *Christopher Street*, No. 158.

TONI MORRISON
Black Matter(s). *Grand Street*, No. 40.

LANCE MORROW
Evil. *Time*, June 10.

MICHAEL NEFF
The Ram in the Thicket. *Exquisite Corpse*, January–April.

KATHLEEN NORRIS
Monks at Play. *Massachusetts Review*, Spring.

JOYCE CAROL OATES
Dracula [Tod Browning, 1931]: The Vampire's Secret. *Southwest Review*, Autumn.

KEVIN ODERMAN
Viburnum: On Moving On. *Shenandoah,* Spring.

DAVID OHLE
The Mortified Man. *Missouri Review,* Vol. 14, No. 3.

IRENE OPPENHEIM
Rocky Redux. *Threepenny Review,* Winter.

SUSAN ORLEAN
Living Large. *The New Yorker,* June 17.

ALICIA OSTRIKER
Esther, or the World Turned Upside Down. *Kenyon Review,* Summer.

GEORGE PACKER
Lost in the 4th Dimension. *Mother Jones,* November/December.

KATHLEEN PARADISO
The Mark of the She-Bear. *New Criterion,* October.

MEG PAVLIK
Cave. *Threepenny Review,* Winter.

GAYLE PEMBERTON
I Light Out for the Territory. *Southwest Review,* Spring.

CARL PFLUGER
On Cranks. *Southwest Review,* Summer.

LANG PHIPPS
Confessions of a Young Wasp. *New York,* September 2.

SAM PICKERING, JR.
Again. *Chattahoochee Review,* Winter.

WILL IT NEVER END. *Southwest Review,* Summer.

KATHA POLLITT
Canon to the Right of Me . . . *The Nation,* September 23.

SARAH PRIESTMAN
Starlight. *Hudson Review,* Autumn.

SUZANNE RHODENBAUGH
Catherine McKinnon, May I Speak? *Michigan Quarterly Review,* Summer.

DAVID RIEFF
The Talk Show Confessional. *XXIst Century,* Winter.

RICHARD RODRIGUEZ
Mixed Blood. *Harper's Magazine,* November.

RICHARD RORTY
Feminism and Pragmatism. *Michigan Quarterly Review,* Spring.

PEGGY ROSENTHAL
The Nuclear Mushroom Cloud as Cultural Image. *American Literary History,* Spring.

DORIEN ROSS
Hands Over Eyes. *Tikkun,* May/June.

MARK RUDMAN
Mexican Mosaic: Hart Crane and Malcolm Lowry. *American Poetry Review,* November/December.

JUDY RUIZ
Lilly, My Sweet. *Missouri Review,* Vol. 14, No. 2.

BRIAN C. RUSSO
The Days of Tiananmen. *Prairie Schooner,* Summer.

SY SAFRANSKY
Native Tongue. *The Sun*, January.

MIKE SAGER
Damn! They Gonna Lynch Us! *GQ*, October.

EDWARD SAID
The Politics of Knowledge. *Raritan*, Summer.

SCOTT RUSSELL SANDERS
Dust. *Kenyon Review*, Summer.
Looking at a River. *Ohio*, April.

REG SANER
Chaco Night. *Michigan Quarterly Review*, Fall.
What's to Become? *High Plains Literary Review*, Winter.

LYNNE SHARON SCHWARTZ
Beggaring Our Better Selves. *Harper's Magazine*, December.

MARY LEE SETTLE
Shared Voices. *Missouri Review*, Vol. 14, No. 3.

ANTON SHAMMAS
Amerka, Amerka. *Harper's Magazine*, February.

ROGER SHATTUCK
Art at First Sight. *Salmagundi*, Fall/Winter.

CHARLES SIEBERT
Where Have All the Animals Gone? *Harper's Magazine*, May.

RAYMOND SOKOLOV
Grasping the Nettle. *Natural History*, August.

MURIEL SPARK
The School of the Links. *The New Yorker*, March 25.

DEANNE STILLMAN
Out There. *Los Angeles Times Magazine*, December 8.

ELIZABETH SWADOS
The Story of a Street Person. *New York Times Magazine*, August 18.

PAUL THEROUX
Memory and Creation: Reflections at Fifty. *Massachusetts Review*, Fall.

QUINCY TROUPE
Up Close and Personal: Miles Davis and Me. *Conjunctions*, No. 16.

MICHAEL VENTURA
A Last Letter to the War. *L.A. Weekly*, March 15–21.

DAVID FOSTER WALLACE
Tennis, Trigonometry, Tornadoes. *Harper's Magazine*, December.

GEORGE WATSON
The Decay of Idleness. *Wilson Quarterly*, Spring.

KATE WHEELER
Ringworm. *Gettysburg Review*, Autumn.

NANCY WILLARD
Something That Will Last. *Prairie Schooner*, Winter.

GEOFFREY WOLFF
Waterway. *Granta*, No. 37.
The Sick Man of Europe. *Paris Review*, No. 120.

CATHY YOUNG
Searching the Soviet Soul. *Reason*, July.